Growing in God's Love

Writers:
Dorothy Brunson
Carrie Chesnut
Peggy DaHarb
Sarah Lyons
Wanda Pelfrey
Kristi Walter

Party Suggestions:
Wendee Haeggberg
Jean Weber

Reproducible
Permission is granted to photocopy patterns and pages from this book (except for lesson plans)—for classroom use only.
The Standard Publishing Company, Cincinnati, Ohio.

Cover design by Coleen Davis and Dale Meyers
Cover illustration by Gerry Oliveira
Inside illustrations by Lynne Marie Davis
Design and typography by Robert E. Korth
Project editor, Marian J. Bennett

The Standard Publishing Company, Cincinnati, Ohio.
A division of Standex International Corporation.

Printed in the United States of America.

04 03 02 01 00 99 98 97 5 4 3 2 1

ISBN 0-7847-0624-7

Table of Contents

Introduction

Welcome to the world of 2's and 3's. This is a world of adventure, fun, new experiences, wonder, and most of all, a world in which you will teach about God and His Son Jesus.

This program endeavors to teach 2's and 3's in the ways they like to be taught and the ways they learn best.

For example . . .

. . . 2's and 3's learn through doing.

Two's and 3's like hands-on activities and lots of action. This program is designed to meet these needs throughout the session—in the learning centers and during the Bible stories.

Two's and 3's are not going to want to sit and listen for any length of time. You will notice in the lesson plan that most of the time will be spent in the learning activities, whether in the centers, or as a group. The children will also be involved in the Bible story, as well as in worship. All this is designed to keep interest high. Remember, a tired and bored child is a problem child. When you involve the whole child, that child will learn!

. . . 2's and 3's learn through play.

They play all day, every day—and toys are their tools. So, much of your time will be spent at play with your 2's and 3's, but not just any play—play with a purpose. The children will play in the learning centers, between quiet times, any time they have an opportunity. And while they play, you will use guided conversation and the materials you have chosen to turn their playtime into learning experiences.

. . . 2's and 3's learn through the use of their five senses.

The more senses 2's and 3's use, the more they learn. This program employs many sensory experiences throughout the lessons—hands-on activities in the centers, worship songs as well as singing games to exercise large muscles, books and pictures to look at and talk about. All of these are fun and exciting for young children (and for teachers too)!

. . . 2's and 3's learn through repetition.

Repetition is very important for 2's and 3's. A child often says, "Read it again," or "Sing it again." A young child will sometimes work the same puzzle over and over until he masters it, or go back to the same activity when he has time. That's why the same theme or focus is used for an entire unit, with a review lesson at the end to make sure the children understand and remember what has been said and done during the unit.

The same simple Bible words are used during the unit, to ensure that the children remember them and can use them. While most 3's can learn much more difficult verses, memorized words without understanding are meaningless. You are encouraged to use these Bible words over and over throughout the lesson—in the learning centers, during worship and story time, in general conversation, as well as reading them directly from the Bible. Make sure that the children have a classroom Bible they can touch and hold. And when the Bible words are highlighted, the children can point to them, "read" them, and know that these words come from the Bible.

A Note on Repetition: These lessons follow the syllabus from Standard Publishing's Sunday school curriculum for 2's and 3's. This provides the repetition and reinforcement that is so important to 2's and 3's. One lesson well learned is worth far more than two or three unrelated lessons. Two's and 3's not only learn through repetition, they like it and feel comfortable with it. These lessons will reinforce the focus of the lessons, and also afford the children many opportunities to apply what they have learned in the morning. The Bible-story presentation, many of the songs and action rhymes, as well as the learning activities, visual aids, and crafts, are different from those used in the morning.

These lessons, however, do not depend upon the Sunday-school lessons. There is plenty of repetition and reinforcement within each lesson and throughout each unit.

How to Use This Course

This book has been designed to allow you as much flexibility as possible. The pages are perforated and reproducible. That means that the book is non-consumable—it can be used over and over if the materials are stored properly. You can use the book in one of two ways. Either pull out pages and give them to the teachers, or photocopy the necessary pages for the teachers and keep your book intact.

Set up a filing system in which to keep your materials. You will need twelve folders, one for each unit. Label these with the quarter title and unit title. Or, if you prefer, use one folder for each lesson. Label these folders with the quarter, unit, and lesson title. As you prepare lessons, store any reproduced material in the appropriate folder. When the lesson has been used, put all materials back in the folder, along with an evaluation of that lesson. This will be helpful for future use.

The book is divided into four quarters, with three related units in each quarter. Each unit is made up of four or five lessons with a common focus. The final lesson reviews and reinforces the previous lessons. This is important for 2's and 3's, as has already been mentioned. The children will be eager to tell you what they know of the past lessons. Make good use of their enthusiasm and interest. If teachers/teams work for short periods, change teachers/teams at the beginning of a new unit rather than at the beginning of a new month. This will give the children the continuity they need, as well as make it easier for the teachers.

Basic Supplies You Will Need

Construction paper
Manila or drawing paper
Shelf paper or butcher paper
Poster board
Tagboard and/or cardboard
Newspaper
Clear, self-adhesive plastic
Tempera paints; finger paints
Painting smocks or old shirts
Jumbo crayons
Play dough
Paper punch
Magazines, catalogs, calendars, old take-home papers (for pictures)
Paper fasteners
Large scissors (for teachers)
White glue; glue sticks
Yarn
Craft sticks
Masking tape
Transparent tape
Clean-up materials

NOTE: If you want an attendance chart to last the entire year, order *Classroom Chart* (#15-01660). This has space for 15 names; each of these books has 216 seals: *Autumn* Seals (#22-01777); *Winter* Seals (#22-01778); *Spring* Seals (#22-01775); *Summer* Seals (#22-01776).

Block Center—large wooden or cardboard blocks, such as Blockbusters; small plastic cars and trucks with wheels that cannot be removed
Family Living Center—dolls, doll clothes, small blankets, plastic dishes, small table and chairs, doll bed (optional), large unbreakable mirror, toy telephones, small cleaning equipment, dress-up clothes
Book/Picture Center—classroom Bible—one that looks like a Bible and has pictures (or add pictures from take-home papers), books and pictures suggested for each unit, small book rack and table and chairs (optional)
Music/Drama Center—cassette tape player/recorder, tapes suitable for children
Game Center—large soft balls (beach balls are good), beanbags
God's Wonders Center—small plants, watering cans, seasonal nature objects (non-poisonous)
Puzzles Center—wooden puzzles with 5 to 8 pieces, homemade ones as suggested in the lessons
Art Center—basic equipment (see above list), plus special needs in lessons

Step by Step Through the Book

Introduction to the Quarter

The introduction tells you what the quarter is about, how the units fit together, as well as goals for the quarter. There are also extra songs and action rhymes to use throughout the quarter as well as very simple party ideas. Each teacher working during this quarter should read these pages.

Introduction to the Unit

These pages give the teachers more specific information to help them understand and prepare for the unit.

Here are unit goals, a unit overview, the Bible words and ways to use them, a list of things to do to get ready, specific resources needed, as well as songs and action rhymes to use. Each teacher for that unit should read these pages along with the Lesson Outlines and Learning Center Cards.

Lesson Outlines

Each lesson consists of two pages that can be folded into a compact four-page outline when pulled out of the book. The lesson will include the lesson value and a list of behavioral goals for the children.

Here is the way the lesson is set up:

Let's Get Ready

This includes specific items needed for the Bible story, plus a listing of the learning centers to use. If you have a very large class, have two of the more popular centers set up at opposite ends of the room, or in smaller rooms. Even though a book center is not suggested in a lesson, this is a good one to add if you have appropriate books and/or pictures. Remember, you will need to have a teacher in each learning center.

Learning Activities

Let's Get Started

This section includes ways to greet the children, what to do when they come, how to get them interested in an activity, and so forth. The class mascot, Zach, will be a helpful friend to use here. Thirty minutes has been allotted for these activities. This includes approximately 10 minutes before the scheduled time for the class to begin—the presession. Getting the children actively involved the minute they enter the classroom is essential.

Three learning activities are suggested here. Materials and teachers should be ready before the first child arrives. The activities will lead up to the worship and story time. A specific learning activity is suggested if there is only one teacher in the classroom. More than one activity can be used, however, by the teacher by using one after the other.

All materials needed, how to prepare them, how to proceed in class, and suggestions for guided conversation are spelled out on the Learning Center Cards that follow the Lesson Outlines. These cards can be pulled out and cut apart if you wish, or you may prefer to photocopy them. You will find the cards much more usable if you copy them, mount them front and back on cardboard, and cover them with clear, self-adhesive plastic. The cards can be placed in the learning centers for the benefit of the teachers, then filed with the lesson materials or placed in a separate file box or drawer.

Worship and Bible Story

Let's Worship God

This may be the only together time the children have. The worship/story area can be a circle of small chairs or just a large rug or individual rugs for the children. The worship suggestions have been kept to a minimum. That's all 2's and 3's can handle at one time. There will be other times of spontaneous worship with the group or with individuals, perhaps as you hold and smell a flower God made. A simple, *"Thank You, God, for this pretty flower,"* is far more meaningful to a young child than is a long prayer given by an adult. A child is also more apt to repeat that short prayer and be encouraged to word his or her own later on.

Let's Learn From the Bible

If your group is small, the Bible story may be told as the children sit in their circle. However, if your group is fairly large or spread apart in age, divide the group into older and younger children or into groups of children who get along well together. You will need a teacher for each group.

Make the Bible story real, exciting, and fun for the children. No one should ever be bored with the Bible! How do you do this?

- Be enthusiastic as you tell the story. If you are excited by the Bible story, the children will be too.
- Keep the Bible story short. Two's and 3's have very short attention spans, especially when it comes to sitting and listening.
- Involve the children. Each lesson has suggestions for doing this. The more the children are involved, the more they will get out of the story.
- Use visual aids. Each story has some type of visual aid to get and hold the children's attention. Some of these are to be made using the patterns on the pages that follow the Learning Center Cards. Others may be pictures or objects that you will find ahead of time.
- Don't sermonize! End the Bible story, then go right into the follow up that is given.

Let's Apply the Lesson

Here is where the lesson is specifically applied to the lives of the children. Zach, the puppet, can be used here to help the children retell the story, ask questions, and so on.

Learning Activities

Let's Play Awhile

By now, the children will be ready to stand up and move around. An action rhyme or song may be suggested here, but if there is none mentioned and your children are unusually restless, use a familiar rhyme, song, or exercise now. Have the suggested learning activity ready to do before going home. If you have a large group and multiple teachers, however, you will want to use several of the centers used previously.

Let's Go Home

Because the children will be tired by now, it is important to keep them occupied in some meaningful activity until parents arrive. Continue with the activity as long as possible, as each child leaves with his or her parent. Make sure the children take home any artwork they have made. Small paper bags are helpful for this purpose. Also, see that parents get their letters at the beginning of each unit.

Extra Helps

Parents' Letters: At the end of each unit is a letter to parents. A copy of this should be given to parents at the end of the first lesson, or better yet, at the end of the previous unit. The letters will help parents repeat and reinforce the lessons.

Unit Planning Sheet: A copy of this 2-page sheet, found on pages 319 and 320, will help you prepare for the entire unit.

Better Safe Than Sorry

Wouldn't it be wonderful just to be able to teach children without worrying about things such as AIDS, abduction by strangers, and child abuse! Wouldn't you love never to worry about a sick child, a fire in the building, or having to handle a medical emergency! Unfortunately, all of these things are realities in today's world, even in the church, and we must be ready to deal with them before they become a problem.

Let's take a look at four areas all churches should plan for . . . just in case! The areas are health and first aid, security, child abuse, and safety. In these few lines we cannot deal extensively with each one, so just consider this a beginning point. Plan to spend time with your leaders to determine your church's policies regarding these areas to insure the health, safety, and well-being of the children who are entrusted to your care.

Health and First Aid

Healthy-Child Policy. Ask a pediatrician to help you draw up guidelines regarding attendance by children who could be ill. Keeping out a child who is contagious will benefit both the child and the class. Promote thorough hand washing by children and teachers to help cut down on germs.

CPR and First Aid. Only a few hours are required to learn CPR techniques needed to save a life. Your local Red Cross chapter will be happy to set up a class for your teachers and interested parents. Costs are usually minimal. How about a good first-aid kit? Do you have one that is well stocked and easily accessible to all your teachers? Once again, your local Red Cross can help you determine what is needed.

Emergency Procedures. Do all your teachers know what to do in an emergency situation? Do they know where the nearest phone is if they need to call 911? Have you implemented a way to contact parents in an emergency (other than running into the auditorium yelling, "HELP!!!")? Determine a plan of action ahead of time—Who will call 911; who will contact the parents; who will stay with the child. The last thing you need during an emergency is panic. The best way to prevent it is to be prepared.

AIDS Awareness. What? In preschool? You've got to be kidding! Unfortunately, no. Even in today's enlightened society, children who are HIV positive or who have AIDS are ostracized. Because of this, a parent is often unwilling to admit his or her child is sick. So, what do you do? The best way is to treat every blood-related incident as though HIV or AIDS were involved. If a child is bleeding in any way, immediately remove him from the other children until the incident is handled. Keep surgical gloves in each classroom to be worn by teachers when cleaning a wound or attending a child with a bloody nose. You can't be too careful!

Security

It is unthinkable that someone would try to take one of your little ones from class without permission. We would all like to think it could never happen in our church. But it might. It almost happened in mine. Almost. But, because we had just begun a security tagging system, the non-custodial mother was prohibited from taking the child because she did not have the proper credentials. The unthinkable part is what might have happened if we hadn't taken proper precautions before the incident occurred.

Tagging. You need to know who all your children are, especially the visitor whose parents you might not recognize on sight. In our church, each child wears a laminated clip-tag that tells the child's name, parent's name and location, and the emergency ID number. You may not need all that on a tag in your church. But think through what you do need, and take action before it's necessary. Then have a way to identify parents when they come to pick up their children. This is especially important for substitute teachers. Of course, *you* know all the parents on sight, but what about that week you're on vacation? Teachers should never be embarrassed to ask a parent for ID. Remember, you are simply protecting that child.

Limited Access. Check your building layout to

see how you can limit the access to your children's area. Put name tags on teachers and other workers so strangers are easily recognized. And never be afraid to ask someone his business! A simple, "May I help you?" may deter someone with improper intentions. Don't leave your hallways empty. Put someone in a prominent place to keep an eye on things while classes are in progress. This is especially important for small churches that have a limited number of people available to help if something should happen.

Abuse Prevention

Here's another subject we'd rather not think about. But we'd better! One case, or even an alleged case, of child abuse in your church could literally close your doors!

Two-Adult Policy. The first, and perhaps easiest, policy to establish is the two-adult rule. Adults who have private access to children have opportunities to harm them. Always have two adults in a classroom with children. This rule not only protects the children, but the workers as well. If a child ever makes an unfounded accusation, the worker has a witness as to his or her actions.

Open-Door Policy. If it is impossible to have two adults in each room, then enforce an open-door policy. People who abuse children need privacy. If doors need to be closed for any reason, fear of escaping children, noise level, and so forth, have your coordinator or another adult drop in on classes unannounced throughout each session.

This same rule applies in the rest rooms. If possible, send same-sex workers with children to the rest rooms. And no adult should go into a stall with a child unless help is requested. Say, "I'll stand outside the door; please call if you need help." With young children, the door can be propped open so both the adult and child can be seen.

Background Checks. Remember the old saying, "He's a wolf in sheep's clothing"? Well, that's what most child molesters/abusers are. They disguise themselves as good, upstanding people. There have been many churches in which trusted workers abused children. Many churches adopt a six-month rule—No one can teach a class until he or she has been a member for at least six months. This is a good rule, but it doesn't weed out "good" abusers. The safest thing to do is have a potential worker fill out an information sheet that includes his or her Social Security number. Then have your law enforcement agency run a background check on that person before he or she enters the classroom.

Train Your Teachers. Children need to be protected, and so do workers! There have been cases of children accusing perfectly innocent people of child abuse. The results can be devastating, both to the teacher and the church. Train your teachers how to conduct themselves in the classroom, rest rooms, and other situations, for their own protection.

Safety

One night, as I was leading a children's choir rehearsal in our auditorium, there was a storm—actually a small tornado—and the steeple blew off the building! The children were hysterical. So was I, almost! We weren't prepared for an emergency of this nature. We are now!

Fire and Storm Plans. Where would you take your class in case of fire? What about a storm that threatened to blow out the windows? What would happen if you lost electricity in a room with no windows? Look at your building, consult the experts, and draw up a plan for any natural disaster you are apt to have—flood, fire, storm, hurricane, tornado, earthquake, and so on. Periodically practice the plan with the children. Post instructions inside each classroom for substitute teachers. An emergency kit that includes a walking rope and a flashlight is a must for each classroom!

Inform Parents. Perhaps your biggest problem in an actual emergency will be the parents who storm the building trying to retrieve their children. That's why it's important to inform them of your procedures so they will know exactly where to get their children should there be a loss of electricity, a fire, or a storm.

Our primary job as teachers, and as Christians, is to teach our little ones about the Lord. But along with that privilege comes the responsibility to keep them as safe and secure as possible while they are in our care. Just a few extra minutes of preparation could make a life-changing difference during an emergency situation. Be prepared!

—Rebecca J. Bennett

Autumn Quarter

Learning to Know God, Who Made Us

Young children are constantly discovering new things and new skills. They are trying hard to learn as much about themselves and their world as they can. What these children are learning now will influence their lives for years to come, as well as for eternity. How important it is for us, as teachers of young children, to help them learn about God's love and care for them while they are in this early and important stage of their development!

Children look to adults to help them understand the meaning of what they are discovering. These lessons are planned to help children discover God and His love and care. Your job is to see that the activities—play, games, songs, stories, crafts, and so forth—are meaningful. You are the link between these activities and the Bible truths the lessons teach. Your attitude—toward God, toward His Son, and toward the Bible, as well as toward the children—may teach more than your words do.

In Unit One, "God Is Great," your respect for God and your thankful attitude about all He has made will leave the impression that God is great and we are to be thankful for all He has made for us.

During Unit Two, "God Is Love," your love for the children will show them that God loves them so much that He gave them special people to love and care for them. Your many expressions of thankfulness will help them to feel thankful to God for those who care for them and will help them to learn to express their thanks to God.

Unit Three, "God Is Good," will encourage children to thank God for everyday things that are usually taken for granted—food, water, clothing, and homes. Use your time well to lead the children, by your teaching and example, to feel and express their thankfulness for God's everyday blessings.

Some children in your class may be hearing about God and His love and care for the very first time. What an opportunity is yours to open the children's eyes and hearts to God and His love! Concepts the children form now will affect their entire lives. Make sure you teach well, show your respect for and thankfulness to God, and above all, let the children know you love them and are glad they are in class with you.

As a result of these lessons, the children will

KNOW

Know that God made the world and everyone in it, and that He continues to provide everyone's basic needs.

FEEL

Feel thankful for all God has done and continues to do for them.

DO

Thank God for His love and care.

Note to those who teach alone: Prepare the learning center suggested in each lesson, but also have one or two others ready to use when the children tire of the first one.

Use these songs and action rhymes throughout the quarter, in addition to those specifically mentioned in the units.

God Is

(Tune: "Farmer in the Dell")

God is great, yes, God is great.
God made the whole world. Yes, God is great.

God is love, yes, God is love.
I love Him and He loves me. Yes, God is love.

God is good, yes, God is good.
He gives us everything we need. Yes, God is great.

Praise Him, Praise Him

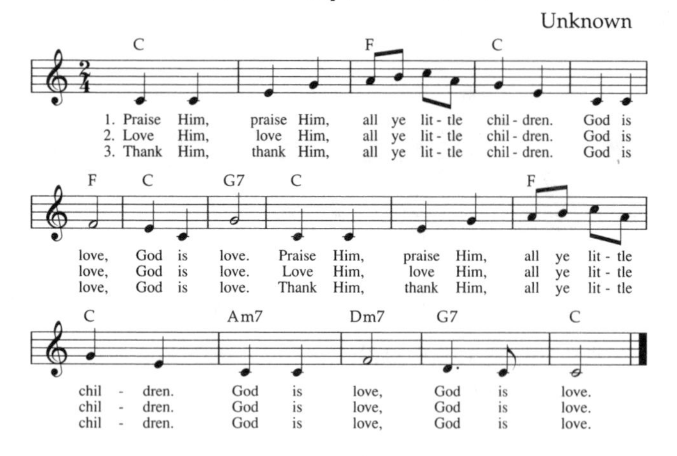

When I Pray

When I pray, I fold my hands
(Fold hands.)
And close my eyes; *(Close eyes.)*
I think about God, and He hears me.
—*Jean Katt*

My Bible

This is my Bible;
(Hands held out in front, palms together.)
I'll open it wide *(Open hands, but keep them touching.)*
And see (or say) what is written on the inside!
(Say Bible verse together.)
—*Jean Baxendale*

My Eyes, My Ears

My eyes, my ears, my nose, my mouth,
My hands and feet so small,
My arms, my legs, my tummy, my head,
I know God made them all!
(Point to each part of the body as you name it.)
—*Sylvia Tester*

Autumn Party Suggestions

September—Nature Hike

Purpose: To enjoy God's creation
When: Saturday or Sunday afternoon
Activity: Go on a nature walk and collect flowers, twigs, pebbles, etc.
Craft: Provide reclosable plastic sandwich bags for nature items. Punch a hole on one side of each bag and tie bags together with yarn to form "books."
Food: Trail mix
Devotion: Review the creation of the world.

October—Noah's Ark Party

Purpose: Alternative to Halloween
When: Saturday or Sunday afternoon, or Halloween.
Preparation: Bring wagons and stuffed animals
Activity: Parents and children decorate wagons with crepe paper streamers. Have a parade with stuffed animals in the wagons.
Game: Play a tape of animal sounds and have the children tell which animal made the sound.
Food: Animal cookies and milk
Devotion: Noah's Ark-boat and God's care. Lead children to thank God for His care.

November—Thanksgiving Party

Purpose: To help the children think of others
When: During class time
Craft: Make "hug" cards. Cut colored paper into 4" x 18" strips. Make handprints on each end of the strips by dipping hands in washable paint. Fold in thirds with the handprints on the inside. On the middle third write:

"May smiles and hugs come your way
To make a happy Thanksgiving Day!"

Game: Toss mini-pumpkins into plastic laundry baskets.
Food: Candy corn and popcorn
Devotion: Lead children to thank God for their families, as well as other blessings.

Unit 1: God Is Great

Lessons 1–4

By the end of the unit, the children will

Know that God is great.
Feel thankful that God created everything.
Pray, "Thank You, God, for the things You made."

Unit Bible Words

"God . . . made the world" (Acts 17:24, *NIV*).

Books

from Standard Publishing
The Story of Creation (24-03791)
God Made Me (24-04230)
God's World (24-03819)
All About Hands (24-03591)
Busy Feet (24-03592)

This Unit at a Glance

1 **God Made the Earth and Sky** **Genesis 1:1-19**
In the beginning, God made the sky, the land, the water, the sun, the moon, the stars, and the plants.

2 **God Made All the Animals** **Genesis 1:20-25**
In the beginning, God made the birds, the fish, and all the animals that live on the land.

3 **God Made the First People, Adam and Eve** **Genesis 1:26, 27; 2:18-22**
In the beginning, God made Adam and Eve. God made everyone.

4 **God Is Great** **Review of Lessons 1-3**

Why Teach This Unit to Young Children?

God is great because He made the world. God is great because He made each animal. And God is great because He made us. Young children are fascinated by God's world. They enjoy exploring it and seeing new things. They like to feel and touch the textures in God's world. They are beginning to recognize and to make animal sounds. They are gaining more freedom of movement and like to use their skills to run, jump, and tumble.

This unit is designed to help the children discover that God created everything that is around them. They will explore some plants that God made. They will examine some animals God made. They will look at God's most wonderful creation—themselves. They will know that God is great. They will feel thankful for all that God has made. And they will prayerfully thank God for the things He has made.

Use the Bible words over and over in your conversation, in the Bible stories, at the learning centers, and in your prayers. For example, **"God made the world." Thank You, God. . . . The Bible tells us that "God made the world." Thank You, God, for the things You made. . . . God made me. "God made the world."**

Have a classroom Bible available in a learning center, at the giving table, or wherever the children will see it. Also have it on your lap or at your side as you tell the Bible story. Have the Bible words highlighted or underlined so the children can see them, point to them, and "read" them.

Things to Do for This Unit

- Photocopy the Learning Center Cards, pages 23-28; cut apart, mount side 1 on cardboard with side 2 on back. Cover with clear, self-adhesive plastic for durability.
- Gather/prepare materials listed on Learning Center Cards.
- Make copies of the Parents' Letter, page 35.
- Prepare borders for Lessons 1-3 (pages 30 and 31).
- Copy and prepare border patterns for matching cards (instructions on page 30).
- For Lesson 3, solicit actors for the parts of Adam and Eve.
- For Lesson 4, copy page 29, cut apart, and glue on craft sticks.

Use These Songs and Action Rhymes During Unit 1

In the Beginning

(Tune: "The Farmer in the Dell")

God made the world.* God made the world.
In the beginning, God made the world.
(*light, sea, sky, animals, etc.)

The man's name was Adam. *(Boys stand and sit.)*
The woman's name was Eve. *(Girls stand and sit.)*
In the beginning, God made Adam and Eve.
(Clap to rhythm.)

God Is Great

(Tune: "London Bridge")

God made all the stars above*, stars above, stars above.
God made all the stars above. God is great.
(*lands and seas, fish and whales, dogs and cats)

God made you and you and me, you and me, you and me.
God made you and you and me. God is great.

A Way to Go

A robin flies, *(Wave arms in flying motion.)*
A bunny hops, *(Hop or jump up and down.)*
A turtle crawls so slow; *(Crawl or step in place very slowly.)*
God gave each animal He made
A special way to go! *("Walk" two fingers up one arm.)*
—Jean Shannon

God Made Me

God made the sun, *(Raise arms in circle over head.)*
God made the tree, *(Spread arms out to indicate branches.)*
God made you, *(Point to another person.)*
And God made me! *(Point to self.)*

God made Adam. *(Bow.)* God made Eve. *(Curtsy.)*
God made you, and God made me. *(Point to another; then to self.)*
—Joy M. Grewell and Kristi Walter

I'm Very Special to God

(Tune: "Hickory, Dickory, Dock")

I'm very special to God. He loves me very much.
He made my hands. He made my feet.
I'm very special to God.

Here's Why God Is Great

God is great. He made the sun.
(Point up; form circle with arms above head.)
God is great. He made the sea.
(Use arms to make waves.)
God is great. He made the stars.
(Hold up hands and wiggle fingers.)
God is great. He made each tree.
(Extend arms like tree branches and sway.)
God is great. He made you and me.
(Point to others. Point to self.)

of board.) What did God say about the sun, moon, and stars? *(Children respond, "This is good.")*

Only our great God could make the world. God made a beautiful world. And God saw that His world was good! God is great.

Let's Apply the Lesson

Point to the visual board. **Where is the sky that God made? Where is the land that God made?**

Jonathan, name one thing God made. When Jonathan answers, use that item in the following rhyme.

God made the water. God made the water.
God made a wonderful world for me.

Ask each child to name one item from the board. Adjust the rhyme to include that item.

We are thankful for the world God made. Thank You, God, for making the world.

Learning Activities

(20 minutes)

Let's Play Awhile

Have the children stand and sing "In the Beginning," then go to the God's Wonders Center. If your class is large and you have several teachers, use the learning activities from the beginning of class.

Let's Go Home

Have Zach tell the children that it's time to clean up after their snack. Direct them to the wastebasket with their napkins. Use wet wipes or a damp cloth to clean hands and faces. Then gather the children in a circle. Lead them in saying the action rhyme, "Here's Why God Is Great."

Since this is the first lesson of the unit, give each child a Parents' Letter.

God Made the Earth and Sky

Genesis 1:1-19

Bible Words: "God . . . made the world" (Acts 17:24, *NIV*).

Lesson Value: Anyone who is building a relationship with God must know and accept God as Creator. He is the creator of the earth, of the animals, and of man. Knowing about God's creation of the earth and its inhabitants is significant because it develops one of the most important relationships between God and man—Creator to creation.

This lesson introduces God as Creator. God is great because He is our creator. Your children will sense awe as they explore the world that God made. Only God could make the world. God is great!

Know: Know that God is great.
Feel: Feel thankful that God created everything.
Do: Pray, "Thank You, God, for the things You made."

Children will accomplish the goals when they:

1. Say the Bible words, "God made the world."
2. Pray, "Thank You, God, for making the world."
3. Sing about the things God created.
4. Examine something that God made.
5. Identify the land and sky that God created.
6. Name something that God has made.

Let's Get Ready

For the Bible story, you will need the classroom Bible, bulletin board (or large poster board), and prepared border visuals (pages 30 and 31). Surround the Bible story area with as many potted plants as possible. Have puppet Zach ready.

Prepare the Book/Picture Center, the Family Living Center, and the Game Center. If you are the only teacher, use just the Family Living Center. Have materials ready for the God's Wonders Center to be used after the Bible story.

Learning Activities

(30 minutes, including 10 minutes presession)

Let's Get Started

Use Zach to greet each child by name. "Hello, Julie. You are a wonderful part of God's big world." Have Zach help the children mark their attendance chart, give their offering, and get involved in one of the learning activities. **Rachel, would you like to look at pictures or help take care of some of God's plants? We're going to have a Bible story about some of the world that God made. Only God could make the world.**

Worship and Bible Story

(15 minutes)

Let's Worship God

Have Zach tell the children, "It's time to put our things away so we can sing and pray to God." Have children gather in the area where the plants will surround them. Begin singing as soon as the children come to the circle. Sing stanza 1 from "In the Beginning" and "God Is Great." **We've been singing about God's world. The Bible says, "God made the world."** Point to the verse in the classroom Bible. Let children "read" the verse from the Bible. Use the rhyme, "When I Pray" (page 12). Then pray, **Thank You, God, for the things You made.**

Let's Learn From the Bible

Introduction: Hide Zach among the plants. **Our room looks like a jungle. Zach is hiding somewhere in this jungle. Can you find him?** After children find Zach, have Zach say, "A jungle would be a great place to play hide-and-seek!" **Who made the jungle plants and all of the plants in our room? Yes, God made the plants. The Bible tells us that "God made the world." The Bible also tells us what God thought about the world He made. Do you know what God said about His world? God said, "This is good." Now you are ready to help me tell the Bible story.** Put Zach away. Place the Bible in your lap.

The Bible Story: Before God began to make the world, there was nothing. No sky, no sun, no trees. There was only darkness. *(Point to the black board.)* What was the first thing that God made? God made the light. God said, "Let there be light." *(Cover over the black paper with white paper.)* So God made day and night. What did God say about the day and night? *(Lead children to say in unison, "This is good.")*

Next, God made the sky. *(Place, or have a child place, cloud border on the board.)* What did God say about the sky? *(Children respond, "This is good.")*

Next, God made the land and the water. He made the mountains and the plains. He made the rivers, lakes, and oceans. *(Place appropriate borders when mentioned.)* What did God say about the water and the land? *(Children respond, "This is good.")*

Next, God made plants to grow on the land. He made flowers, grass, trees, and jungles. *(Place borders.)* What did God say about the plants? *(Children respond, "This is good.")*

Next God made lights for the day and night. He made the sun for the day. *(Place sun in day section of board.)* He made the moon and the stars for night. *(Place moon and stars in night section*

We are thankful that God made animals for us to love. How can we love God's animals? Accept a variety of answers. **We show we are thankful for God's animals when we are kind to them and take care of them. Thank You, God, for making the animals.**

Learning Activities

(20 minutes)

Let's Play Awhile

Have children stand and do the action rhyme, "A Way to Go," then take children to the Art Center. If your class is large and you have multiple teachers, use the other activities from the beginning of the lesson as well.

Let's Go Home

Have Zach tell the children that it's time to clean up. If a child is reluctant to help, give him a specific job to do. When all materials are picked up and put away, gather the children in a circle. Lead them in playing "Duck, Duck, Goose." Each child must choose two different animals to name as he walks around the circle (i.e. "Lion, lion, tiger," or "Doggie, doggie, kitty").

Take one child at a time to the door as parents arrive. Make sure children take home their thumbprint art.

God Made All the Animals

Genesis 1:20-25

Bible Words: "God . . . made the world" (Acts 17:24, *NIV*).

Lesson Value: Young children love animals. These children are just beginning to learn how to care for animals. Perhaps they have pets at home. Today's lesson will teach them that God made all of the animals. God is great because He made the animals. Your children will learn that God gave them the special job of taking care of animals. They will spend some time today practicing their animal care skills. They will discover that God shows His love for them by giving them animals to care for. This will lead them to feel thankful for God's animals.

Know: Know that God is great.
Feel: Feel thankful that God created everything.
Do: Pray, "Thank You, God, for the things You made."

Children will accomplish the goals when they:

1. Say the Bible words, "God made the world."
2. Pray, "Thank You, God, for making the animals."
3. Sing about the animals that God made.
4. Examine an animal that God made.
5. Identify animals that God made by naming them or pointing to them in pictures.
6. Name two animals that God has made.

Let's Get Ready

For the Bible story, you will need the classroom Bible, puppet Zach, the bulletin board visual from last week, and prepared animal borders (page 31).

Prepare the Game Center, the Family Living Center, and God's Wonders Center. If you are the only teacher, use just the God's Wonders Center. Have materials prepared for the Art Center to use after the Bible story.

Learning Activities

(30 minutes, including 10 minutes presession)

Let's Get Started

Have Zach greet each child by name. "Jenny, do you have an animal at home? Tell me about your animal. How do you take care of your animal? God made animals."

After children have marked the attendance chart and have given their offering, direct them to get involved in the learning activities. Say, **Michael, today we will learn about God's animals. Would you like to pretend you're an animal, or name the animals?**

Worship and Bible Story

(15 minutes)

Let's Worship God

Have Zach tell the children, "It's time to put our things away so we can sing and pray to God." Begin singing as soon as the first child sits in the circle with you. Sing "God Is Great" followed by "In the Beginning," using the names of animals the children suggest. **Our Bible words say, "God made the world." Can you say that with me?** Do so. **God made the animals for us to love.** Do the action rhyme, "When I Pray," then pray, **Thank You, God, for making the animals.**

Let's Learn From the Bible

Introduction: Point to the board prepared during last week's lesson. **The Bible says, "God made the world." He made the day and night. He made the sun, moon, and stars. He made the land and sea. He made the plants. What did God say about the world He made?** Children should answer, "This is good." **These are not the only things God made in His world. God also made the animals. Help me by making the sound of each animal that I name.**

The Bible Story: God looked at the world that He made. He saw that it was a beautiful world. It had beautiful flowers and rivers. It had lovely mountains and valleys. The night sky was wonderful to see. God said, "My world is good."

But God wasn't finished. He'd just begun!

God made fish to live in the water. *(Have children make a "fish" face. Add fish to board in the water area.)*

God made birds to fly in the air. *(Have children chirp and tweet. Add birds in the sky area.)*

After God made animals for the sky and sea, He made animals for the land. He made the lions. *(Have children roar. Add lions.)* God made the sheep. *(Have children baa-aa. Add sheep.)*

What other animals did God make? *(Call on children one at a time. Children make the animal's noise and you name the animal.)* God was very busy the day He made the animals. What did God say about the animals that He made? *(Children should answer, "This is good.")* God liked the animals He made!

Let's Apply the Lesson

Our Bible words say, "God made the world." Have children say the Bible words with you. Then have each child name one animal that God made. Use two animal names at a time in the following song to the tune of "London Bridge":

God made all the fish and whales, fish and whales,
fish and whales.
God made all the fish and whales. God is great!

Let's Apply the Lesson

If the children have any questions for Adam and Eve, allow them to ask. Then help them say good-bye to Adam and Eve.

Our Bible words say, "God made the world." Adam and Eve, the first people, were a part of that world. Let's say our Bible words together. Do so. Have the children stand and lead them in verse 2 of "God Made Me."

Adam and Eve were God's special friends. You and I are God's special friends too. We are special because God made us. Pray, **Thank You, God, for making Adam and Eve and me.**

Learning Activities

(20 minutes)

Let's Apply the Lesson

Lead the children in singing "God Is Great." Then direct the children to the Family Living Center. If your class is large and you have multiple teachers, use the other activities from the beginning of the lesson as well.

Let's Go Home

Have Zach tell the children that it's time to clean up. Gather the children in a circle. Say this rhyme.

Listen to what I can say.
I've learned some Bible words today.
"God made the world."

Adam and Eve were a special part of the world that God made. You and I are also a special part of God's world. Lead the children to sing stanza 2 of "In the Beginning." Then lead them in singing "I'm Very Special to God."

We are special to God. We are special because God made each one of us. Pray with the children, **Thank You, God, for making Adam and Eve and me.**

Lesson 3
Date: ____________

God Made the First People, Adam and Eve

Genesis 1:26, 27; 2:18-22

Bible Words: "God . . . made the world" (Acts 17:24, *NIV*).

Lesson Value: God had made a beautiful world to be the home for people. Everything in God's world was ready for the creation of Adam and Eve. God's most valuable and most wonderful creation is man. People are God's most special creation because they are made in God's image. God made people to be His friends. Two's and three's can be God's friends. During today's lesson, your children will discover that they are important to God because He made them. What did God think about the people He made? God looked at everything He had made, and it was very good.

Know: Know that God is great.
Feel: Feel thankful that God created everything.
Do: Pray, "Thank You, God, for the things You made."

Children will accomplish the goals when they:

1. Say the Bible words, "God made the world."
2. Pray, "Thank You, God, for making Adam and Eve and me."
3. Sing about Adam and Eve and the people God made.
4. Point to Adam and Eve on the creation board.
5. Tell the names of the first man and woman.
6. Pretend to be Adam and Eve.

Let's Get Ready

For the Bible story, you will need the classroom Bible, puppet Zach, prepared Adam and Eve figures (page 31), and two adults who will present the first-person Bible story.

Prepare the Game Center, the Book/Picture Center, and the Art Center. If you are the only teacher, use just the Book/Picture Center. Have materials ready for the Family Living Center to be used after the Bible story.

Learning Activities

(30 minutes, including 10 minutes presession)

Let's Get Started

As children arrive, greet each one with the rhyme, "God Made Me." Substitute each child's name in place of the word *you*. Also substitute other items of creation for the words *sun* and *tree*.

God made the sun. God made the tree.
God made you, and God made me.

Direct each child to the attendance chart and offering container. Then direct her to get involved in one of the learning activities.

Worship and Bible Story

(15 minutes)

Let's Worship God

Have Zach tell the children, "It's time to put our things away so we can sing and pray to God." Begin singing as soon as the first child sits in the circle with you. Sing songs from the unit page or have children suggest songs to sing. If you know the song, "He's Got the Whole World in His Hands," sing this, using the children's names in place of the words *you* and *me*. "He's got Molly and Rachel in His hands. He's got Randy and Brock in His hands," etc. Lead children in saying the Bible words, "God made the world." If you have time, let the children take turns holding the Bible, pointing to the words, and "reading" them. Then pray, **Thank You, God, for making Adam and Eve and me.**

Let's Learn From the Bible

Introduction: Have Zach say, "I wonder what it was like for Adam and Eve to be the first people on earth." **I've wondered that too, Zach. It must have been very special to be the only people on earth. God gave them a wonderful place to live. Adam and Eve are here to visit us and tell us what it was like to be the first people and to live in God's beautiful garden. Let's welcome Adam and Eve.** Adam and Eve enter the room and greet each child with a hug, handshake, or pat on the head.

The Bible Story: *(The two adults will present the following first-person stories as Adam and Eve:)*

Adam: Hi, boys and girls. My name is Adam. God created me. Do you remember how God made the world? He made the day and night. He made the mountains and seas. He made the sun, moon, and stars. He made the fish and whales. He made the birds to fly in the sky. God made the dogs and cats and all the animals. What did God say about His world? *(Children should answer, "This is good.")*

God wasn't finished. After He created the animals, He had more creating to do. He created people. He created me. I was the first man. I'm very special because God made me. He made me to be His friend.

Eve: I'm God's special friend too. I was the first woman. Hi, boys and girls. My name is Eve. God created me. God created me to be Adam's friend.

God made a home for us in His beautiful garden. We lived there together. We took care of God's beautiful plants and animals. We were happy in the beautiful garden that God made. What did God say about the people He made? *(Children should answer, "This is very good.")*

stars. God is great because He made the sun, moon, and stars. . . . Show me the flowers and trees. God is great because He made the flowers and trees. . . . Show me the fish, bird, and animals. God is great because He made the fish, birds, and animals. . . . Show me the people. God is great because He made people. God is great because He made you and me.

Sing "God Is Great," holding up the appropriate fans.

Learning Activities

(20 minutes)

Let's Play Awhile

Our Bible words say, "God made the world." Have the children say the Bible words with you. Then have the children play the game from this session's Game Center.

Let the children make their creation booklets in the Art Center. If your group is large and you have multiple teachers, use the other activities from the beginning of class as well.

Let's Go Home

Have Zach tell the children that it's time to clean up. Gather the children in a circle. Bring a mirror or several mirrors to the circle. Let children look at themselves in the mirror(s). Lead them in saying this action rhyme.

I look in the mirror. What do I see? *(Look in the mirror.)*
I see someone God made. *(Point up.)*
That someone is me! God made me. *(Point to self.)*

I look in the mirror. What do I see? *(Look in the mirror.)*
I see someone who knows God is great. *(Point up.)*
That someone is me! God made me. *(Point to self.)*

I look in the mirror. What do I see? *(Look in the mirror.)*
I see someone God loves. *(Cross arms across chest.)*
That someone is me! God loves me. *(Point to self.)*

God Is Great

Based on Lessons 1—3

Bible Words: "God . . . made the world" (Acts 17:24, *NIV*).

Lesson Value: God created a beautiful world as a home for people and animals. He created amazing animals for people to enjoy. God's world shows us that He loves us. God's world shows us that He exists. Today, as your children review the days of creation, they will express thankfulness for everything that God created. They will know that God is great because of His great creations. They will also know that they are special to God because He created them.

Know: Know that God is great.
Feel: Feel thankful that God created everything.
Do: Pray, "Thank You, God, for the things You made."

Children will accomplish the goals when they:

1. Say the Bible words, "God made the world."
2. Pray, "Thank You, God, for making the world."
3. Sing about the things God has made.
4. Examine something God has made.
5. Point to a picture of something God made.
6. Name three things that God has made.

Let's Get Ready

For the Bible story, you will need the classroom Bible, puppet Zach, and one set of fans for each child (page 29).

Prepare the Game Center, the Book/Picture Center, and the Family Living Center. If you are the only teacher, use just the Game Center. Have materials ready for the Art Center to be used after the Bible story.

Learning Activities

(30 minutes, including 10 minutes presession)

Let's Get Started

Have Zach hold one of the creation fans and greet the children as they arrive. **Ryan, here's something that God made. What is something else that God made? Yes, God made the sun. Our Bible words say, "God made the world." God's world shows us that He loves us.**

Direct each child to complete the attendance chart, to deposit his offering, and to get involved in one of the learning activities.

Worship and Bible Story

(15 minutes)

Let's Worship God

Have Zach tell the children, "It's time to put our things away so we can sing and pray to God." Begin singing as soon as the first child sits in the circle with you. Sing songs from the unit page or have children suggest songs to sing. Sing "I'm Very Special to God." Then pray, **Thank You, God, for making the world.**

Let's Learn From the Bible

Introduction: Close your eyes. What do you see? I see darkness. That is what the world was like before God made anything. It was dark and empty. But God made a beautiful world. What did God say about the world He made? Children should answer, "This is good." **God made amazing animals. What did God say about the animals He made?** "This is good." **God made people His special friends. What did God say about the people He made?** "This is very good."

The Bible-story Review: *(Pass out the sky/water/land fans.)* God made the world. He made the sky, the water, and the land. We breathe the air God made. We drink water God made. And we get our food from the land God made. God loves us. Thank You, God, for the sky, land, and water.

(Pass out the sun/moon/stars fans.) God made the world. He made the sun, the moon, and the stars. The sun lights the day. The moon and the stars light the night. Thank You, God, for the sun, moon, and stars.

(Pass out the tree/flower fans.) God made the world. He made the beautiful flowers and tall trees. We like to look at flowers and we like to sit in the shade of big, tall trees. God made all the plants that grow on the land and in the water. God loves us. Thank You, God, for the plants.

(Pass out the fish/bird/animal fans.) God made the world. He made the animals. He made fish to swim in the water. He made birds to fly in the sky. He made animals to walk on the land. He made our pets. God loves us. Thank You, God, for making the animals.

(Pass out the people fans.) God made the world. He made all the people. He made Adam and Eve, the first man and woman. He made our moms and dads. He made our grandmas and grandpas. He made our brothers and sisters. He made our friends. He made each one of us. All of the people God made are very special. We are God's special friends. God loves us. Thank You, God, for making people.

Let's Apply the Lesson

God is great because He made such a beautiful world. What did God say about the world He made? "This is good." **God made a good world. God is great.**

Show me the sky, land, and water. God is great because He made the sky, land, and water. . . . Show me the sun, moon, and

Book/Picture Center

Unit 1—God Is Great

Items to Include:

Lesson 1
Copies of pages 30 and 31

Lesson 3
All About Hands
Busy Feet

Purpose: The child will examine something God has made and will feel thankful that God made everything.

Things to Do and Say

Lesson 1

Copy two sets of the border patterns (excluding the animals and people). Cut them out and mount them on cardboard to make matching cards.

In class, turn one set of pictures face up on the floor. Show one card from the second set. Ask children to name the item and then find the matching item among the pictures on the floor. When the match is located, have children stand and imitate that item. For the tree, children will stand and stretch out their arms. As children imitate the item, lead them to say the Bible words, "God made the world." Also lead children to pray, "Thank You, God, for trees."

Lesson 3

God made you! He made your wonderful hands and busy feet. Our hands and feet are remarkable because they can do many things! Thank You, God, for making our hands and feet.

What can you do with your hands? What can you do with your feet? Have children look through the books and tell what they can do with their hands and feet. As the opportunity presents itself, have children do what is shown on the page, such as clap and

Art Center

Unit 1—God Is Great

Items to Include:

Lesson 2
Copies of page 27
Washable ink pads in a variety of colors
Wet wipes

Lesson 3
Copies of page 32
Polaroid® camera and film

Purpose: The child will name things God has made and will thank God for what He has made.

Things to Do and Say

Lesson 2

Here are pictures of some animals God made. Let's name these animals. Thank You, God, for animals. Let's add our thumbprints to color the animals.

Use one color at a time. Manipulate each child's thumb. Roll each thumb from side to side across the ink pad. Then place the thumb in position on each animal and again roll the thumb from side to side. If available, use red ink for the ladybug, green for the frog, pink for the pig, and so on. Use the wet wipes to clean off the ink from the thumbs.

Our Bible words say, "God made the world." These animals are a part of God's world. God made the animals. Let's name these animals. Thank You, God, for ladybugs. Lead children to thank God for each animal.

NOTE: If you do not have a Polaroid® camera, take the children's pictures this week and have the film developed before next week's session.

Lesson 3

Cut open the windows on copies of page 32. Give each child a page to color. Take a Polaroid® picture of each child. Cut pictures slightly larger than the size of the opening. Tape the child's photograph behind the opening in his picture. Mount the entire page

Art Center, continued

Scissors (for teacher)
Glue
Transparent tape
Construction paper

Lesson 4
Copies of pages 33 and 34
Stickers from page 28
Stapler and staples
Scissors (for teacher)
Crayons or washable markers
Cotton balls
Small twigs
Leaves

on a piece of construction paper. Help each child open the “window” and pray, “Thank You, God, for making (name of child).”

Lesson 4

Prepare creation booklets by copying pages 33 and 34 back-to-back. Cut each page in half lengthwise. Stack the two pieces together so that pages are in order and place two staples in the “spine.” Prepare the stickers according to the instructions on page 28.

Our Bible words say, “God made the world.” We are going to make a book about the world God made. Read each page and help the children add the items to the page as follows: (1) Add the child's name. (2) Read. (3) Color the sky blue and add cotton clouds. (4) Add twigs and leaves for trees. (5) Add the sun, moon, and star stickers. (6) Add the fish and bird stickers. (7) Add the animal stickers. (8) Add the people stickers.

Children may color any part of the book they wish. Have children identify items. **These cotton balls look like something God made. Yes, they look like the clouds God made. Thank You, God, for the beautiful clouds. God is great because He made the beautiful clouds.**

Book/Picture Center, continued

Lesson 4
Creation books listed on page 13

wave and hop and run. Then sing “I'm Very Special to God.”

If you do not have access to these two books, find books and/or pictures of children and talk about what they are doing with their hands and feet.

Lesson 4

The Bible tells us that “God made the world.” Look at these books about God's world. What do these pictures show us that God made? . . . Thank You, God, for making the world. Place books where children can look at the pictures and name the things God made.

Family Living Center

Unit 1—God Is Great

Items to Include:

Lesson 1
A variety of potted plants (or a trip outdoors)
A package of seeds (i.e. bean, corn)
Potting soil in paper cups
Watering cans
Water (optional)

Lesson 2
A variety of stuffed animals

Purpose: The child will feel thankful that God created everything.

Things to Do and Say

Lesson 1

Let children water (or pretend to water) the potted plants or plants outside around the building. Also let the children plant a seed in one of the paper cups and water it. Discuss how the soil and water will help the seed grow into a plant.

God made the world. He made all the plants. Some plants give us food. Some plants have flowers. Other plants give us shade. Thank You, God, for plants.

When God made people, He gave them the job of taking care of the plants. How can we take care of the plants? Have children answer. **Plants need water to grow. Sometimes God waters the plants with rain. Sometimes people water the plants.**

Lesson 2

God made the world. God made the animals. God made the first people, Adam and Eve. God gave Adam the job of naming all the animals. Let's be Adam and name the animals. Have children touch or hold each stuffed animal and give the animal a name. These names can be the kind of animal or a personal name for the animal. **Adam and Eve must have felt thankful for the animals God made. Thank You, God, for the animals.**

Game Center

Unit 1—God Is Great

Items to Include:

Purpose: The child will say the Bible words, "God made the world."

Things to Do and Say

Lessons 1 and 4

Our Bible words say, "God made the world." Thank You, God, for making the world. Let's play a game to help us remember that God made the world.

Play ring-around-the-rosy to this rhyme. On the word *me,* children fall down. Repeat several times.

God made the world, God made the sea,
God made the animals; and God made me!

Lesson 2

Play follow-the-leader by imitating animals. Have children suggest animals to imitate. Announce each animal. **Here's an elephant God made.** Act like the animal. Then lead the children to say the Bible words, "God made the world." Ways to imitate animals:

- Elephant—walk bent over; clasp hands and swing arms like a trunk.
- Horse—gallop and neigh.
- Bird—flap arms and tweet and chirp.
- Duck—waddle and quack.
- Dog—walk on hands and knees and bark.

Game Center, continued

Lesson 3

Group the children in pairs as Adam and Eve. Call out the following instructions for each pair to follow together. After two or three commands, repeat the "spread out" command.

- Adam and Eve, spread out.
- Adam and Eve, touch hands.
- Adam and Eve, touch feet.
- Adam and Eve, smell the flowers.
- Adam and Eve, thank God.
- Adam and Eve, pick fruit.
- Adam and Eve, pet the animals.
- Adam and Eve, say the Bible words, "God made the world."

Family Living Center, continued

Lessons 3 and 4
Items from
Lessons 1 and 2

Lessons 3 and 4

Have children pretend to be Adam and Eve. They may take care of the garden and feed and name the animals. They may pretend to eat fruit from the trees in the garden. They may mountain climb or swim in the water.

God made the world. God made a beautiful world with mountains and rivers, plants and animals, and people. Thank You, God, for making the world.

After God made the world, He made people. He made the first man and woman, Adam and Eve. God told Adam and Eve to take care of the world God made. What did Adam and Eve do to take care of the plants? What did Adam and Eve do to take care of the animals? What did Adam and Eve drink? What did Adam and Eve eat? God made all these things.

God made the animals.

God's Wonders Center

Unit 1—God Is Great

Items to Include:

Lesson 1
A variety of plant foods such as carrots, green beans, strawberries, apples
Napkins
Wet wipes

Purpose: The child will examine something God made and will feel thankful that God made everything.

Things to Do and Say

Lesson 1

Prepare some of the food for a snack. Prepare some food for examination. If possible, provide the food with leaves attached, such as a carrot with the green top still attached.

Show the children the food. **God made the world. He made the earth, the sun, the stars, and the plants. He made plants that give us food. Look at the leaves on these foods. These foods grow on the plants that God made. Let's name these foods. Do you eat apples? Thank You, God, for apples. Thank You, God, for plants that give us food.**

Allow children to handle and examine the foods and the leaves attached to them. Point out how each leaf is different and how each food is different.

Before children eat their snacks, pray, **Thank You, God, for making plants that give us food.** As the children eat the snack, continue to talk about how God made food plants. **God made plants that grow food. We can thank God for our food. Thank You, God, for carrots, strawberries, and green beans.**

Instructions for Making Stickers
1. Mix two parts white glue and one part vinegar.
2. Add a few drops of peppermint extract if desired.
3. Lightly "paint" mixture onto backs of uncut stickers. Let dry.
4. Allow children to color (or print on colored stock).
5. Cut apart stickers and let children lick and stick.

Autumn, Unit 1—Lesson 4
Art Center

God's Wonders Center, continued

Lesson 2
Magnifying glass
A child's bug collection

Lesson 2

If a bug collection is not available, collect a few bugs in small glass jars. Punch air holes in the jar's covering. Bring the bugs to class, sealed in the glass jars. Or, if the weather permits, take children on a walk around the building to look for bugs. Prepare a jar with air holes in which to place the bugs. Bugs can be examined and released.

Have children gather around the bug display. **God made the world. He made the earth, the sun, the stars, the plants, and God made the animals. He made the bugs. Look at these bugs. Have you ever seen one of these bugs? What kind of bug is this? Thank You, God, for bugs.**

Let the children examine the bugs. Tell them the names of each one. Let the children use the magnifying glass to take a closer look at the bugs.

Lead the children to pray, "Thank You, God, for the things You have made."

Instructions for Making Fans

1. Copy fans on heavy paper or mount on cardboard.
2. Glue or tape craft sticks to fans for handles.
3. Make one set of fans for each teacher and child.

Directions for Border Visuals for Autumn, Unit 1—Lessons 1-3

Use a bulletin board, portable board, or wall area as background. Copy or trace patterns. Choose paper suitable for each pattern (construction paper, wrapping paper, shelf paper, tissue paper, newspaper, or paper sacks). Cut the selected paper to height of each pattern and length desired. Accordion-style fold paper to pattern's width. Place pattern on top of prepared paper and cut out shape. Unfold strip.

Completely cover background area with black paper. To use, distribute strips to children to hold until strips are ready to be added to board. For large group, cut strips into sections. Join sections on board.

Lesson 1: Add white or light blue paper over black to cover 3/4 of board. *(See sketch.)* Add clouds across top of sky area. Add land border across lower half of board. Add water border across bottom of board as shown. Add tree border at top of land border. Cut one sun and add to sky. Cut one moon and add to black area. Add stars across black area.
Lesson 2: Add birds, fish, and animals. Children may glue cotton balls to sheep.
Lesson 3: Add Adam and Eve silhouettes.

Border Visuals for Autumn, Unit 1—Lessons 1-3

"God . . . made the world"
Acts 17:24, NIV
God made me!

Dear Parent:

During this unit your child will learn about God's world in these lessons.
Lesson 1—*God Made the Earth and Sky* (Genesis 1:1-19)
Lesson 2—*God Made All the Animals* (Genesis 1:20-25)
Lesson 3—*God Made the First People, Adam and Eve* (Genesis 1:26, 27; 2:18-22)
Lesson 4—*God Is Great* (Review of Lessons 1-3)

Your child will discover that God is great. God is great because He created the world, the animals, and the people. God is great because He created each one of us. Your child will know that God is great and will feel thankful for the things God created. Your child will respond by thanking God for the things He made.

Here are some ways to reinforce these lessons at home:

- Point out things God made. Name each one. Say, "Thank You, God, for the *(name item)*."
- Tell your child why you are thankful for something God made. Say something like, "I'm thankful for apples because they taste so good."
- Play "I See Something God Made." Take turns guessing what the other one sees that God made.
- Encourage your child to "help" take care of house plants, the yard or garden, or any animals that you have.
- Pray this prayer with your child, "Thank You, God, for the things You made."
- Remind your child that God made the world because He loves him or her.
- Say the Bible words with your child every day: "God . . . made the world" (Acts 17:24, *NIV*).
- Sing these songs and repeat these action rhymes during the unit:

I'm Very Special to God

(Tune: "Hickory, Dickory, Dock")

I'm very special to God. He loves me very much.
He made my hands. He made my feet.
I'm very special to God.

God Made Me

God made the sun, *(Raise arms in circle over head.)*
God made the tree, *(Spread arms out to indicate branches.)*
God made you, and God made me! *(Point to another; then to self.)*

God made Adam. *(Bow.)* God made Eve. *(Curtsy.)*
God made you, and God made me. *(Point to another; then to self.)*

—*Joy M. Grewell and Kristi Walter*

Your child's teacher,

God Is Great

(Tune: "London Bridge")

God made all the stars above*, stars above, stars above.
God made all the stars above. God is great.
(*lands and seas, fish and whales, dogs and cats)

God made you and you and me, you and me, you and me.
God made you and you and me. God is great.

A Way to Go

A robin flies, *(Wave arms in flying motion.)*
A bunny hops, *(Hop up and down.)*
A turtle crawls so slow; *(Crawl in place very slowly.)*
God gave each animal He made
A special way to go! *("Walk" two fingers up one arm.)*

—*Jean Shannon*

Unit 2: God Is Love

Lessons 5–8

By the end of the unit, the children will

Know that God is love.
Feel happy about families.
Pray, "Thank You, God, for families."

Resources

Attendance chart
Heart stickers

Books

from Standard Publishing
God Cares for Me! (24-03112)
God's Love (24-03702)
My Family and Friends (24-03114)
My Family and Me (24-03701)
I'm Glad I'm Your Grandma (24-04210)

This Unit at a Glance

5 God Made Mothers — **1 Samuel 1:1-11, 19, 20**
Hannah is blessed by God with a son, Samuel.

6 God Made Fathers — **1 Samuel 17:12-20**
Jesse shows love and care for the physical needs of his children.

7 God Made Families — **Genesis 4:1, 2**
Adam and Eve, the first parents, are blessed by God with two sons, Cain and Abel.

8 God Is Love — **Review of Lessons 5–7**

Why Teach This Unit to Young Children?

As you teach this unit you will help children recognize and appreciate the many ways their parents show love on a daily basis. Young children recognize and feel love when it comes in the form of a big kiss or hug, when a trip to the park is planned, or ice cream and other treats are on the menu. A young child does not, however, appreciate that mom is showing love when she makes the child take a bath or lie down for a nap.

Daddies and mommies who go to work each day are showing their love by being faithful providers. Young children fail to understand that. During this unit you will help children understand that cooking, cleaning, mowing the lawn, and teaching them about God are some of the many ways moms and dads say, "I love you." The children will also be taught that it was our loving God who thought up the wonderful idea of families and it is He who puts each family together. They will be encouraged to be happy, to sing, and to pray, "Thank You, God, for my family."

A word of caution: Be aware of the different family settings your children may come from. Be alert and sensitive to any special needs that may arise during this unit.

The Bible words may seem to be short and simple, of little importance. But when we think of them as small seeds planted today that will produce a harvest of fruit in years to come, their value increases greatly.

Use the Bible words any time, when greeting children, in learning centers, songs, rhymes, prayers, at play, snack time, and when saying good-bye. **Sarah, look at the heart. Hearts make me think of our Bible words, "God is love." Let's sing, "God is love." . . . . Here is how we say our Bible words in sign language. . . . Now we can even tell people who can't hear that "God is love."**

Place Bibles with bookmarks and highlighted words in your learning centers for children to read. Always have your Bible near you when you tell the Bible story.

Things to Do for This Unit

- Make copies of the Parents' Letter, page 59, and the Unit Planning Sheet, pages 319 and 320.
- Photocopy the Learning Center Cards, pages 47-52; cut apart on solid lines; glue side 1 on cardboard, then side 2 on back of cardboard. Laminate for durability (optional).
- Gather/prepare materials listed on Learning Center Cards.
- Photocopy pages 53-55; add color; mount on construction paper for teaching pictures.
- Make felt figures from patterns and instructions on pages 56 and 57.
- For Lesson 5, find pictures of mothers and children.
- For Lesson 6, find pictures of dads working or doing things with children.
- For Lesson 7, you will need a large sheet or blanket and a picnic basket.
- For Lesson 8, make four large red hearts from felt

Use These Songs and Action Rhymes During Unit 2

God Made My Family

J. M. G. Joy M. Grewell

It's Time to Worship

A. K. Alice Koerner

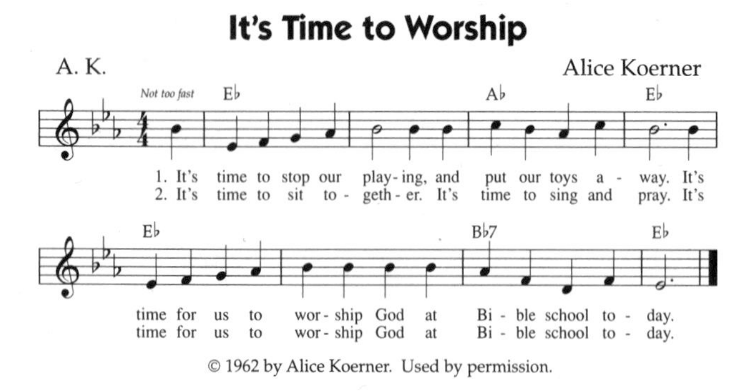

© 1962 by Alice Koerner. Used by permission.

I Can Talk to God

G. S. Gertrude Shannon

Ab Eb
I can talk to God. I can talk to God. I
Eb7 Ab
know that He is lis-ten-ing. I can talk to God.

We Thank You, Thank You, God

S. T. Sylvia Tester

God's World

J. M. G. Joy M. Grewell

My Mother and Daddy

My mother loves me very much, *(Hug self.)*
When I'm sleeping, when I play.
(Pretend to sleep; then clap hands.)
My mother takes good care of me, *(Point to self.)*
And I am happy every day! *(Smile.)*
(Repeat, substituting "daddy" for "mother.")

—Sandra Maddux

kneel to pray, sit up and smile, then cradle the new baby. Show the picture of Hannah and Samuel. Zach asks the following questions:

- "Who gave baby Samuel to Hannah?" (God.)
- "Did God love baby Samuel?" (Yes.) **God knew baby Samuel would need a mommy to take care of him.**
- "Did Hannah love Samuel?" (Yes.) **She took care of him and taught him about God's love.**
- "Does God love you?" (Yes!) **God knew you would need a mommy to take care of you.**
- "Does your mommy love you?" (Yes!) **She takes care of you and teaches you about God's love.**

Can you tell me one way your mommy loves and takes care of you? Older children may be able to answer; young children may only point as you hold up a picture. **Yes, Rachel, your mommy makes sure you eat good food.** Sing, "We Thank You, Thank You, God" (for our mommies).

Learning Activities

(20 minutes)

Let's Play Awhile

Do the rhyme, "My Mother and Daddy." Have the God's Wonders Center activity ready. Explain what you will be doing.

Let's Go Home

Sing as the children pick up, "This is the way we pick up the toys (blocks, dolls, trucks) . . . when we pretend to be mommy."

Read a book until parents arrive. Or, if the children need action, play "Mommy Says." Give simple instructions for the children to follow. Make sure each child has his coloring page and a Parents' Letter to take home.

God Made Mothers

1 Samuel 1:1-11, 19, 20

Bible Words: "God is love" (1 John 4:8, *NIV*).

Lesson Value: A little one easily recognizes the comforting side of mom's love—a hug or kiss, soothing words for an "owie," or listening to a story or song while sitting on mom's lap. This lesson will help the young child identify other ways his mother shares God's love daily. The child will learn that he has a mother because of God's love. The child will be encouraged to feel happy God gave him a mother and to give thanks for her. Make sure you substitute another caregiver for a child who has no mother.

Know: Know that God is love.
Feel: Feel happy about families.
Do: Pray, "Thank You, God, for my mommy."

Children will accomplish the goals when they:

1. Say the Bible words, "God is love."
2. Tell who gave baby Samuel to Hannah.
3. Sing about mommies.
4. Pray, "Thank You, God, for my mommy."
5. Pretend to be a mommy taking care of her child.
6. Point to or name the mommy in the Bible story.

Let's Get Ready

For the Bible story, you will need your classroom Bible and a bookmark with a heart sticker at the top. Have heart stickers and pictures of mothers loving and caring for their children. Make a flannel Hannah and baby Samuel (patterns on pages 56 and 57) and have a flannelgraph board ready. Also, make a copy of the picture of Hannah and baby Samuel from page 53. Add color, mount on construction paper, and cover with clear, self-adhesive plastic (optional).

Prepare the Family Living Center, the Book/Picture Center, and the Art Center. If you are the only teacher use just the Family Living Center and include items from the other two centers. Have the God's Wonder's Center ready to use after the Bible story.

Learning Activities

(30 minutes, including 10 minutes presession)

Let's Get Started

Have Zach hold a small plastic or stuffed animal or baby as he welcomes the children. "Hi, Rachel. I'm so happy your mommy (daddy, etc.) brought you to church to learn about God's love. I brought my baby with me. Miss Becky will help you get settled and then you can find a baby to love and care for." Make sure each child becomes involved in a learning activity.

Worship and Bible Story

(15 minutes)

Let's Worship God

Zach lays his baby down and says, "Let's clean up while our babies rest. Then we will learn about God's love." Give specific help as needed. **Hunter, thank you for putting that truck on the shelf.**

Sing "God Made My Family"; then sing "I Can Talk to God."

Pray, **Thank You, God, for giving us mommies.** Open your Bible and read 1 John 4:8. Sing to the tune of "Farmer in the Dell":

"God is love." Yes, "God is love."
My Bible tells me that "God is love."

When you hear your name, stand up and say our Bible words and I will give you a heart sticker. If a child is reluctant, simply trace the words in your Bible with his finger as you say, **"God is love." God loves Jacob.**

Let's Learn From the Bible

Introduction: Have your Bible open on your lap as you hold up Zach. Say, **Where is your baby, Zach?** "He is sleeping," Zach replies. **Yes, a good mommy makes sure her baby gets lots of rest. Our Bible story is about a good mommy named . . .** *(pause, allowing children to answer)* **Hannah and her baby . . .** *(pause)* **Samuel.** Lay Zach aside.

The Bible Story: The Bible tells us that Hannah was sad because she had no children. *(Lay Bible aside, kneel, bow head, and fold hands as if praying. Pretend to cry. Watch children carefully. If some seem upset, reassure them before you continue.)* "O, dear God, this is Hannah. I'm asking You again for a baby. Please God, if You will give me a baby boy I will teach him about You and Your great love."

(Sit up as you place the sad Hannah on the board.) Why was Hannah sad? *(Let children answer.)* Yes, because she had no baby to love. *(Smile.)* She would soon be happy though!

(Turn the figure over to happy Hannah.) God heard Hannah's prayer. God gave Hannah a beautiful baby boy! What did she name her baby? . . . Yes, Samuel! *(Place Samuel in Hannah's arms.)* Oh, how happy Hannah was that God had given her baby Samuel to care for and love!

Let's Apply the Lesson

Zach says, "May we help you tell the story?" **That's a great idea!** Lead the class in acting out the story. Look sad as you

Let's Apply the Lesson

Have Zach call on children to answer questions. Repeat the questions as needed, giving heart stickers as children answer.

- "What is the daddy's name (or point to the daddy)?" **Yes, Jesse is the daddy in our story who loved his children.**
- "What is the son's name (point to the son)?" **You're right, David is the name of the son in our story.**
- "What kind thing did Jesse do to show he loved his sons?" **Yes, he sent them food to eat.**
- "Tell me (point to) one thing your daddy does to show he loves you." Hold up pictures; help as needed.
- "Who gave your daddy to you?" **Yes, God knew you would need a daddy. God loves you and gave you a daddy.** Also mention other male caregivers.

Sing "Thank You, Thank You, God" (for my daddy, grandpa, etc.). Repeat several times.

Learning Activities

(20 minutes)

Let's Play Awhile

Do the action rhyme, "My Mother and Daddy," and sing the Bible words song used earlier. Then go to the Block Center. If you have more than one teacher also use the previous activities.

Let's Go Home

Zach says, "Let's pretend we are daddies driving big machines that pick up toys." Make engine noises as your "claws" pick up toys. **That's right, Elizabeth, your truck must be strong to pick up three blocks at one time. Wow!**

Quiet option: Read books or talk about pictures. Active option: Play "Daddy Says." (Daddy says, "Hammer a nail . . . shave your face, etc.")

Make sure each child has his coloring page from the Book/Picture Center as he goes home.

God Made Fathers

1 Samuel 17:12-20

Bible Words: "God is love" (1 John 4:8, *NIV*).

Lesson Value: This lesson will help children appreciate the many ways their fathers show love toward them, from playing "rough" on the floor to getting up each morning and going to work so that their physical needs can be met. The child will learn that it is because of God's love she has a father. She will also be encouraged to feel happy God gave her a father, and to give thanks for her daddy (or a father substitute).

Know: Know that God is love.
Feel: Feel happy about families.
Do: Pray, "Thank You, God, for my daddy."

Children will accomplish the goals when they:

1. Say the Bible words, "God is love."
2. Point to or name Jesse and David in a picture.
3. Pray, "Thank You, God, for my daddy."
4. Pretend to be a daddy.
5. Name things about daddies that are good.

Let's Get Ready

For the Bible story, you will need the classroom Bible, Zach, the flannelgraph figures of Jesse, David, and his bundle (patterns on pages 56 and 57), flannelgraph board, heart stickers, and pictures of fathers working or doing things with children. Also, copy the picture of Jesse and David (page 54); color; mount on construction paper; cover with clear, self-adhesive plastic (optional).

Prepare the Family Living Center, the God's Wonders Center, and the Book/Picture Center. If you are the only teacher use just the Family Living Center, incorporating the others as you can. Have the Block Center ready to be used after the Bible story.

Cut heart-shaped pieces of bread with cookie cutters to use when children arrive.

Learning Activities

(30 minutes, including 10 minutes presession)

Let's Get Started

Be seated as you greet children so you and Zach can be on their eye level. Zach says, "Hello, Sarah, here is some bread. In our Bible story, David's father, Jesse, asked him to take some bread to his brothers who were away from home. Jesse loved his sons. Would you like a bite before you put your heart sticker on our chart? Hearts remind us that 'God is love.'" Help as needed, then guide each child to a learning center.

Worship and Bible Story

(15 minutes)

Let's Worship God

Zach begins singing "It's Time to Worship" as he picks up several toys. Begin singing "God Made My Family" as the first children arrive. Do the rhyme, "My Mother and Daddy." Sing, "God's World" and "I Can Talk to God." Say, **Let's pray together, "Thank You, God, for giving us daddies."** By telling what you will pray before you pray, the children will be apt to say the words with you. Place your Bible on your lap and do the rhyme, "My Bible" (page 12). Then sing this Bible words song to the tune of "Farmer in the Dell":

"God is love." Yes, "God is love."
My Bible tells me that "God is love."

Let's Learn From the Bible

Introduction: Hold Zach up and have him pretend to be chewing. He swallows and says, "That was good bread!" **Zach, did you know that someone had to work so that we would have money to buy that bread?** Zach shakes his head and says, "No, I never thought of that." To the children he says, "Have YOU ever thought about that?"

Lay Zach down as you say to the children, **Our daddies work hard so that we will have money to buy food, clothes, and other things we need. Our daddies love us. Let's find out about a daddy in the Bible who loved his children.**

Tell the children they are going to help you with this story. Explain that they will need to listen and watch carefully so they will know what to do. Practice these actions with them: Place hands around mouth as though calling; pat thighs to simulate running; look sad (pull corners of mouth down); point away from you; rub tummy; hug yourself; clap hands. Do these actions where indicated in the story. Place your Bible on your lap.

The Bible Story: *(Place figure of Jesse holding the bundle on the flannelboard.)* What is this daddy's name? Yes, his name is Jesse.

One day, Jesse called, "David, David, come here. *(Calling motion.)* I have a special job for you."

David ran quickly to his father. *(Pat thighs. Make flannelgraph David "run" to Jesse.)* "What do you want me to do, Father?"

(Look sad.) Jesse told David, "I miss your big brothers who are away from home. Maybe they do not have enough food to eat. *(Rub tummy.)* Please take this food to them *(place bundle in David's hands)* so they will know that I love them very much." *(Hug self.)*

What kind of good food is in the bundle? . . . Yes, bread for David's big brothers. David said, "I will take this food to them and find out how they are doing." *(Clap.)*

Let's Apply the Lesson

Zach asks the following questions while you and the children answer enthusiastically.

- "Who gives us mommies?" **God.**
- "Who gives us daddies?" **God.**
- "Who gives us our families?" **God.**
- "Does God love you?" **Yes!**
- "The Bible says, 'God is what?'" **"God is love."**
- Zach whispers, "The Bible says, 'God is what?'" You and children whisper, **"God is love."**
- Zach says in a strong voice, "The Bible says, 'God is what'?'" You and children reply in strong voices, **"God is love."**

Zach says, "There is one more thing in our picnic basket." Give a cookie to each each child. **I'm so happy that God thought of families.** As children eat their cookies, show them the picture of the first family and help them identify each person.

Learning Activities

(20 minutes)

Let's Play Awhile

Zach says, "Let's stand up and do our rhyme, "My Mother and Daddy." Children will then go to the Art Center. If you have more than one teacher, offer several learning centers.

Let's Go Home

Zach says, "Moms and dads will be coming soon for their boys and girls. Let's put away our toys so we will be ready." Sing, "This is the way we pick up the toys . . . and put them all away." Encourage children by including their names in the song.

Divide children into small groups and give each child her flannelgraph family from the Art Center. Let children tell the names of the people in their families. Then play, "I'm Looking for a Family." Describe a family until a child recognizes it as his family. Be as specific as needed.

God Made Families

Genesis 4:1, 2

Bible Words: "God is love" (1 John 4:8, *NIV*).

Lesson Value: God loved us from the very beginning, and out of this love came God's plan for the family. This lesson will help children celebrate the families God has given them. Children will be encouraged to name things about their families that are good. They will sing about families, pretend to be a family, and pray, thanking God for their families. As throughout all of this unit, be sensitive to those children who may come from broken or troubled homes. As you prepare for this lesson spend extra time in prayer asking God to give you the words that would encourage these young children.

Know: Know that God is love.
Feel: Feel thankful for families.
Do: Pray, "Thank You, God, for my family."

Children will accomplish the goals when they:

1. Say the Bible words, "God is love."
2. Pray, "Thank You, God, for my family."
3. Pretend to be a family.
4. Sing about families.
5. Name one thing about families that is good.
6. Point to or name the people in the Bible story.

Let's Get Ready

For the Bible story, you will need Zach, a large sheet or blanket to sit on, a picnic basket with the following: a Bible with small scene to represent "world" placed in Genesis 1 and heart placed in 1 John 4; flannelgraph family (pages 56 and 57); picture of Bible-times family (page 55) prepared as a teaching picture; tiny heart-shaped cookies.

Prepare the God's Wonders Center, the Family Living Center, and the Book/Picture Center. If you are the only teacher, use just the Book/Picture Center. Have materials ready for the Art Center to use after the Bible story.

Learning Activities

(30 minutes, including 10 minutes presession)

Let's Get Started

Place a heart sticker on Zach's cheek and paint a small heart on your own cheek. As children arrive, Zach excitedly shows them his "heart." "Hi, Devon. Look, I have a heart on my cheek. It reminds me of our Bible words, 'God is love.' You may have a heart after you put your sticker on our chart." Follow your usual routine; then direct children to the God's Wonders Center.

Worship and Bible Story

(15 minutes)

Let's Worship God

Zach sings "It's Time to Worship" as a signal to clean up. Have children sit on the blanket as they arrive. Do the rhyme, "My Mother and Daddy"; repeat it several times. Sing "God Made My Family" and "I Can Talk to God." Pray, **Thank You, God, for loving us. Thank You, God, for our families.** With hands still folded and head bowed, sing "We Thank You, Thank You, God" (for our families). Ask several children, **Why do you have a heart on your cheek? . . . That's right! The Bible tells us "God is love."** Do the rhyme, "My Bible." **God loves us and gave us our families.**

Let's Learn From the Bible

Introduction: Zach pulls or pushes a picnic basket out where children can see it. Ask, **Zach, are you going on a picnic?** He answers, "Yes! I heard our Bible story was about a family and picnics are one of the best things families can do together!" Lay Zach aside, keeping the basket close. **Zach is right, picnics can be lots of fun. Let's see what is in our basket.** As you pull out each item, allow a child to hold it as you talk about it, then put it down.

The Bible Story: *(Pull out Bible)* What is this? . . . Yes, a Bible. In the beginning of our Bible we read that God made the world. *(Show the scene secured in Genesis.)* Who can tell me the name of the first man God made? . . . You are right, Adam was the first man God made and he was the first daddy. *(Pull out the flannelgraph father and put it on the board.)*

Who can tell me the name of the first woman God made? . . . Great! Eve was the first woman God made and she was the first mommy. *(Pull out the flannelgraph mom and place it next to Adam. Next place the two sons on the board.)*

Our Bible tells us God gave Adam and Eve two children to love and take care of. Can anybody remember their names? . . . Cain was the older brother and Abel was the younger brother.

(Pull out or point to picnic basket.) Maybe they went on picnics together just like our families do today. *(Turn to 1 John in your Bible and show the heart.)* "God is love." He knew we would need our families. I'm so happy that God loves us and gives us our families! Let's say thank-you to God. *(Prompt children by counting and holding up fingers.)* One, two, three *(very enthusiastically)*, "Thank You, God!" Yes, thank You, God, for families. *(Sing "God Made My Family.")*

Let's Apply the Lesson

Moving quickly through this activity, Zach calls a child by name, the child stands and answers one of the questions below. Give the child a sticker and have him remain standing. When all children are standing, do the rhyme, "My Mother and Daddy."

- Does God love you?
- Does your mommy love you?
- Who gave you a mommy?
- Does your daddy love you?
- Who gave you a daddy?
- Does your family love you?
- Who gave you a family?

Learning Activities

(20 minutes)

Let's Play Awhile

Do the rhyme, "My Mother and Daddy," then go to the Block Center. If you are the only teacher and have not done the God's Wonders Center, pull out the cookies from your basket and allow children a few minutes to eat them before you begin the blocks activity.

Let's Go Home

Sing songs from this unit and repeat the action rhymes. Have a book used earlier in this unit ready in case parents are delayed. Make sure children take home their picture frames and their Art Center activity.

God Is Love

Review of Lessons 5–7

Bible Words: "God is love" (1 John 4:8, *NIV*).

Lesson Value: The Bible stories and Bible words from this unit will be reviewed and the lessons applied. Children will be reminded once again that it is because of God and His love for them that they have families. They will be encouraged to feel happy and to thank God for their families. This lesson will be a celebration in honor of families and will reinforce the ideas taught earlier in this unit.

Know: Know that God is love.
Feel: Feel happy about families.
Do: Pray, "Thank You, God, for my family."

Children will accomplish the goals when they:

1. Say the Bible words, "God is love."
2. Sing about families.
3. Pretend to be part of a family.
4. Pray, "Thank You, God, for my family."
5. Identify people in the Bible stories.
6. Answer, "God", when asked, "Who loves us and gives us families?"

Let's Get Ready

Make sure you have the pictures and frames together before class, as directed in the Family Living Center.

For the Bible story, you will need Zach, a large blanket, flannelgraph board, picnic basket filled with the following: Bible with heart marking 1 John 4:8, four large red felt hearts to go on the flannelgraph board, flannelgraph figures from Lessons 5-7, and heart stickers.

Prepare the Family Living Center, the Art Center, and the God's Wonders Center. If you are the only teacher use just the Family Living Center. Have the materials ready for the Block Center to be used after the Bible story.

Learning Activities

(30 minutes, including 10 minutes presession)

Let's Get Started

Zach greets each child by name and with a big hug. "Hi, Elizabeth *(hug)*. I am so glad you came to learn about God's love." Help each child put a heart sticker on the chart and then move to a learning center.

Worship and Bible Story

(15 minutes)

Let's Worship God

Have Zach signal the children to clean up by singing, "It's Time to Worship." Be seated on the blanket as you did last week. Sing "God Made My Family" and do the rhyme, "My Mother and Daddy." Sing "I Can Talk to God." Pray, **Thank You, God, for loving us. Thank You for giving us families.** Sing "We Thank You, Thank You God" (for our families).

Let's Learn From the Bible

Introduction: Zach says, "We are sitting on our blanket again today. I wonder if we will go on another picnic." Zach pulls the picnic basket out front again as he did last week. Ask, **Zach, would you like to go on another picnic?** He says, "Yes, I had so much fun last week that I want to do it again." Zach turns toward children, "Don't you?" **OK, let's see what we have in our basket today.** Lay Zach aside as you pull the basket close.

The Bible-story Review: *(Pull out your Bible and turn to 1 John 4:8 and the big red heart. Say the following rhyme.)*

This is my Bible; I'll open it wide
And see what is written on the inside! "God is love."

Say those words with me, "God is love." Every time I pull out a big red heart you say the Bible words with me. *(Pull out a heart.)* "God is love." Great!

Our Bible tells us about a woman who was sad. *(Pull out sad Hannah and place her on the board.)* Do you remember her name? . . . Yes, Hannah. She talked to God and he gave her a little baby boy to love. *(Turn Hannah over; place Samuel next to her.)* His name was *(pause)* . . . Samuel. You are right. God loved Samuel and he knew Samuel would need a good mommy. *(Pull out a red heart.)* "God is love."

Our Bible tells us about a daddy named Jesse. *(Remove Hannah and Samuel; put Jesse on the board.)* He loved his sons and wanted to be sure they had enough food so he sent his son *(pause)* David to take food to his big brothers. *(Put David and bundle up.)* God knew children would need daddies to love and help take care of them. *(Pull out heart.)* "God is love."

Our Bible tells us about the first family God made. *(Remove Jesse, David, and bundle; put up family.)* Let's see if we can remember their names. The daddy . . . Adam, the mommy . . . Eve, and the children . . . Cain and Abel. Super! God gives us families to love and take care of us. *(Pull out heart.)* "God is love." Let's thank God again. Sing "God Made My Family."

Book/Picture Center

Unit 2—God Is Love

Items to Include:

- Books (List on page 37.)
- Felt figures, pages 56, 57
- Pictures of mothers and children, fathers and children, fathers working, and families
- Copies of coloring pages, 53-55
- Crayons or washable markers.

Purpose: The child will identify family members from the Bible stories and from modern-day pictures.

Things to Do and Say

Lesson 5

Before children arrive make copies of page 53 and arrange the teaching materials in a way that invites the children to come and handle them.

Talk with each child about the picture of Hannah holding Samuel. **This mommy is named Hannah. She was sad because she had no baby to love. She asked God for a baby and he gave her Samuel. God gives us our mommies to love and care for us. Selena, who gave baby Samuel to Hannah? . . . Yes, God did. Sutton, who gave you your mommy? . . . You are right! God did. Let's say, "Thank You, God, for mommy."**

Lesson 6

Make copies of page 54 and have appropriate materials displayed for children before they arrive. Use this center as a time for holding and hugging children as you read, talk, and help them.

Emily, this is David and his daddy, Jesse. Jesse loved his sons very much, just like your daddy loves you. Point to the daddy. . . . Yes, his name is Jesse. What is his son's name? . . . Great, David is right! Who gave you a daddy? . . . God did, because He loves you. Let's pray, 'Thank You, God, for my daddy."

God's Wonders Center

Unit 2—God Is Love

Items to Include:

Lesson 6

- Toaster (optional)
- Sliced bread
- Butter
- Plastic knives
- Heart-shaped cookie cutters

Purpose: The child will learn the Bible words while enjoying hands-on activities.

Things to Do and Say

Lesson 5

Before class ask a mom to bring her baby to visit your classroom. If this is not possible, plan to take a walk to the church nursery to view the babies.

As children look at the baby, comment on how little she is and on how much work it is to care for a baby. **Mommies have to work hard to take care of their babies. Kordell, can you name one thing your mommy does for you? . . . Good, she bakes you cookies. . . . Yes, Sue, she pushes you on the swing. Mommies love their children very much and work hard to take care of them. Let's sing softly for the baby.** Sing "God Made My Family," and then "We Thank You, Thank You, God" (for our mommies).

Lesson 6

If you choose to use the toaster make proper safety arrangements. Toast the bread and let children press the cookie cutters into the toast making hearts. Let them use plastic knives to spread butter on their "hearts" and then eat the hearts.

Hearts make us think of love. Our Bible tells us that "God is love." As children work, sing to the tune of "Farmer in the Dell":

"God is love." Yes, "God is love."
My Bible tells me that "God is love."

Book/Picture Center, continued

Lesson 7

Copy page 55 and display the material you have selected for this lesson.

Connie, look at this family. We read about them in our Bible. The daddy's name is Adam, the mommy's name is Eve, and their sons are Cain and Abel. Can you tell me who gives us our families? . . . Yes, the Bible says God gives us our families. Thank You, God, for Connie's family. What do you like to do with your family? Help as needed. . . . **Thomas is looking at a book about families. Maybe we could pretend I am the mommy** (daddy, grandmother) **and you are my children. I'll read the book to you.**

God's Wonders Center, continued

Napkins
Classroom Bible
Heart stickers.

Kevin, what does our Bible say? . . . Yes, "God is love." Here is a heart sticker. When daddy asks, "Why do you have that sticker?" you can say, "Because 'God is love.'"

Sing "God's World" (God made daddies).

Lesson 7
Face paint
Handheld mirror
Bible
Small bowl of water
Damp washcloth
Paper towels.

Lesson 7

Arrange your open Bible and materials on a table. Have one adult-size chair facing a child-size chair. As children arrive, explain that this is a special paint for faces and that it will wash off easily. If some children are hesitant, offer to paint their hands. If you have time you may want to paint faces and hands. **Peter, you may choose a color and I will paint a heart on your cheek. This will help you remember our Bible words. Can you say them? . . . Yes, "God is love."**

As you paint, sing "God Made My Family," "God's World" (God made families), and "God Is Love" (see Lesson 6). Let each child see his face in the mirror when you have finished. **Janet, when Mommy or Daddy asks, "Why do you have a heart on your face?" what will you say? . . . Great, "God is love."**

Lesson 8
Heart-shaped sugar cookies
Plastic knives
Paper towels
Frosting, butter, or peanut butter
Bible
Clean-up supplies

Lesson 8

Hold up a cookie. **Who can tell me what shape this cookie is? What does a heart make us think about? . . . Yes, Hunter, God's love. Let's say our Bible words together. One, two, three. "God is love."** Sing, "God Is Love" (Lesson 6).

Let children help pass out paper towels, cookies, and knives. Explain that they will spread frosting on their cookies and then eat them. Choose songs from this unit to sing as you help the children work.

Block Center

Unit 2—God Is Love

Items to Include:

Large blocks

Lesson 6
A piece of cloth

Lesson 8
Doll
Blanket
Picnic basket

Purpose: The child will act out the Bible stories.

Things to Do and Say

Lesson 6

Use the blocks to make a sheep pen, house, and road. Tie the cloth around a block to look like a bundle of food. Act out the story as many times as you can. Several children can be sheep to which David waves good-bye when he hears his father call.

Help children by telling them exactly what to say. **Caleb, you are the daddy, Jesse. Call, "David, David, come here, Son." Jacob, you run to your daddy and say, "Here I am."** You may have to speak for young children but they will enjoy being a part. **Tori, give your son David a big hug and say, "I love you," just the way your daddy does when you leave him.**

Lesson 8

Act out the Bible stories taught in this unit. **Noah, let's wrap the doll in this blanket and pretend he is baby Samuel. We can build a church with these blocks and you can pretend to be sad Hannah asking God for a baby. When God gave Hannah the baby boy she had prayed for, Hannah loved her baby Samuel. Your mommy loves you, too, Emily.**

Anna, let's pretend you are Eve, the first mommy God made. We can take Cain and Abel on a picnic. Why don't we ask Mark and Tom to be your sons? . . . Our Bible

Family Living Center

Unit 2—God Is Love

Items to Include:

Camera and film
Dolls and clothing
Dishes and food
Housecleaning items

Lesson 5
Pictures of mommies with children
Women's dress-up items

Lesson 6
Pictures of daddies with children or working

Purpose: The child will pretend to be various family members.

Things to Do and Say

Lesson 5

Have small Bibles with the Bible words highlighted in this center. Take pictures of the children as they play. Make sure you get a picture of each child. Do this during the first three lessons. **Emily, I like the way you are rocking your baby. Smile, and I will take your picture.**

As children play, comment on ways they are showing love to their babies. Remind them that their mommies love them in the same ways. **Sally, I can see you are feeding your baby. You must love your baby. What good food does your mommy feed you? . . . She must love you. Let's thank God for your mommy.** Help children pray, "Thank You, God, for my mommy."

Lesson 6

Encourage even girls to pretend to be daddies taking care of children or going to work. **Kyle, I see you are dressed up. Are you going to work? . . . What kind of work do you do? . . . You must love your family to work so hard for them. Does your daddy work hard? . . . What other good things does he do for you?** Help as needed, using the pictures you have available. **Does he love you? . . . Let's thank God for your daddy.** Help children pray.

Family Living Center, continued

Plastic tools
Riding cars and trucks
Men's dress-up items
Old watches, briefcases, calculators

Lesson 7
Pictures of families

Lesson 8
Pictures used during this unit
Pictures taken in Lessons 5-7
Construction paper
Magnetic tape
Glue stick
Copies of frame on page 52

Lesson 7

Encourage children to form family groups and suggest activities that they can do together (go to church, the park, the store, out to eat, on vacation, or to Grandma's house).

Being together with our families is fun. Chase, are you taking your family to church to learn about God's love? . . . Brook, your family is going to visit Grandmother? What fun! Thank You, God, for giving us families. Arrange chairs in the form of a car and use old belts as seatbelts. As you speak with the children, give each an opportunity to pray. **Carolyn, God gave you a special family. Let's thank Him.** Help as needed. **Thank You, God, for my family.**

Lesson 8

Before class make copies of the frame on page 52. If possible, use colored paper. Cut out the centers. Using a glue stick secure a picture behind the frame by gluing only the frame around the picture, not the picture itself. Glue the frame to construction paper. Parents can later remove the picture. Write the child's name on the line. Secure magnets to the back.

During class allow children to pretend as in previous lessons. Show them their pictures and give them opportunities to pray. **Holly, here is a picture of you pretending to be a mommy loving her baby. God loves us so much he gives us our families. Let's thank Him.**

Block Center, continued

words say, "God is love." God made families to love each other. Adam and Eve loved their little boys. Your family loves you!

Come to a Family Celebration

Who: Families and close friends of young children—moms, dads, brothers, sisters, grandmas and grandpas, but no pets!

When: ______________________________

Where: ______________________________

What to bring: ______________________________

Whom to call: ______________________________

Come and join the fun as we celebrate God's love
for our children and our families.

Art Center

Unit 2—God Is Love

Items to Include:

Lesson 5
Play dough
Heart-shaped cookie cutters
Spatulas
Plastic knives
Cookie sheets
Heart stickers.

Lesson 7
Bible
Felt figures made from patterns on pages 56 and 57
Washable markers
Small plastic bags

Purpose: The child will say the Bible words, "God is love."

Things to Do and Say

Lesson 5

Have the classroom Bible, play dough, and accessories on the table when children arrive. Hold up a cookie cutter. **When we see a heart we think of love.** Hold up the open Bible. **The Bible says, "God is love."**

As children play, work your way around the table helping with the play dough. Show little ones how to make a pancake and then press a cutter into the dough. Go around the table a second time with your Bible and stickers allowing children to "read" the words and receive a sticker. **Aaron, what do our Bible words say? . . . Yes, "God is love." Here is a sticker. When mommy asks why you have a sticker tell her, "God is love."**

Lesson 7

Before class cut out enough felt figures so that each child will have his family members. Patterns are on pages 56 and 57. Put each child's family figures in a plastic bag with the child's name written on it with permanent marker, or put a piece of paper with the child's name on it in the bag.

During class give each child her bag. **Lisa, who did God put in your family? . . . Right, here is your mommy, daddy, and two sisters. What does your family like to do together?** Help as needed. **You like to play together? That is a good thing for families**

Art Center, continued

Yarn and small pieces of cloth (optional)

Lesson 8
Copies of page 58
Finger paint or sponges and tempera paint (light colors will work best)
Paper towels
Damp washclothes
Towels
Newspaper
Large paint shirts
Glitter or colored sugar (optional)

to do together. Our Bible says, "God is love." God gave you a family, Lisa. He loves you. Children may scribble-color faces and clothes on their families or use the other materials you supply.

Lesson 8

Before class make copies of page 58 and prepare your work area. First, remind children that hearts make us think of love. Tell them that the words on their papers say "God is love." As they work make your way around the table helping and talking with each child.

Devon, can you "read" what these words say? . . . Yes, you know the Bible words, "God is love." Kara, what do these hearts make you think about? . . . I think of love from God too. God loves us and gives us families. Can you tell me one thing about your family that is good? (Give help as needed—play together, work together, go to church, help and care for each other., etc.) If you want, sprinkle glitter or colored sugar on the paint before it dries.

Hannah loved her
baby Samuel.

Jesse loved David
and his brothers.

Adam and Eve loved their family.

Autumn, Unit 2

Bulletin Board Suggestion

Use patterns to make construction-paper people to put on board. Make copies of the coloring pages (53-55) and put these on board also. Cut out letters or write "God is love" on board. Place words low enough for children to point to as they learn the Bible words. Make a border of hearts to go around the board.

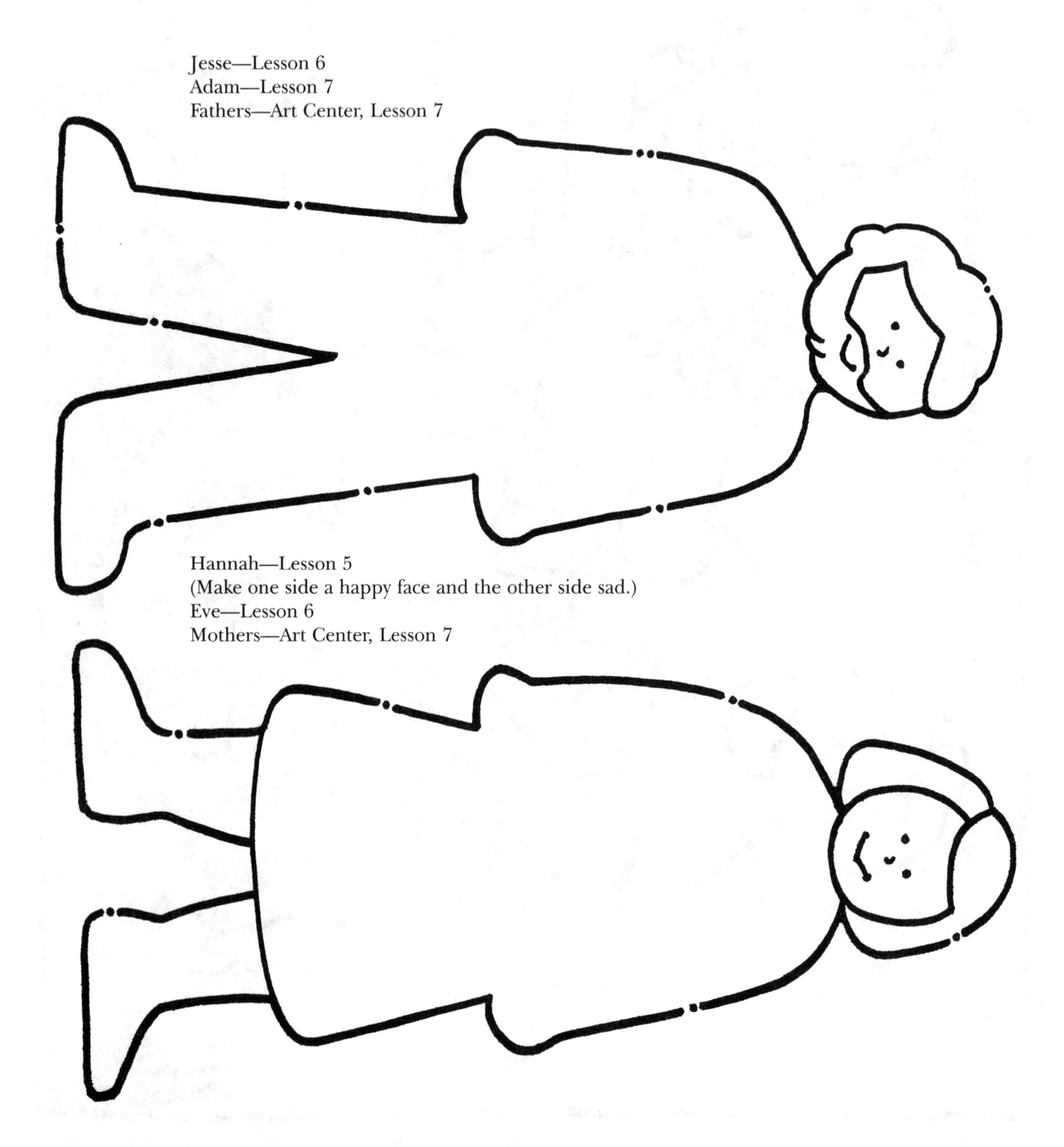

Instructions

1. Make a copy of all patterns. Cut out.
2. Lay patterns on felt and trace. Cut out.
3. Add faces and other details as desired for visuals.
4. For Art Center, Lesson 7, you may prefer to make figures out of construction paper or poster board. Leave plain for children to decorate.

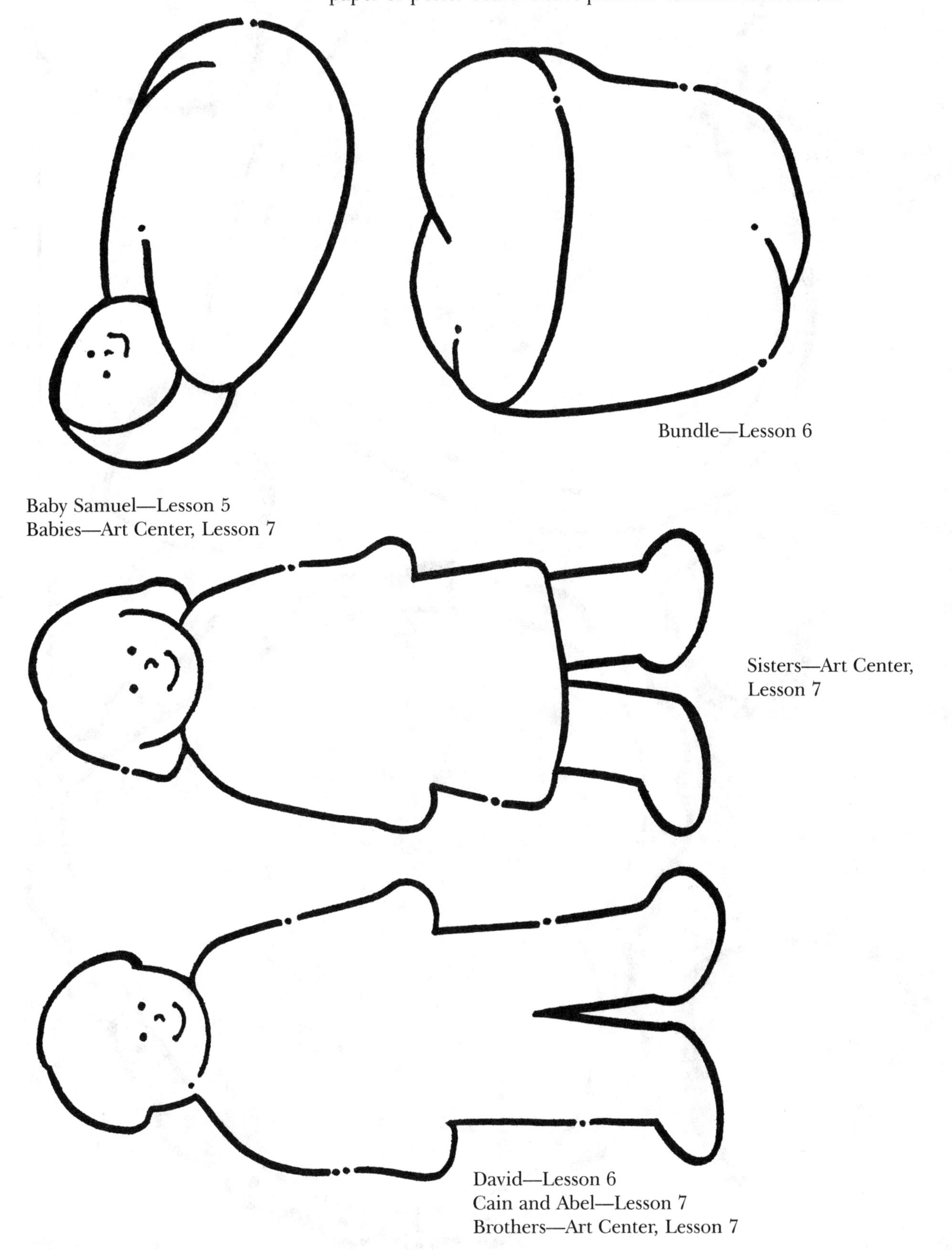

Bundle—Lesson 6

Baby Samuel—Lesson 5
Babies—Art Center, Lesson 7

Sisters—Art Center, Lesson 7

David—Lesson 6
Cain and Abel—Lesson 7
Brothers—Art Center, Lesson 7

God Is Love

God loves ____________.

Dear Parent:

This month our lessons are all about YOU and the sweet family with which God has blessed you! Here are the Bible stories we will be using.

- *God Made Mothers* (1Samuel 1:1-11, 19, 20)
- *God Made Fathers* (1 Samuel 17:12-20)
- *God Made Families* (Genesis 4:1, 2)
- *God Is Love* (a review and reinforcement of the first three lessons)

Your child will be learning that it is because of God's love he has a family. We will encourage him to feel happy about his family, to think of good things he does with his family, and to thank God for his family.

Our Bible words for this month are from 1 John 4:8, "God is love."

Below are some ways you can help your child at home to remember what we talk about at church.

- Read the Bible stories from a children's picture Bible.
- Place a bookmark in a Bible your child can handle. Help her find the Bible words and "read" them together.
- Print the Bible words on a piece of construction paper and let your child decorate around the words. Make a hanger for this and hang it on a doorknob or drawer knob where your child will see it often.
- Encourage everyone in the family to memorize the Bible words and say them together before meals.
- Use heart-shaped cookie cutters to make sugar cookies, play with play dough, or make beautiful pictures for family members near or far.
- Look at family photo albums and thank God for each family member.
- Sing "God Is Love" to the tune of "Farmer in the Dell":

"God is love." Yes, "God is love."
God gave me mommy (daddy, a family). Yes, "God is love."

- Do this rhyme often.

My mother loves me very much, *(Hug self.)*
When I'm sleeping, when I play.
(Pretend to sleep; then clap hands.)
My mother takes good care of me, *(Point to self.)*
And I am happy every day! *(Smile.)*
(Repeat, substituting "daddy" for "mother.")
—Sandra Maddux

May God bless your family as you spend time together.

Unit 3: God Is Good

Lessons 9–13

By the end of the unit, the children will

Know that God is good.
Feel happy that God takes care of us.
Pray, "Thank You, God, for the things You give to us."

Unit Bible Words

"God is good" (Psalm 73:1, *NIV*).

This Unit at a Glance

9 God Gives Good Food — **1 Kings 17:8-16**
God provides food for Elijah, a widow, and her son during a severe drought.

10 God Gives Water — **Exodus 17:1-6**
God provides water for Moses and the Israelites in the desert.

11 God Gives Clothes — **1 Samuel 2:19**
Hannah sews new clothes for the growing Samuel.

12 God Gives Homes — **Genesis 6:14-22; 7; 8:1-20**
Noah obeys God's instructions and builds the ark that saves him, his family, and the animals.

13 God Is Good — **Review of Lessons 9-12**

Why Teach This Unit to Young Children?

In today's hurried pace, we often forget that God is caring for us and providing our basic needs. This unit introduces to young children the fact that God is good and that He takes care of us by providing our daily needs. This month the children will enjoy seeing, tasting, and identifying various foods; playing and experimenting with water, as well as drinking it; trying on clothes and discovering the feel of different textures; and seeing pictures of different homes. Through these hands-on activities the children will gain a better understanding of God's love and care. "God is good"!

The Bible words should be used over and over in your conversation, in the Bible stories, at the learning centers, and in your prayers. For example, **"God is good." He cares for us. . . . God made the oranges. "God is good."**

Have a classroom Bible available in a learning center, at the giving table, or wherever the children will see it. Also have it on your lap or at your side as you tell the Bible story. Have the Bible words highlighted or underlined so the children can see them, point to them, and "read" them.

Things to Do for This Unit

- Photocopy the Parents' Letter (page 86) and the Unit Planning Sheet (pages 319 and 320).
- Photocopy the Learning Center Cards (pages 73-78); cut apart on solid lines; glue side 1 to cardboard and side 2 to back of side 1. Laminate for durability (optional).
- Gather/prepare materials listed on Learning Center Cards.
- Copy and color pages 79-82 for visuals.
- For Lesson 9, make a house for Zach (if you don't already have one) from a shoe box or something similar. Zach can stay in his house when you are not using him.

Use These Songs and Action Rhymes During Unit 3

It's Time to Put the Toys Away

(Tune: "Mary Had a Little Lamb")

It's time to put the toys away, toys away, toys away.
It's time to put the toys away, so we know where to find them.

God Cares for Me

(Tune: "Farmer in the Dell")

God cares for me, and God cares for you.
All the time, from morning 'til night,
Yes, God cares for us.
(Point to yourself and to others at appropriate times.)

God's World

God Is Good

(Tune: "God Is So Good")

God is good. God is good.
God is good. God is good to me.
(Also sing, "God gives me food, etc.; God cares for me.")

Listening Rhyme

First our feet go tap-tap-tap. *(Tap feet on floor.)*
Then our hands go clap-clap-clap. *(Clap hands.)*
We look with both our eyes,
(Make glasses by circling fingers around eyes.)
We hear with both our ears, *(Cup hands behind ears.)*
And then our hands fall in our laps. *(Fold hands in lap.)*
—*Dorothy Fay Richards*

We Thank You, Thank You, God

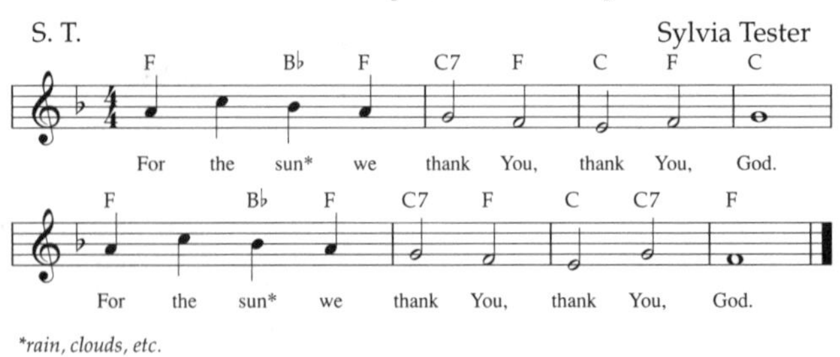

hungry? Does your tummy ever say, "Gr-r-r-r," because it is hungry? "God is good" to us. He cares for us by giving us the food we need. Why does God give us food? Yes, because "God is good." Show the children those words in the Bible. If there is time, let each child have a turn to hold the Bible and point to or "read" the highlighted words.

Learning Activities

(20 minutes)

Let's Play Awhile

Have the children stand up and sing "We Thank You, Thank You, God," using "food" in the place of "sun." Then have the children go to the Game Center. If yours is a large class, also offer the learning centers used earlier.

Let's Go Home

Let Zach sing "It's Time to Put the Toys Away." Encourage the children to clean up by helping them to pick up the toys and put them away. As soon as a few children have finished, start the following song to the tune of "Mary Had a Little Lamb":

Sit like a pumpkin, a pumpkin, a pumpkin.
Sit like a pumpkin, just like this.
(Sit with legs crossed and arms forming circle in front.)

Add other actions, such as, rock, roll, spin, and wobble, to do as parents come to pick up their children. Make sure the children take home their Parents' Letters and artwork.

God Gives Good Food

1 Kings 17:8-16

Bible Words: "God is good" (Psalm 73:1, *NIV*).

Lesson Value: A severe drought had been in the land for several years. God had taken care of Elijah by providing food brought by birds and water from a small brook. Eventually the brook dried up and the birds quit bringing the food. God sent Elijah into town to a widow's house where God provided the items she needed to make bread every day. God provides for us and our daily needs. Often we don't even think about how God is providing for us unless there is something special or unique about the situation. This lesson will help your children understand that God cares for them by providing food, a basic need.

Know: Know that God is good.
Feel: Feel happy that God takes care of us.
Do: Thank God for food.

Children will accomplish the goals when they:

1. Say the Bible words, "God is good."
2. Name foods they like, or point to pictures of foods they like.
3. Handle some food that God made.
4. Pray, "Thank You, God, for giving us food."
5. Sing about the food God gives.

Let's Get Ready

For the Bible story, you will need the classroom Bible, Zach, a plastic spoon, and a plate or bowl. Also have the teaching picture of Elijah, the widow, and her son (page 79).

Prepare the Art Center, the Family Living Center, and God's Wonders Center. If you are the only teacher, prepare just the Family Living Center. Use the Game Center after the Bible story.

Learning Activities

(30 minutes, including 10 minutes presession)

Let's Get Started

Use Zach to greet each child by name. "Hi, Sarah. What a pretty smile you have on today. I think you are smiling because 'God is good.' Is that right?" Follow your usual procedure; then direct her to one of the learning centers.

Worship and Bible Story

(15 minutes)

Let's Worship God

Zach says, "It's time to put our things away so we can sing and pray to God." Start singing as soon as children begin coming to the circle. This will encourage others to finish their jobs and come to the circle. Begin with "God's World," using various foods. Then sing "Praise Him, Praise Him," using "God is good" in place of "God is love." Introduce "Listening Rhyme." This transition rhyme is good to get children ready to pray and listen to the story. **Our Bible words tell us that "God is good." God takes good care of us in many ways. Let's bow our heads, fold our hands, and close our eyes; then we can tell God, "Thank You, God, for loving us and caring for us. Thank You for giving us good food."** Pray in those words. Telling the children ahead of time what you will be saying encourages children to pray with you.

Let's Learn From the Bible

Introduction: Before the story, attach a plastic spoon to Zach's paw. Bring Zach out of his house with a bowl or plate. **Zach, what are you doing?** Zach answers, "I'm getting ready to eat. I'm hungry. I've already thanked God for my food." **Zach, our story is about someone who was very hungry. God provided food for him. Let's find out how God did that.** Put Zach and the bowl out of sight. Have your open Bible on your lap or next to you.

The Bible Story: Elijah was very hungry! It had been a long time since he had anything to eat. His stomach was saying, "Gr-r-r-r!" Elijah was walking and walking. He was going to a town where God had told him to go.

When Elijah reached the town, he saw a woman who was picking up sticks. Elijah said to her, "Would you bring me a cup of water?" As the woman went to get the water, Elijah added, "And bring me a piece of bread too."

The woman told Elijah, "I have no bread. I have only a little flour and oil at home. I'm gathering sticks to make a fire. Then I'm going to bake a little loaf of bread for my son and me."

Elijah said, "Don't worry. Go home and make a loaf of bread for me and bring it to me. Then you can make more bread for you and your son. God said there will be enough flour and oil. You and your son will not go hungry."

So the woman did what Elijah told her to do. Every day there was enough flour and oil to make more bread, just as God had promised. Perhaps Elijah, the woman, and her son told God every day, "Thank You, God, for our bread."

Let's Apply the Lesson

Show the teaching picture. Retell the story with the children's help. Ask the children to point to Elijah, the woman, and her son.

Show some of the plates of food from the Art Center. **Seeing this food makes me feel hungry. Have you ever been really**

Learning Activities

(20 minutes)

Let's Play Awhile

Have the children stand up and sing "God Is Good"; then go to the Game Center. If your class is large you may want to repeat the centers you had at the beginning of the hour.

Let's Go Home

Let Zach tell the children it's time to put the toys away. The children may be getting tired at this point and may be a little fussy. Encourage the children with a little help. As soon as most of the toys are put away, start the following activity: Have pairs of children face each other sitting on the floor and holding hands with their legs crossed or out in front of them. The young two's who cannot get this concept can be a boat all by themselves. Sing the traditional song, "Row, Row, Row Your Boat." As you sing, let the children rock back and forth like a boat. Sing this several times—with a deep voice for a big boat, a high voice for a small boat. Let the children come up with some ideas for other boats: sail boat, motor boat, tug boat; sing it fast, sing it slowly, sing it fast. Make sure the children take home the fish they made in the Art Center.

God Gives Water

Exodus 17:1-6

Bible Words: "God is good" (Psalm 73:1, *NIV*).

Lesson Value: The Israelites had been without water. They were tired, hot, and thirsty. What would you do in circumstances such as these? Probably the same as the Israelites—complain. When they complained to Moses, he was upset with them because God had already proven how well He could take care of them. God told Moses to hit a rock and He would cause water to flow out of it. Moses did as God said and the Israelites had all the water they could drink. It is easy to complain when things aren't going as we would like for them to. God can and will take care of us. We just have to trust Him to do as He has promised. The children can learn that God does care, that He provides for our needs, and we can trust Him to keep His word.

Know: Know that God is good.
Feel: Feel happy that God takes care of us.
Do: Thank God for water.

Children will accomplish the goals when they:
1. Say the Bible words, "God is good."
2. Play with water.
3. Tell what God gave the people to drink in the Bible story.
4. Use water in some way.
5. Thank God for the water He gives us daily.

Let's Get Ready

For the Bible story, you will need the classroom Bible, puppet Zach, a small plastic cup, and a rock (as large as you can easily bring in the classroom). Also, have flannel-backed figures from pages 80 and 81.

Prepare the Art Center, God's Wonders Center, and the Music/Drama Center. If you are the only teacher, prepare just the Art Center. Use the Game Center after the Bible story.

Learning Activities

(30 minutes, including 10 minutes presession)

Let's Get Started

As Zach greets each child by name, help the children put in their offerings and put their stickers on the attendance chart. Then encourage the children to get involved in a learning center by saying, **"God is good" to us. He gives us water to drink and to use. We are going to be talking about water today. What would you like to do first—play in the God's Wonders Center or make a fish in the Art Center?**

Worship and Bible Story

(15 minutes)

Let's Worship God

Let Zach tell the children, "It's time to put our things away so we can sing and pray to God." As soon as the first child arrives in your worship area, start singing "God Is Good" (using the words, "God gives me water"), and "God Cares for Me." Sing "We Thank You, Thank You, God" (substituting "food" and then "water" for "sun"). **We have been singing about ways "God is good" to us. Let's say our Bible words together, "God is good."** Then pray, **Thank You, God, for giving us water. Thank You for being so good to us.**

Let's Learn From the Bible

Introduction: Have Zach carry in an empty cup. **Zach, you look thirsty. I wonder what Zach wants in his cup. Oh! Maybe he wants some water!** Have Zach nod his head. **Water is what we like when we are thirsty. Today our Bible story is about some very thirsty people who wanted some water. Let's find out how they got their water.** Put Zach aside; hold your Bible on your lap. Have the large rock behind you. Place the flannelgraph figures in your Bible.

The Bible Story: Mothers and daddies and their children were walking and walking in the hot desert. The people had been walking for a very long time. They were tired. They were hot. They were very thirsty.

The mothers and daddies went to Moses and said, "We are thirsty and we want some water. Ask God to give us some water."

Moses said, "Why are you angry with me?" Then Moses prayed to God. He told God that the people wanted water to drink. He asked God, "What should I do?"

God said, "Moses, use your walking stick to hit a big rock I will show you. I will make water come out of the rock."

So Moses obeyed God. He hit the rock and, just as God promised, water came pouring out of that rock! The mothers and daddies and their children had lots of water to drink. God took care of them. "God is good"!

Let's Apply the Lesson

Who was thirsty in our Bible story? Who did they talk to? Who did Moses talk to? What did God tell Moses to do? Who made the water come from the rock?

Have you ever seen water come from a rock? Do you think water will come from this rock if I hit it? No! Do so. **I can't make water come from a rock. Only God can do that. . . . Have you ever been thirsty? Did you ask your mother or daddy for a drink of water? Water is good. It helps us not to be thirsty. God made the water and He gave it to us to drink. God is good.**

Let's Apply the Lesson

Everyone stand up and show me how you are growing. Are you getting taller? Yes, you are! Does anyone have new clothes? New clothes are fun, especially when you are growing and your clothes don't fit anymore.

Who got new clothes in our story? Who made the clothes for Samuel? Hold up the picture of Hannah. **That's right. His mother, Hannah. God helped Hannah to make the new coat for Samuel. God helps your mommies and daddies provide clothes for you. "God is good" to give us clothes to wear.**

Learning Activities

(20 minutes)

Let's Play Awhile

Dismiss the children to the Music/Drama Center. If you have a large group of children you may want to do all of the learning centers from earlier allowing the children to try new activities.

Let's Go Home

Use Zach to tell the children it is time to put the toys away. Some simple instructions may be helpful for the children. **Jaime, please put this pair of boots in the box for me.** When most of the toys are put away, gather the children into a circle and start singing "This is the way . . . " Review the two previous lessons by singing about eating foods and ways to use water, as well as stanzas about clothes, such as the following: "This is the way we pull on our boots, . . . so early in the morning."

Make sure all children have their paper dolls and clothing from the Art Center to take home. As each child leaves, try to say something positive to his parents about his behavior. **Adam was a willing helper when we picked up our toys.** Some specific praise will encourage Adam to continue being a willing helper, perhaps even at home.

God Gives Clothes

1 Samuel 2:19

Bible Words: "God is good" (Psalm 73:1, *NIV*).

Lesson Value: Hannah prayed for a son and God honored that prayer. Hannah named her son Samuel. She loved him very much. When Samuel was still a child she took him to the tabernacle to work with the priest, Eli. Hannah still loved Samuel very much and showed her love by making new clothes for him every year and taking them to him. God blessed Hannah with more children after that. Through the story of Hannah and Samuel, your children will learn that God loves them and cares for them. One way He does this is by providing clothing, one of our basic needs. God is good!

Know: Know that God is good.
Feel: Feel happy that God takes care of us.
Do: Thank God for clothes.

Children will accomplish the goals when they:

1. Say the Bible words, "God is good."
2. Sing about God's goodness.
3. Tell one thing that God has given them.
4. Pray, "Thank You, God, for giving me clothes."

Let's Get Ready

For the Bible story, you will need the classroom Bible, the

picture of Hannah (page 82), puppet Zach, an item of clothing Zach can wear or carry in for the story, and a large piece of cloth and a large plastic needle (or just pretend to have the needle). Also have small pieces of cloth for the children.

Prepare the Family Living Center, Art Center, and the Game Center. If you are the only teacher prepare just the Art Center. Have materials ready for the Music/Drama Center for after the Bible story. Also have the Family Living Center available, if possible.

Learning Activities

(30 minutes, including 10 minutes presession)

Let's Get Started

Let Zach greet the children. By now the children will probably be fond of Zach and really enjoy his greeting. Have Zach make a comment about the clothing that each child is wearing. "Alicia, you have roses on your dress. What a pretty dress. 'God is good' to give us clothes to wear." After the child has put in her offering and placed her sticker on the attendance chart, help her choose a learning center. Offer a choice of two, either of which is acceptable to you. **Would you like to dress the doll babies or make your own paper doll and clothes?**

Worship and Bible Story

(15 minutes)

Let's Worship God

Let Zach tell the children it is time to put the toys away. As soon as the first child is ready, start your music time with "God Cares for Me." Sing it several times while the children are gathering. Then sing "God Is Good" and "We Thank You, Thank You, God" (for our clothes). **"God is good" to us. Let's bow our heads and tell Him, "Thank You, God, for our clothes. Thank You for taking care of us."** Pray in those words.

Let's Learn From the Bible

Introduction: Bring Zach out with his jacket or hat. **Zach has his jacket to keep him warm. Clothes are very important. We wear heavy clothes in the winter to keep us warm and lighter clothes in the summer to keep us cool. Each of you is growing and as you grow, what happens? Your clothes seem too small. Then you need new clothes. Our Bible story is about a little boy who was growing just the way you are growing. He needed new clothes just like you do sometimes. Let's listen very quietly to the story about this little boy and his new clothes.**

Put Zach back in his house or at least out of sight so he doesn't distract the children. Bring out the classroom Bible and hand out the pieces of cloth. Demonstrate sewing motions for the children. Then have them try the motions. Explain that you will be sewing throughout the story. When they see you sewing they are to do the sewing motions with you.

The Bible Story: Hannah wanted to be a mommy, but she didn't have any children. So, Hannah asked God for a baby boy. And God gave her a baby boy. Hannah named her baby boy Samuel. Hannah loved her little boy very much. She took good care of him.

Samuel was like all little boys. He was growing and growing. He was getting taller and taller. His clothes began to feel smaller and smaller. His shirt was too tight. His coat was too short.

Hannah looked at Samuel and said, "You need some new clothes."

Samuel looked at himself and said, "I need a new shirt and a new coat." Hannah cut some pretty new cloth to make a coat for Samuel. Then she sewed and sewed. *(Make large sewing motions with your hands.)* Sometimes she picked up her sewing and looked at it. *(Hold up the cloth and look at it.)* Would the coat fit Samuel?

Then she tried the new coat on Samuel. It fit just right! Samuel liked his new coat. He said, "Thank you, Mother, for my new coat." And Hannah smiled.

ground was all covered with water. But Noah and his family and the animals were safe and dry in their ark home.

Then the rain stopped and the sun came out and started drying up the water.

When the ground was dry, Noah and his family and the animals came out of the ark-boat. *(Everyone can climb back out of the boat.)*

Noah and his family thanked God for giving them a home on the water.

Let's Apply the Lesson

Do you live in a house like Noah's ark-boat? No! What does your house look like? Some houses are very big and some are small. Do you have any animals at your house? Make sure each child has a chance to tell about his pet. God has helped each of us to have a home. Let's tell God thank-you right now for our homes and for taking care of us.

Learning Activities

(20 minutes)

Let's Play Awhile

Encourage the children to put their stuffed animals into a box or laundry basket, then go to the God's Wonders Center. If your class is large and you have multiple teachers, use the other activities from the beginning of the lesson as well.

Let's Go Home

Let Zach sing "It's Time to Put the Toys Away." **Amy, what is your favorite animal? . . . What does the lion say? How does the lion walk?** Let's all be lions. Let each child pick a favorite animal and act it out as a class. Or, sing "God's World," using animal names the children suggest. Have animal pictures for the children to hold up.

Make sure the children have their ark pictures to take home.

God Gives Homes

Genesis 6:14-22; 7; 8:1-20

Bible Words: "God is good" (Psalm 73:1, *NIV*).

Lesson Value: Noah loved and obeyed God in a world that wanted nothing to do with Him. God decided to destroy the disobedient people leaving only a remnant to repopulate the earth. He gave Noah instructions for building a floating home for his family and the many animals God would send to Noah. (We trust Noah was an animal lover!) All children seem to love the story of Noah and his ark, probably because of the animals. This lesson gives a little different twist to the story by teaching the children that God cares for us by providing our homes.

Know: Know that God is good.
Feel: Feel happy that God takes care of us.
Do: Thank God for giving us homes.

Children will accomplish the goals when they:

1. Say the Bible words, "God is good."
2. Sing about God's love.
3. Tell one thing God has given them.
4. Tell who gives us homes (God).
5. Pray, "Thank You, God, for giving me a home."

Let's Get Ready

For the Bible story, you will need the classroom Bible,

puppet Zach, Zach's home, and a Noah's ark puzzle or toy, or just a picture of Noah's ark. Also have a refrigerator box to be used as the ark and a stuffed animal for each child.

Prepare the Art Center, the Family Living Center, and the Music/Drama Center. If you are the only teacher prepare just the Family Living Center. Have materials ready for the God's Wonders Center to use after the Bible story.

Learning Activities

(30 minutes, including 10 minutes presession)

Let's Get Started

Have Zach greet each child. After the child has put her attendance sticker on the chart show her Zach's home and ask, **Paige, does Zach's home look like your home? We are going to be learning about different kinds of homes and how God takes care of us.** Then encourage each child to get involved in one of the learning centers.

Worship and Bible Story

(15 minutes)

Let's Worship God

Let Zach tell the children, "It's time to put our things away so we can sing and pray to God." Zach can sing the song, "It's Time to Put the Toys Away." Begin singing as soon as children come to the circle. Sing "God Cares for Me" and do the rhyme, "Noah."

Hammer, hammer, hammer. *(Pound fists together.)*
Saw, saw, saw. *(Move one hand across opposite arm.)*
Noah built a boat big and tall.
(Spread arms out wide; then lift arms up high.)
—Sandra Maddux

Then use "Listening Rhyme." Open your Bible and say, **God cares for each of us. The Bible tells us that "God is good." Let's say our Bible words together.** Do so. Then pray, **Thank You, God, for taking care of us. Thank You for giving us homes.**

Let's Learn From the Bible

Introduction: Have Zach beside you, but still inside his house. **Where, oh where is Zach?** Zach pops out of his house. **There you are, Zach. You were inside your house where it is safe and warm. Our Bible story is about a special house. I want each of you to hold an animal for me, because animals are part of our Bible story.** Pass out a stuffed animal to each child. **Let's listen very carefully to this story.** Put Zach away.

The Bible Story: One day, God talked to a man named Noah. He said, "Noah, I am going to send a big flood. It will cover the earth. I want you to build a very big boat—an ark."

Noah obeyed God and he and his sons began to work on the big ark-boat. First, Noah and his sons sawed and sawed until they had plenty of boards. *(Move hand back and forth and say, "ZZZZZZZ." Have the children do this with you also.)* Then Noah and his sons hammered and hammered. *(With fist hit palm of hand and have children imitate you.)*

Noah and his sons worked for a long, long time. Then one day the ark was finished.

Noah's wife and his sons' wives must have put lots of food on the boat—food for themselves and food for animals. Do you know why? Yes, God was going to send lots of animals to live on the ark with Noah and his family.

When everything was ready, the animals began to come. The big elephants walked slowly. The monkeys hurried. The horses ran to get on the ark-boat. There were so many animals! *(Help the children get in the "ark" with their stuffed animals.)*

Do you know what happened then? Yes, it started to rain. *(Pat hands on thighs to make sound of rain.)* It rained and rained. Soon the ark started to move. *(Sway from side to side.)* Finally, the

Let's Apply the Lesson

Place the pictures/visuals in front of the children. Tell them to point to or name the people when you ask the questions. **God took care of these Bible people. Whom did he give food to? . . . Who asked him for water? . . . Who made clothes for her little boy? . . . What kind of a home did God give Noah? Who took care of all these people? God did! Who takes care of you? God does! Let's tell God thank-you.** Let children suggest what to thank God for. Make sure you cover all the subjects of the stories. Encourage any child who is willing to pray aloud but don't insist on a child doing this.

Learning Activities

(20 minutes)

Let's Play Awhile

Remind the children of the learning centers that are available. Encourage them to do something they have not done previously. If you are the only teacher, use the Game Center.

Let's Go Home

Let Zach sing, "It's Time to Put the Toys Away." As soon as most of the toys are put away, gather the children into a circle. Sing the action song used in the Music/Drama Center during this unit. Add as many stanzas as possible, until all the children have gone home.

Make sure the children have their cookies from the Family Living Center to take home.

Lesson 13
Date: ______

God Is Good

Review of Lessons 9–12

Bible Words: "God is good" (Psalm 73:1, *NIV*).

Lesson Value: God is a loving God. He provides for us in many ways. He provided food for Elijah when it looked hopeless. He provided water for the Israelites when there was no water and they could have died. Hannah sewed clothes for her son God had given her. God told Noah how to build the ark, providing a safe home for him, his family, and the animals. God loves us and wants us to have what we need. He often provides for our needs without our even realizing it. This review should help to reinforce in the minds of the children that God is good, that He loves them, and that He takes care of their daily needs.

Know: Know that God is good.
Feel: Feel happy that God takes care of us.
Do: Thank God for giving food, water, clothes, and homes.

Children will accomplish the goals when they:

1. Say the Bible words, "God is good."
2. Sing about God's goodness.
3. Say one thing God has given them.
4. Pray, "Thank You, God, for all the good things You give us."

Let's Get Ready

For the Bible story, you will need the classroom Bible, puppet Zach, Zach's hat or jacket, Zach's house, and a flannelboard. Place the pictures/visuals from previous lessons in your Bible.

Prepare the God's Wonders Center, the Family Living Center, and the Music/Drama Center. If you are the only teacher prepare just the Family Living Center. Use the Game Center after the Bible story.

Learning Activities

(30 minutes, including 10 minutes presession)

Let's Get Started

Let Zach greet each child. Always make sure all children feel loved and wanted in the classroom. Follow your usual schedule. Let Zach encourage the children to choose learning centers. Remember, however, that some young children need a little time to warm up in the classroom and may need to sit and watch other children for a few minutes before they become involved. Just make sure that they join in the activities as soon as possible.

Worship and Bible Story

(15 minutes)

Let's Worship God

Let Zach start the song, "It's Time to Put the Toys Away." Sometimes young children have trouble making the transition from one activity to another so make this time as pleasant as possible. Begin singing as soon as children come to the circle. Sing "God Is Good," "God Cares for Me," and "God's World." Open your Bible and say, **We have been singing about how good God is to us. The Bible says, "God is good." Let's say that together: "God is good." Now let's tell God, "Thank You, God, for all the good things You give us. We love You."** Then pray in those same words.

Let's Learn From the Bible

Introduction: Bring out Zach, his house, and his jacket or hat. **Zach, you look like you are well taken care of. You have a home and clothes and we know you have food and water. You must be very happy. We have those things too, because God gives them to us. God loves us and provides for us. Let's remember our stories about some people God cared for.** Put Zach and his things away. Hold your Bible on your lap.

The Bible-story Review: Elijah was very hungry. God told him to tell a woman to bake him some bread. Elijah told the woman what God had said and she obeyed. God provided food for Elijah, the woman, and her son for a long time. *(Show the teaching picture. Let the children point to Elijah, the woman, and her son.)*

(Let several older children place the figures on the flannelboard as you tell the story.) The Israelites were very thirsty while they were in the desert. There was no water. Moses asked God what to do and God told him to hit a rock. Moses obeyed and water came pouring out of the rock. The Israelites had water to drink.

Samuel was growing and growing, just like you are growing. *(Have the children stand up and show you how they are growing and then sit down.)* Samuel was getting too big for his clothes. His mother, Hannah, made him some new clothes. Samuel liked his new clothes. Hannah was glad. *(Show the picture of Hannah. Let the children tell you what she is doing.)*

God told Noah to build a big ark-boat because there was going to be a flood. Noah obeyed God. Then what happened? *(Let the children tell you about the animals.)* Yes, God sent lots of animals to get in the ark with Noah and his family. And then . . . *(wait for the answer)* it rained and rained. Noah and his family and the animals were all safe on their ark-boat home. God took care of them.

Art Center

Unit 3—God Is Good

Items to Include:

Lesson 9
Magazine pictures of foods
Paper plates
Glue sticks

Lesson 10
Fish pattern (page 83)
Crayons
Colored sugar and glue (optional)

Purpose: The child will come to a better understanding of how God is good by engaging in creative play.

Things to Do and Say

Lesson 9

Cut a variety of pictures of foods from magazines. Choose foods children normally like, such as macaroni and cheese, hot dogs, and desserts, along with fresh fruits and vegetables. Let children look for their favorite foods to glue onto the paper plates. Write on the edge of each paper plate, "God gives Brittany's favorite foods to her." Encourage children to choose foods from several food groups.

What is your favorite food, Brittany? What else do you like? Oh, that is good for you! It will make you grow up big and strong. "God is good" to make food for us that makes us healthy.

Lesson 10

Before class make a copy of the fish pattern on construction paper. Provide crayons or washable markers for the children to color the fish. Talk about the pretty colors of fish they have seen or may even have at home. Provide colored sugar for the older children to glue on the fish to make them pretty.

Has anyone ever caught a fish? What did your fish look like? Where do fish live? That's right, in the water. Can fish live without water? No. "God is good" to provide

Family Living Center

Unit 3—God Is Good

Items to Include:

Lesson 9
Toaster
Bread
Margarine
Cinnamon-sugar mix
Napkins
Clean-up supplies

Lesson 11
Dolls and/or teddy bears
Doll clothes
Blankets

Purpose: The child will learn that God is good, through a variety of hands-on activities.

Things to Do and Say

Lesson 9

Caution: Make sure you are aware of any food allergies before you use this activity.

Before you begin, warn the children that the toaster is very hot and no one must touch it. Have your toaster sitting in a safe position so the cord cannot be tripped over, or where the toaster is tempting to touch. Toast the bread for the children, and then allow them to butter the bread and sprinkle on the cinnamon and sugar. The younger the child the more assistance you will need to give.

As you and the children work, say, **"God is good" to give us our food. He gives us crunchy toast, smooth butter, tasty cinnamon, and sweet sugar. Isn't God good to us! What other foods does God give us? Which food is your favorite?**

Lesson 11

Provide dolls and/or teddy bears of various sizes. Let the children dress up the dolls and teddy bears as they see fit. They will need a little help now and then. Also provide blankets so younger children can easily wrap up their babies.

What would you like to put on your baby, Aaron? Do you think your baby is cold or hot? What do you think your baby needs to stay warm/cool? . . . Maria, what do

Art Center, continued

water for the fish to live in. Can we live without water? Of course not! God gives us water to drink, to take baths in, and to swim in. "God is good"!

Lesson 11
Paper doll pattern (page 84)
Textured fabrics
Glue
Crayons

Lesson 11

Before class follow instructions for preparing paper dolls. Older children can use glue sticks with your help, then add the clothing. For younger children, put on the glue and help them place the clothing.

You can color your paper doll to look like you or like a friend. What color is your hair? Yes, Jennifer, your hair is a pretty red. Can you find a red crayon to color your doll's hair? . . . What would you like to put on your doll, Brandon? Here are some boy's clothes. How does this shirt feel? Is it soft (rough, smooth)? **"God is good" to give us clothes.**

Lesson 12
Ark pattern (page 85)
Animal stickers (pages 77 and 78)
Construction paper or manila paper
White glue
Vinegar
Peppermint extract (optional)

Lesson 12

Make copies of the ark pattern from page 85 on poster board or cardboard and cut them out. Make animal stickers according to directions on page 77. Help the children glue their arks onto light shades of construction paper or manila paper, then lick and stick their animals wherever they please.

Do you know what this boat was called? Yes, an ark. We'll call it the ark-boat. The Bible tells us that a man named Noah was told by God to build this big ark-boat. Then God told Noah to bring lots of animals to put in the ark-boat. Noah, his family, and the animals lived on the ark-boat for a long time. God took care of them. "God is good"!

Family Living Center, continued

you have on today? Yes, a pretty red dress. Your mommy made the dress? "God is good" to give us clothes to wear. Thank You, God, for helping Maria's mommy make her pretty dress.

Lesson 12
Cleaning cloths

Lesson 12

Provide plenty of soft cloths and perhaps a child-size broom or two. Let the children sweep the floor and/or use the dust cloths to clean the tables and chairs and other items in the room.

As the children work, say, **When we clean we are taking care of our classroom that God has given us. Do you help your mommy clean at home, too? "God is good" to us. He helps us have homes to live in. Thank You, God, for my home.**

Lesson 13
Cookies or graham crackers
Frosting
Sprinkles
Sandwich bags
Plastic knives or craft sticks
Napkins
Paper cups

Lesson 13

Let the children spread frosting on their cookies or graham crackers. If you want, you can let them also add sprinkles. Do this over a cookie sheet to catch the extra sprinkles. Children love the many colors, but can get carried away with sprinkling, so be careful! Check for any food allergies before this activity. Provide cups of water to drink with the cookies.

Do you help make cookies at home? Mommy lets you help her mix the cookies, Amy? What fun! . . . What foods do you help fix at home, Michael? Aren't you glad God gives us our food? Thank You, God, for these good cookies. And thank You, God, for water to drink. If there is time and you have extra cookies, let the children make seconds and put them in sandwich bags to take home.

God's Wonders Center

Unit 3—God Is Good

Items to Include:

Lesson 9
Fruits and vegetables
Plastic knives
Large plates

Lessons 10 and 13
Plastic aprons
Tub of water
Items that float
Items that sink
Shower curtain

Purpose: The child will discover ways God provides for him.

Things to Do and Say

Lesson 9

Provide a variety of fruits and vegetables that children are apt to like. Also have one or two unusual ones for them to try out. Wash the food and cut into halves, etc. Help the children use the plastic knives to cut these into bite-size pieces; then let them arrange the foods on the large plates. When they have done this, let them sample the fruits and vegetables.

How does this food taste? Is it sweet? sour? soft? crunchy? "God is good." He gives us food every day. Let's tell God thank-you for this good food. . . . You are doing a good job cutting that apple, Andrew. Do you like apples? So do I! . . . Abbie, let's try a bite of this melon. Umm, it tastes sweet! . . . "God is good." He gives us good food! Thank You, God, for all this good food.

Lessons 10 and 13

Put plastic aprons on the children to keep their clothes as dry as possible. If you do not have plastic aprons, large bath towels will also work. Cover the tables with absorbent towels. A shower curtain under the table will help protect your carpet if you don't have a tile floor. Provide some items that will sink and some that will float. Let the children test the items to see if they float or sink.

Game Center

Unit 3—God Is Good

Items to Include:

Lesson 9
Fruits and vegetables
Pillow case

Lesson 10
Blue cloth or felt
Toy boats
Paper or felt fish
"Fishing" gear (optional)

Purpose: The child will learn that "God is good" because God provides for his needs in various ways.

Things to Do and Say

Lesson 9

Use fruits such as an apple, orange, and banana (not too ripe), and vegetables such as a carrot, some string beans, and a potato. Place one of your food items in the pillow case or a bag, without the children seeing what you put in.

Have a child reach inside the bag and feel the food. Ask, **What does this food feel like? Is it hard or soft? Is it round? What food do you think it is?** After the child guesses let him pull it out and see if he was right. If he is wrong say something like, **Oh, I think you found an apple, but it does feel a little like an orange. That was a good guess. . . . "God is good." He gives us good food. Thank You, God, for apples.**

Lesson 10

Cut a large circle or oval shape out of blue fabric or felt. Place the "lake" on the floor. Put a variety of boats in the lake and add some felt or construction paper fish for the children to play with. *Optional:* Add paper clips to the fish. Make fishing poles from dowel rods and string, with magnets tied on the ends. Let the children go fishing.

As the children play, say, **This looks like a lake. Boats can float on top of the water in the lake. Fish can swim in the water. God made water to be something special.**

God's Wonders Center, continued

For Lesson 10: **I like to float boats in the water, don't you? God gives us water to play in. He also gives us water to drink. Our Bible story tells of a time when a lot of people were very thirsty. God told Moses just how to get water for the people. "God is good." . . . Your parents need water to wash your clothes. How else do you use water? Yes, Taylor, you take a bath in water. I'm glad God gives us water to use all these ways. "God is good" to us.**

Add this conversation for Lesson 13: **Justin, is that plastic boat floating on the water? Yes, it is floating. The big boat that God told Noah to build floated on the water. Noah, his family, and many animals lived on the ark-boat for a long time. God took care of them while they lived in their ark-boat home. God was good to Noah. He helps us have homes to live in too. "God is good."**

Lesson 12
Play dough
recipe:
1 cup cold water
1 cup salt
2 T. cornstarch
3 cups flour
2 tsp. oil
Food coloring
Animal cookie cutters
Shower curtain

Lesson 12

A shower curtain laid on the floor under the tables will help protect your floor. Mix the water, salt, oil and enough food coloring to make a bright color. (Dough can also be left white). Gradually work flour and cornstarch into the mixture until it reaches a bread dough consistency. Let the children knead the dough and experiment with it for a while. Then encourage them to roll out (or pat) the dough and make animals with the cookie cutters. Some children may want to make a house or ark.

Joshua, what animal did you make? Do you think giraffes were on the ark-boat? Oh, yes, God had Noah put giraffes on the ark. . . . What other animals were on the ark-boat? Let children name animals they know. **The ark-boat was like a house on water for Noah, his family, and all the animals. Does it look like your house? No! Your house does not need to float on the water. . . . "God is good." He provides a house for each of us to live in.**

Game Center, continued

What can we do with the water? . . . That's right, we can swim in it, drink it, wash with it, and play in it. "God is good" to give us water. Let's tell Him thank-you for the water He has given us.

Lesson 11
Shoes, boots, etc.
Dress-up clothes and accessories

Lesson 11

Gather several pairs of shoes and boots (galoshes, cowboy), as well as various types of adult clothing that are easy for the children to put on and play in. Accessories such as purses, shoes, hats, and ties are of great interest to the children.

The children will enjoy walking around in the shoes, boots, and clothing. As they are doing this, say, **Who do you think wears shoes like this? A mommy or a daddy? . . . When would someone wear boots like this? Yes, when it rains. "God is good" to give us clothes to wear to keep us warm and boots to keep our feet warm and dry. . . . Rachel, you look like a mommy in that pretty dress! Where would you go in that dress? Yes, to church! Thank You, God, for giving us pretty dresses to wear to church.**

Lesson 13
Blue sheet, cloth, or construction paper

Lesson 13

Prepare a "river" for the children with your blue sheet, cloth, or pieces of construction paper laid lengthwise. Or, if you prefer, use blocks to make the river. The river should be narrow enough for the children to be able to jump over it easily. Some children may want to just step over. You may need to hold the hands of younger children. Let the children practice jumping over the river. You can have this as controlled as you want, allowing one child at a time to jump or two or more to jump at once.

After the children jump over the river help them say the Bible words, "God is good."

Review ways God is good. As a child jumps the river, say, **"God is good." He gives Tony good food to eat. . . . God gives Derek clothes to wear. "God is good."**

Instructions for Making Stickers:

1. Make copies of animals on various colors of paper or allow children to color in class (before cutting apart animals).
2. Mix 2 parts white glue and 1 part vinegar.
3. Add few drops of peppermint extract if desired.
4. Lightly "paint" mixture on backs of uncut stickers. Let dry.
5. Cut apart stickers. Children will add these to the ark-boat on page 85.

Music/Drama Center

Unit 3—God Is Good

Items to Include:

A tape player with a tape of the tune, "Mulberry Bush" (optional)

Purpose: The child will feel happy that God takes care of us.

Things to Do and Say

Lesson 10

Make, or have someone else make, a tape of the tune to "Mulberry Bush." Tell the children you are going to sing a song and act out ways we use the water God gives us. Sing, "This is the way we take a bath, so early in the morning." Then let the children think of other ways we use water (drink our water, water the flowers, wash our hands, swim in the pool, and so forth, . . . so early in the morning, afternoon, or evening). When you have finished, have everyone say, "Thank You, God, for giving us water."

Lesson 11

Let the children listen to the tape as you sing such words as, "This is the way we put on our hats, . . . before we go to church." Go through the motions of putting on a hat as you sing those words. Then stand in a circle, or just anywhere the children want, and go through a variety of items of clothing.

That was fun! I'm glad God has given us so many different kinds of clothing. "God is good."

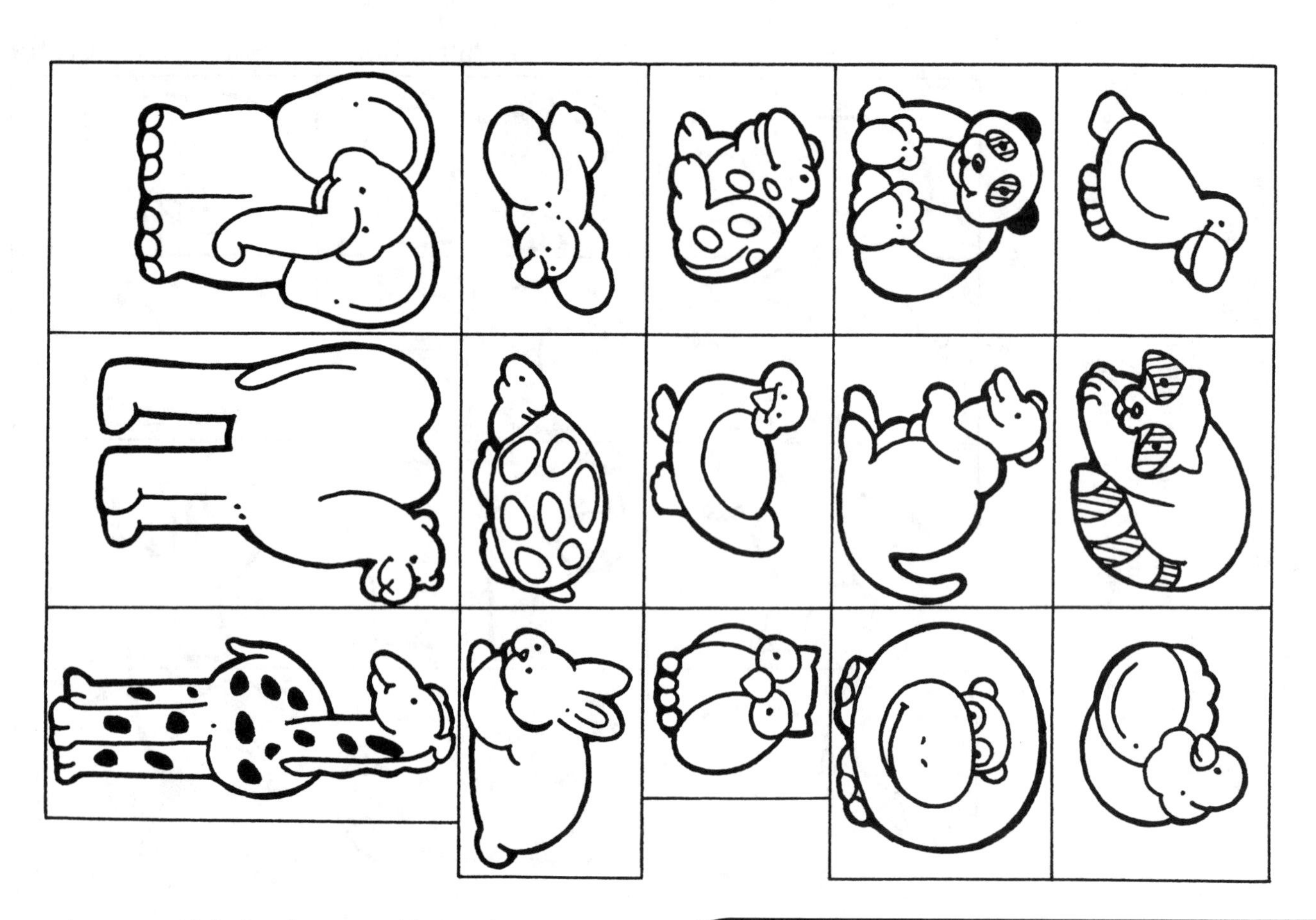

Autumn, Unit 3—Lesson 12 Art Center

Music/Drama Center, continued

Lesson 12

Have the children make a circle. If your children are young, they may do better if you use masking tape on the floor to mark their spots. Once in the circle talk about how various animals move—bunnies hop, frogs jump, birds fly, snakes slither, bugs crawl, etc. Have the children move like each animal. The children will enjoy thinking up their own animals to imitate. Then sing the "Mulberry" tune with these words: "This is the way the bunny hops, . . . so early in the morning" (or, "all around the town," etc.) Continue as long as children are interested.

Lesson 13

Use the singing game from previous weeks to review all the ways "God is good."

"This is the way we eat our apples, . . . so early in the morning." "This is the way we drink our water, take a bath," etc. . . . "This is the way the bunny hops, the fish swims," etc. End with, "This is the way we thank God, . . . because 'God is good.'" Bow your head and fold your hands as you sing this.

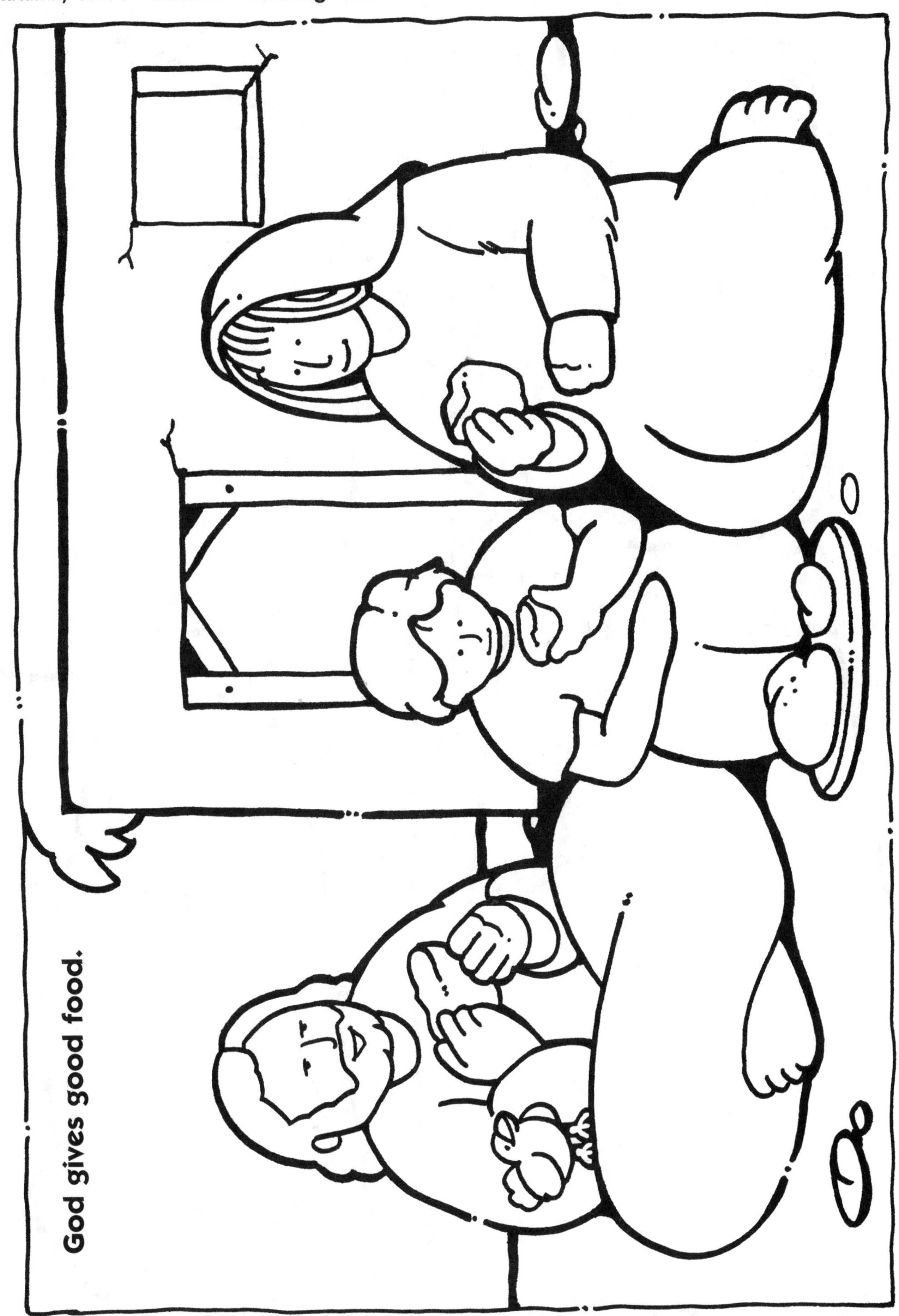
God gives good food.

Autumn, Unit 3—Lesson 10
Figures for Flannelboard

Instructions for Making Flannelgraph Figures

1. Copy figures onto construction paper or poster board.
2. Add color as desired.
3. Cut out figures.
4. Glue pieces of flannel (or fine sandpaper) to backs.
5. Place on flannelboard as directed in lesson.

God helps us have clothes.

God made pretty fish to swim in water.

Instructions for Paper Dolls

1. Make multiple copies of doll on card stock or poster board and cut out one doll per child. Children will color these in class.
2. Cut clothing from various colors and textures of cloth.
3. Allow children to choose clothing.
4. Help children glue clothing to dolls.

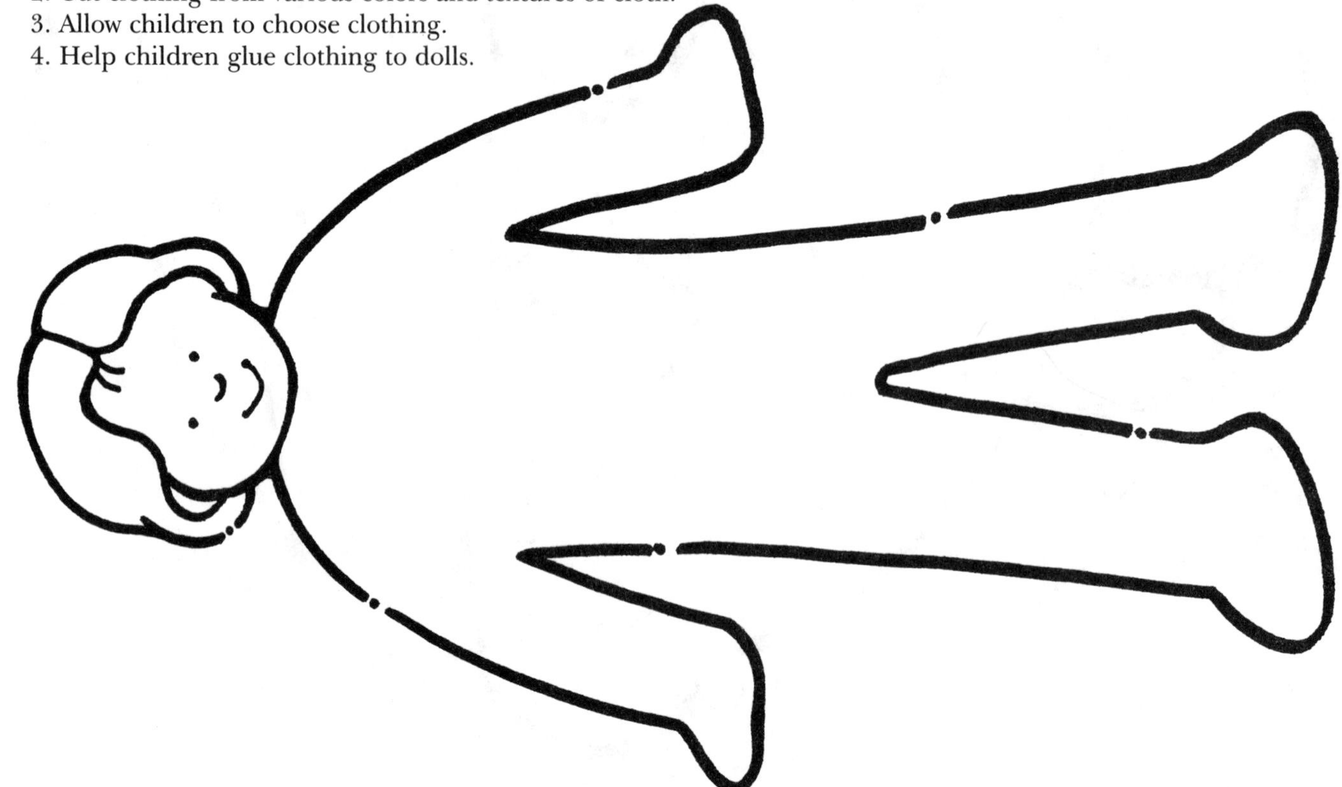

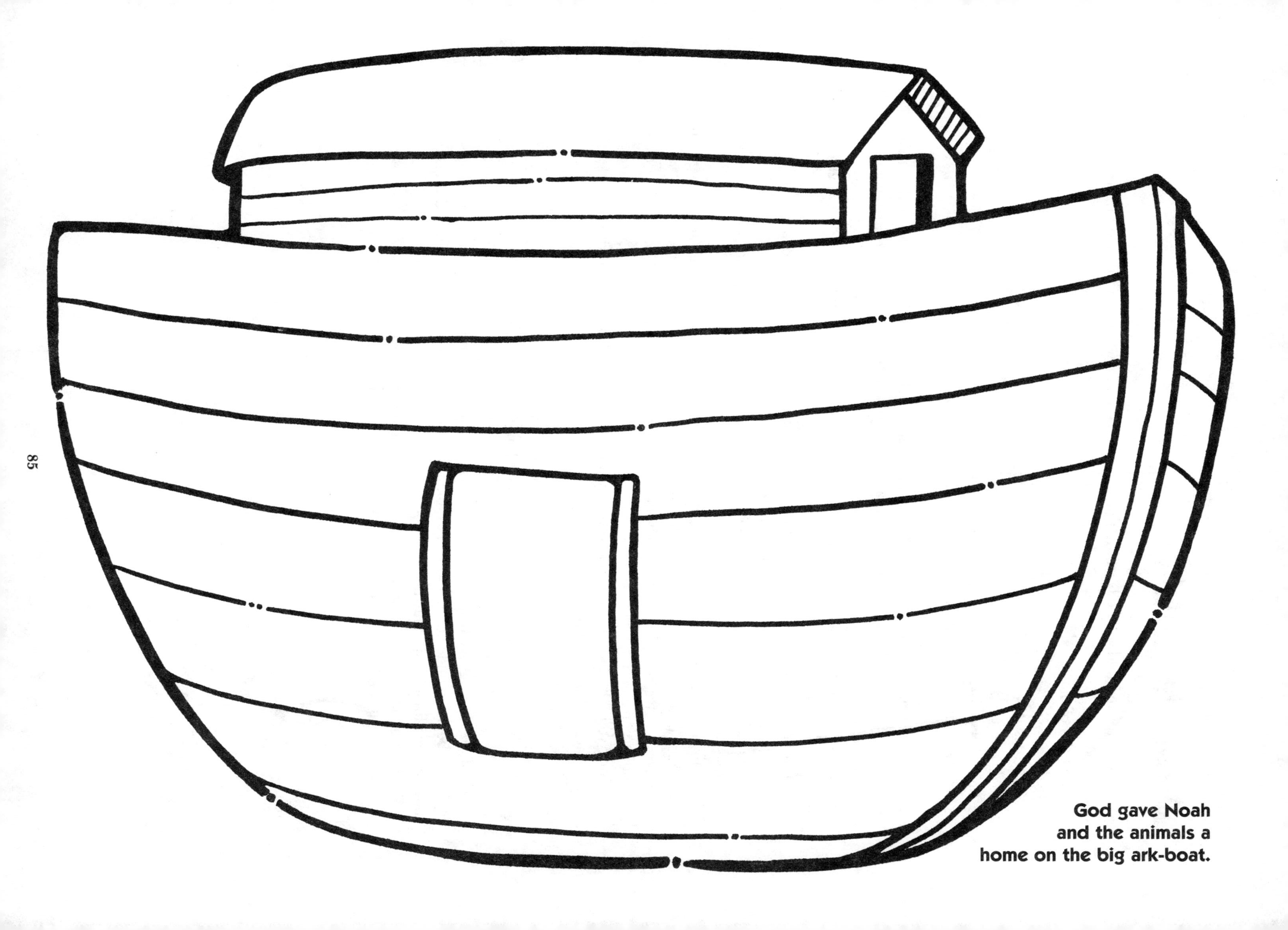

God gave Noah
and the animals a
home on the big ark-boat.

Dear Parent:

This unit your child will be learning that God is good. She will learn that God provides our daily needs.

The titles of our lessons are:

God Gives Good Food (1 Kings 17:8-16)
God Gives Water (Exodus 17:1-6)
God Gives Clothes (1 Samuel 2:19)
God Gives Homes (Genesis 6:14-22; 7; 8:1-20)
God Is Good (a review of the previous lessons)

Our Bible words are "God is good," found in Psalm 73:1. Your child will soon realize that these words are from the Bible if you will read them from your Bible often and help your child "read" them too.

You can reinforce your child's learning by talking about the simple things God has given to your child personally or to your family.

- Before meals, when you thank God for the food that He has provided, talk about how "God is good" to provide the food for your family.
- As you help your child dress in the morning, talk about how "God is good" to give her the clothes she likes to wear.
- When you have gone shopping or to church and come home, say, "God is good" to give us our nice home.
- When you give your child a drink of water, or give your child a bath, talk about how "God is good" to give us water.
- A song your child will learn is one you may want to learn and sing along with her. It goes to the tune of "Farmer in the Dell."

God cares for me, and God cares for you.
All the time, from morning 'til night, yes, God cares for us.

All of these things seem so simple, but through your words and example of thankfulness, your child will begin to understand and feel thankful for the fact that God loves him and cares for him by providing for his daily needs.

In our hurried world it is important for us to remember to give God the credit for meeting our daily needs. Let's remember to give Him thanks and praise for all He provides. "God is good"!

Your child's teacher,

Winter Quarter

Learning to Know Jesus, God's Son

Perhaps the most compelling, delightful Bible event to tell is the birth of Jesus, especially if your listeners are wide-eyed young children, eager for you to get to the part about the special baby, Jesus. The story has all the elements of mystery and familiarity to please children—angels and shepherds and wise men, a mother and father and baby boy—and it is usually the first Bible event a young child learns about at home. Young children love the story, and so do you, their teacher!

But the story doesn't end there. Jesus did not stay a baby. He grew up, becoming a man who said to His disciples, "Let the children come to me," and on the cross, "Father, forgive them." As the circumstances of His birth were not ordinary, so He was not an ordinary man.

The quarter theme is "Learning to Know Jesus, God's, Son." The first unit, "God Sends His Son, Jesus," contains five lessons about baby Jesus. The three lessons in the middle unit, "God's Son, Jesus, Grows Up," deal with Jesus as a boy. "God's Son, Jesus," the third unit, has five lessons from the life of Jesus as a full-grown man.

Children need to know that the baby Jesus did not stay a baby but grew up just as they are growing. They also need to know that Jesus who loves them, watches over them, and hears their prayers and songs is the grown-up, strong, and powerful Son of God.

As a result of these lessons, the children will

KNOW

That God's Son, Jesus, came to earth as a baby and grew up to be the man Jesus who could do wonderful things.

FEEL

Feel happy that God's Son, Jesus, came to earth.

DO

Thank God for His Son, Jesus.

Note to those who teach alone: Prepare the learning center suggested in each lesson, but also have one or two others ready to use when the children tire of the first one.

Use these songs and action rhymes throughout the quarter in addition to those specifically mentioned in the units.

I'm So Happy Today

D. F. R. Dorothy Fay Richards

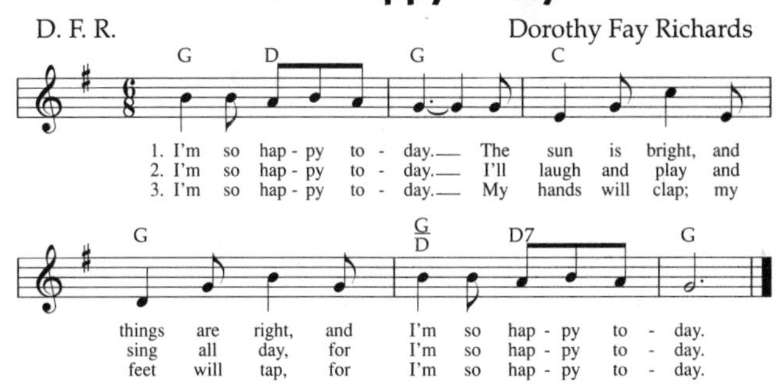

Let's Be Very Quiet

D. F. R. Dorothy Fay Richards

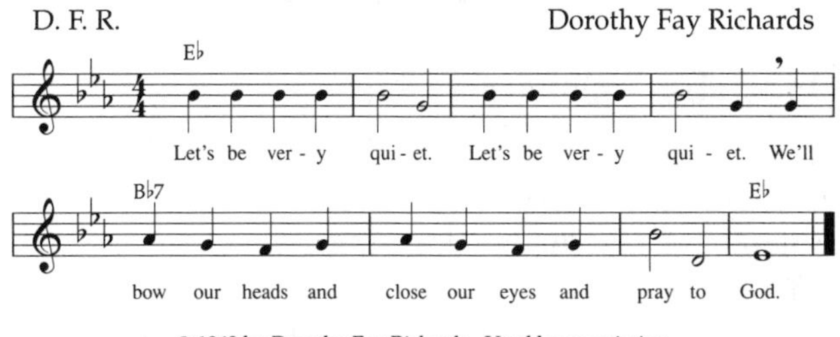

Busy Fingers

Busy little finger people, *(Hold up closed hands.)*
Who will put the toys (wraps, etc.) away?
(Look at hands.)
"I will," "I will," "I will," "I will," "I will," all the fingers say.
(Raise fingers one at a time beginning with thumbs.)
—*Louise M. Oglevee*

My Bible

This is my Bible; *(Palms held together.)*
I'll open it wide *(Open hands; keep them touching.)*
And see (or say) what is written
On the inside! *(Say Bible verse together.)*
—*Jean Baxendale*

Winter Party Suggestions

December—Christmas Party

Purpose: To help the children learn the Christmas story
When: During class time
Game: Hide the nativity figures around the room. Let the children find them and bring them to the stable. Talk about who the people are and what they are doing.
Activity: Make play dough cakes and decorate with plastic flowers and candles.
Food: Decorated cupcakes. Sing "Happy Birthday" to Jesus.
Devotion: Tell the Christmas story; let children thank God for baby Jesus.

January—Joseph's Pretty Coat

Purpose: To help the children understand their parents' love and care for them
When: During class time
Craft: Make coats like Joseph had. Cut 6" circles from the bottoms of large grocery bags. Cut 4" holes on sides for arms. Split bags from neck opening to tops of bags to form "coats." Let children paint in bright colors.
Food: Peanut butter and jelly sandwiches cut in various shapes with cookie cutters
Devotion: Story of Joseph and his father who gave him the beautiful coat because he loved him.

February—Valentine Party

Purpose: To help the children show love to family and friends
When: Saturday or Sunday afternoon
Activity: Bake and decorate cookies to give to others (If time is limited, bake cookies ahead of time.)
Preparation: Refrigerator cookie dough, frosting, heart-shaped cookie cutters, plastic knives or spreaders, plastic sandwich bags
Food: Decorated cookies and milk or water
Devotion: Jesus fed the multitude (many people) because He loved them. He could do wonderful things because He is God's Son!

Unit 1: God Sends His Son, Jesus

Lessons 1–5

By the end of the unit, the children will

Know that the baby God sent was His Son, Jesus.
Feel happy because God sent Jesus.
Thank God for Jesus.

Unit Bible Words

"God . . . sent His Son" (1 John 4:10, *NIV*).

Books

from Standard Publishing
The Littlest Sheep (24-03907)
One Tiny Baby (24-04219)
Thank You, God, for Christmas (24-04221)
The Very Special Night (24-04222)
The Very Special Visitors (24-03595)

This Unit at a Glance

1 An Angel Tells About God's Son — **Luke 1:26-38**
An angel tells Mary she is to be the mother of God's Son, Jesus.

2 God's Son, Jesus, Is Born — **Luke 2:1-7**
Jesus is born in an ordinary stable.

3 The Shepherds Go to See God's Son — **Luke 2:8-20**
The shepherds leave their flocks to go see the baby the angel told about.

4 Wise Men Worship God's Son — **Matthew 2:1, 2, 9-11**
Wise men follow a star for a long time so they can worship the baby Jesus.

5 God's Son, Jesus — **Review of Lessons 1–4**

Why Teach This Unit to Young Children?

The children in your class are hearing a lot about Christmas. In fact, they have been hearing about it since last October. They do not have a vast memory reserve to draw from, so everything sounds new and exciting. Unfortunately, most of what they have heard stresses the emphases we prefer not to place on Christmas.

The lessons in this unit seek to tie the things they see at home, in day care, and in the mall to the real meaning of Christmas, the birth of Jesus, so He is the one they think about when they see trees and stars.

Highlight the Bible words in your classroom Bible and let your children hold the Bible, point to the words, and "read" them. Use the words often in conversation, prayers, in the learning centers, during worship, and any other time you can. Make God's Word real to the children!

Things to Do for This Unit

- Make copies of Parents' Letter (page 114) and Unit Planning Sheet (pages 319 and 320).
- Photocopy the Learning Center Cards (pages 101-106); cut apart on solid lines. Glue side 1 to cardboard; then glue side 2 to back of cardboard. Laminate for durability (optional).
- Gather/prepare materials listed on Learning Center Cards.
- Obtain two flashlights for use during the unit.
- For Lesson 1, obtain a square cardboard box with a lid. Cut out an angel from one side using the pattern on page 107.
- Also find a letter, a toy telephone, and a newspaper.
- For Lesson 2, wrap a small empty gift box attractively and a small trinket gift in a plain box for each child. Have extras for visitors.
- Also cut the manger out of side 2 of the cardboard box, using the pattern on page 108.
- For Lesson 3, cut the shepherd from page 109 out of side 3 of the box.
- For Lesson 4, cut a star in side 4 of the box, using the pattern on page 110.
- Make paper hearts with the children's names on them, using the pattern on page 111.
- Obtain a picture of a newborn baby.
- For Lesson 5, cut from poster board or construction paper several of each shape used on the box.

Use These Songs and Action Rhymes During Unit 1

The Shepherds Walked on Tiptoe

My Bible

This is my Bible; *(Palms held together.)*
I'll open it wide *(Open hands; keep them touching.)*
And see (or say) what is written
On the inside! *(Say Bible verse together.)*
—*Jean Baxendale*

Let's Be Very Quiet

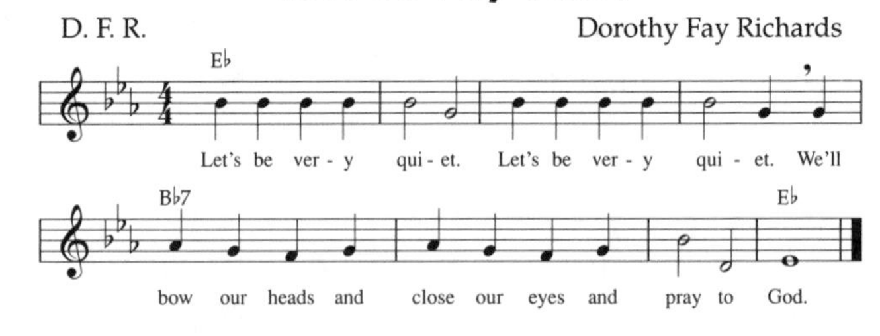

The Baby Jesus

A stable, *(Make house with hands.)*
A manger, *(Make box with hands.)*
A baby, *(Cradle "baby.")*
With animals all around. *(Arms outstretched.)*
The baby is sleeping. *(Folded hands against cheek.)*
Let's tiptoe, *(Walk on tiptoe.)*
And not make even a sound. *(Sh-h-h!)*
—*Dana Eynon*

Jesus Is the Son of God

(Tune: "London Bridge")

Jesus is the Son of God, Son of God, Son of God.
Jesus is the Son of God. Thank You, God, for Jesus.

You can repeat this as often as you wish. If your class is large and you have multiple teachers, offer all the learning centers.

Let's Go Home

Have Zach begin the action rhyme, "The Busy Fingers" (page 88). Begin cleaning the room and encourage the children to help. Say, **Our room will look so pretty with all the decorations. Let's make sure everything is put away.**

When the room is neat, have the children join hands and walk in a circle singing these words to the tune of "London Bridge."

An angel brought Mary happy news,
Happy news, happy news.
An angel brought Mary happy news.
The Bible tells me so.

Make sure each child has his art project and the Parents' Letter to take home. Take one child at a time to the door as parents arrive. Keep the other children occupied until their parents come.

Smile, Mary, Smile

B. E. — Barbara Ebert
Arr. by Morine Barnes

1. Smile, Ma-ry, smile. Hap-py news was told to you. Smile, Ma-ry, smile.
2. Smile, Ma-ry, smile. Hap-py news was told to you. Smile, Ma-ry, smile.

You will have a ba - by boy. You will have a ba - by boy.
God's Son, Je - sus, will bring joy. God's Son, Je - sus, will bring joy.

An Angel Tells About God's Son

Luke 1:26-38

Bible Words: "God . . . sent His Son" (1 John 4:10, *NIV*).

Lesson Value: Children naturally sense a spirit of excitement at Christmas. They can easily become confused, however, about the cause of all the excitement. Giving a meaning for that excitement and the things that are done to express joy at Christmas will begin to give them a basis on which to build their Christmas experience.

Know: Know that the baby God sent was His Son, Jesus.
Feel: Feel happy because God sent Jesus.
Do: Thank God for Jesus.

Children will accomplish the goals when they:

1. Say the Bible words, "God sent His Son."
2. Pray, "Thank You, God, for baby Jesus."
3. Tell why we do happy things at Christmas.
4. Experience ways of sharing happy news.

Let's Get Ready

For the Bible story, cut out an angel from one side of a cardboard carton using the pattern on page 107. Place a flashlight inside the carton. Have a letter, a toy telephone, and a newspaper ready, and three cloths to cover them.

Prepare the Art Center, the Family Living Center, and the Book/Picture Center. If you are the only teacher, use just the

Family Living Center now. Have materials for the Game Center ready to be used after the Bible story.

Learning Activities

(30 minutes, including 10 minutes presession)

Let's Get Started

Have Zach greet each child with, "Oh, good! You came to hear the happy news!" Guide each child to hang up his coat, record his attendance, and get involved in a learning activity. Offer a child two choices if you have multiple learning centers. Then make sure she gets involved in the one she chooses. Making a choice is a good learning experience for a child. Learning to stick with that choice is also good.

Worship and Bible Story

(15 minutes)

Let's Worship God

Have Zach give the children a three-minute warning before actually asking them to clean up. As soon as a few children finish and go to the circle, begin singing "Let's Be Very Quiet." Then sing "Smile, Mary, Smile," and "Jesus Is the Son of God." Say, **A baby's birth is always good news. The birth of baby Jesus was especially good news!** Use the action rhyme, "My Bible," before saying the Bible words, "God sent His Son." Pray, **Thank You, God, for sending baby Jesus. We are happy that He was born.**

Let's Learn From the Bible

Introduction: Have the letter, a toy telephone, and a newspaper on the floor or a small table in front of you, each covered with a cloth. **I wonder what is under each cloth.** Have Zach remove the cloths. **You know, we can get news from each of these things. Sometimes we get bad news. Sometimes we get good news. Let's hear some good news.** Pick up and open your Bible.

Show the children how to make "angels" by locking their thumbs and holding fingertips up to make wings. Tell them to make their angels when you say the word *angel.* Turn off your lights and open your classroom door so you will have only a small amount of light in the room. The flashlight in the box will show up better this way.

The Bible Story: We read in the Bible about a young woman named Mary. God had good news for Mary. *(Turn on flashlight in the box.)* God sent an angel *(make angel with hands)* to Mary. *(Put hands down.)*

The angel *(make angel)* said to Mary, "God has sent me to tell you some good news. You are going to be a mother. God is going to give you a special baby. He will be God's own Son. His name will be Jesus." *(Put hands down.)*

Mary was surprised! She was happy to hear this good news.

The angel *(make angels)* left. *(Put hands down.)*

Then Mary thanked God for this very happy news.

Let's Apply the Lesson

Who did God send with good news? . . . An angel, that's right. What was the name of the lady God sent the angel to? . . . Mary, yes. What was the good news? Yes, God was going to send her a baby boy, whose name was Jesus. This happy news is for us too. It is the reason why we are happy at Christmas time.

Learning Activities

(20 minutes)

Let's Play Awhile

Have the children stand and sing again "Smile, Mary, Smile." Then play the game suggested in the Game Center.

in a plain stable. God's Son, Jesus, was born in a stable that was a home for animals. How do we feel about Jesus, God's greatest gift? . . . Yes, we are happy that He was born!

Learning Activities

(20 minutes)

Let's Play Awhile

Have the children stand and sing "Jesus Was Born," and then move to the God's Wonders Center. If you have a large class and multiple teachers, also use the learning centers that were offered at the beginning of the lesson.

Let's Go Home

Have Zach begin the action rhyme, "The Busy Fingers." Begin straightening the room with the children.

After the room has been cleaned up, have the children join hands and walk in a circle singing these words to the tune of "London Bridge."

Jesus was born in a stable plain,
Stable plain, stable plain.
Jesus was born in a stable plain.
The Bible tells me so.

Make sure the children take home their hay wreaths when their parents arrive. Try to tell each parent something good her child did during the session. **Bethany did a good job picking up in the Family Living Center today.** Constructive praise encourages good behavior.

God's Son, Jesus, Is Born

Luke 2:1-7

Bible Words: "God . . . sent His Son" (1 John 4:10, *NIV*).

Lesson Value: If there is one thing all young children like, it is to get gifts. This lesson will help them begin to see Jesus as the greatest gift ever given, even though He came wrapped in very plain packaging.

Know: Know that the baby God sent was His Son, Jesus.
Feel: Feel happy because God sent Jesus.
Do: Thank God for Jesus.

Children will accomplish the goals when they:

1. Say the Bible words, "God sent His Son."
2. Pray, "Thank You, God, for baby Jesus.
3. Tell what the greatest gift ever given was.
4. Experience joy because Jesus was given.

Let's Get Ready

For the Bible story, you will need to wrap for each child one beautiful but empty package and one plain package in which you have placed a small trinket or treat. Put the attractive packages in one carton and the plain ones in another carton and place both cartons near the door. Cut out the manger/baby stencil from the second side of the box used last week. Use the pattern on page 108.

Prepare the Family Living Center, the Art Center, and Block Center. If you are the only teacher, use just the Family Living Center now. Have materials ready for the God's Wonders Center to be used after the Bible story.

Learning Activities

(30 minutes, including 10 minutes presession)

Let's Get Started

Use Zach to welcome each child by name and encourage him to hang up his wrap and put a sticker on the attendance chart. Have Zach point to the two cartons of packages and ask, "Which packages do you think have the best gifts?" After the child has answered, offer him the choice of two learning centers and make sure he becomes involved in the activity of his choice.

Worship and Bible Story

(15 minutes)

Let's Worship God

Let Zach tell the children, "It's time to put our work away so we can learn about a special gift." This will be more effective if the children get a two- or three-minute warning.

Begin singing "Jesus Was Born." Then sing "Jesus Is the Son of God" and "Let's Be Very Quiet." Pray, **Dear God, You give us many gifts. Thank You for the very best gift of all. Thank You, God, for Jesus.** Do the action rhyme, "My Bible," then say the Bible words, "God sent His Son."

Let's Learn From the Bible

Introduction: Have Zach push over both cartons of gift boxes he pointed out earlier. **I am going to give each of you one pretty package and one plain package to hold. Hold one in each hand and do not open them until I tell you.** Give out gifts and pick up your Bible and flashlight. Open your classroom door and turn off the lights.

The Bible Story: We read in the Bible that Mary and her husband, Joseph, had to make a long trip. It was almost time for Mary's baby to be born.

Finally they arrived in Bethlehem. They must have looked forward to finding a nice, comfortable room where they could rest. But there were many other people who had come to Bethlehem before them. There were no rooms to be found!

But wait! The innkeeper told Joseph about a stable.

A stable! A stable was for animals! But it was better than no place at all.

Mary and Joseph moved their things into the stable. It was probably very dark and rough. It probably smelled of hay and animals. It may have even had a few animals still in it.

And there in that plain, plain place, God gave His greatest gift. *(Turn on flashlight in box.)* What was that gift? Yes, God's Son, Jesus, was the greatest gift ever given! How happy Joseph and Mary must have been when baby Jesus was born!

Let's Apply the Lesson

Tell the children to unwrap their fancy packages. **Not everything that looks pretty on the outside is worth anything on the inside.**

Now let them open their plain gifts. **That's better. See, good things can come in plain packages. What was the best gift ever given? . . . Jesus! Where was Jesus born? In a fancy palace? No,**

Was it important for the shepherds to watch their sheep? . . . Yes. Was it more important for them to go see the baby Jesus? . . . Yes. Did they love the baby Jesus? . . . Yes, they did. Is it important for us to come to church to learn about baby Jesus? . . . Yes. Do we love the baby Jesus? . . . Yes, we do! Let's thank God for baby Jesus again.

Learning Activities

(20 minutes)

Let's Play Awhile

Let the children make the shepherds with candy cane staffs suggested in the Art Center. Use the other learning centers if needed.

Let's Go Home

Have Zach begin the action rhyme, "The Busy Fingers." Help the children straighten the room. Then have the children join hands and walk in a circle singing the following words to the tune of "London Bridge":

Shepherds left their flocks of sheep.
Flocks of sheep, flocks of sheep.
Shepherds left their flocks of sheep
To find the baby Jesus.

Continue to sing this song, including the words from the past two weeks, until parents arrive. Take one child at a time to the door as her parents come. Make sure the children take home their candy-cane shepherds.

The Shepherds Go to See God's Son

Luke 2:8-20

Bible Words: "God . . . sent His Son" (1 John 4:10, *NIV*).

Lesson Value: The story of the shepherds is a story of priorities. Before the angel came with the good news, the shepherds were doing something important. They were tending their sheep. After the angel came, they had something more important to do. They needed to see God's Son. This is a good place for these little ones to begin organizing their priorities.

Know: Know that the baby God sent was His Son, Jesus.
Feel: Feel happy because God sent Jesus.
Do: Thank God for Jesus.

Children will accomplish the goals when they:

1. Say the Bible words, "God sent His Son."
2. Pray, "Thank You, God, for Jesus."
3. Tell what the shepherds left to go see Jesus.
4. Experience something of a shepherd's life.

Let's Get Ready

For the Bible story, cut shepherd and sheep stencil from the third side of the box used the past two weeks.

Prepare the Family Living Center, the Block Center, and the God's Wonders Center. If you are the only teacher, use just the Family Living Center now. Have materials prepared for the Art Center to be used after the Bible story.

Learning Activities

(30 minutes, including 10 minutes presession)

Let's Get Started

Have Zach greet each child by name and say, "I'm so glad you could come. After you have hung up your wrap and put on your attendance sticker, you can join the others in the Family Living Center or the Block Center." Suggesting two centers, either of which is acceptable to you, allows the child to make a choice, and making a choice is a good learning experience for a young child.

Worship and Bible Story

(15 minutes)

Let's Worship God

Have Zach encourage the children to finish their work, pick up materials, and come to the circle. Gather the cotton-ball "sheep" from the Block Center. Sing "Jesus Was Born," "Jesus Is the Son of God," and "The Shepherds Walked on Tiptoe." Use the action rhyme, "My Bible," to introduce the Bible words, "God sent His Son." Lead the children to pray, **Thank You, God, for Jesus.**

Introduction: Have Zach point out the cotton-ball "sheep" and ask the children if they remember what the cotton balls are supposed to be. Have him invite each child to choose one. **I want each of you to pretend to be a shepherd. When you hear me say the word *sheep*, hold up your sheep and say "Baa."** Pick up your Bible and turn the box so the shepherd and sheep cutout is facing the children. Turn on your reading flashlight, open your door, and turn off the lights.

The Bible Story: We read in the Bible that on the night Jesus was born, there were shepherds caring for their sheep *(Baa.)* on a hill outside of Bethlehem. It was very dark. There were no street lights. There were no flashlights. Perhaps there was a campfire. Perhaps it was clear and the moon and stars shone brightly. Perhaps some of the shepherds were dozing by the fire. Perhaps some were with the sheep. *(Baa.)*

Shepherds had very important jobs. They were trusted to care for many sheep. *(Baa.)* Sheep *(Baa.)* were very valuable to their owners.

Suddenly it wasn't dark any longer! An angel was right there with them! The angel told them good news! God's Son had been born! God's Son had been born close by in Bethlehem! Then more angels came to praise God.

As soon as the angels left, the shepherds decided what to do. They left their sheep. *(Baa.)* They hurried to Bethlehem. They found baby Jesus. They saw God's Son!

When they had seen baby Jesus, they went back to their sheep. *(Baa.)* They were so happy they praised God. Perhaps they said, "Thank You, God, for baby Jesus."

Let's Apply the Lesson

Pretend you are shepherds and I am an angel. I will tell you good news. Stand up. **God's Son has been born. He is in a stable in Bethlehem.** Sit down. **Now, leave your sheep** (cotton balls) **on the floor and let's go look for baby Jesus.** You may need to remind the children of the manger scene in the Family Living Center. **When you find the baby Jesus, you can come back.**

But even if you don't bring money, you can tell Jesus how wonderful He is. You can give Him your love.

Turn the box to the manger cutout and invite children to drop their paper hearts into the box. Explain to the children that giving God their love means that they will love the people around them—their parents, grandparents, sisters and brothers, neighbors, and so forth. It also means that they will obey their parents, teachers, and so forth.

Learning Activities

(20 minutes)

Let's Play Awhile

If possible take the children to an unused room and play the game suggested in the Game Center. If you must use your room, take the children on a walk in the halls while another teacher prepares for the game. If your class is large and you have multiple teachers, have the centers used earlier ready as well.

Let's Go Home

Lead the children in "The Busy Fingers." Have the children join hands and sing these words to the tune of "London Bridge."

Wise men came to worship Jesus,
Worship Jesus, worship Jesus.
Wise men came to worship Jesus,
And brought gifts to Him.

Repeat as long as there are children left in the room. Use the stanzas from the previous lessons too. Make sure the children take their cookie gift bags to their mothers.

Wise Men Worship God's Son

Matthew 2:1, 2, 9-11

Bible Words: "God . . . sent His Son" (1 John 4:10, *NIV*).

Lesson Value: Worship is a hard concept for young children to grasp because they are so self-centered. They can, however, understand that all newborns get a lot of attention. If we speak of the baby Jesus in an attitude of reverence, perhaps they can begin to understand that He was the most special baby ever born, who deserved more attention than other babies.

Know: Know that the baby God sent was His Son, Jesus.
Feel: Feel happy because God sent Jesus.
Do: Thank God for Jesus.

Children will accomplish the goals when they:

1. Say the Bible words, "God sent His Son."
2. Pray, "Thank You, God, for Jesus."
3. Tell why Jesus was special.
4. Experience a moment of worship.

Let's Get Ready

For the Bible story, you will need to cut the star stencil in the fourth side of the box. Make paper hearts with each child's name on one. Have a picture of a newborn baby ready.

Prepare the Family Living Center, the Art Center, and the God's Wonders Center. If you are the only teacher, combine the activities of the Family Living Center and Art Center. Have materials ready for the Game Center to be used after the Bible story.

Learning Activities

(30 minutes, including 10 minutes presession)

Let's Get Started

Have Zach hold a picture of a newborn from your church or community where the children will see it as they enter the room. Let him great each child by saying, "Hi, Julie. This is baby Jason. He is brand new. Isn't he special?" Have Zach encourage the child to hang up his coat and join a learning activity.

Worship and Bible Story

(15 minutes)

Let's Worship God

Have Zach encourage the children to stop their play and begin to clean up, and then join the activities at the circle. Sing, "Jesus Was Born," "Jesus Is the Son of God," and "Let's Be Very Quiet." Ask the children to close their eyes and stay very quiet and listen while you whisper special things about baby Jesus. Slowly, with a pause between each, whisper, **Baby Jesus was a gift from God. Baby Jesus was God's own Son.** Pray, **Thank You, God, for baby Jesus.** Read the Bible words from your classroom Bible. Then let the children take turns holding the Bible, pointing to the highlighted words, and "reading" them.

Let's Learn From the Bible

Introduction: Pose three children so they appear to be praying, singing, and giving. Have the other children guess what they are doing. **We are going to talk about worship. When we worship God, we tell or show Him how wonderful we know He is. We can sing. We can pray. We can give Him offerings and gifts.** Give each child a paper heart with his name written on it. Tell the children they will use these later. Put Zach away. Then pick up your Bible and turn the box to show the star cutout. Turn on your flashlight, open the door, and turn off the lights.

The Bible Story: We read in the Bible that when baby Jesus was born a special star appeared in the sky.

The Bible says that there were some wise men who lived in a faraway country who saw the new star. They knew that the new star meant that a special baby was born. The wise men were very excited. They decided to follow the star to find the special baby.

The wise men gathered some gifts to take to the special baby. They began to follow that star. The wise men traveled a long, long way. They kept watching for the new star, and finally they found the special baby!

Do you know what they did? The Bible tells us that they went into the house where little Jesus was, bowed down, and worshiped Him. Then they gave Him their gifts and left.

Just think! Those wise men traveled all that way just to see little Jesus and tell Him how special they knew He was and to give Him gifts to show they loved Him.

Let's Apply the Story

How did the wise men know where Jesus was? . . . That's right. They followed the star. Did they take anything to Jesus? . . . Yes, they took Him gifts. What did they do when they found Jesus? . . . They bowed, they worshiped Jesus, and they gave Him gifts. How can we worship Jesus? . . . That's right, Brandon. We can sing to Him. And we can tell Him that He is great! Yes, Erin, we can bring our money to give to God.

Learning Activities

(20 minutes)

Let's Play Awhile

Play the Christmas cookie-cutter game suggested in the Game Center. If you need more than one activity at this time, use those suggested at the beginning of the lesson. Remember, in order to make these activities meaningful, you need a teacher to lead each one.

Let's Go Home

Have Zach encourage the children to straighten the room and then gather together. To the tune of "London Bridge," have the children sing all four stanzas as they hold hands and walk in a circle.

1. An angel brought Mary happy news, etc.
   The Bible tells me so.
2. Jesus was born in a stable plain, etc.
   The Bible tells me so.
3. Shepherds left their flock of sheep, etc.
   To find the baby Jesus.
4. Wise men came to worship Him, etc.
   And brought gifts to Him.

Make sure each child has everything he brought ready to take home when his parents arrive. See that each parent and child leaves with a positive feeling toward you and your class.

God's Son, Jesus

Review of Lessons 1–4

Bible Words: "God . . . sent His Son" (1 John 4:10, *NIV*).

Lesson Value: By the time this lesson is presented, Christmas day will have passed, but the children may still be tired, cranky, and over-stimulated. By reviewing what they have learned about baby Jesus, you can help them switch their focus from the worldly glitter of Christmas to the real meaning of Christmas.

Know: Know that the baby God sent was His Son, Jesus.
Feel: Feel happy because God sent Jesus.
Do: Thank God for Jesus.

Children will accomplish the goals when they:

1. Say the Bible words, "God sent His Son."
2. Thank God for Jesus
3. Tell briefly about Jesus' birth
4. Express joy because Jesus was born.

Let's Get Ready

For the Bible story, you will need to use the stencils from the first four lessons to cut out several of each shape from poster board or construction paper. You will also need the box and flashlight used in the earlier lessons.

Prepare the Family Living Center, the Book/Picture Center, and the God's Wonders Center. If you are the only teacher, do the activities in the Family Living Center now. Have the materials ready for the Game Center to use after the Bible story.

Learning Activities

(30 minutes, including 10 minutes presession)

Let's Get Started

Have Zach greet each child, direct her to hang up wraps, and help her select a learning center. If a child brings in a Christmas toy, have Zach admire it and suggest it be placed on a shelf where it can be seen but not bothered by others. Then make sure the child becomes involved in a learning activity.

Worship and Bible Story

(15 minutes)

Let's Worship God

Let Zach encourage the children to begin putting away their work and moving to the circle. Sing "Smile, Mary Smile," "Jesus Was Born," and "Jesus Is the Son of God." Using the action rhyme, "My Bible," say the Bible words, "God sent His Son." Pray, **Dear God, thank You for Your Son, Jesus.**

Let's Learn From the Bible

Introduction: Have Zach invite each child to reach in the light box and choose one shape. Then put Zach away. **Each of you has a shape which is like one of the cutouts in our light box. When I turn the side that matches your shape to the front, hold up your shape.** Pick up your Bible, turn on your story and box flashlight, open the room door, and turn off the room lights.

The Bible-story Review: *(Turn angel shape to front.)* Do you remember that we read in the Bible that an angel told Mary she would have a baby? The baby would be God's own Son. What was that baby's name? . . . Yes, Jesus.

(Turn box to manger cutout.) Mary's baby was born while she and Joseph were in Bethlehem. Mary and Joseph could not find a room to stay in. Where did they stay? . . . Yes, in a stable.

(Turn box to shepherd cutout.) The Bible tells us about the first visitors the baby Jesus had. Who were they? . . . Yes, the shepherds were the first people to see the baby Jesus. The shepherds left their sheep and went to see baby Jesus. What did they do after they saw baby Jesus? . . . Yes, they praised (thanked) God for His Son, Jesus.

(Turn box to star cutout.) Some wise men followed a star for a long time to find little Jesus so they could worship Him. What did they bring little Jesus? . . . Yes, they brought Him fine gifts.

Let's Apply the Lesson

If you have an angel, stand up. Who did the angel tell? (Mary.)

If you have a manger, stand up. Who was laid in the manger? (Baby Jesus.)

If you have a shepherd, stand up. What did the shepherd leave behind? (Their sheep.)

If you have a wise man, stand up. Who did the wise men want to worship? (Little Jesus.)

If you love Jesus, stand up. Yes, we all love Jesus!

Family Living Center

Unit 1—God Sends His Son, Jesus

Items to Include:

Lesson 1
Artificial tree
Manger scene
Unbreakable decorations

Lesson 2
Baby layette items
Manger from manger scene

Purpose: The child will tell why we do happy things at Christmas.

Things to Do and Say

Lesson 1

Let the children decorate the Christmas tree and arrange the manger scene. As they work, ask, **How many of you have already decorated your home for Christmas? What did you do? We do happy things this time of year to celebrate the birth of God's Son, Jesus. Jesus was the special baby the Bible tells us about. The Bible says, "God sent His Son." Those are our Bible words for this month.**

Lesson 2

Let the children examine the items with eyes and hands. Say, **Someone went to a lot of trouble to get these nice things ready for a baby. See how pretty the work is? I am sure the baby has a nice place to live. She was born in a nice clean hospital.**

Let's see the kind of place Jesus was born. Look at the manger scene. **This looks like a barn for animals. In fact, that is what a stable is. The Bible tells us that Jesus, God's Son, was born in a stable. His mother laid Him in a manger to sleep. We are happy because Jesus was born.**

Art Center

Unit 1—God Sends His Son, Jesus

Items to Include:

Lesson 1
Sponges
Angel stencil (page 111)
Tempera paint
Butcher paper

Lesson 2
Cardboard or poster board
White glue
Bits of straw or hay
Self-stick Christmas stickers

Purpose: The child will express joy because God sent His Son, Jesus.

Things to Do and Say

Lesson 1

Ahead of time, cut out several angel shapes from sponges using the pattern on page 111. Cut the butcher paper into manageable lengths. Let the children sponge paint gift-wrap paper.

Say, **God used an angel to tell Mary some happy news. Do you know what that news was? Yes, she was going to have a baby boy named Jesus. Mary was excited to know this happy news. We are happy that Jesus was born.**

Lesson 2

Cut wreath shapes from cardboard or poster board. Make these about 10" in diameter and about 3" wide. Let the children place bits of straw and hay on the glue you have spread on the cardboard wreaths. The children can then decorate them with stickers.

Say, **This straw wreath will help you remember that Jesus was born in a stable. His mother laid Him in a bed of straw. How happy she must have been when Jesus was born! We are happy too.**

Art Center, continued

Lesson 3
Shepherd pattern (page 112)
Construction paper or tagboard
Tempera or watercolor paint
Paint brushes
Candy canes
Transparent tape

Lesson 4
White paper lunch sacks
Star stickers

Lesson 3

Make copies of the shepherd from page 112 on construction paper or tagboard. Let each child paint a shepherd. Help each one tape a candy cane staff to his shepherd's hand.

Shepherds were busy people. They took care of many sheep. They used a long cane shaped like this to help them take care of the sheep. It was called a staff. The shepherds were excited and happy when they went to see baby Jesus. We are happy that Jesus was born. . . . Thank You, God, for Jesus. We are happy that He was born.

Lesson 4

Have the children decorate white lunch sacks with stars. Say, **We will use these lunch sacks to hold gifts. Christmas gifts remind us of God's great gift, His Son, Jesus. They also remind us of the gifts the wise men brought to little Jesus. We are happy that Jesus was born. Thank You, God, for Your Son, Jesus.**

Family Living Center, continued

Lesson 3
Spray bottle with water
Small broom(s)
Dust cloths

Lesson 4
Cookies
Frosting
Decorative candies
Plastic knives or spreaders

Lesson 5
Packing boxes

Lesson 3

Let the children clean the area to get ready for visitors.

We love to get our homes ready for company during the Christmas holidays. We clean and decorate and cook. Mary could not do that for the first Christmas visitors. She was in a stable. There were visitors who came to see the special baby, Jesus. Who were they? . . . Yes, they were shepherds. They were excited and happy to see God's Son, Jesus. We are happy that Jesus was born too.

Lesson 4

Let each child decorate several cookies as a special gift for his family. Place these in sacks decorated at the Art Center.

How good these cookies look! It's fun to give gifts to people we love. Today we will learn about some people who brought gifts to show their love for little Jesus. Your families will be happy to get these good cookies. Giving gifts to others makes us feel happy.

Lesson 5

Let the children take down and pack away decorations.

It is time to put away our decorations, but the joy of Christmas can stay in our hearts all year long. We are happy that Jesus was born.

Book/Picture Center

Unit 1—God Sends His Son, Jesus

Items to Include:

Lesson 1
Books and pictures showing angels

Lesson 5
Books covering all stories
Pictures and visuals from past lessons

Purpose: The child will feel happy that God sent His Son, Jesus.

Things to Do and Say

Lesson 1

Demonstrate how to turn the pages of a book carefully. Help the children find pictures of angels. **What do you think an angel would look like? How do you think you would feel if an angel came to your house?** Let the children discuss. **The Bible tells us that an angel came to a young woman named Mary. Mary was surprised. She had never seen an angel before. He had some happy news to tell her. I'm going to tell you this happy news in our Bible story in a few minutes.**

Lesson 5

Review the stories with the children. Let them tell you the stories. You may need to ask easy questions to elicit responses. After the children have told what they know, say, **You have learned a lot about the birth of Jesus. We can be happy all year long about Jesus' birth.**

God's Wonders Center

Unit 1—God Sends His Son, Jesus

Items to Include:

Lesson 2
Straw or hay
Piece of wood
Leather strap
Bucket of water
Blanket from barn

Lesson 3
Live sheep or lamb
Wool or woolen cloth
Book about sheep

Purpose: The child will use his senses more fully to understand the Bible story.

Things to Do and Say

Lesson 2

Let the children examine the animal barn items. Encourage the children to use their senses of touch and smell especially. **Most babies are born in hospitals that smell like medicine. Baby Jesus was surrounded by the warm smells of a barn.**

Lesson 3

Take the children outside or to a nearby farm to see sheep. (You could have the lesson at the farm.) If this is impossible, plan to take the children to a live nativity scene nearby, or perhaps you can video tape some sheep to show the children. **The first visitors baby Jesus had were shepherds. They are people who care for sheep. How would you take care of sheep? . . . The shepherds were happy to know that Jesus was born. They went to see Jesus in the stable.**

God's Wonders Center, continued

Lesson 4
Books or videos
about stars

Lesson 4

If you are meeting after dark, take the children outside to look at stars. If that is not possible, read a simple book or show a video about stars. Be sure to preview the video ahead of time.

Many years ago people used the stars to guide them. The wise men saw a special star. That star led them to the house where little Jesus was living. They took Jesus gifts to show they loved Him.

Lesson 5
Cinnamon
Cedar or pine
Ginger
Hay
Small paper sacks

Lesson 5

Place each of the four scents in separate paper sacks. Let the children smell and guess what is in each. **These are the smells of Christmas. I love these smells, don't you? Even when I smell them during other times of the year, I remember Jesus' birthday. We are happy that Jesus was born. Thank You, God, for Your Son, Jesus.**

Block Center

Unit 1—God Sends His Son, Jesus

Items to Include:

Large cardboard blocks

Lesson 2
Animal toys in scale with blocks

Lesson 3
Cotton balls

Purpose: The children will enjoy hands-on activities to help visualize the Bible stories.

Things to Do and Say

Lesson 2

Encourage the children to build a stable. Let them place animals in it.

The Bible tells us that Jesus was born in a stable. A stable is a sort of barn where animals sleep. Maybe it looked something like this. There probably were animals nearby. How would the cows sound? What sounds would the sheep make? What about a donkey?

Lesson 3

Use a black felt-tip pen to make eyes on the cotton balls. Encourage the children to build a pen for the cotton ball "sheep." As they work, talk about taking care of sheep, what sounds sheep make, and so forth. **The Bible does not say anything about the shepherds taking time to put their sheep in a pen before they went to find baby Jesus. They were in a big hurry to see baby Jesus. They were very excited and happy that Jesus was born! We are happy Jesus was born too.**

Game Center

Unit 1—God Sends His Son, Jesus

Items to Include:

Lesson 1
Unbreakable angel decoration, 3" to 6" tall

Lesson 4
Flashlight
Star cutout (page 112)

Lesson 5
Christmas cookie cutters

Purpose: The child will feel happy because God sent Jesus.

Things to Do and Say

Lesson 1

Before the class begins, hide the angel decoration in the room. Let the children look until they find it. If time and interest permit you may want to repeat. **The Bible tells us that an angel gave Mary the happy news about baby Jesus. He told her that she would have a baby boy and should name Him Jesus. We are happy that Jesus was born.**

Lesson 4

Take the children to a room that is a little dark. Warn the children that it will be dark. Ask them to hide their eyes while a teacher hides the star. The teacher will quietly conceal herself and turn on the flashlight shining it through the star cut out.

Can you find the star? The wise men had to look up in the sky each night for the star. The star helped them find baby Jesus. They were happy to find Him. They loved little Jesus.

Lesson 5

Hide Christmas cookie cutters around the room and let the children find them. When they have located them all, let them talk about the meaning of each. Even those shaped like toys can have meaning.

We do happy things at Christmas because we are glad Jesus was born. The wise men gave Jesus gifts because they were happy He was born. We like to give gifts to people too. We are happy that Jesus was born.

Winter, Unit 1—Lesson 1 Visual

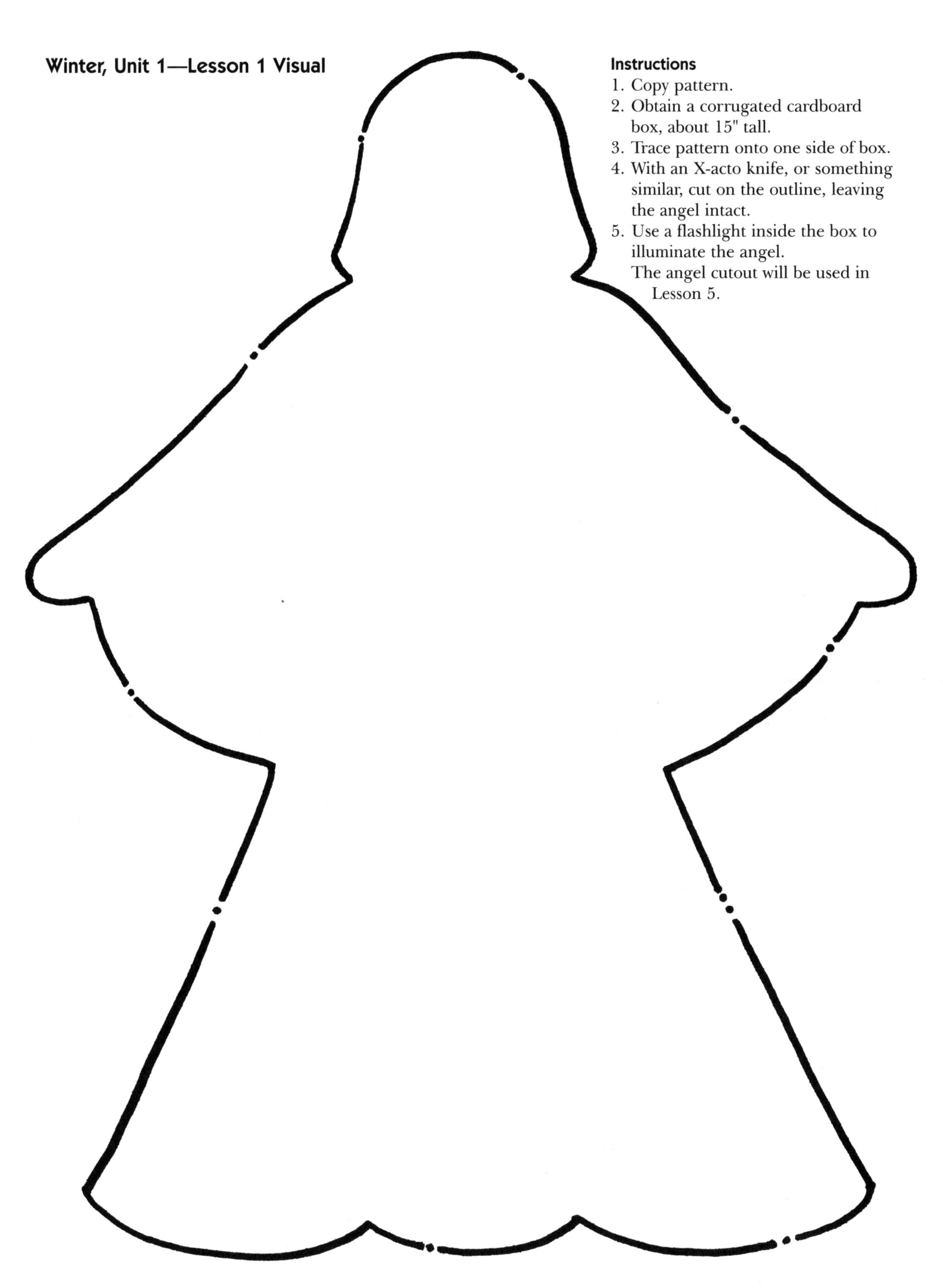

Instructions

1. Copy pattern.
2. Obtain a corrugated cardboard box, about 15" tall.
3. Trace pattern onto one side of box.
4. With an X-acto knife, or something similar, cut on the outline, leaving the angel intact.
5. Use a flashlight inside the box to illuminate the angel.

The angel cutout will be used in Lesson 5.

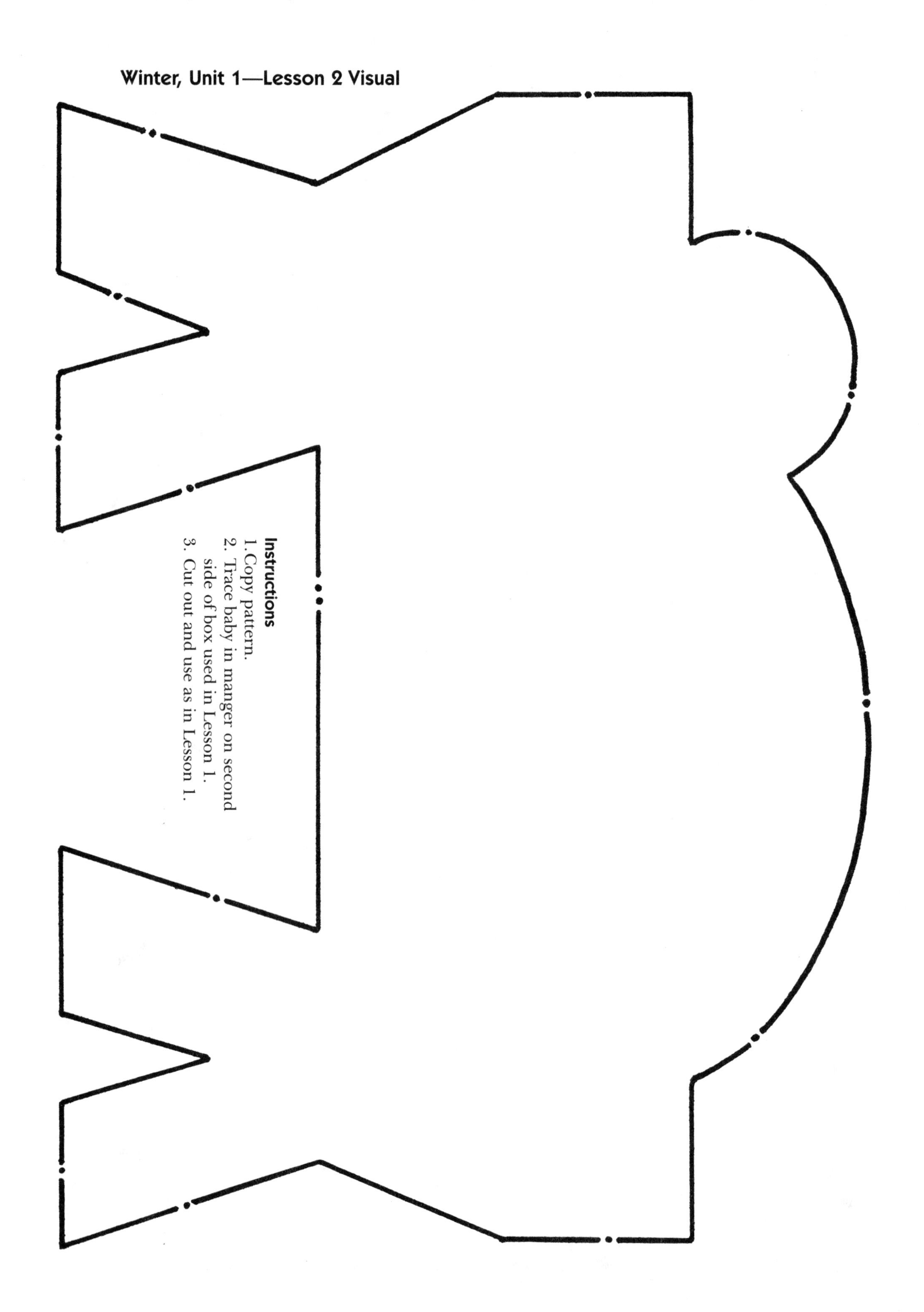
Instructions
1. Copy pattern.
2. Trace baby in manger on second side of box used in Lesson 1.
3. Cut out and use as in Lesson 1.

Winter, Unit 1—Lesson 3 Visual

Instructions

1. Copy pattern.
2. Trace shepherd and sheep pattern on side 3 of box used previously.
3. Cut out and use as in Lesson 1.

Winter, Unit 1—Lesson 4 Game Center

Winter, Unit 1—Lesson 4 Visual

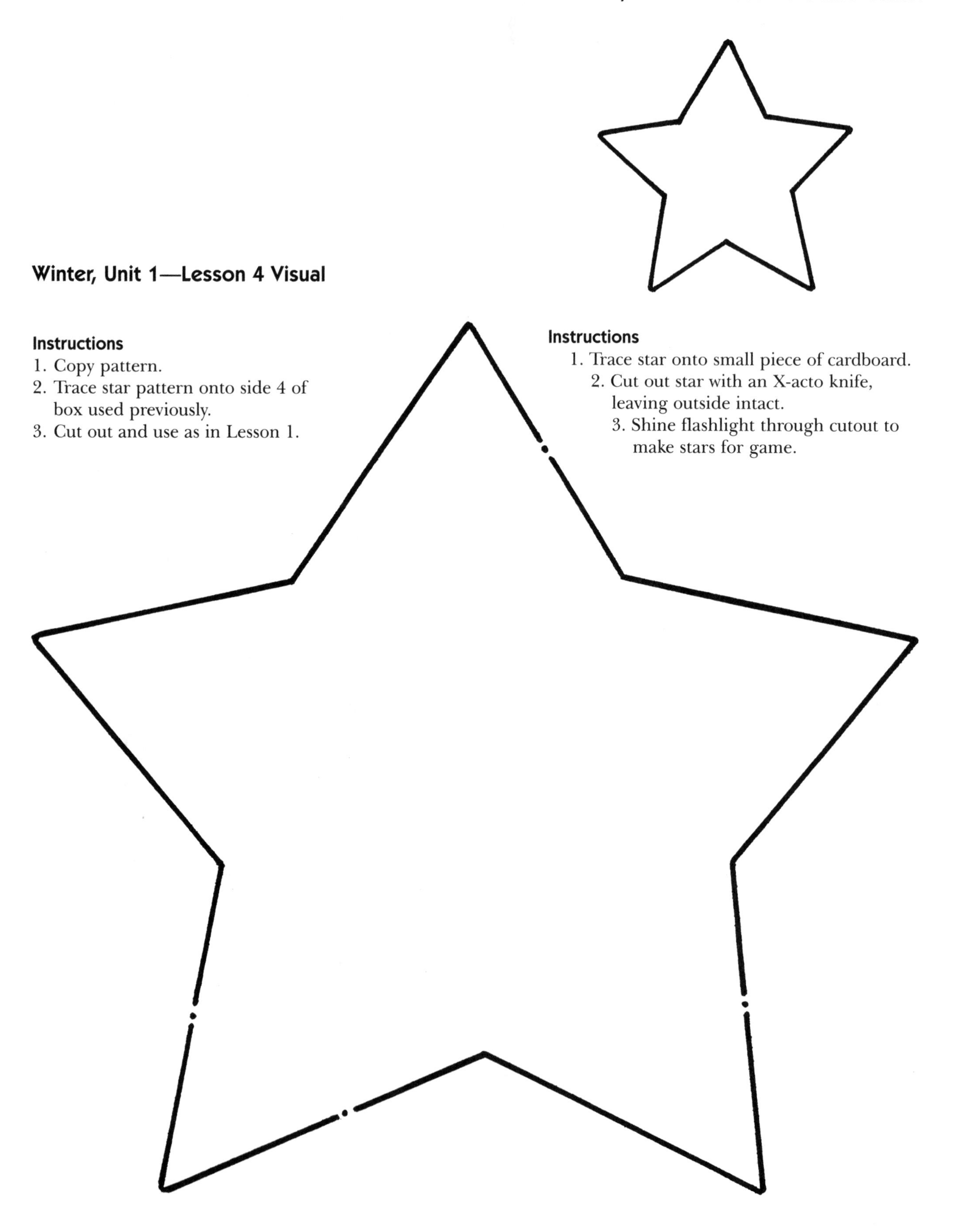

Instructions

1. Copy pattern.
2. Trace star pattern onto side 4 of box used previously.
3. Cut out and use as in Lesson 1.

Instructions

1. Trace star onto small piece of cardboard.
2. Cut out star with an X-acto knife, leaving outside intact.
3. Shine flashlight through cutout to make stars for game.

Winter, Unit 1—Lesson 1 Art Center

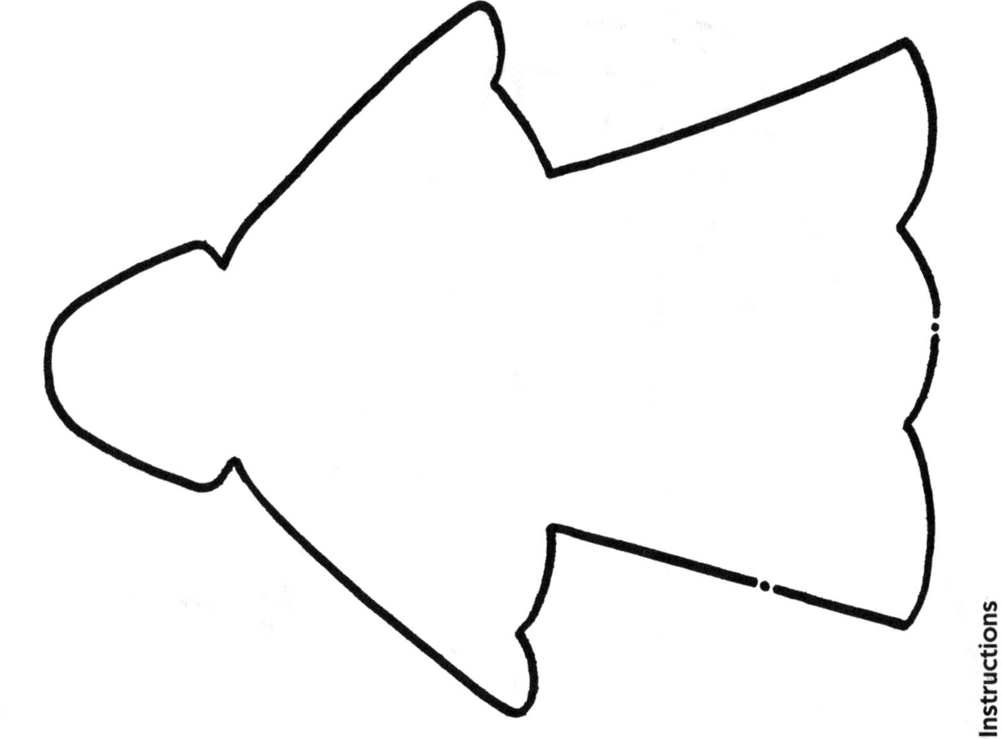

Instructions
1. Copy angel pattern.
2. Trace pattern onto cardboard or poster board.
3. Cut out pattern and use to cut several sponges.
4. Use sponges to paint gift-wrap paper.

Winter, Unit 1—Lesson 4

Instructions
1. Copy heart pattern.
2. Trace heart onto cardboard; cut out heart.
3. Make a construction-paper heart for each child in your class.
4. Print a child's name on each heart.
5. Use as directed in Lesson 4.

Instructions

1. Copy shepherd pattern onto construction paper, one per child.
2. Print on papers, "Shepherds came to see God's Son, Jesus."
3. Children may scribble-color if there is time.
4. Help each child tape a candy cane onto shepherd's hand for a staff.

We are happy that Jesus,
God's Son, was born.
"God . . . sent His Son"
(1 John 4:10).

Dear Parent:

December is such a busy month! There are so many things you want to do. There are so many things you know you ought to do. May we make a suggestion? Take a moment to pencil in on your calendar the things that will be of greatest spiritual benefit to you and your family. Attend as many special church programs as possible; go to see an outdoor creche; listen to and sing Christmas carols; decorate your home with meaningful items and explain the significance of angels, stars, and so forth; let your child help you prepare gifts for others and talk about the happiness we receive when we give to others. Make Christmas truly a celebration of Jesus' birthday, not just a time for hectic shopping, wrapping, and receiving presents.

During December we want to help your child experience in our classroom the wonderful gift of God—Jesus, His Son. Our theme is "God Sends His Son, Jesus," and our Bible words are, "God . . . sent His Son" (1 John 4:10, *NIV*). Our weekly lessons are:

- *An Angel Tells About God's Son* (Luke 1:26-38)
- *God's Son, Jesus, Is Born* (Luke 2:1-7)
- *The Shepherds Go to See God's Son* (Luke 2:8-20)
- *Wise Men Worship God's Son* (Matthew 2:1, 2, 9-11)
- *God's Son, Jesus* (based on previous lessons)

Sing this song with your child to the tune of "London Bridge":

1. An angel brought Mary happy news, happy news, happy news.
   An angel brought Mary happy news. The Bible tells me so.
2. Jesus was born in a stable plain, stable plain, stable plain.
   Jesus was born in a stable plain. The Bible tells me so.
3. Shepherds left their flocks of sheep, flocks of sheep, flocks of sheep.
   Shepherds left their flocks of sheep to find the baby Jesus.
4. Wise men came to worship Jesus, worship Jesus, worship Jesus.
   Wise men came to worship Jesus and brought gifts to Him.

Here is an action rhyme we will be using before our Bible words each week.

My Bible

This is my Bible; *(Palms held together.)*
I'll open it wide *(Open hands; keep them touching.)*
And see (or say) what is written
On the inside! *(Say Bible verse: "God sent His Son.")*
—*Jean Baxendale*

Have a blessed Christmas season with your child.

Unit 2: God's Son, Jesus, Grows Up

Lessons 6–8

By the end of the unit, the children will

Know that Jesus pleased God.
Feel that they want to be like Jesus.
Please God by helping and obeying like Jesus did.

Unit Bible Words

"Jesus . . . pleased God" (Luke 2:52, *ICB*).

Books

from Standard Publishing
Jesus Grew (24-03115)
Look, I'm Growing Up (24-04233)

This Unit at a Glance

6 Jesus Is a Helper — **Luke 2:40, 52**
Jesus grows and helps as a child.

7 Jesus Obeys Mary and Joseph — **Luke 2:40-52**
Jesus is found in the temple as He talks to the teachers.

8 The Boy Jesus — **Review of Lessons 6 and 7**

Why Teach This Unit to Young Children?

Seeing Jesus grow up serves as a bridge between the sweet baby Jesus and the strong man Jesus the children will be learning about from now until Easter. That bridge will help them begin to realize that Jesus was a real person. Seeing Jesus as a child will also help the children to understand that Jesus not only knows about children but understands them because He once was one.

Highlight the Bible words in your classroom Bible and use them often in conversation with the children. Let the children hold the Bible and help them "read" the words for themselves.

Things to Do for This Unit

- Make copies of the Parents' Letter (page 133) and Unit Planning Sheet (pages 319 and 320).
- Photocopy the Learning Center Cards (pages 123-128). Cut apart on solid lines. Glue side 1 of a card onto cardboard; then glue side 2 to back of card. Laminate for durability (optional).
- Prepare/collect materials suggested on the Learning Center Cards.
- For Lesson 6, trace the outline of a boy in your class. Cut out and mount outline on wall. Copy the face of the little-boy Jesus on page 129.

- Make a paper doll for each child (page 132).
- For Lesson 7, trace the outline of a 12-year-old boy. Cut out and mount outline on wall. Copy the face of the older-boy Jesus on page 130.
- Collect items a 12-year-old boy might like, such as baseball cards or bottle caps.
- For Lesson 8, make an outline of a grown man. Cut out and mount outline on wall. Copy the face of the man Jesus on page 131.

Use These Songs and Action Rhymes During Unit 2

Jesus Grew and Grew

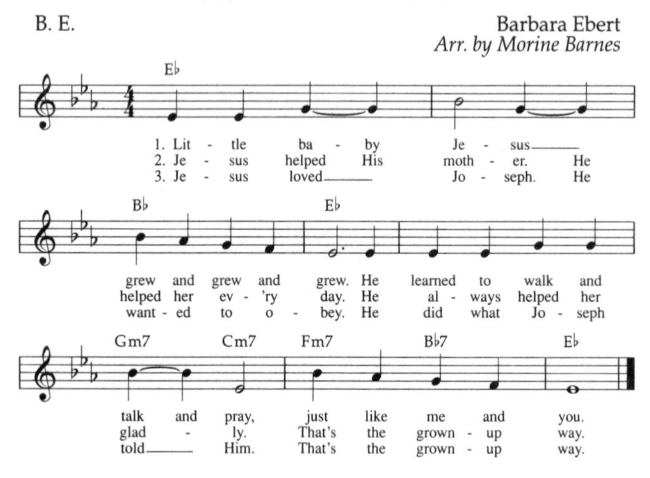

A Helper I Will Be

(Tune: "Farmer in the Dell")

A helper I will be; a helper I will be.
There's work to do, there's work to do in my family.

I love to help my mom; I love to help my dad.
I love to help; it makes God glad.
A helper I will be.

When I Pray

When I pray, I fold my hands *(Fold hands.)*
And close my eyes; *(Close eyes.)*
I think about God, and He hears me.

—*Jean Katt*

The Growing Song

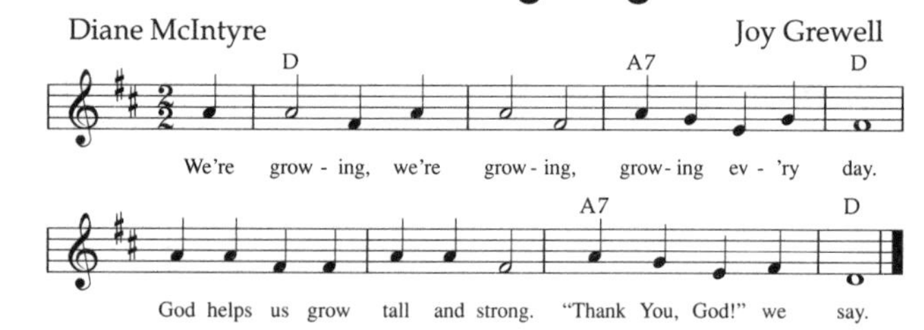

My Bible

This is my Bible; *(Palms held together.)*
I'll open it wide *(Open hands; keep them touching.)*
And see (or say) what is written
On the inside! *(Say Bible words together.)*

—*Jean Baxendale*

you getting big enough to help? Of course you are! What are some ways you can help your mommies? How can you help your daddies? You please God when you help others. Use grandparents and any other adults who are caregivers. Repeat the song, "Jesus Grew and Grew."

Learning Activities

(20 minutes)

Let's Play Awhile

Have the children carry blocks as you set up the game described in the Game Center. When the game is finished, say, **You could not be a helper when you were one-year-olds. You are growing. You are big enough to help. Every day you learn more ways to be helpers. When you help others you please God. That's what Jesus did!**

Let's Go Home

Have Zach encourage the children to put away the blocks they got out. Introduce the song, "A Helper I Will Be," as you guide the children to pick up and put away materials.

After the blocks are put away, show the children how to go about the room using their dust cloths. Remind the children to be helpers at home. Give each child his paper doll and dust cloth to take home. Also send home a copy of the Parent's Letter.

As a parent picks up her child, say something positive about the child, if possible. **Derek was a good helper. He picked up lots of blocks!** Positive reinforcement goes a long way in encouraging good behavior!

Jesus Is a Helper

Luke 2:40, 52

Bible Words: "Jesus . . . pleased God" (Luke 2:52, *ICB*).

Lesson Value: Adults find great comfort in knowing that Jesus dealt with the same problems while on earth that they deal with. Two's and 3's can experience that same comfort when they come to understand that Jesus probably had skinned knees, had to learn to dress himself, and had to deal with new babies in the house several times. In gaining that understanding, they can also begin to see that Jesus did not wait until He was grown to begin pleasing God.

Know: Know that Jesus pleased God.
Feel: Want to be like Jesus.
Do: Please God like Jesus did (help).

Children will accomplish the goals when they:

1. Say the Bible words, "Jesus pleased God."
2. Discover ways they are like Jesus.
3. Sing about Jesus.
4. Practice ways to help.
5. Pray, "Help us be helpers like Jesus was."

Let's Get Ready

For the Bible story, trace the outline of one of your boys. Place the face of the boy Jesus from page 129 on it. Cut out a paper doll shape for each child (page 132).

Prepare the Art Center, the Family Living Center, and God's Wonders Center. If you are the only teacher, use just the Family Living Center now. The Game Center will be used after the Bible story.

Learning Activities

(30 minutes, including 10 minutes presession)

Let's Get Started

Have Zach greet each child by name and suggest that he help by hanging up his coat and placing his attendance sticker on the chart. Let each child choose from two learning centers you suggest. By making suggestions, you can keep the groups fairly even in number. Always make sure that the child becomes involved in an activity. A shy child may want to watch for a few minutes before joining the others, but soon guide him gently to a place at the table, or wherever the action is, so that he becomes a part of the group.

Worship and Bible Story

(15 minutes)

Let's Worship God

Have Zach tell the children when it is time to finish their work and clean up. As they begin to gather for worship, sing "I'm So Happy Today" (page 88). Then sing "Jesus Grew and Grew," and "The Growing Song." Show the children the Bible words highlighted or underlined in your Bible. Say, **The Bible tells us "Jesus pleased God."** Use the action rhyme, "When I Pray" to prepare the children to pray. **Now, let's pray, "Dear God, thank You that we are growing like Jesus did. Help us be helpers like Jesus was."** Then pray in those words. The children will soon learn to follow you when you tell them ahead of time what you will be praying. This is a first step in praying aloud.

Let's Learn From the Bible

Introduction: Have Zach appear with a measuring tape and measure each child. Record each child's height on a paper doll and let her hold her doll as you tell the Bible story. **Children come in many different sizes. Jesus was once a small baby. But, did He stay a baby? No! Let's see what the Bible tells us about Jesus growing up.** Put Zach and tape measure away and open your Bible.

The Bible Story: When we read the Bible, it does not tell us a lot about the time Jesus was your age. It does tell us that Jesus grew from a baby to a man, so at one point He must have been just this size. *(Point to "boy Jesus" on wall.)* He may have been tall for His age. He may have been short for His age. *(Indicate size with your hands.)* The Bible just says that He grew.

He must have eaten the good food His mother cooked for Him.We read in the Bible that Jesus became strong. A child's body does not become strong if that child doesn't eat good food or just sits around. Jesus probably ran and climbed and played stick ball with His friends.

Jesus also probably helped Mary around the house. And perhaps He helped Joseph in the carpentry shop too.

We read that Jesus was filled with wisdom. He must have listened carefully when He was being taught God's Word.

The Bible also tells us that Jesus grew in favor with God and men. That means that God was pleased with Jesus, and people—even grownups, liked Him too. I think He must have been a kind and polite little boy.

Let's Apply the Lesson

Make your paper dolls become puppets. Let them answer my questions. What are some ways Jesus might have helped His mother around the house? . . . What are some ways He might have helped Joseph? You may need to give some time and cultural clues here.

Are you growing the way Jesus did? Yes, you are! . . . Are

obeys, thank him and return the cap. Repeat with each child. Ask, **Are you getting big enough to obey? Yes, you are! Whom are you to obey?** Let the children list people. If they do not respond readily, suggest people. **Should you obey your mommies? Yes! Should you obey your daddies? Of course! You please God when you obey your parents.**

Learning Activities

(20 minutes)

Let's Play Awhile

If possible, move to a larger room to play the game described in the Game Center. If that's not possible, and you did not use all of the learning centers suggested earlier, you might prefer to use one of those. If you have a large class and multiple teachers, offer several of the learning activities used earlier.

Let's Go Home

Have Zach encourage the children to straighten the room and gather their belongings.

Sing the song, "A Helper I Will Be," substituting the words "to obey" for "to help" in the second stanza. If you have extra time, stand in a circle and make up helping/obeying actions and sing to the tune of "Mulberry Bush." For example, "This is the way we pick up our toys, . . . we're big enough to help." Or, "This is the way we obey our mommies, . . . we're big enough to obey." Do an action such as going to sleep or washing hands.

As parents arrive to pick up their children, mention a way each child is helping and/or obeying in class. Stress the fact that the child is getting big enough to do these things. Some parents do not expect young children to obey and/or help. Your encouragement can help parents realize the importance of teaching and expecting their children to obey and help.

Jesus Obeys Mary and Joseph

Luke 2:40-52

Bible Words: "Jesus . . . pleased God" (Luke 2:52, *ICB*).

Lesson Value: Most children feel that as soon as they are "a little older" they can do as they please. Emphasizing the fact that Jesus, as an older child, honored Mary and Joseph's wishes to return home with them, even though He seemed to wish to remain in God's house, should make an impression on these little ones. Jesus was a big boy, almost a man by Jewish standards, but He quietly stayed under the authority His Father had arranged for Him.

Know: Know that Jesus pleased God.
Feel: Want to be like Jesus.
Do: Please God like Jesus did (obey).

Children will accomplish the goals when they:

1. Say the Bible words, "Jesus pleased God."
2. Discover ways they are like Jesus.
3. Sing about Jesus.
4. Practice ways to obey.
5. Pray, "Help us obey like Jesus did."

Let's Get Ready

For the Bible story, trace the outline of a twelve-year-old boy the children know. Place the outline on the wall beside the "child" outline from the last lesson. Have a copy of the face from page 130 ready to add during the story time.

Prepare the Family Living Center, the Block Center, and the Art Center. If you are teaching alone, use just the Family Living Center now. The Game Center will be used after the Bible story.

Learning Activities

(30 minutes, including 10 minutes presession)

Let's Get Started

Use Zach to greet each child and have him say something such as, "I'm glad I can count on you to remember our rules about hanging up wraps and putting on attendance stickers. You are getting big. You are learning to obey!" After each child has done those things, allow her to choose between two of the learning centers.

Worship and Bible Story

(15 minutes)

Let's Worship God

Have Zach announce when it is time to finish work and put things away. Sing "I'm So Happy Today" several times as the children gather. Then sing "Jesus Grew and Grew" and "The Growing Song." As you say, **The Bible tells us, "Jesus pleased God,"** show the highlighted words. Let each child have a turn to hold the Bible and "read" the words aloud. Before praying, say the action rhyme, "When I Pray." Then pray, **Dear God, help us to please You. Help us obey like Jesus did.**

Let's Learn From the Bible

Introduction: Give Zach a selection of things twelve-year-old boys might like, such as baseball cards or bottle caps. Allow each child to choose one thing. **Do you see the outline on the wall? That is Eric Smith's outline. Eric is twelve years old. Let's add the big-boy Jesus face.** Do so. **Jesus was once the same age as Eric. Jesus did not collect bottle caps or baseball cards because there were no milk bottles or baseball games then. Perhaps He collected pretty rocks or something like that. Please hold your** (name items) **quietly while you listen to the Bible story.** Have Zach leave and pick up your Bible.

The Bible Story: We read in the Bible that when Jesus was twelve, He got to make a special trip with Mary and Joseph. He got to go to Jerusalem for Passover. This was a time when the people would pray and thank God all day long.

Now Jerusalem was a very special city. God's beautiful temple was there. The temple was something like a big church building.

When Passover was finished, Mary and Joseph started to go back home. They had come with a big group of people. They were going back with the same people.

We do not know what happened. Maybe Jesus went back for just one more look at the temple. Maybe He just started talking to one of the teachers and lost track of time. All the Bible tells us was that when the group Mary and Joseph were with stopped to camp for the night, Jesus was not with them.

Mary and Joseph hurried back to Jerusalem. They must have been so worried! Can you guess where they found Jesus? *(Let children guess.)* They found Him in God's temple-church. Jesus was surprised that they had looked anywhere else.

It must have been hard for Jesus to leave God's beautiful temple-church. But Jesus did not argue. Jesus did not beg to stay a little while longer. Jesus went back home with Mary and Joseph. He knew God would want Him to obey them.

Let's Apply the Lesson

What does it mean to obey? . . . Yes, it means to do what you have been told to do. Tell the children you are going to play a game about obeying. Choose a compliant child to play first. **Patrick, please give me your bottle cap.** When the child

at the picture you are holding. What do you think Jesus would have been like when He was the age of that child?

The Bible does tell us about Jesus after He grew up. Perhaps He was as tall as Mr. Bill. *(Point to outline. Add grown-up face.)* We will be learning about the grown-up Jesus next week.

Let's Apply the Lesson

We've learned that Jesus pleased God by helping and obeying. Let's think about what Jesus might have done to help Mary and Joseph. Help children suggest ways to help. **Can you do some of those things? Yes, you can! Jesus also obeyed His parents. That means that He did what His parents wanted Him to do. Let's name some ways you can obey your parents.** (Go to bed without complaining, eat what mommy gives you, put away toys when told, etc.) **You please God when you help others and when you obey your parents.**

Learning Activities

(20 minutes)

Let's Play Awhile

Use the suggestion on the Game Center card. Remind the children to remember to please God when they see their milk caps. If your class is large and you have multiple teachers, also offer the other learning activities from the beginning of the lesson.

Let's Go Home

After the children have helped straighten the room, sing "A Helper I Will Be." Make sure each child has her art activity and milk cap when she leaves. Remind her to be like Jesus and look for ways to please God.

The Boy Jesus

Review of Lessons 6 and 7

Bible Words: "Jesus . . . pleased God" (Luke 2:52, *ICB*).

Lesson Value: We know very little about the childhood of Jesus; however, it is very important that the children fully appreciate the fact that Jesus was a child with the same needs and problems they have. This lesson will serve to emphasize that fact as well as form a bridge from the Christmas story to the man Jesus they will be learning more about in later lessons.

Know: Know that Jesus pleased God.
Feel: Want to be like Jesus.
Do: Please God like Jesus did (help, obey).

The children will accomplish the goals when they:

1. Say the Bible words, "Jesus pleased God."
2. Discover ways they are like Jesus.
3. Point out a way Jesus pleased God.
4. Point out ways they can please God.
5. Pray, "Help us please You like Jesus did."

Let's Get Ready:
For the Bible story, trace the outline of a man in his early 30's, someone the children will know. Mount this on the wall beside the last two figures. Cut out the man Jesus' face from page 131. Collect pictures of children your class will recognize—from newborn to twelve, and write their ages on the backs of their pictures.

Prepare the Family Living Center, the Art Center, and God's Wonder's Center. If you are the only teacher, use just the Family Living Center. Have the Game Center ready to use after the Bible story.

Learning Activities

(30 minutes, including 10 minutes presession)

Let's Get Started
Let Zach greet each child by name and ask him to tell something fun he did during the past week. This may require some prompting. After the child responds, direct him to hang up his coat, place a sticker on the attendance chart, and choose a learning center. Give a child two choices, either of which is acceptable to you. That way, the child will have an opportunity to make a choice, and you will be happy with his choice.

Worship and Bible Story

(15 minutes)

Let's Worship God
Have Zach encourage the children to finish what they are doing and clean up the room. Begin singing "Jesus Grew and Grew," "I'm So Happy Today," and "The Growing Song." Say, **I heard some of you telling Zach about the fun you had this past week. All children like to have fun. I'm sure that even while you were having fun you were also pleasing God and your parents. The Bible says, "Jesus pleased God."** Use the action rhyme, "When I Pray," before you pray, **Dear God, help us please You like Jesus did.**

Let's Learn From the Bible
Introduction: Give each child one of the pictures of children you have collected. **Each one of you is holding a picture of a boy or girl. Can you tell me who you have?** Let a child who has a picture of someone he knows identify that person. **You're right! That's Jeremy's big sister, Julie. Let's see how old Julie is.** Look on the back of the picture. Identify the remaining pictures and note the ages. **It seems as if we have a picture of someone for almost every growing-up year. Let's put you in order according to the age of the child in the picture you have.** Do so and ask the children to stay that way during the story. Put Zach away and have your Bible on your lap or nearby.

The Bible-story Review: We had a story in the Bible about when Jesus was born. Brittany is holding a picture of a newborn. We don't know much about Jesus when He was one year old or two or three *(indicate children holding pictures of children this age)* or four or five or six or seven or eight or nine or ten or eleven. About all we know is that Jesus grew bigger and learned more about God's Word and pleased God and the people around Him. The Bible tells us that. Are those things all children can do? *(Let children respond.)*

When Jesus was twelve, we know He went on a special trip. Do you remember where He went? *(Let children respond.)* He went to Jerusalem with Mary and Joseph. He probably would have liked to stay in Jerusalem because God's temple was there. Mary and Joseph wanted Him to go home with them. Did Jesus go? *(Let children respond.)* Jesus obeyed His parents. Is that something all boys and girls can do? *(Let children respond.)*

The Bible doesn't tell us much about Jesus while He was growing up, but we do know that Jesus always pleased God. Look

Game Center

Unit 2—God's Son, Jesus, Grows Up

Items to Include:

Lesson 6
Dowel rods
Large cardboard blocks

Lesson 7
Poster board or cardboard
Felt marker

Purpose: The child will learn that he is growing the way Jesus grew.

Things to Do and Say

Lesson 6

Stack two sets of blocks the same height as a one-year-old might crawl under. Stack a second two sets the height a two-year-old might walk under. Stack a third set the height a three-year-old might walk under.

Let the children take turns crawling and walking under the dowels. Say, **You are not the same size now you were when you were one year old. You are growing. The baby Jesus grew the way you are growing. He grew to be a bigger boy, big enough to help his mother and Joseph.**

Lesson 7

If possible, play this game in a large room. Post a sign reading "Jerusalem" at a distance from the group. Tell the children that, to get to Jerusalem, they must follow directions. Say something like, **Take five little tiny steps toward the mail box.** Continue giving directions until the group reaches Jerusalem.

When Jesus grew to be a big boy, He went on a long trip to Jerusalem. He was big enough to go with His mother and Joseph. He was big enough to follow directions. You are growing the way Jesus grew. I'm glad you are growing big enough to follow directions.

God's Wonders Center

Unit 2—God's Son, Jesus, Grows Up

Items to Include:

Lesson 6
Mother and baby animal (or pictures of these)

Lesson 8
Rocks
Unusual sticks
Seashells

Purpose: The child will learn that he is growing up just like Jesus did.

Things to Do and Say

Lesson 6

Bring a mother and baby animal to class. If this is impossible, find or take pictures of an animal mother and baby or babies. Instruct the children about handling and being quiet before introducing the animals to the classroom.

This mother cat was once small like her kitten. What happened? Yes, she grew up. What do animals need to make them grow? Help children to think of food, water, sleep, exercise, and so forth.

Are you growing? Yes, you are! You are growing every day. What do you need to make you grow? (Good food, water, plenty of sleep, exercise, fresh air, and so forth.) **Jesus grew up just the way you are growing. He grew big enough to help His mother and Joseph. You are getting big enough to help too.**

Lesson 8

Arrange the nature items to attract the children. Make sure nothing is harmful to young children! Encourage the children to look at the things you have displayed.

Do babies play with rocks and sticks and bugs. . . . No! Do some bigger boys and

Game Center, continued

Lesson 8
Milk caps

Lesson 8

Print "Jesus" on each milk cap or circle of cardboard. Hide the milk caps (circles) in your classroom. Tell the children to look until each child has found one cap or circle.

The cap you find will have the name of someone who obeyed. Help the children to "read" the name of Jesus. **Can we put on the other side the name of someone else who will obey? Yes, we can! Jeremy is big enough to obey. Let's write Jeremy's name on his cap. Write each child's name on the cap he finds. Stress that the child is big enough to obey.** Being big enough to do "important" things means a great deal to a young child.

God's Wonders Center, continued

Worms (in a jar of soil)
Bugs (in a jar with holes)
Other nature items

girls like these things? . . . Yes! Did Jesus play with bugs and rocks when He was a baby? . . . Of course not. How about when Jesus grew to be a bigger boy? . . . Yes, He probably did. Even in Bible times there were rocks and sticks and worms and bugs. I'm sure Jesus spent time looking at things like these. What other things do you think the boy Jesus might have liked to look at? *(Let the children discuss.)* **The Bible tells us that Jesus grew up. He pleased God. You are growing just the way Jesus did. You are getting bigger every day. You are getting big enough to help and obey the way Jesus did. And that pleases God!**

Block Center

Unit 2—God's Son, Jesus, Grows Up

Items to Include:

Large cardboard blocks

Purpose: The child will learn that he is growing big enough to obey the way Jesus did.

Things to Do and Say

Lesson 7

Help the children begin to build a large temple. Talk to them as you work.

In our Bible story, Jesus grew big enough to go with His mother and Joseph to the big temple in Jerusalem. The temple was a large building something like our church building. We'll call it a temple-church. Jesus had to obey His parents by staying with them as they walked to Jerusalem, and by being quiet in the temple-church. I'll tell you the story in a little while. . . . I'm glad that you are growing big enough to work together. That is a fine temple-church you are building.

Younger children may prefer to build a road to follow to the temple-church. Show them how to "walk" with their fingers along the road. **I'm glad you are getting big enough to play with me here in our block area.**

When it is time to pick up, talk about the fact that the children are big enough to pick up the blocks, big enough to obey you, and so forth. Praise them for being helpers.

Family Living Center

Unit 2—God's Son, Jesus, Grows Up

Items to Include:

Lesson 6
- Vegetables and fruits
- Plastic knives
- Paper plates

Lesson 7
- Ingredients for cookies
- Cooking equipment

Purpose: The child will learn that Jesus experienced normal growth, just as he is.

Things to Do and Say

Lesson 6

Have the vegetables and fruits cut into manageable sizes. Show the children how to use plastic knives to cut up the fruits and vegetables into bite-size pieces. You may need to hold the hands of the younger children as they cut. Emphasize that they are using plastic knives, and must always have an adult to help them, and never use a sharp knife. Young children may prefer using a brush to wash carrots, etc., rather than try to cut them.

These fruits and vegetables look good! These are good for you too. I'm glad God has given us good food to help us grow. . . . Jesus probably ate some of these same fruits and vegetables when He was growing up. You are growing up just like Jesus did. . . . You are getting big enough to help your mommies prepare good foods like this at home. . . . We're going to save these to eat later. We will share them with the rest of the class.

Lesson 7

Have the ingredients for making cookies already measured so the children can simply add and stir. Or, to save time, have prepared cookie dough, either some you have made or ready-prepared rolls. Let the children place the cookie dough on cookie sheets.

We are going to bake "Obedience" cookies. If you obey me, we will have good

Family Living Center, continued

cookies to eat. Give each child a specific job to do. Have an adult ready to take the cookies to bake in a preheated oven. Serve the cookies at the end of class time.

If you do not have time or facilities to bake cookies, provide cookies or graham crackers and frosting for the children to spread with plastic knives. Comment on the children's obedience as they work. **I like the way you are working together. Sharing your knife with Katy was a good thing to do, Mark. These are going to be good "Obedience" cookies!**

Lesson 8
Home safety items

Lesson 8

Bring electric outlet covers, a smoke detector, an empty box of matches, and so forth. Let the children tell you what they know about each item you have. If they don't know what an item is, explain to them the function and reason for its being. Make this simple and short!

Let's talk about family safety rules. Should you obey the rules your mommies and daddies make for you? Why? (Because they know what is best, to keep us safe, etc.) . . . **Jesus grew up to be a big boy. He obeyed Mary and Joseph. You are growing up the way Jesus did. Do you ever get too big to obey rules? Of course not! Even parents have to obey safety rules.**

Art Center

Unit 2—God's Son, Jesus, Grows Up

Items to Include:

Lesson 6
12" squares of soft fabric (1 per child)
Fabric paint
Shallow pan
Large sponge

Lesson 7
Non-menthol shaving cream

Purpose: The child will learn more about growing while enjoying sensory experiences.

Things to Do and Say

Lesson 6

Before class, ask a mother of a small baby to provide you with a painted handprint of her baby. In class, have fabric paint in a shallow pan with a sponge in it. The children will first measure their hands to the baby's print. Then let each child press her hand on the sponge and make a handprint on her fabric square to make a dustcloth.

When your hand was as little as the baby's, you could not help. You could not even feed yourself. But you are growing. You are big enough to help. You are big enough to do lots of things. Jesus grew the way you are growing. He grew from a baby to a little boy, and then to a big boy.

Lesson 7

Tell the children they can finger paint with shaving cream if they obey the rules. Give the rules one at a time and let each child comply before giving the next rule. 1) Roll or push up your sleeves. 2) Put on a paint shirt. 3) Stand without touching your neighbor. 4) No splashing.

You have grown up enough to follow rules. You are getting bigger. You can do many things you couldn't do when you were smaller. Jesus grew up that way too. He grew big enough to help, and big enough to obey His parents.

Lesson 8
Construction paper
Patterns from page 132
Yarn

Lesson 8

Make copies of the patterns on page 132 in the original size, one per child. Then make copies of these enlarged a small amount; then make copies by enlarging the enlargements. Now you will have three sizes of paper dolls, a set for each child. On each of the smallest ones print "Jesus"; on the middle-sized ones print "pleased"; and on the largest ones, print "God (Luke 2:52)." Punch a hole in the top of each paper doll.

In class, give each child a piece of yarn to string through the three construction paper dolls. Watch to be sure they are kept in order. Show the children how to make their dolls grow as they say the Bible words.

Instructions

1. Copy boy Jesus' head onto flesh-tone construction paper.
2. Add color and cut out head.
3. Glue face to outline of boy, as suggested in Lesson 6.

Instructions

1. Copy young Jesus' head onto flesh-tone construction paper.
2. Add color and cut out head.
3. Glue onto outline of 12-year-old boy as suggested in Lesson 7.

Instructions

1. Copy Jesus' head onto flesh-tone construction paper; color and cut out.
2. Glue head to outline of man, as suggested in Lesson 8.

Instructions
1. Copy onto flesh-tone construction paper; add color and cut out.
2. Or, copy dolls onto various colors of paper.
3. Use as directed in Lesson 6.

Dear Parent:

Your child probably knows about the baby Jesus and the man Jesus by now. This little unit will serve as a bridge between the baby and the man. The unit focuses on Jesus' childhood. The thrust of these lessons is to help your child become like Jesus. Your child is growing the way Jesus did, he can help the way Jesus probably did, and he can learn to obey the way Jesus did. All of this is pleasing to God. That is, it makes God happy.

Here are the lessons we will be studying:
Jesus Is a Helper (Luke 2:40, 52)
Jesus Obeys Mary and Joseph (Luke 2:40-52)
The Boy Jesus (based on the previous lessons)

Take time to speculate with your child about what Jesus' childhood might have been like. Remind your child that she is growing, and is getting big enough to help and to obey, just the way Jesus did. The Bible tells us that Jesus was pleasing to God as well as to people. What better goal than to please God and people!

Give your child plenty of opportunities to help. For example, let your child help you make beds, dust furniture, do the dishes, empty wastebaskets, set the table, fold laundry, help wash and prepare vegetables, and so forth. Comment on your child's achievements, the fact that she is big enough to help, and thank her for her help. Be specific about the help given and honest in your praise. Talk about the fact that Jesus probably helped His mother and Joseph, and that helping others makes God happy (pleases Him).

Talk about what obedience is—doing what you are told to do, and praise your child for obeying you. Again, be specific and honest in your praise. Remind him that he is doing what Jesus did, and that obeying is one way to please God (make God happy).

Sing these words with your child:

A Helper I Will Be
(Tune: "Farmer in the Dell")

A helper I will be; a helper I will be.
There's work to do, there's work to do in my family.

I love to help* my mom; I love to help* my dad.
I love to help*; it makes God glad. A helper I will be.
*to obey

Do the following rhyme before praying with him at bedtime:

When I Pray

When I pray, I fold my hands
(Fold hands.)
And close my eyes; *(Close eyes.)*
I think about God, and He hears me.
—*Jean Katt*

Your child's teacher,

Unit 3: God's Son, Jesus

Lessons 9–13

By the end of the unit, the children will

Know that Jesus can do wonderful things because He is God's Son.
Want to thank God for wonderful things Jesus did.
Thank God for wonderful things Jesus did.

Unit Bible Words

"Jesus is the Son of God" (Acts 9:20, *NIV*).

Books

from Standard Publishing
God Cares for Me! (24-03112)
No Problem! (24-03594) (healing of lame man)

This Unit at a Glance

9 Jesus Helps His Friends Catch Fish — **Luke 5:1-9**
At Jesus' suggestion, His friends fish on the opposite side of the boat with amazing results—a miraculous catch of fish!

10 Jesus Stops a Storm — **Luke 8:22-25**
Jesus commands the wind and waves to be still and has miraculous obedience from nature!

11 Jesus Heals Two Blind Men — **Matthew 20:29-34**
When two blind men ask for healing, Jesus touches their eyes and they receive their sight instantaneously—another of Jesus' miracles!

12 Jesus Makes a Lame Man Walk — **Mark 2:1-12**
Four friends bring a lame man to see Jesus and the crowd is amazed to see him come down through the roof, and even more amazed when Jesus miraculously heals him!

13 Jesus Is God's Son — **Review of Lessons 9–12**

Why Teach This Unit to Young Children?

These lessons will help your children begin to associate positive feelings and words with Jesus, God's Son. They will feel happy when they remember how Jesus helped the people in these Bible stories. The children will associate the fact that Jesus changed sad to happy, fear to safety, blindness to sight, and lameness to health. When these children hear the words, "Jesus, God's Son," they will see mental images of happiness, joy, and wonder. They will be thankful to have a friend who can do wonderful things!

The Bible words should be used in general conversation, during learning centers, worship, and Bible story time. It is important to emphasize this unit's Bible words immediately after telling about something wonderful Jesus did. **Jesus made the storm be quiet. He could do that because "Jesus is the Son of God"!** Have the classroom Bible in prominent places. Hold it on your lap during Bible story time. Highlight the Bible words so that children easily can see, point to, and "read" them with you.

Things to Do for This Unit

- Photocopy the Parents' Letter (page 160) and the Unit Planning Sheet (pages 319 and 320).
- Copy the Learning Center Cards (pages 147-152); cut apart on solid lines. Glue first side to cardboard and second side to back of the cardboard. Laminate for durability (optional).
- Gather/prepare materials listed on Learning Center Cards.
- For Lesson 10, obtain a life preserver, boat, or fishing net for Zach.
- For Lesson 12, find a square box with loose-fitting lid. Cut a square section from the center of the lid, but don't discard the cutout. Draw a door (don't cut it out) and an outside stairway. Also have plenty of straight clothespins.

Use These Songs and Action Rhymes During Unit 3

It's Time to Worship

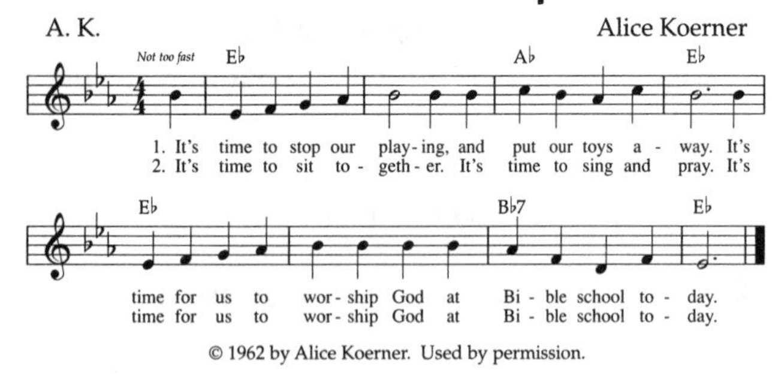

**Use "our classroom" in place of "Bible school."*

Jesus Is the Son of God

(Tune: "London Bridge")

Jesus is the Son of God,
Son of God, Son of God.
Jesus is the Son of God.
Thank You, God, for Jesus.

Jesus helped His friends catch fish,*
Friends catch fish, friends catch fish.
Jesus helped His friends catch fish.
Thank You, God, for Jesus.

*3. Jesus stopped a storm at sea, etc.
*4. Jesus made a blind man see, etc.
*5. Jesus made a sick man walk, etc.

I Will Help

(Tune: "Row, Row, Row Your Boat")

I will help at church. I will help at church.
I am big enough to help.* I will help at church.

*2. My hands will pick up toys and share.
*3. My eyes will look for ways to help.
*4. My ears will listen carefully.
*5. My mouth will gladly say, "I will."

When I Pray

When I pray, I fold my hands *(Fold hands.)*
And close my eyes; *(Close eyes.)*
I think about God, and He hears me. —*Jean Katt*

I'm So Glad!

I'm so glad *(Clap hands.)*
The sun* I see; *(Make big round sun with arms.)*
I'm so glad *(Clap hands.)*
God loves me! *(Point to self.)*

*Snow *(Flutter fingers to the floor.)*
*Rain *(Flutter fingers to the floor, quickly.)*
*Birds *(Waves arms at sides.)*

—*Jean Baxendale*

Wait! I see our friend Jesus! Let's show how we feel when we see Jesus! *(Wave; excited, happy faces.)* **Jesus will help His friends. Let's show how Jesus helped!** *(Pull in heavy nets of fish; happy faces.)* Show the picture of the net full of fish. Have the children tell (point to) the wonderful thing Jesus did. **Jesus could do wonderful things because He is the Son of God! Those are our Bible words. Let's say them together.** Do so.

Learning Activities

(20 minutes)

Let's Play Awhile

Have the children stand and sing these words to the tune of "Fishers of Men." Add actions if you wish.

Jesus helped His friends catch lots of fish,
Catch lots of fish, catch lots of fish.
Jesus helped His friends catch lots of fish.
He's the Son of God!

Have the children go to the Game Center for the fishing game. If you have a large class and several teachers, open the centers used at the beginning of the lesson. This will allow the children to enjoy activities they didn't have time for earlier.

Let's Go Home

Use Zach to sing, "I Will Help." Encourage reluctant children by giving them specific tasks to do. **Abby, please put the block in the closet. . . . Luke, that puzzle goes on the shelf.** As soon as children have finished picking up, sing "Jesus Is the Son of God." Encourage children to pretend to lift a heavy net of fish as they sing the second stanza.

Jesus Helps His Friends Catch Fish

Luke 5:1-9

Bible Words: "Jesus is the Son of God" (Acts 9:20, *NIV*).

Lesson Value: When Jesus caused the fishermen's nets to overflow with fish, Peter, James, and John were convinced to follow Jesus. This miracle was the beginning of their understanding of who Jesus was and that He was special. The story of the fish will be an exciting one for your children. Encourage them to share the fishermen's excitement as they begin to learn how special Jesus, the Son of God, is!

Know: Know that Jesus can do wonderful things because He is God's Son.
Feel: Want to thank God for wonderful things Jesus did.
Do: Thank God for wonderful things Jesus did.

Children will accomplish the goals when they:

1. Say the Bible words, "Jesus is the Son of God."
2. Discover how Jesus and His friends caught fish.
3. Sing about Jesus.
4. Point to or name a wonderful thing Jesus did.
5. Pray, "Thank You, God, for the wonderful things Jesus did."

Let's Get Ready

For the Bible story, you will need the puppet Zach, a produce sack (Zach's net), bucket (Zach's fishing hole), the classroom Bible, and a completed copy of page 153.

Prepare the God's Wonders Center, the Art Center, and the Book/Picture Center. If you are the only teacher, use just the God's Wonders Center now. Have materials ready for the Game Center to use after the Bible story.

Let's Get Started

Have pictures of fish, water, boats, and anything else that pertains to fishing near the door where children will see them as they enter. Let Zach tell the children about some of the pictures. After a child has hung up his coat, added a sticker to the attendance chart, and is ready for a learning center, offer him two learning activities from which to choose. **Joshua, you may go to the Art Center to make a picture of some men fishing, or you may watch the fish in the God's Wonders Center and try to catch fish in our "pond." Which do you want to do first?** When Joshua has decided, see that he gets involved in the activity he has chosen.

Learning Activities

(30 minutes, including 10 minutes presession)

Let's Worship God

When it is time to pick up the toys, use Zach to help you sing "It's Time to Worship." As soon as the first children come to the worship area, begin to sing "I'm So Happy Today" (page 88). Then sing the first stanza of "Jesus Is the Son of God." Use the rhyme "My Bible" (page 88) to introduce this unit's Bible words, "Jesus is the Son of God." After saying the Bible words ask the children to say them with you. Use the rhyme, "When I Pray," to prepare the children for prayer. Then say, **Now we're ready to pray, "Thank You, God, for the wonderful things Jesus did."** Then fold your hands and pray those words. The children will soon learn to say them with you.

Let's Learn From the Bible

Introduction: Have Zach hold a fishing net (produce sack) and begin to fish in the bucket. **Zach is trying to catch something for his dinner. What do you think Zach is trying to catch?** (Fish!) **Let's let Zach keep trying while we listen to a Bible story about some fishermen who were friends of Jesus!** Set Zach and the bucket of water aside. Place your Bible open to Luke 5:1-9 on your lap.

The Bible Story: Some friends of Jesus had been fishing all night on the sea. Over and over they would throw their nets into the water, then bring them up, but their nets were empty. They couldn't catch any fish! *(Show the children how to throw a net into the water, then pull it in and lift empty hands. Look very sad.)*

Finally the fishermen got tired They decided to stop fishing and bring their boats back to shore. *(Ask children to act as though they are tired—yawn, stretch, and rub sleepy eyes.)*

As the fishermen were washing their nets, they saw their friend, Jesus. *(Shade your eyes with your hand as though you see Jesus.)* Jesus sat down in Peter's boat. Jesus asked Peter to move his boat away from the shore. Then Jesus talked to the people who had gathered on the shore.

When Jesus was finished talking to the people, He told Peter to row back out to the deep water and fish some more. *(Encourage the children to row their boats; then throw out their nets.)* When Peter did this, the net became so full of fish, he had to ask his friends, James and John, to come and help him! Everyone was amazed at what had happened. The fishermen had never seen so many fish! Jesus can do wonderful things because He is the Son of God!

Let's Apply the Lesson

Let's show how the fishermen looked when they fished all night and didn't catch any fish! *(Sad faces, angry faces, empty hands.)* **Let's show how the fishermen felt when they decided to stop fishing.** *(Tired faces, yawns, rubbing eyes.)*

Learning Activities

(20 minutes)

Let's Play Awhile

Have the children stand and do the action rhyme, "I'm So Glad," then go to the Block Center. If you have more than one teacher you may wish to use other activities from the beginning of this session as well.

Let's Go Home

Use Zach to sing "I Will Help." Guide children in cleaning up and putting away toys by suggesting simple tasks as you and Zach walk about the room. **Chelsea, please put the book on the shelf. . . . Jeff, bring me the crayons so I can put them in the cabinet. Thank you.** As soon as there is one child who is finished with room cleanup begin the rhyme, "I'm So Glad. " Sing these words to the tune of "Fishers of Men."

Jesus stopped the storm on the sea,
Storm on the sea, storm on the sea.
Jesus stopped the storm on the sea.
He's the Son of God.

Jesus Stops a Storm

Luke 8:22-25

Bible Words: "Jesus is the Son of God" (Acts 9:20, *NIV*).

Lesson Value: What makes a person special? Being able to do what no one else could set Jesus apart from the crowd. His miraculous abilities were part of what shaped His disciples' attitudes about who Jesus was. What an incredible experience to watch someone command the wind and waves to be still—and it happens! Communicate that excitement to your class today. Let them see in your face and hear in your voice how special Jesus is. Let them experience the wonderful things Jesus can do!

Know: Know that Jesus can do wonderful things because He is God's Son.
Feel: Want to thank God for wonderful things Jesus did.
Do: Thank God for wonderful things Jesus did.

Children will accomplish the goals when they:

1. Say the Bible words, "Jesus is the Son of God."
2. Discover what a storm on a lake is like.
3. Sing about Jesus.
4. Point to or name a wonderful thing Jesus did.
5. Pray, "Thank You, God, for the wonderful things Jesus did."

Let's Get Ready

For the Bible story you will need the puppet Zach, a sailing or boating prop for Zach (life vest, life preserver, boat, fishing net. etc.), Bible open to Luke 8:22-25.

Prepare the Book/Picture Center, the Art Center, and the God's Wonders Center. If you are the only teacher, prepare just the Art Center. Have the Block Center ready to use after the Bible story.

Learning Activities

(30 minutes, including 10 minutes presession)

Let's Get Started

Use Zach to greet each child by name. "Hi, Kaitlyn! I'm glad you're here. . . . I see Michael coming through my door. I'm so glad you're here today, Michael!" Assist children with wraps, offering, and attendance stickers at this time. Direct each child to a learning center.

Worship and Bible Story

(15 minutes)

Let's Worship God

Use Zach to sing "It's Time to Worship." As soon as children come to the worship circle, begin singing "I'm So Happy Today." Use the rhyme, "My Bible." Display the classroom Bible and point to the Bible words as you say them. Sing "Let's Be Very Quiet." Then pray, **Thank You, God, for the wonderful things Jesus did.** Sing the first two stanzas of "Jesus Is the Son of God."

Let's Learn From the Bible

Introduction: Present Zach prepared for a boat ride (life jacket, life preserver, boat, etc.) to the children. **I see Zach has something special today! He is going to go for a ride in a boat! Are you excited to go on a boat ride, Zach?** Zach nods his head. **Bye, Zach. Have a safe trip!** Set Zach aside and pick up the Bible. I want to tell you a Bible story about a time when Jesus and His friends were on a boat.

The Bible Story: Jesus and His friends stepped into a boat. *(If your group is small, use the boat from the block area. If not, just make your fingers go step, step.)* Careful now! Don't tip over the boat! *(Rock gently from side to side.)* Jesus and His friends rode in their boat on the Sea of Galilee. *(Pretend to trail your fingers in the water; make rippling motions.)* Soon Jesus became very sleepy. *(Yawn; stretch arms.)* Jesus lay down in the boat to take a nap. *(Close eyes; folded hands against cheek.)*

While Jesus was sleeping the weather started to change. The wind got stronger; it was blowing hard! *(Make wind noises; hold arms to protect yourself from the wind.)* The waves got higher and the boat rocked back and forth! *(Rock back and forth; look frightened.)* Jesus' friends were afraid. They said, "Jesus, wake up! Help us! We will drown!"

Jesus woke up. Jesus was not afraid. He stood up and spoke to the wind and the waves. He said, "Storm, be quiet!" And the storm stopped! What a wonderful thing Jesus did for His friends. Jesus could do wonderful things because He is the Son of God.

Let's Apply the Lesson

Who can show how Jesus and His friends rode in a boat? Step, step; be careful! Don't rock the boat! **Who can show Jesus when He was sleepy?** Close eyes, yawn, stretch. **What's happening? A storm! Who can show the wind?** Blow; wave arms. **The waves are getting stronger. Who can show what the waves do to the boat?** Rock back and forth. **Jesus wakes up!** Open eyes. **He tells the wind and waves, "Storm, be quiet!"** Children say, "S-h-h-h" to the wind and waves. **The wind and waves listen to Jesus. They are quiet. Who can say who Jesus is?** ("Jesus is the Son of God"!) Sing "Jesus Is the Son of God," adding the third stanza.

Let's Apply the Lesson

Who can show what it means to be blind? Show the picture from page 154. **Being blind means not being able to see. Who was walking down the road?** (Jesus!) **Who was sitting on the road waiting for Jesus?** (Two blind men.) **What did Jesus do to make the blind men see?** (He put his hands on their eyes.) Use Zach to put his hands on the eyes in the picture. Then add the stick-on eyes. **The men could see! Jesus can do wonderful things! Who can tell who Jesus is? Yes, "Jesus is the Son of God"!**

Learning Activities

(20 minutes)

Let's Play Awhile

Have the children stand and do the action rhyme, "I'm So Glad!" then sing these words to the tune of "Fishers of Men."

Jesus helped the blind men to see,
Blind men to see, blind men to see.
Jesus helped the blind men to see.
He's the Son of God!

Now go to the God's Wonders Center. This activity should help the children appreciate their eyesight.

Let's Go Home

Use Zach to help you sing "I Will Help." Encourage children to participate in room cleanup by walking from area to area with Zach. "I see Kylie putting away a book. I'm glad Kylie is a helper." As soon as one or two children finish, begin the song, "Jesus Is the Son of God." Teach the children the new stanza about today's lesson.

Jesus Heals Two Blind Men

Matthew 20:29-34

Bible Words: "Jesus is the Son of God" (Acts 9:20, *NIV*).

Lesson Value: Young children should certainly have an experience in common with the Bible characters found in today's lesson. The two blind men wanted to be heard and everyone around them wanted the men to be quiet! Jesus heard the request of these men who were blind. He understood that they knew He was someone special. Jesus gave the blind men sight. He demonstrated to all that He could do wonderful things. He does wonderful things because He is the Son of God!

Know: Know that Jesus can do wonderful things because He is the Son of God.
Feel: Want to thank God for wonderful things Jesus did.
Do: Thank God for wonderful things Jesus did.

Children will accomplish the goals when they:

1. Say the Bible words, "Jesus is the Son of God."
2. Discover what it means to be blind.
3. Sing about Jesus.
4. Point to or name a wonderful thing Jesus did.
5. Pray, "Thank You, God, for the wonderful things Jesus did."

Let's Get Ready

For the Bible story, you will need the puppet Zach, a blindfold for Zach, your classroom Bible open to Matthew 20:29-34, a copy of page 154 and the eye stickers from page 159.

Prepare the Book/Picture Center, the Art Center, and the Family Living Center. If you are the only teacher, use just the Family Living Center. Use the God's Wonders Center after the Bible story.

Learning Activities

(30 minutes, including 10 minutes presession)

Let's Get Started

Be sure to make good use of the words *see, sight, eyes,* and *look* throughout the session. Use Zach to greet each child by name. "I see you, Karen! I'm glad I can see your blue Bible. . . . I'm looking at Rob. He has on a brown shirt today. I'm glad I can see brown! . . . I see Jaimie! Jaimie, can you see where your sticker goes? . . . I'm glad you're here today, Greg. Do you see a book you might like to look at over here?" Involve each child in one of the learning centers at this time.

Worship and Bible Story

(15 minutes)

Let's Worship God

Use Zach to sing "It's Time to Worship." Begin singing as soon as children come to the circle. Sing "I'm So Happy Today" and "Jesus Is the Son of God" using the first three stanzas. Use the rhyme, "I'm So Glad!" Then use the rhyme, "My Bible," finishing with the Bible words, "Jesus is the Son of God." Sing "Let's Be Very Quiet"; then pray, **Thank You, God, for the wonderful things Jesus did.**

Let's Learn From the Bible

Introduction: Bring Zach to the worship circle blindfolded. Say, **There is something different about Zach today, children. Who can tell me** (point to) **what is different about Zach? You're right! His eyes! Zach, can you see Karen?** Zach shakes his head no. **Zach, can you see Mark?** Zach shakes his head no. **Zach, can you see me?** Zach shakes his head no. **Zach, would you like to see Karen, Mark, and me?** Zach nods his head yes. Take off Zach's blindfold. **Zach is happy to see me!** Zach nods his head yes. Set Zach aside and put your Bible open to Matthew 20:29-34 on your lap.

The Bible Story: Jesus was walking to Jerusalem. *(Let children "walk" with their hands.)* Many people were following behind Jesus. *(Have children use both hands to represent many people walking.)* The people wanted to be with Jesus. They wanted to hear Him talk.

Along the road where Jesus was walking sat two men who couldn't see. *(Have children cover their eyes with their hands.)* Even though they couldn't see Jesus, they could hear Him! *(Children step-step-step with their hands.)* When they knew Jesus was close by, the blind men called out, "Jesus, Jesus! Please help us!" *(Children may cup their hands to their mouths and call, "Jesus!")*

But the people who were following Jesus told the blind men, "Sh-h-h! Be quiet! Don't bother Jesus!" *(Children may put their fingers to their lips and say, "Sh-h-h!")* But the blind men just called more loudly, "Jesus! Please help us!"

Jesus heard the men. He asked them, "What do you want?"

"We want to see!" the two blind men said.

So Jesus put his hands on their eyes *(Instruct the children to put hands on their eyes.)* and the men could see! Just like that!

"Thank You, Jesus! We can see!" the happy men said.

Jesus could do this wonderful thing for the blind men because He is the Son of God.

one finger. **Two people?** Hold up one finger on each hand. **No! Many people!** Wiggle all your fingers. **Someone came to see Jesus. He needed help. Let's show the man who couldn't walk.** Have children lie down as if on a mat, or give each child a clothespin to lay on the floor. **Jesus made the man well. Let's show the wonderful thing Jesus did!** Children should jump up or stand up their clothespins. Ask children to sing "Jesus Is the Son of God," using the stanza, "Jesus made a sick man walk."

Learning Activities

(20 minutes)

Let's Play Awhile

Have the children sing the following song to the tune of "Fishers of Men," and then go to the Game Center. If you have more than one teacher available, also use the activities from earlier in this session.

Jesus told the sick man to walk,
Sick man to walk, sick man to walk.
Jesus told the sick man to walk.
He's the Son of God.

Let's Go Home

When it is time to pick up and put away toys, have Zach start saying the action rhyme, "I Will Help." Move about the room encouraging children to pick up. **I see Nathan is using his strong legs to help pick up the blocks. . . . I like the way Brian walked over here on his strong legs to sing with me.**

Sing all stanzas of the song above. As parents come, take one child at a time to the door while the others continue to sing.

Jesus Makes a Lame Man Walk

Mark 2:1-12

Bible Words: "Jesus is the Son of God" (Acts 9:20, *NIV*).

Lesson Value: In today's lesson your children will be introduced to another group of men who went to great lengths to get Jesus' attention. Whether or not these men were convinced as to who Jesus really was, we are not sure. What we do know is that these men knew Jesus was special. Reports of the wonderful things Jesus had done had reached their ears and they were determined to see Jesus for themselves. Their persistence paid off. They were witness to Jesus' miraculous power—power that came from being the Son of God. This is one more lesson to help your children understand that Jesus could do these wonderful things because He is the Son of God.

Know: Know that Jesus can do wonderful things because He is God's Son.
Feel: Want to thank God for wonderful things Jesus did.
Do: Thank God for wonderful things Jesus did.

Children will accomplish the goals when they:
1. Say the Bible words, "Jesus is the Son of God."
2. Discover how Jesus made a sick man walk.
3. Sing about Jesus.
4. Point to or name a wonderful thing Jesus did.
5. Pray, "Thank You, God, for the wonderful things Jesus did."

Let's Get Ready

For the Bible story, obtain a box with a lid. Draw a door but don't cut it out. Draw steps going up the side of the box. Cut a section from the lid to make a hole in the "roof." You will also need non-snap clothespins, Zach, and the classroom Bible.

Prepare the Family Living Center, the Block Center, and the Art Center. If you are the only teacher, use just the Art Center now. Have the Game Center ready to use after the Bible story.

Learning Activities

(30 minutes, including 10 minutes presession)

Let's Get Started

Use Zach to greet the children. "I see Daniel walking into our classroom! . . . There is Austin walking to learn more about Jesus!" Assist children with coats, attendance stickers, and offering. Guide each child to participate in a learning center. If one center is filled, suggest one or two others from which the child can choose.

Worship and Bible Story

(15 minutes)

Let's Worship God

Have Zach sing "It's Time to Worship." Begin singing as soon as children come to the circle. Sing "I'm So Happy Today" and "Jesus Is the Son of God" (the first four stanzas). Use the rhyme, "My Bible," ending with the Bible words. If you have time, allow the children to take turns holding the classroom Bible and pointing to and/or saying the highlighted words. Say the rhyme, "When I Pray." Then say, **Now we are ready to pray, "Thank You, God, for the wonderful things Jesus did."** Then pray in those exact words. By now most of the children will say them with you.

Let's Learn From the Bible

Introduction: Have Zach come to the worship circle pushing the box with the lid on top. **Zach wants to visit someone in this house. He is walking all around the house** (Have Zach do this.) **but he can't get in! Zach has an idea! He's making a hole in the roof** (Take off pre-cut section of lid.) **and in he goes!** Set Zach aside. Place the Bible open to Mark 2:1-12 on your lap. **Listen to a story from the Bible about some others who made a hole in the roof.**

The Bible Story: Jesus was teaching inside a house. The house was full of people who had come to hear Jesus. There were so many people there was no place to stand, not even outside the door! *(Set clothespins all around the box.)*

Now there was a man who couldn't use his legs. He knew Jesus was nearby. He wanted to see Jesus and ask Jesus to make his legs well.

Friends of the man who couldn't walk said, "We will carry you to Jesus!" And so they did! *(Place a clothespin lying flat in your hand.)*

But when the men got to the house they couldn't get in! They tried to get near the door and the windows but there were too many people. Finally the friends had an idea! They climbed the outside stairs and took the man up to the roof of the house. Then they cut a hole in the roof and lowered their friend inside. *(Place clothespin inside box.)*

Jesus saw the man who couldn't walk. He said, "Pick up your mat and go home."

The man got up! He could walk! Jesus had made his legs well. Everyone in the room was amazed! The man and his friends were very happy! Jesus could do a wonderful thing like this because He is the Son of God.

Let's Apply the Lesson

Let's show where Jesus was teaching. Make a house shape with hands by touching finger tips together. **Let's show how many people came to hear Jesus teach. One person?** Hold up

Let's Apply the Lesson

Show the happy/sad face plate to the children. **When you see this happy face, make a happy face; make a sad face when I show you this sad face.**

Show how Jesus' friends felt when they didn't catch fish. (Sad) **Show how Jesus' friends felt when He helped them catch lots of fish!** (Happy)

Show how Jesus' friends felt during the storm. (Sad) **Show how Jesus' friends felt when He made the storm be quiet.** (Happy)

Show how the blind men felt because they couldn't see. (Sad) **Show how the men felt when Jesus helped them.** (Happy)

Show how the man who couldn't use his legs felt because he couldn't walk. (Sad) **Show how the man felt when Jesus helped him.** (Happy)

Show how you feel because you know that Jesus is God's Son. (Happy!)

Learning Activities

(20 minutes)

Let's Play Awhile

Have the children stand and do the action rhyme, "I'm So Glad," and then go to the Family Living Center or whatever center you have decided to use. If you have more than one teacher available use additional activities from the beginning of this session.

Let's Go Home

As soon as everything is picked up and put away, gather the children in a circle and sing one or more of the songs from this unit that tell the stories you have studied. Let the children add any actions they want to go along with the words. Continue singing until all parents have come for their children. Make sure the children take home anything they have left in the classroom during this unit.

Jesus Is God's Son

Review of Lessons 9–12

Bible Words: "Jesus is the Son of God" (Acts 9:20, *NIV*).

Lesson Value: As a teacher of young children, your goals for this unit will have more to do with how your children feel about Jesus than what they know. Your class should not be expected to remember names, dates, and places. Rather, the most important concept for them to have grasped is attitude. How will they feel, not what they will know, about Jesus is the aim. When they hear the name *Jesus,* your children will associate such words as *happy, wonderful,* and *glad.* Thank You, God, that Jesus does wonderful things!

Know: Know that Jesus can do wonderful things because He is God's Son.
Feel: Want to thank God for wonderful things Jesus did.
Do: Thank God for the wonderful things Jesus did.

Children will accomplish the goals when they:

1. Say the Bible words, "Jesus is the Son of God."
2. Review how Jesus did wonderful things.
3. Sing about Jesus.
4. Point to or name a wonderful thing Jesus did.
5. Pray, "Thank You, God, for the wonderful things Jesus did."

Let's Get Ready

For the Bible story, you will need a net (produce sack), toy boat (or sponge boat in bottle), blindfold, box with lid (from last week), a happy/sad paper plate face (draw a sad face on bottom of plate and a happy face on top), the puppet Zach, and the classroom Bible.

Prepare the Game Center, the God's Wonders Center, and the Book/Picture Center. If you are the only teacher, use just the God's Wonders Center now. After the Bible story, use any of the activities from previous weeks that the children especially liked, or that could be used to review the lessons. For example, the Family Living Center is an area that lends itself to conversation among teachers and children. As the children play, ask questions about the stories and get the children to tell you what they remember.

Learning Activities

(30 minutes, including 10 minutes presession)

Let's Get Started

Let Zach greet the children again today. "I'm glad you are here, Josh! Thank you for coming to learn about Jesus, Emily!" Help children with coats, offering, and attendance stickers. Let Zach direct each child to a learning center.

Worship and Bible Story

(15 minutes)

Let's Worship God

Have Zach sing "It's Time to Worship." As the first children sit down with you, begin to sing "I'm So Happy Today" and then "Jesus Is the Son of God" (all stanzas). Then use the rhyme, "My Bible" with the Bible words at the end. Use the rhyme, "When I Pray," and then tell the children you will be praying these words, **"Thank You, God, for the wonderful things Jesus did."** Then pray in those same words.

Let's Learn From the Bible

Introduction: Have Zach bring out each prop (net, boat, blindfold, and house/clothespin) one by one. When Zach has finished, say, **Thank you, Zach, for being a helper. We need to remember what these things remind us of!** Set Zach aside, and place your open Bible on your lap.

The Bible-story Review: *(Hold up the net.)* What wonderful thing that Jesus did does this net remind you of? *(Let children tell you.)* Yes, the net reminds us that Jesus helped His friends catch lots and lots of fish. Let's show how many fish Jesus' friends caught. *(Everyone pretends to struggle with heavy nets. Then sing stanza 2 of "Jesus Is the Son of God.")*

(Hold up the toy boat.) Who can tell me what wonderful thing this little boat reminds us of? Yes, Jesus went out in a boat with His friends and a storm came up. What did Jesus say to the storm? . . . "Sh-h-h-h. Be quiet!" Let's show what the storm did. *(Sit very still and be quiet.)* Yes! The storm was quiet. *(Sing the next stanza of "Jesus Is the Son of God.")*

(Hold up the blindfold.) Who can tell me what this reminds us of? Jesus made the blind men's eyes see again. That's right! Show me how the men's eyes were before they met Jesus. *(Children cover their eyes.)* How were the men's eyes after Jesus healed them? *(Children uncover their eyes. Sing the next stanza of "Jesus Is the Son of God.")*

(Show the box house.) What wonderful thing did Jesus do in a house? Jesus helped a man walk again! Show me the man before Jesus healed him. *(Children lie down.)* Now show me the man after Jesus healed him. *(Children stand up. Sing the last stanza of "Jesus Is the Son of God.")* Let's tell God thank-You for the wonderful things Jesus did.

God's Wonders Center

Unit 3—God's Son, Jesus

Items to Include:

Lesson 9
Fishbowl with fish
Two buckets
Small sponges
Fish pattern (page 159)
Net or large strainer

Lesson 10
2-liter bottle
Blue food coloring

Purpose: The child will point to or name a wonderful thing Jesus did.

Things to Do and Say

Lesson 9

Place the fish bowl where the children can see it easily. Have a bucket half full of water with sponges cut into fish shapes in it. The children will "catch" a fish and place it in the empty bucket. You may want to place the buckets on a sheet of plastic to protect the floor.

Allow the children to observe and talk about the fish in the fish bowl. Explain to the children that God made many kinds of fish. **God made many pretty fish for us to look at and enjoy. He made others that are good to eat. Thank You, God, for making fish.**

Our Bible story is about a wonderful thing Jesus did. He helped His friends catch lots and lots of fish. . . . Would you like to catch some fish? You can take turns using this net (strainer) **to catch some of these fish and put them in the empty bucket. . . . Who can tell me** (point to) **what wonderful thing Jesus did for His friends? . . . Yes, He helped them catch lots of fish. I'll tell you the whole story in a little while.**

Lesson 10

Insert a small sponge cut in the shape of a boat into a clear 2-liter bottle. Fill bottle two-thirds full of water; add blue food coloring. Have about 2" of water in the large container.

Block Center

Unit 3—God's Son, Jesus

Items to Include:

Large cardboard blocks

Lesson 10
Net produce bags

Lesson 12
Picture of Jesus
Blanket
Baby doll

Purpose: The child will know that Jesus can do wonderful things because He is God's Son.

Things to Do and Say

Lesson 10

Help children build a boat from blocks. Make an area in the center large enough for several children to sit. Tell the children they are going out in their boat to fish. Show them how to throw the net into the water and draw it up.

After the children have had an opportunity to fish say, **I see Jesus and His friends in a boat over there. Jesus' friends are fishing.** Point to an imaginary boat. **Jesus must be tired. He is asleep in the boat. . . . I feel the wind getting stronger! Do you feel the wind rocking your boat?** Sway back and forth as though the boat is rocking. **The waves are getting bigger! They make our boat rock even more!** Rock harder. **Jesus' friends are afraid! They are waking Jesus. He is standing up and speaking. . . .** Stop rocking. **Jesus has made the storm stop. He can do that because He is the Son of God. Those are our Bible words. Say them with me: "Jesus is the Son of God."**

Lesson 12

Help children build the outline of a house with an opening for a door. Place the picture of Jesus in the house. Explain that Jesus is inside the house and people are crowding around to hear Him. Tell the children they will be the crowd. Have four children ready

God's Wonders Center, continued

Sponge
Boat pattern (page 159)
Large container for water
Toy boat

Show the children the bottle. Ask them to tell about what they see. Slowly rock the bottle back and forth, creating a "storm." Ask the children to tell about what is happening.

Direct the children's attention to the container of water. Place the toy boat on the water and tell the children to create a storm by blowing (wind) and making storm noises. **Jesus helped His friends during a storm. He told the wind and waves to stop! He kept His friends safe on the boat. Now the storm is over. Thank You, Jesus, for stopping the storm! Who can tell me** (point to) **something wonderful Jesus did?**

Lesson 11
Cardboard tubes
Aluminum foil

Lesson 11

Make "spy glasses" from cardboard tubes covered with aluminum foil. Tell the children they will be going on a "wonder hunt," looking for wonderful things God has made. Lead the children around the room or on an outdoor walk. Ask the children to stop and cover the ends of their spy glasses with their hands. **What do you see?** (Nothing; dark; my hand.) **Open your spy glasses. Now what do you see?** Let children tell you.

Our Bible story is about two men who couldn't see. They were blind. Jesus did a wonderful thing! He made the blind men be able to see! They could see all the things God made. . . . I'm glad we can see. Let's thank God for our eyes and for all the wonderful things we can see. Do so. . . . **What wonderful thing did Jesus do for the blind men? . . . Yes, Derek, He made them be able to see.**

Lesson 13
Spy glasses used earlier
Visuals/pictures from this unit

Lesson 13

Set up this unit's visuals/pictures around the room. Let the children use the spy glasses to look for wonderful things Jesus did—for His fishermen friends, when there was a storm at sea, for the blind men, and for the sick man. Encourage the children to find these things, point to them, and tell you about them.

Block Center, continued

to carry the blanket with the doll on it.

Jesus was in a house one day. Many people wanted to hear Him. They crowded around Him so no one could get in the door. Some friends brought their sick friend to see Jesus. They carried him on a bed something like this. But when they got to the house they couldn't get their friend in the door to see Jesus. They finally did get in to see Jesus and He did make the sick man well. Jesus could do this wonderful thing because He is God's Son.

Book/Picture Center

Unit 3—God's Son, Jesus

Items to Include:

Lesson 9
Books about Jesus and fishermen
Pictures of fish
Picture of fishermen (page 153)
Bible

Lesson 10
Pictures of storms
Bible

Purpose: The child will point to and/or name wonderful things Jesus did.

Things to Do and Say

Lesson 9

Ahead of time, copy the picture from page 153. Color it and add some stick-on fish. Display pictures and books so children will want to pick them up and look at them. Look at pictures/books of fish and thank God for fish. Read a book if you have an appropriate one, or "picture read"—that is, tell what is happening in a picture, ask the child to point to specific things/people, and so forth.

Show the children the picture of Jesus' friends fishing. **These are some of Jesus' friends. They are fishermen. When they couldn't catch any fish, Jesus went out with them and helped them catch so many fish that their nets began to break. Jesus could do that because He is God's Son.** Ask the children to name or point to something special Jesus did. (The net with fish.)

Show the children the highlighted Bible words in your classroom Bible and help them "read" the words. Pray with the children, **Thank You, God, for the wonderful things Jesus did.**

Lesson 10

Have a completed two-sided picture made from pages 155 and 156. Display this along with the other pictures and books.

Game Center

Unit 3—God's Son, Jesus

Items to Include:

Lesson 9
Fish crackers
Paper cups with handles
Grocery sack

Lesson 12
Baby blankets or large towels

Purpose: The child will say the Bible words, "Jesus is the Son of God."

Things to Do and Say

Lesson 9

Have the fish crackers in a large grocery sack. Seat the children in single file on the floor or low chairs. Explain that they are going to pretend to fish. Give each child a paper cup with a handle on it.

Let's play like we are Jesus' friends sitting in a boat trying to catch fish. Have the children pretend to scoop up fish on one side of them. **No fish! Let's row back to shore.** Pretend to row.

Then say, **Now let's pretend that Jesus is in the boat with us. He is telling us to put our nets on the other side.** Go along the row of children with the sack full of fish. Let each child scoop up some of the fish. **Look at all the fish Jesus helped us catch! Jesus could do this because He is God's Son. Let's say those Bible words together.** Do so. Then let the children eat their crackers.

Lesson 12

If you have an older child who could pretend to be Jesus, have him come to the group and say the words, "Pick up your mat and walk," when you get to that part of the story.

Hand each child a blanket or towel. Ask the children to lie down on their mats. Say, **Let's pretend we are like the sick man who couldn't walk. We will lie on our mats**

Book/Picture Center, continued

Stormy/calm pictures (pages 155 and 156)
Books about God's care

Ask the children to point to and name what they see in the pictures. Talk about storms. **What does a storm sound like? . . . What does a storm look like? . . . How do you feel when there is a storm?** Encourage the children to make sounds and motions for wind and rain. Then read a book on God's care, or talk about the fact that God cares for us when there is a storm.

Look at the picture of the rocking boat on the stormy sea. **Jesus was in a boat with His friends when a big storm came up. Do you know what Jesus did? He stopped that storm!** Turn over to side 2. **Jesus could do this because He is the Son of God.** Look at the Bible words and say them with the children. Then pray, **Thank You, God, for the wonderful things Jesus did.**

Lesson 11
Books and pictures of animals, scenes, flowers, foods, etc.
Picture of blind man (page 154)
Bible

Lesson 11

Display the pictures of interesting things to see. Ask a child to point to and name things she likes to see. When Jade does this, say, **Thank You, God, for Jade's eyes. Thank You for wonderful things to see.**

Look at the picture made from page 154. **In our Bible story, Jesus met some men who could not see.** Name some things they couldn't see. **Do you know what Jesus did? Jesus touched their eyes and at once they could see! Jesus could do this because He is the Son of God. Thank You, God, for the wonderful things Jesus did.**

Lesson 13
Books and pictures from past weeks

Lesson 13

Use the pictures and books to review the past lessons. Ask questions to encourage the children to tell you what they remember, and also to name the wonderful things Jesus did because He is the Son of God.

Game Center, continued

until Jesus comes to help us! . . . Oh, here is Jesus. What does He say? . . . Yes, pick up your mat and walk. Encourage the children to do this. **We can walk! How could Jesus do this? Our Bible words tell us. Let's say them together. "Jesus is the Son of God."**

Lesson 13
Tape player (optional)

Lesson 13

Use this musical game as a review of all the lessons. If you want, tape an instrument playing "London Bridge." Or, just sing these words with the children. Encourage them to add motions to fit the words. Remind the children that they are singing the Bible words, "Jesus is the Son of God."

Jesus is the Son of God, Son of God, Son of God.
Jesus is the Son of God. Men caught lots of fish!*
*2. Blind eyes could see!
*3. Jesus stopped the storm!
*4. A sick man could walk!

If you want, let the children sing this and play as they would "London Bridge." Let the "bridge" come down on the last word. Then ask the children what wonderful thing they just sang about.

Art Center

Unit 3—God's Son, Jesus

Items to Include:

Lesson 9
Copies of page 153
Fish stickers (page 159)
Crayons or washable markers

Lesson 10
Back-to-back copies of pages 155 and 156
Moon and cloud stickers (page 159)
Crayons

Purpose: The child will learn through creative activities that Jesus could do wonderful things because He is God's Son.

Things to Do and Say

Lesson 9

Make fish stickers (instructions on page 159). Cut them apart ahead of time.

Talk about the picture as the children color theirs. Ask who is in the boat, what the men are doing, and so forth. Then say, **These men don't have any fish in their nets. When Jesus went out in the boat with the men He helped them catch lots and lots of fish! Jesus could do this because He is the Son of God. . . . Let's put some fish in the nets.** Give the children one or two fish stickers at a time. As you give a child his stickers, help him say the Bible words, "Jesus is the Son of God."

Lesson 10

Have cloud and moon stickers cut out ahead of time. If you cannot copy the pages back-to-back, make copies of each and glue sets together. Let children color the stormy side first.

What do you see in this picture? (Lots of waves.) **What is this?** Hold up a cloud sticker. **There are lots of dark clouds during a storm.** Help children add these. Point to the boat. **Jesus' friends were in the boat. Jesus was asleep. When the waves got too high, the men were afraid of the storm. They woke Jesus.**

Family Living Center

Unit 3—God's Son, Jesus

Items to Include:

Lesson 11
Blindfolds
Sunglasses (for 2's)
Table and chairs
Toy telephone
Dishes, etc.

Lesson 12
Doll babies
Blankets and clothing

Purpose: The child will discover that Jesus could do wonderful things.

Things to Do and Say

Lesson 11

Have a small table and chairs, along with dishes, a toy telephone, and so forth. Explain to the children that they are going to see what it would be like to be blind. Blindfold two children at a time. **Note:** Use sunglasses for 2's who might be afraid of being blindfolded.

Ask the blindfolded children, **What can you see? . . . That's the way it is for blind people.** Help a child sit down at the table. Ask her to answer the phone. Let another child try to set the table. Help the children see how difficult it would be to be blind. Let children take turns doing various jobs around the "house."

When Jesus met two blind men, He helped them. He touched their eyes and at once they could see! How do you think the blind men felt after Jesus helped them to see? . . . Yes, happy and excited! How would they have felt when they were blind? Jesus could do this because He is the Son of God.

Lesson 12

Let some children play like their babies are sick. Have several children be doctors and/or nurses. The "mommies and daddies" will take their sick children to the doctor's office. Show the children how to use a stethoscope, perhaps put on bandages, and so forth.

Art Center, continued

Turn over to side 2. Point to Jesus. **There's Jesus! Jesus wasn't afraid. He said, "Waves be still; wind, stop blowing." And the storm stopped! Jesus could stop the storm because He is the Son of God. After you color this picture, you may put a moon in the sky.**

Lesson 11
Copies of page 154
Eye stickers (page 159)
Crayons or washable markers
Yarn and glue (optional)

Lesson 11
Let the children color the picture of the blind man. Talk about what it would be like to be blind. Then tell the children, **Jesus touched the blind man's eyes and he was able to see—just like that! Jesus could do that because He is the Son of God.** Help the children add the eye stickers. Then say the Bible words together. If there is time, let the children glue short pieces of yarn on the man's hair and beard.

Lesson 12
Back-to-back copies of pages 157 and 158
Crayons or washable markers
Cloth scraps
Glue
Transparent tape

Lesson 12
Ahead of time, cut small pieces of cloth to put on the man's garment in the first picture, and roll pieces of felt or burlap and glue them shut for the second picture.

After the children color their picture of the sick man, help them add pieces of cloth to the man's clothing. **Some friends brought this man to see Jesus. The man was lying on a mat because he couldn't walk. Jesus said to the man, "Get up and carry your mat."**

Now turn over your pictures. . . . And the man got up and carried his mat! Let the children color this side and then give each child a roll of cloth to put in the man's hands. **How do you think the man felt when he could walk? . . . Yes, he must have been very happy! Jesus could do this because He is the Son of God.**

Family Living Center, continued

Doctor and/or nurse kits

What happens at your house when you are sick or get hurt? . . . Yes, your mommy or daddy takes you to see the doctor. What does the doctor do? Encourage children to mention things such as, "looks at me, listens to me, gives me medicine," and so forth.

One day some friends brought a man to Jesus. The man was lying on a mat because he couldn't walk. What do you think Jesus said to the man? He said, "Take up your mat and walk." And do you know what the man did? . . . Yes, he got up, picked up his mat, and walked away! Jesus could make the man well that way because Jesus is the Son of God! Let's say those Bible words together. Do so.

Jesus told His friends where to fish and they caught many fish.
"Jesus is the Son of God" (Acts 9:20).

Jesus touched the eyes of this blind man and he could see.

"Jesus is the Son of God" (Acts 9:20).

When Jesus and His friends were caught in a big storm, . . .

Jesus stopped the storm!
"Jesus is the Son of God" (Acts 9:20).

Four men brought their sick friend to Jesus.

"Jesus is the Son of God" (Acts 9:20).

Instructions for Making Stickers

1. Make copies of sticker art on white paper or various colors of construction paper.
2. Mix 2 parts white glue and 1 part vinegar. Add a few drops of peppermint extract if desired.
3. Lightly "paint" mixture on backs of uncut stickers. Let dry.
4. If children will be coloring their stickers, leave stickers uncut.
5. Cut stickers apart and let children lick and stick them in place.

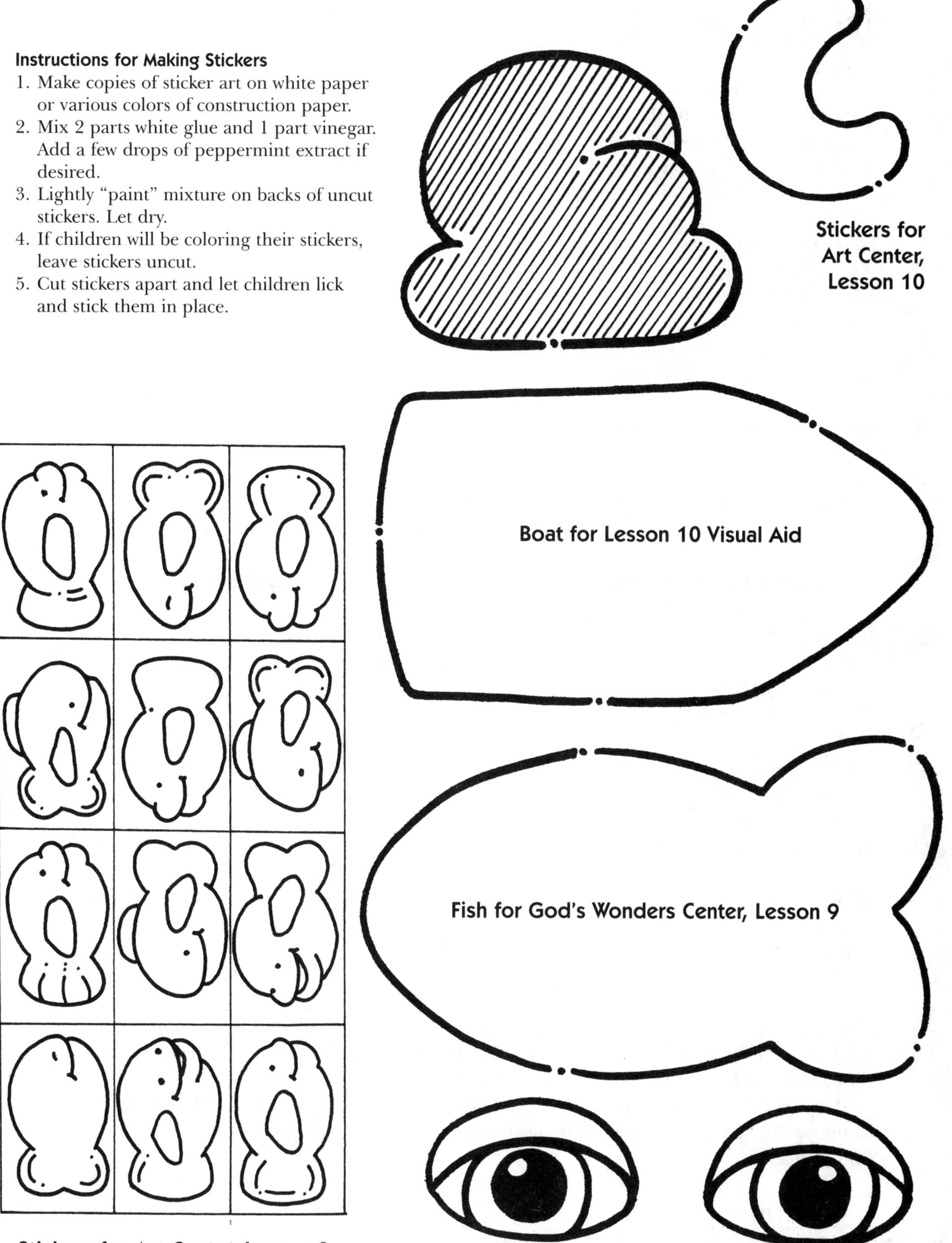

Stickers for Art Center, Lesson 10

Stickers for Art Center, Lesson 9

Stickers for Art Center, Lesson 11

Dear Parent:

The stories in this unit will teach your child the wonderful things Jesus did as a man. Four miraculous events will be shared in the Bible stories, songs, rhymes, and other learning activities. The goal for the children is to begin to associate the words *happy* and *wonderful* with the concept of Jesus, God's Son. When your child hears stories about God's Son, Jesus, he will know something wonderful is about to happen!

Here are the Bible lessons your child will be learning:
Jesus Helps His Friends Catch Fish (Luke 5:1-9)
Jesus Stops the Storm (Luke 8:22-25)
Jesus Heals Two Blind Men (Matthew 20:29-34)
Jesus Makes a Lame Man Walk (Mark 2:1-12)
Jesus Is God's Son (review of previous lessons)

Here are ways to bring the lesson home.

Sing this song to the tune of "London Bridge."

Jesus Is the Son of God

Jesus is the Son of God,
Son of God, Son of God.
Jesus is the Son of God.
Thank You, God, for Jesus.

Jesus helped His friends catch fish,*
Friends catch fish, friends catch fish.
Jesus helped His friends catch fish.
Thank You, God, for Jesus.

*3. Jesus stopped a storm at sea, etc.
4. Jesus made a blind man see, etc.
5. Jesus made a sick man walk, etc.

Use the following rhyme with your child:

My Bible

This is my Bible; *(Palms held together.)*
I'll open it wide *(Open hands; keep them touching.)*
And see (or say) what is written on the inside!
(Say the Bible words, "Jesus is the Son of God.")
—Jean Baxendale

Highlight this unit's Bible words from Acts 9:20 in a Bible your child can handle. Point to the words as you read them. Then let your child practice "reading" them with you. Remind your child often that Jesus is wonderful because He is God's Son.

Daily life provides many opportunities for seeing God's care in our lives. Food, clothing, nature, safety, and warm relationships are all reminders that Jesus helps us, too, because He is God's Son!

Your child's teacher

Spring Quarter

Learning to Know Jesus, Who Loves Us

This quarter will help the children learn more about Jesus who, in the last unit of the Winter quarter, was introduced as the Son of God who could do wonderful things. This quarter will make Jesus seem more real to the children—a friend who cares about them, who listens to them, who loved children when He was here on earth, and who loves them.

In Unit One, "We Can Know Jesus Is Our Friend," the children will be learning that Jesus had friends, that we are His friends, and that He loves us. To help each child know that Jesus is his friend and that He loves each one is the focus of the lessons. For young children, much of their knowing comes from feeling. When you show the children gentleness, openness, delight, and concern, you are letting them know that the Jesus you teach about also is like that. So, let the Lord Jesus love each child through you.

Unit Two, "We Can Know Jesus Is Close to Us," will help the children want to sing and pray to Jesus, and to know that when they do, Jesus is listening. Let your own love for God's Son, Jesus, be seen by your children as you sing with enthusiasm and pray sincerely.

Unit Three, "We Can Be Jesus' Helpers," will encourage each child to find ways he can respond to Jesus' love. Even 2's and 3's can begin to learn that Jesus wants them to help others. They are ready to begin to tell other people, "Jesus loves you." Your enthusiasm and willingness to obey your Lord will teach more than your words can. What goes on in the classroom can be "caught" by these impressionable young children!

Remember, you are teaching about the One who said, "Let the little children come to me. Don't stop them. The kingdom of God belongs to people who are like these little children" (Mark 10:14, *ICB*).

Note to those who teach alone: Prepare the learning center suggested in each lesson, but also have one or two others ready to use when the children tire of the first one.

As a result of these lessons, the children will

KNOW

Know that Jesus is a friend who cares about them and loves them, and who listens to them when they pray and sing to Him.

FEEL

Feel happy to know that Jesus is a caring, loving friend.

DO

Thank God for their friend Jesus.

Use these songs and action rhymes throughout the quarter, in addition to those specifically mentioned in the units.

I'm So Glad

I'm so glad *(Clap hands.)*
The sun I see. *(Make big round sun with arms.)*
I'm so glad *(Clap hands.)*
That Jesus loves me! *(Point to self.)*

—Jean Baxendale

Jesus Loves Little Ones

I Am Jesus' Special Friend

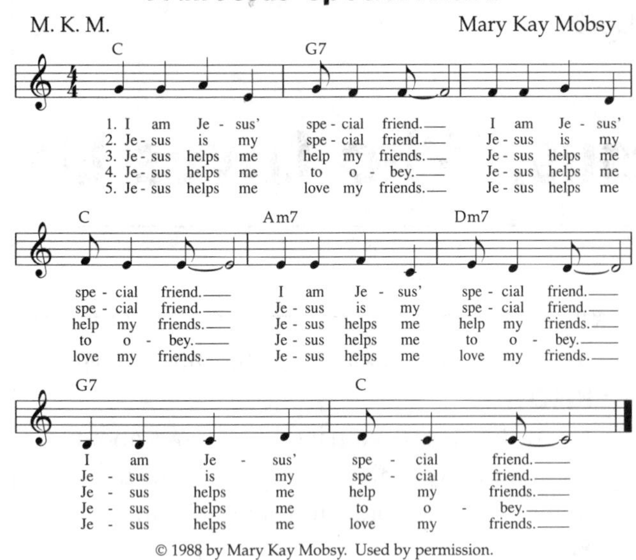

I Love Jesus

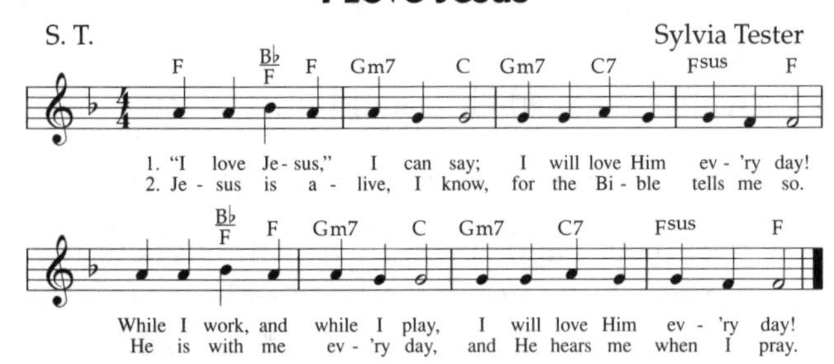

Additional, Optional Verses:

3. I will use my helping hands.
I will use my helping hands.
Pick up toys and share with friends.
I'll be Jesus' helper.

4. I will use my helping eyes.
I will use my helping eyes.
Look for things to do to help.
I'll be Jesus' helper.

5. I will use my helping ears.
I will use my helping ears.
Listen when my mommy calls.
I'll be Jesus' helper.

6. I will use my helping mouth.
I will use my helping mouth.
I will tell of Jesus' love.
I'll be Jesus' helper.

Jesus' Love

Jesus loves all children—
The ones still very small,
(Use hand to indicate knee-high child.)
The baby in the cradle,
(Fold arms to form cradle and rock.)
The ones so big and tall.
(Hands high over head.)

—Thea Cannon

I Stand on Tiptoe

I stand on tiptoe, *(Stand on tiptoe.)*
And ring the bell, *(Pretend to ring doorbell.)*
Because I have something *(Point to self.)*
I want to tell. *(Cup hands to mouth.)*
Jesus loves you! *(Point to another person.)*

—Marjorie R. Miller

Spring Party Suggestions

March—Kite Party

Purpose:	Fun!
When:	Saturday or Sunday afternoon
Activity:	Flying kites
Preparation:	Ask parents to bring kites—homemade or bought.
Food:	Rice cereal treats and fruit punch
Devotion:	Jesus calms the storm—Jesus can do wonderful things!

April—Easter Party

Purpose:	To help the children know how to worship and praise Jesus
When:	During class time
Craft:	Make musical instruments—String jingle bells on chenille wires; put beans in paper towel tubes, staple ends and cover with tape.
Activity:	Play instruments and sing songs that praise Jesus. Talk about how we can praise Him.
Food:	Fruit and crackers
Devotion:	The triumphal entry; thank God for Jesus.

May—Mother's Day Party

Purpose:	To help children show love to their mothers
When:	During class time
Preparation:	Provide Styrofoam cups, dirt, and small flowering plants, self-stick seals; small pictures of the children, craft sticks, and glue.
Activity:	Let the children decorate their cups with seals and plant flowers in them. Glue a picture of each child on a craft stick and push in the dirt beside his or her plant.
Devotions:	Let children tell why they love their mothers; thank God for each mother.

Unit 1: We Can Know Jesus Is Our Friend

Lessons 1–4

By the end of the unit, the children will

Know that Jesus is a friend.
Feel happy and loved by Jesus.
Label Jesus as a friend.

Unit Bible Words

"You are my friends" (John 15:14, *NIV*).

Books

from Standard Publishing
Jesus Is My Special Friend (#24-04211)
Zaccheus Meets Jesus (#24-03598)

This Unit at a Glance

1 Jesus Calls Four Fishermen to Be His Friends — **Matthew 4:18-22**
Jesus calls Peter, Andrew, James, and John to become followers and friends.

2 Jesus Visits in the Home of His Friends — **Luke 10:38-42**
Jesus is invited into the home of Mary and Martha.

3 Jesus Makes a New Friend — **Luke 19:1-6**
Jesus meets Zaccheus, who invites Jesus to his home.

4 I Know Jesus Is My Friend — **Review of Lessons 1-3**

Why Teach This Unit to Young Children?

"Greater love has no one than this, that he lay down his life for his friends. You are my friends" (John 15:13, 14, *NIV*). Jesus has already proven His great love for us by giving up His sinless life on the cross in the place of our sinful and ruined lives. He loves each precious little child in your class and wants each one to know of His unending love.

Much of the theology and terminology associated with Christ's death is too difficult for little ones to understand but they are old enough to recognize a friend who truly loves and cares for them.

This unit gives you the opportunity to introduce children to this special friend who will never leave them, never be too busy for them, who will never say mean words, get angry with them, or reject them. The children will learn that Jesus is their forever friend, and they will be happy knowing He loves and cares about them.

Every teacher and helper needs to know the Bible words and be looking for opportunities to use them throughout the lesson. Follow the suggestions given in the lesson plans, and add others you think of. The Bible words can be used when greeting children, in the learning centers, at the worship and story area, during snack and restroom breaks, and when saying good-bye. Display many Bibles, with the words highlighted and marked with a bookmark, so that children can find and "read" them easily.

Things to Do for This Unit

- Make copies of the Parents' Letter (page 186) and the Unit Planning Sheet (pages 319 and 320).
- Copy the Learning Center Cards (pages 173-178); cut apart on solid lines and glue side 1 of each card to cardboard and side 2 to the back of the cardboard. Laminate for durability (optional).
- Gather/prepare materials listed on the Learning Center Cards.
- Gather pictures of Jesus with children, write the Bible words on or under the pictures, and place them at the children's eye level.
- Put up a bulletin board or make one from poster board.
- For Lesson 4, mail party invitations (page 177) to your children.
- Decorate your classroom for the party.

Use These Songs and Action Rhymes During Unit 1

You Are My Friends

(Tune: "Row, Row, Row Your Boat")

_____ is Jesus' friend; _____ is Jesus' friend.
The Bible tells us Jesus said, "You are my friends."

Pat the Bible

(Tune: "Did You Ever See a Lassie?")

Oh, I love to pat* the Bible, the Bible, the Bible.
Oh, I love to pat the Bible, for it is God's Word.
I'll pat it and pat it, and pat it and pat it.
Oh, I love to pat the Bible, for it is God's Word.

*Also use "read" in place of "pat."

It's Time to Worship

I Can Talk to God

Listening Rhyme

First our feet go tap-tap-tap, *(Tap feet on floor.)*
Then our hands go clap-clap-clap. *(Clap hands.)*
We look with both our eyes,
(Make glasses by circling fingers around eyes.)
We hear with both our ears, *(Cup hands behind ears.)*
And then our hands fall in our laps.
(Fold hands in lap.) —*Dorothy Fay Richards*

Zaccheus

Actions:
(1) Hands in front, right palm raised above left palm.
(2) Bring palms a little closer together.
(3) Alternate hands in climbing motions.
(4) Shade eyes with right hand and look down.
(5) "Walk" fingers of right hand up left forearm.
(6) Shade eyes with right hand and look up.
(7) Words are spoken, while looking up and shaking finger in admonition.
(8) Clap hands on accented beat.

Bible tells us these men were Jesus' friends. Can you tell me their names? . . . Good! Peter and Andrew were brothers, and James and John were brothers.

Jesus has many friends right here in this room. Zach and I will come around and let you look at one of Jesus' special friends. Zach holds a small mirror so each child can see herself. As a child looks in the mirror, ask one of the following:

- **Which special friend of Jesus do you see? . . . Yes, Kara, you are a special friend of Jesus!**
- **How do you feel about being Jesus' friend?** *(Smile.)* **Yes, we feel happy that Jesus is our friend!**
- **Can you name a place your friend Jesus will go with you?** You may need to help with this one. **Will Jesus go with us to the park? . . . Yes, He is with us wherever we go.**

Learning Activities

(20 minutes)

Let's Play Awhile

Put Zach and the mirror down. Say, **Let's play a game. When you hear your name, stand up and come make a circle of Jesus' friends.** Sing, "You Are My Friends," naming each child. Make sure no one is left out. Leave an adult for last if possible. When the children are all holding hands walk around in your circle singing the words, "We are Jesus' friends." Dismiss to the Block Center. If you have several teachers also have activities used earlier.

Let's Go Home

Zach signals clean-up time by singing "This is the way we pick up the toys . . . and put them all away." Change the words to encourage children who need specific instructions. Do the rhyme, "Jesus Is a Friend," and read a book about friends. If children are restless, repeat the game played earlier. Make sure the children take their fish pictures and their letters to parents.

Jesus Calls Four Fishermen to Be His Friends

Matthew 4:18-22

Bible Words: "You are my friends" (John 15:14, *NIV*).

Lesson Value: Jesus is a friend like no other. He never has to go home, He never moves away, He never is too busy, and He is never mean or selfish. This lesson will encourage children to begin to think of Jesus as a friend who is always near and ready to help. If they are sad, afraid, or lonely, He is there. If they need someone to talk to, Jesus is the friend on whom to call. The children will feel happy as they learn about Jesus' love for them.

Know: Know that Jesus is a friend.
Feel: Feel happy and loved by Jesus.
Do: Label Jesus as a friend.

Children will accomplish the goals when they:

1. Say the Bible words, "You are my friends."
2. Pray, "Thank You, Jesus, for being my special friend."
3. Sing about their friend Jesus.
4. Name or point to friends (children in room, Jesus).
5. Tell (show) how they feel about being Jesus' friends.

Let's Get Ready

For the Bible story, you will need the classroom Bible, puppet Zach, small fishing pole, paper-doll visual (page 179), picture of the fishermen with Jesus (page 180), and unbreakable hand mirror.

Prepare the God's Wonders Center, the Art Center, and the Family Living Center. If you are the only teacher, use the God's Wonders Center now. Have materials ready for the Block Center to be used after the Bible story.

Learning Activities

(30 minutes, including 10 minutes presession)

Let's Get Started

On a low table by the door, place an open Bible with the Bible words highlighted, a basket of fish crackers, and/or a small bowl with live fish. As you greet the children, have Zach say, "Hello friend Kordell, it's good to see you." Let Zach ask questions about fishing. Then say, **Our Bible story is about four friends of Jesus who used big nets to catch fish.** Allow each child to look at the fish or eat a couple of crackers. Then direct him to a learning center.

Worship and Bible Story

(15 minutes)

Let's Worship God

Zach signals that it is clean-up time by singing, "It's Time to Worship." As the first children arrive at the worship area begin singing "Jesus Loves the Little Ones." Then sing "I Am Jesus' Special Friend" (stanzas 1 and 2). Songs are on pages 161 and 162. Do the rhyme, "Jesus Is a Friend," then sing "I Can Talk to God" and pray, **Thank You, Jesus, for being my special friend.**

Hold up your Bible. **What is this? . . . Yes, this is the Bible. Inside are some new Bible words for us to learn.** Open your Bible to the highlighted words. (Keeping a large colorful bookmark at that place is helpful.) Read the words, then sing "You Are My Friends" inserting each child's name.

Let's Learn From the Bible

Introduction: Hold Zach up with a fishing pole in his hands (small stick with string or yarn attached to the end). Say, **Zach, you must be going fishing.** He answers, "Yes, I heard Jesus had some friends who were fishermen." **You are right, Zach, but Jesus' friends didn't use fishing poles; they used big fishing nets.** Zach answers, "Oh, maybe I should sit down and listen to the Bible story before I go fishing." **Good idea, Zach!** Lay Zach, aside, pick up your Bible and open it to where you have placed your paper-doll visual.

The Bible Story: *(Hold up the paper dolls so that only Jesus is showing.)* One day Jesus went for a walk by the Sea of Galilee. *(Pretend to make Jesus walk.)* He saw two brothers fishing with a big net. *(Open the dolls to show two men.)* Their names were Peter *(point)* and Andrew *(point)*. "Come follow me, Peter," Jesus said. "Come follow me, Andrew." Peter and Andrew put down their fishing net and followed Jesus.

In a little while Jesus saw two more brothers *(open to show two more people)*. Their names were James and John *(point as before)*. They were helping their father get their nets ready to fish. Jesus said, "Come follow me, James. Come follow me, John." James and John put down their nets, said good-bye to their father, and went with Jesus.

Let's Apply the Lesson

Close the paper dolls so that only Jesus is showing. Say, **Jesus wanted to be friends with Peter and Andrew** *(show Peter and Andrew)*. **Jesus wanted them to be with Him. Jesus wanted to be friends with James and John** *(show James and John)*. **Jesus wanted them to be with Him.** *(Act surprised.)* **Look, I have one more person here!** *(Open to the last doll.)* **That is YOU! The Bible tells us that Jesus wants to be your special friend. He will always be with you.** Sing, "I Am Jesus' Special Friend" (stanzas 1 and 2).

Hold up the picture of Jesus and the four fishermen. Say, **The**

- **Who do you see? . . . Are you Jesus' special friend? Yes, Jesus said, "You are my friends."**
- **Can you show me how it feels to be Jesus' special friend?** Encourage children to smile or laugh. **We feel happy because Jesus is our special friend.**
- **Does Jesus love you, Caleb? . . . Yes, the Bible tells us that Jesus loves us.**
- **Can you show me how it feels to be loved by Jesus?** Again encourage children to smile. **I'm happy to know that Jesus loves me!**

Learning Activities

(20 minutes)

Let's Play Awhile

Let's play the game we learned last week. When I sing your name come up and help me make a circle of Jesus' friends. When we are all holding hands we will walk around as we sing. Begin singing "You Are My Friends," inserting the children's names. Dismiss to the Block Center. If your class is large, also use the other activities suggested earlier.

Let's Go Home

Zach signals clean-up time by singing to the tune of "Mulberry Bush," "This is the way we help our friends . . . pick up all the toys."

While waiting for parents, read *Jesus Is My Special Friend* or another appropriate book. For more action, divide the children into small groups and sit on the floor in circles. As you roll a ball to Maria, say, **Maria is Jesus' friend.** Go around the circle several times letting children decide where the ball should go and helping them say the words.

Since there is no art project to take home, let children take home copies of the teaching picture to color.

Jesus Visits in the Home of His Friends

Luke 10:38-42

Bible Words: "You are my friends" (John 15:14, *NIV*).

Lesson Value: Jesus is a friend who will be with us always. His desire is to be included in every part of our lives. He wants us to remember that He is present, not only when we worship on Sunday, but all through the week—as we drive in the car, do the shopping, visit friends, play outside, and in the privacy of our homes. This lesson gives you the opportunity to teach children that Jesus is a friend who will be with them morning, noon, and night. Children will learn that their young lives are important to Him and He loves and cares for them. Encourage your children to feel happy knowing that this special friend will be with them always.

Know: Know that Jesus is a friend.
Feel: Feel happy and loved by Jesus.
Do: Label Jesus as a friend.

Children will accomplish the goals when they:
1. Say the Bible words, "You are my friends."
2. Pray, "Thank You, Jesus, for being my special friend."
3. Sing about their friend Jesus.
4. Name or point to friends (children in room, Jesus).
5. Tell (show) how they feel about being Jesus' friends.

Let's Get Ready

For the Bible story, you will need the classroom Bible, Zach, feather duster or cloth, paper-doll visual (page 179), the teaching picture (page 181), and a small mirror.

Prepare the Family Living Center, the Art Center, and the Game Center. If you are the only teacher use just the Family Living Center. Have the Block Center ready to use after the Bible story.

Learning Activities

(30 minutes, including 10 minutes presession)

Let's Get Started

As Zach cheerfully greets the children have him hold a feather duster or cleaning cloth. Place an empty (for safety) bottle of cleaner on the table near him so the children understand that he has been cleaning. "Hello friend Holly, I knew you were coming so I have been cleaning. Do you ever help Mommy clean house when company is coming? . . . Jesus visited at the home of His friends, Mary and Martha. I'm sure they wanted everything to look just right." Help each child as needed then direct her to a learning center.

Worship and Bible Story

(15 minutes)

Let's Worship God

Zach puts his cleaning supplies away and says, "We have done a great job of cleaning. Now it is time to sit and listen." Zach sings "It's Time to Worship." Sing "Jesus Loves Me," "Jesus Loves the Little Ones," and "I Am Jesus' Special Friend" (stanzas 1 and 2). Sing enthusiastically, using lots of eye contact, facial expressions, and any motions you know or can make up. Move from one thing to the next to keep the children's attention. Do the rhymes, "Jesus' Love" (page 182) and the "Listening Rhyme." Sing "I Can Talk to God," then pray, **Thank You, Jesus, for being my special friend.** Sing "Pat the Bible," letting each child pat and "read" the Bible as you hold it for him. **Our Bible words are, "You are my friends." Let's say them together. One, two, three, "You are my friends." I'm glad Jesus is our friend!**

Let's Learn From the Bible

Introduction: Zach pops up with the feather duster in his hands, acting tired. **Zach, I thought you had finished cleaning. What are you doing now?** He replies, "Oh, I found some more dirt so I thought I'd clean it up while you told the story." **You know, Zach, Jesus' friend, Martha, was like you. But Jesus wanted her to listen. Let me tell you the story now.** Lay Zach aside, open your Bible to your visuals, and hold up the paper dolls so that only Jesus is showing.

The Bible Story: Jesus and some of his friends had walked a long way. *(Make figure walk.)* They came to the town where Mary and her sister, Martha, lived. Perhaps Martha opened the door and said, "Come in friend Jesus." *(Show Martha and Mary.)* Mary probably said, "Friend Jesus, You are welcome here."

Jesus came in. He sat down and rested. He talked to his friends. Mary sat down and listened to Jesus while Martha worked. Jesus said, "Come friend Martha, sit down, rest, and listen." Jesus liked being with his friends, Mary and Martha. Jesus likes being with you too! *(Open visual to show the last figure.)*

Let's sing "You Are My Friends." *(Hold up visual and sing Mary and Martha first. Put visual away, hold up your Bible, and sing the names of children in your class.)*

Let's Apply the Lesson

Hold up the teaching picture. Let the children name Jesus' friends in the picture. Zach then comes up holding the mirror as he did last week. As each child takes a turn, ask one of the following questions:

was happy to be Jesus' friend! *(Section 4.)* Repeat as time and the children's interest allow.

Pick up Zach and let him ask the children to name or point to various places their friend Jesus will go with them. Use the pictures of children you have gathered to help with answers. **Here are some children playing outside** (sleeping, riding in the car, at church, etc.). **Is their special friend Jesus with them? . . . Yes, Jesus will be with us wherever we go. I'm glad that Jesus is my friend! Thank You, God, for our friend Jesus.**

Learning Activities

(20 minutes)

Let's Play Awhile

Zach says, "Let's sing 'Zaccheus' again." Sing as you did earlier using Zach to help with the motions. Lay Zach down and make a circle with the children holding hands. Sing "You Are My Friends" as you walk around in your circle.

Dismiss to the Block Center. If you have more than one teacher use the other centers as well.

Let's Go Home

Zach says, "Friends, it is time to clean up. Let's sing as we help each other." Sing to the tune of "Mulberry Bush," "This is the way we help our friends . . . pick up all the blocks," using words to fit the materials that need to be picked up. When the room is neat, read *Zaccheus Meets Jesus* or another appropriate book. Sing "Zaccheus" and other songs from this unit until parents come.

Jesus Makes a New Friend

Luke 19:1-6

Bible Words: "You are my friends" (John 15:14, *NIV*).

Lesson Value: The details of this story may be familiar to many of your children. The song about Zaccheus is fun and is known by many preschoolers. However, the song does not mention that Jesus wanted to be a friend to Zaccheus and it does not include Zaccheus' reaction when he is told that Jesus is coming to his home. Luke 19:6 says that Zaccheus "welcomed him [Jesus] gladly." This lesson will give you the opportunity to teach children that Jesus and Zaccheus became friends, and that Zaccheus was happy to be considered a friend of Jesus. You will also continue teaching children that Jesus wants to be their friend and to stay with them always. Encourage them to be like Zaccheus—glad that Jesus is their special friend.

Know: Know that Jesus is a friend.
Feel: Feel happy and loved by Jesus.
Do: Label Jesus as a friend.

Children will accomplish the goals when they:

1. Say the Bible words, "You are my friends."
2. Pray, "Thank You, Jesus, for being my special friend."
3. Sing about their friend Jesus.
4. Name or point to friends (children in the room, Jesus).
5. Name places their friend Jesus will go with them.

Let's Get Ready

For the Bible story, you will need the classroom Bible, Zach, the pictures of Jesus and Zaccheus from pages 182 and 183 (cut apart on solid lines into sections 1-4), and pictures of children (Bible times and present day).

Prepare the Art Center, the Game Center, and the God's Wonders Center. If you are the only teacher use just the Art Center. Have materials ready in the Block Center to use after the Bible story.

Learning Activities

(30 minutes, including 10 minutes presession)

Let's Get Started

As Zach greets each child, have him use the word *friend.* "How is my friend Ashley today? . . . I'm so glad to see my friend Aaron!" Also, let Zach remind the children that he was named after the Bible man in the Bible story. Make sure each child chooses and gets involved in a learning activity.

Worship and Bible Story

(15 minutes)

Let's Worship God

Zach signals clean-up time by saying, "Friends, let's help each other clean up." Sing "It's Time to Worship." At the worship area sing "You Are My Friends" and then "Pat the Bible." Let each child pat the Bible as you hold it; repeat the song if necessary. Do the Rhyme, "My Bible," then sing "I Am Jesus' Special Friend" (page 162, stanzas 1 and 2). Do the rhyme, "Jesus' Love"; then use "When I Pray" to prepare the children for prayer. Say, **Now we are ready to pray, "Thank You, Jesus, for being our special friend."** Then pray in those words.

Let's Learn From the Bible

Introduction: Say, **Today we are going to learn about another friend of Jesus. His name is . . .** Zach pops up and interrupts, "Hey, wait a minute. Didn't you forget a song? You know, "Zaccheus." **Oh, yes. We probably should sing that song because Zaccheus is the friend of Jesus we will be talking about. Will you help us sing, Zach?** "Yes ma'am," he replies. Sing "Zaccheus," letting Zach do the motions. Repeat if you wish and then set Zach aside and pick up your Bible.

The Bible Story: *(Speak in a loud voice and with expression.)* Oh, what a day! Everyone in Jericho was talking about it. *Jesus* was coming to town! *(Put up section 1.)* All the people wanted to see Jesus so they ran out to the road to get a good look as He passed by. *(Place hands above eyes, as if looking for Jesus. Encourage children to make motions with you.)*

Zaccheus ran out to the road, too, but he could not get a good look at Jesus. He was too short to see over the crowd. *(Squint as if trying to see; then shake head sadly.)* But, Zaccheus was smart. *(Tap head with index finger.)* He knew which way Jesus would be going. *(Point "down" the road.)*

Zaccheus ran ahead of the people and climbed *(Pretend to climb.)* up into a big sycamore tree. *(Put up section 2.)* When Jesus got there He looked up at Zaccheus and smiled. *(Smile, looking up.)* Jesus said, *(Shake finger as in song.)* "Zaccheus, you come down, for I'm going to your house today."*(Put up section 3.)*

(Put up section 4.) Zaccheus came down quickly. He was very happy that Jesus was coming to his home. Jesus was his friend!

Let's Apply the Lesson

Hand out the sections of the visual aid; briefly retell the story, letting the children bring up their sections at the correct time. **Jesus was coming to town.** *(Section 1.)* **Zaccheus could not see Jesus so he climbed up a tree.** *(Section 2.)* **When Jesus got to the tree, He smiled and said, "Come down, friend Zaccheus."** *(Section 3.)* **Jesus went to Zaccheus' house. Zaccheus**

Let's Apply the Lesson

Zach holds a small mirror. He says, "Jesus has many friends right here in this room. When you see yourself in my mirror, smile to show me you are happy to be Jesus' friend." As Zach holds the mirror for Anna you say, **Anna is happy she is Jesus' friend.**

Learning Activities

(20 minutes)

Let's Play Awhile

Sing "You Are My Friends," handing each child a sticker as you sing his name. Do the rhyme, "Jesus' Love," then go to the God's Wonders Center. If you have multiple teachers use the other centers as well.

Let's Go Home

Zach says, "We have had a wonderful party with all of our friends. Now it is time to help each other put away the toys." Sing, "This is the way we help our friends . . . " For a quiet option, read a book or two from this unit that the children enjoyed and/or sing several songs. For an active option, play a game from this unit that the children enjoyed and/or do some action rhymes. Make sure each child has the book he made in the Art Center.

I Know Jesus Is My Friend

Review of Lessons 1–3

Bible Words: "You are my friends" (John 15:14, *NIV*).

Lesson Value: Children get excited about going to a party. They remember the fun and the good feelings that come from being together with friends, playing, and celebrating. This lesson will be a party—a celebration of Jesus' friendship. Children will associate the happy feelings they have with the fact that Jesus is their friend. The children will be encouraged to call Jesus a friend. They will again be taught that Jesus will be with them always. They will also be given the opportunity to thank Jesus for being their special friend.

Know: Know that Jesus is a friend.
Feel: Feel happy and loved by Jesus.
Do: Label Jesus as a friend.

Children will accomplish the goals when they:
1. Say the Bible words, "You are my friends."
2. Pray, "Thank You, Jesus, for being my special friend."
3. Sing about their friend Jesus.
4. Name or point to Jesus' friends in the Bible stories.
5. Tell how they feel because Jesus is their friend.
6. Name or point to friends (children in the room, Jesus).

Let's Get Ready

For the Bible story, you will need the classroom Bible, Zach, visuals from past lessons, small mirror, and Jesus and the children stickers.

Before children arrive, decorate your classroom with colorful streamers and balloons. Prepare the Art Center, the Game Center, and the Family Living Center. If you are the only teacher use just the Art Center now. Have the God's Wonders Center ready to use after the Bible story.

Learning Activities

(30 minutes, including 10 minutes presession)

Let's Get Started

Zach greets his friends holding a picture of Jesus and the children with the Bible words written on it. "Hello, friend Peter. I'm happy to see you. I have a picture of our friend Jesus here and these are our Bible words. Do you remember them? That's right! Jesus said, 'You are my friends.' After you put your sticker on our chart you may go find something fun to do at our 'Friends of Jesus' party." Help as needed and then direct each child to an activity.

Worship and Bible Story

(15 minutes)

Let's Worship God

Zach signals clean-up time by singing "It's Time to Worship." Stand at the worship area and begin singing these words to the tune of "London Bridge": "Head and shoulders, knees and toes . . . clap your hands for Jesus." Repeat the song, this time ending with the words,"We are Jesus' friends." **Let's make Bible books with our hands.** Do the rhyme, "My Bible." Sing, "I Am Jesus' Special Friend," then do the rhyme, "Jesus' Love." Whisper, **Let's sit down now.** Sing quietly, "I Can Talk to God." Pray, **Thank You, Jesus, for being my special friend. I love You.**

Let's Learn From the Bible

Introduction: Zach pops up and says, "Happy Birthday!" Look puzzled as you say, **Zach, this is not a birthday party. This is a party for all** *(point to the children)* **of Jesus' friends.** He says thoughtfully, "Oh, can I be Jesus' friend?" Answer, **Yes, Zach, Jesus wants to be friends with everyone. He loves all of us.** *(Point to the children again.)* Zach says, "I'm glad we're having a 'Friends of Jesus' party. I'm glad Jesus is *my* friend." **Me too!** Lay Zach aside as you put your Bible in your lap and pick up your visuals.

The Bible-story Review: *(Hold up the paper dolls of Jesus and the fishermen.)* Let's see how smart you are. You remember that Jesus went walking by the water and met four fishermen who would become His very good friends. Let's see, what were their names? . . . Yes, that's right, Peter and his brother Andrew left their fishing nets to be friends with Jesus. Who were the other two fishermen? *(Pause again; encourage children to answer.)* You are right. James and John said good-bye" to their father and went to be Jesus' friends. You remember a lot about that Bible story.

(Hold up the paper dolls of Mary, Martha, and Jesus.) Jesus also had some friends who invited him to stay in their home and rest. Now, what were their names? . . . Good. Mary, who sat down and listened to Jesus talk, and her sister Martha, who kept on working until Jesus told her to come and listen to Him. Jesus likes for us to listen to Him too.

(Hold up the picture of Zaccheus.) You remember who this is. *(Point to Zaccheus.)* . . . Yes, Jesus' friend Zaccheus. Let's sing about Zaccheus. *(Do so.)* How did Zaccheus feel when he heard that Jesus was going to come to his house? . . . Yes, he was happy that Jesus was going to be his friend.

Family Living Center

Unit 1—We Can Know Jesus Is Our Friend

Items to Include:

Lesson 1
- Dress-up items
- Full-length mirror
- Several unbreakable hand mirrors.

Lesson 2
- Sugar cookies shaped like girls and boys
- Plastic knives
- Prepared frosting
- Napkins
- Cups/water
- Sprinkles or other decorations (optional)

Purpose: The child will recognize Jesus as a special friend.

Things to Do and Say

Lesson 1

Secure your full-length mirror so that it is safe. Let children dress up and pretend that they are going somewhere with their friends (church, park, store, etc.). If dolls are available, children may want to take their "babies."

Encourage the children to look at themselves in the mirrors. **Nathan, I see a friend of Jesus in the mirror. Who is that? . . . Yes, Nathan is a special friend of Jesus. You are all dressed up.** Ask questions, such as, **Where are you going? Who is going with you? What are the names of your friends? What do you like to do with your friends? . . . Jesus is a special friend who is always with us. Thank You, God, for our special friend, Jesus.**

Lesson 2

Give each child a paper plate with a cookie and a plastic knife. Show the children how to take a small amount of frosting on their knives and spread it carefully on their cookies. This will be messy, so be prepared with wet cloths and towels to wipe hands as needed. Towels or aprons tied around children would keep frosting off clothing.

Sutton, my friend, you have done a great job spreading frosting on your cookie. These boy and girl cookies make me think of what Jesus said, "You are my friends."

Block Center

Unit 1—We Can Know Jesus Is Our Friend

Items to Include:

- Large blocks

Lesson 1
- Several towels
- Picture of fishermen using nets

Purpose: The child will act out the Bible stories.

Things to Do and Say

Lesson 1

Help the children use the blocks to make outlines of two boats. Demonstrate how to use the towels as nets by throwing them out into the "water" and then slowly pulling them back. Show the picture of people using nets to fish.

Act out the Bible story with the children taking turns being Jesus and His fishermen friends. **Sarah, you pretend to be Jesus taking a walk by the water. You can call your friends to come and follow you. Do you remember the names of Jesus' fishermen friends? . . . Yes, Peter and Andrew were brothers and James and John were brothers. They were Jesus' friends and He wanted to be with them. Jesus is your friend. He is always with you.**

Lesson 2

Encourage the children to make a house and then act out the story. Leave a door for "Jesus" to come through as Martha and Mary invite Him to sit and rest. Jesus' friends can sit and listen as Jesus tells them, "You are my friends." You could include a review of last week's lesson by having some children pretend to be Jesus' fishermen friends.

Repeat as you have time, changing characters as the children desire. **Kyle, it's your turn to pretend to be Jesus going to visit His friends. . . . What were their names? . . .**

Family Living Center, continued

Clean-up supplies
Towels or aprons

He wants all boys and girls to be his friends. He wants to be your friend.

When the children have had time to spread the frosting, say, **Before we eat, let's thank God for our food and for our special friend, Jesus.** Pray, **Thank You, God, for our cookies and for our special friend, Jesus.**

Lesson 4
Household equipment
Cleaning supplies
Aprons

Lesson 4

Let children pretend they are cleaning up and getting ready for company. A friend is coming to visit, perhaps Jesus. Talk about the previous lessons as the children work.

Susan, I see you are busy washing the dishes. Do you have a friend coming to visit?. . . Oh, what is her name? . . . I know her, she is my friend too. Do you think Mary and Martha cleaned their house before Jesus visited? Yes, I think so too. I'm glad Jesus is our special friend.

Jeremy, I see that you are setting the table for dinner. Do you think Zaccheus gave Jesus something to eat when Jesus went to his house? . . . Zaccheus was so happy to have Jesus as his friend! Jesus is your friend, Jeremy. I'm glad that Jesus is my friend too. Thank You, God, for our special friend, Jesus.

Block Center, continued

Jesus liked to be with Mary and Martha. He liked to talk to them. He likes for people to listen to what He says. The Bible tells us that Jesus said, "You are my friends."

Lesson 3
Small stepstool

Lesson 3

Use the blocks to build a house for Zaccheus and a road on which Jesus can walk. Use the stepstool as the tree, letting children take turns "climbing up" while holding to an adult hand. Act out the story.

Holly, you be Zaccheus and climb up in the tree. Emily can be your friend Jesus. When Jesus asks you to come down, come quickly and show us how happy you feel to be Jesus' friend. I am glad Jesus wants to be my friend, too, and that He is with me wherever I am.

God's Wonders Center

Unit 1—We Can Know Jesus Is Our Friend

Items to Include:

Lesson 1
Fishbowl with fish
Large plastic containers
Newspapers
Plastic liner
Towels
Aprons
Small plastic boats and people
A hair net

Lesson 3
Pinecones

Purpose: The child will pray, "Thank You, Jesus, for being my special friend."

Things to Do and Say

Lesson 1

Prepare your area and put small amounts of water in the containers. Set these aside. Cover a large table with plastic and put the fishbowl on this.

When children arrive let them look at the fish in the bowl. **We are going to meet four friends of Jesus who were fishermen. They caught fish much bigger than these. Have you ever been fishing? . . . Did you use a fishing pole? . . . Jesus' friends used nets that looked like this** *(show hair net)* **but were much larger.**

Remove the fish and place your water containers on the table. Let the children play with the plastic boats and people. **Let's pretend we are Jesus' fishermen friends, Peter, Andrew, James, and John. Let's sail our boats and try to catch some fish. I'm sure Peter, Andrew, James, and John were glad Jesus was their friend. Maybe they said, "Thank You, Jesus, for being our friend." Let's thank Jesus too. Thank You, Jesus, for being our special friend.** As children play speak with each one, giving her an opportunity to pray.

Lesson 3

Gather as many nature items from trees as possible. Arrange these attractively so the

Art Center

Unit 1—We Can Know Jesus Is Our Friend

Items to Include:

Bible

Lesson 1
Page 184
Pastel paint
Black marker
Paint shirts
Newspapers
Clean-up supplies
Sponges
Hair nets (optional)

Lesson 2
Play dough
People cookie cutters
Jesus stickers (optional)

Purpose: The child will say the Bible words, "You are my friends."

Things to Do and Say

Lesson 1

Prepare the area and have your Bible open. Show the children the Bible words. **Jacob, here are our new Bible words. Jesus said, "You are my friends." Let's say them together. . . . In our story Jesus met some fishermen friends. They used nets when they fished.** Show a hair net.

Here is a picture of a fish for you to paint. Print the child's name by taking his hand as he holds a marker. **This says, "Jacob is a friend of Jesus."** Point to the words and read them. Encourage the child to do this after you.

Let the children finger paint or sponge paint. Sing, "You Are My Friends." Optional: Tape a hair net over the fish when the child has finished painting his picture.

Lesson 2

Have the Bible open and materials, except play dough, on the table. When the children are seated, go around the table letting each child "read" the Bible words and get a sticker. **Andrea, this sticker will remind you that Jesus is your special friend.**

Hand out play dough. Show how to make a pancake and press the sharp edge of the cutter into the dough. If you do not have cookie cutters, show children how to make "a friend of Jesus" by attaching a small ball to the end of a "snake" (body), then wrapping

God's Wonders Center, continued

Acorns Tree branch Twigs Leaves Pictures of trees

children will be drawn to them. Have the pictures of trees displayed on the wall at the children's eye level or laid on a table where they can handle the pictures and look at them. Make sure that no tree item is dangerous for the children to handle.

As a child picks up an item, give a brief explanation of what part of a tree it is. **That is an acorn. It is a seed from a large oak tree. If the acorn is planted in the ground, a tree will grow from it. . . . Our Bible story has a tree in it. A man named Zaccheus climbed up in the tree to get a better look at Jesus. Zaccheus became a friend of Jesus. I'll tell you the whole story in a little while. Jesus is my friend. Thank You, Jesus, for being my friend. . . . Jesus is your friend, too, Katie. Would you like to thank Him for being your friend?** Help the child thank Jesus for being her friend but don't force her to say this aloud.

Lesson 4
Nature items
Sandpaper
Plastic containers with lids
Coffee cans with lids

Lesson 4

Let the children make rhythm instruments out of tree items, perhaps items you had for Lesson 3. Children can put acorns or tiny pieces of tree limbs into plastic bottles with lids. Short pieces of branches (about 10" to 12" long and about 1" thick) can be sanded to make rhythm sticks. Small pinecones can be placed in coffee cans with lids. Don't worry about gluing lids on containers. The children won't be using the instruments that long. As children work, talk about the story of Zaccheus climbing the tree.

Show the children how to use the various instruments. **We are going to have a "Friends of Jesus" parade. Let's make a line and march as we play our instruments. I'll be the leader, so follow me.** Sing, "Jesus Loves Me" several times. Allow an older child to be the leader. Sing, "You Are My Friends" as you march this time. Collect the instruments when you have finished marching.

Art Center, continued

another "snake" around the middle of the body for arms and a third "snake" at the bottom for legs. As children work, sing "You Are My Friends."

Lesson 3
Figures from page 79
Crayons
Construction paper
Glue sticks

Lesson 3

For each child, make a copy of the male figure from page 179 (with Jesus' face) and a boy or girl figure. The children will color the paper dolls and then glue them, hand in hand, to sheets of construction paper. Print the child's name and "Jesus" under the appropriate dolls. Print the Bible words on the sheets before class.

As you work with a child, say, **Here is a paper doll for you to color, Katie. Give her a blue dress like the one you are wearing. We will call her, "Katie." After you color the paper doll of Jesus, you can glue both dolls on this pretty paper. . . . Do you know what these words say? Yes, they are our Bible words, "You are my friends." Jesus is your friend, Katie.**

Lesson 4
Copies of page 185
Crayons or washable markers

Lesson 4

Ahead of time, make copies of page 185. Fold each one on the solid line, and then on the dotted line. Have booklets and crayons or washable markers on the table when children arrive.

Andre, here is a little book for you to color. Jesus said, "You are my friends." Point to the front page. Print the child's name and help him "read" the words, *Andre is Jesus' friend*. As children color talk about each page of the booklet. **I'm so glad our friend Jesus will be with us, when we are outside playing, and when we are inside our homes. . . . How do we know Jesus is our friend? . . . Yes, the Bible tells us. Let's say our Bible words together.** Do so. Then sing, "You Are My Friends."

Game Center

Unit 1—We Can Know Jesus Is Our Friend

Items to Include:

Lesson 2
Dinner-size paper plates
Black marker

Lesson 3
Dinner-size paper plates
Markers

Purpose: The child will tell how she feels because Jesus is her friend.

Things to Do and Say

Lesson 2

Use a black marker to make plates into steering wheels, one for each child and teacher.

Hold up a steering wheel and say, **Who can tell me what this is? . . . That's right, Brian. It's a steering wheel like the one in your car. I'm going to give you a steering wheel so you can play like you are driving a car. We can "drive" wherever we want and our friend Jesus will go with us. How does it make you feel to know that Jesus is your friend, Abbie? . . . Yes, it makes you feel happy! I'm happy that Jesus is my friend too.**

Pass out the steering wheels and lead the children around your classroom. If your room is small, lead the children around the church building. Stop frequently to pretend you are in a new place. **Here we are at Grandma's house** (the store, at home, over the mountains, etc.). **Thank You, friend Jesus, for always being with us.**

Lesson 3

Draw happy faces on the paper plates, one for each child and teacher.

Hold up a happy face. **Can you look like this? Let me see you smile. Great! That is how Zaccheus, the man in our Bible story, must have looked. He felt very happy when Jesus became his friend. How do we feel knowing that Jesus is our friend? . . . Yes,**

Game Center, continued

Michael, we are happy too! Show me your smile.

Let's play a game. You will put your head down and close your eyes. You will feel just like Zaccheus did in our Bible story when he couldn't see over people's heads. I will hide these happy faces and then you can find them. Now, everyone hide your eyes. Hide the happy faces. Then say, **OK, friends of Jesus, let's see if you can find the happy faces.** Encourage children who find many to share with those who have few. Play until it is time for another activity.

Lesson 4
Cupcakes
Napkins
Cups (optional)

Lesson 4

I'm so happy that all of you friends of Jesus could be here for our "Friends of Jesus" party. Show me how you feel because Jesus is your friend. . . . Great, I see lots of smiles. Let's thank Jesus for being our special friend. I'll say one, two, three *(raise your fingers as you count)* **and we will all say, "Thank You, Jesus, for being my special friend." Ready? One, two, three . . . Now let's whisper. One two, three . . . OK, let's say it one more time in our strong voices. One, two, three . . . I'm sure our friend Jesus is smiling right now.**

Have children sit down at a table. Say, **Thank You, God, for our cupcakes.** Pass out the cupcakes. You may also want to have cups of water to drink with the cupcakes. If you have time left, play the hide-and-seek game from last week.

Spring, Unit 1—Paper Dolls

Directions:

1. Copy each pattern onto cardboard and cut out.
2. Fold construction paper accordion style so the edges of the pattern are even with folds of paper.
3. Trace pattern, cut out, add faces, names, other details. Use "Jesus" face on Jesus.

For Lesson 1: Cut 6 men; tape hands together as needed.
For Lesson 2: Cut 1 man and 3 women; tape as needed.
For bulletin board: Use patterns for borders (see page 178).

"You are my friends."
John 15:14

Jesus called four fishermen to be His friends.

"You are my friends."
John 15:14
Jesus liked to visit
in the home of His friends, Mary and Martha.

Directions:

1. Copy pages 182 and 183.
2. Cut sections apart; color; glue to cardboard.
3. Attach pictures to wall or poster board when telling story.

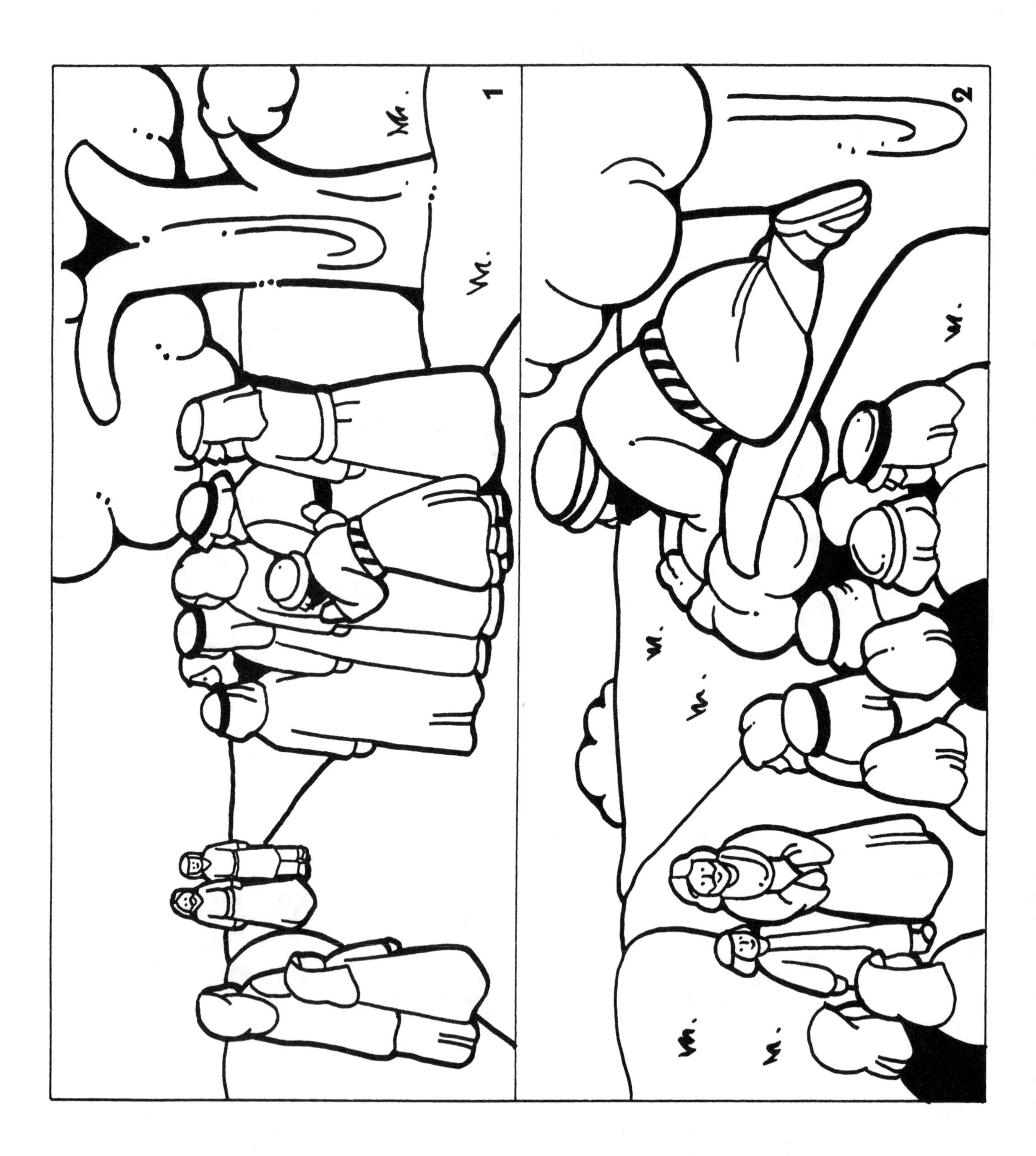

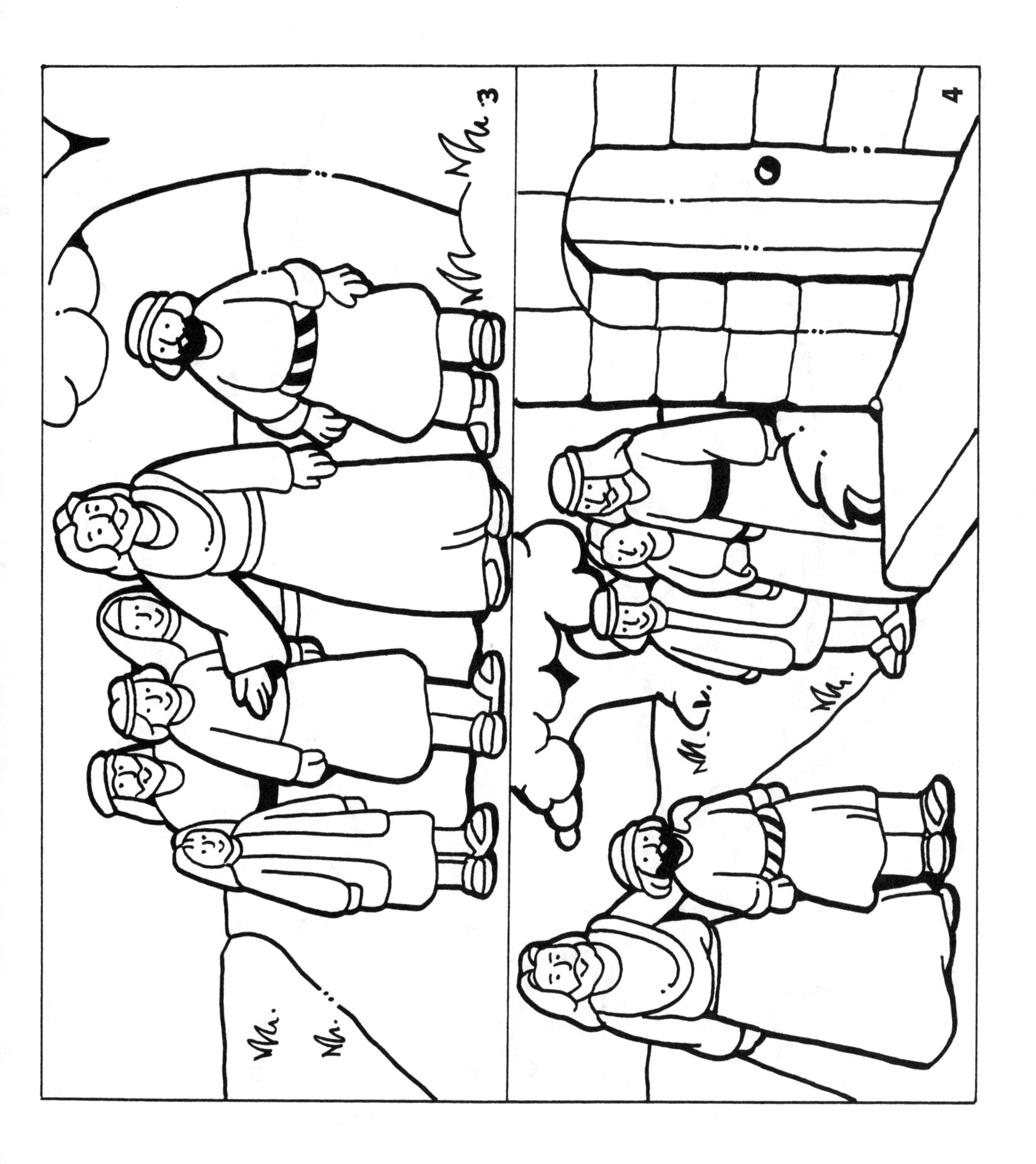
3
4

is a friend of Jesus.

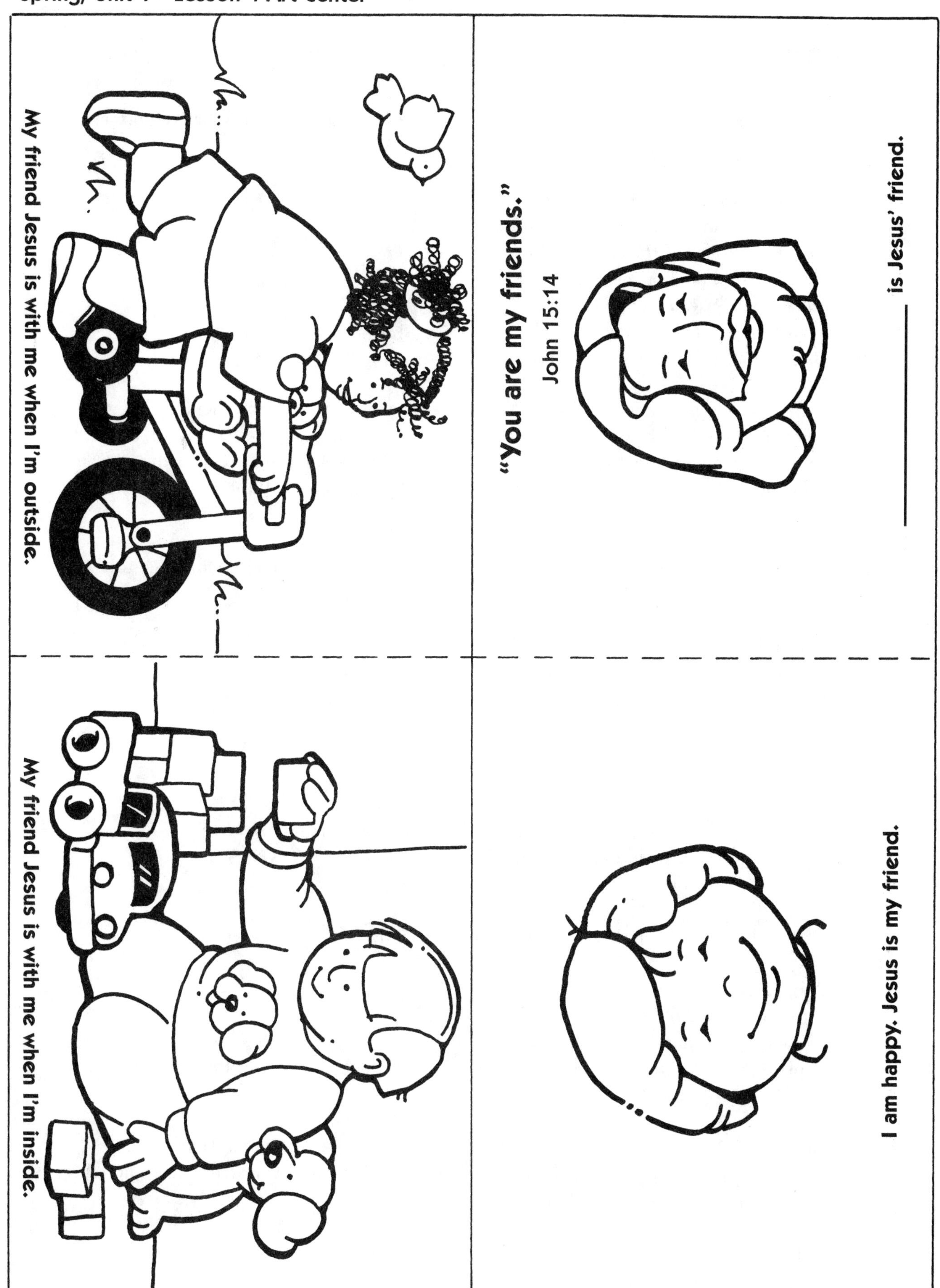
My friend Jesus is with me when I'm outside.
My friend Jesus is with me when I'm inside.
"You are my friends."
John 15:14
________ is Jesus' friend.
I am happy. Jesus is my friend.

Dear Parent:

Your child is beginning a new unit this week, entitled "We Can Know Jesus Is Our Friend." The stories we will be learning are:

Jesus Calls Four Fishermen to Be His Friends—Matthew 4:18-22
Peter, Andrew, James, and John follow Jesus.
Jesus Visits in the Home of His Friends—Luke 10:38-42
Jesus is a guest in the home of Mary and Martha.
Jesus Makes a New Friend—Luke 19:1-6
Zaccheus becomes Jesus' friend.
I Know Jesus Is My Friend—a review and reinforcement of previous lessons.

Our new Bible words are found in John 15:14, where Jesus says, "You are my friends." The goal of this unit is to introduce the children to a special friend who will always be with them, a friend who will always love them, a forever friend. We want your child to know that Jesus is this special friend. We want your child to feel happy that he is loved by Jesus and to think of Jesus as a friend.

Below are some activities that you and your child can do together at home to help reach this goal.

- Sing together to the tune of "Farmer in the Dell":

  _____ is Jesus' friend. _____ is Jesus' friend.
  The Bible tells us Jesus said, "You are my friends."
  (Insert the names of family members.)

- Say this action rhyme together:

  Jesus is a friend to children—
  The ones still very small, *(Use hand to indicate knee-high child.)*
  The baby in the cradle, *(Fold arms to form cradle, and rock.)*
  The ones so big and tall. *(Hands high over head.)*

- Pray together: "Thank You, Jesus, for being my special friend."

- Read together:

—Bible stories from a children's Bible;
—Papers your child brings home from church;
—The book, *Jesus Is My Special Friend* (#24-04211, Standard Publishing), or other appropriate books.

- Play together: Look at pictures of family and friends and talk about what a friend is. Talk about the ways Jesus is a friend. Make a collage of pictures of places your child goes and talk about how Jesus will always go with us.

His friend and yours,

Unit 2: We Can Know Jesus Is Close to Us

Lessons 5–9

By the end of the unit, the children will

Know that Jesus is alive.
Feel happy that Jesus is alive.
Sing and talk to Jesus.

Unit Bible Words:
"We love him" (1 John 4:19, *KJV*).

Books
from Standard Publishing
The Boy Who Couldn't (24-03879)
Jesus Is My Special Friend (24-04211)
Jesus Loves Me All the Time (24-04212)
A Child's Story of Jesus (24-04217)
The Best Story About Jesus (24-04226)
Look, I'm Growing Up (24-04233)

This Unit at a Glance

5 Jesus Is Alive! — John 18—21
After Jesus' resurrection, He makes breakfast for His friends.

6 Nicodemus Talks to Jesus — John 3:1-21
An important Jewish leader talks to Jesus at night.

7 Children Come to Jesus — Mark 10:13-16
Jesus tells the disciples, "Let the children come to me."

8 People Praise Jesus — Mark 11:1-10
The people shout, "Hosanna!" when Jesus enters Jerusalem.

9 I Know Jesus Is Close to Me — Review of Lessons 5–8

Why Teach This Unit to Young Children?

Preschoolers love to talk and sing! They are learning new words, learning how to express themselves, and how to communicate with others. They are also learning to talk to Jesus!

The Bible stories in this unit give examples of Bible people who sang and talked to Jesus, and Jesus listened to them. Children are important to Jesus, and He listens to them when they sing and talk to Him. He hears them because He is alive. The children will express happiness because Jesus is alive. They will discover that singing and talking to Jesus is an important way to tell Him that they love Him.

Use the Bible words in your conversation, in the Bible stories, at the learning centers, and in your prayers. For example, **Jesus loves us. "We love him." . . . We are happy because Jesus is our friend. "We love him." . . . Thank You, God, for making Jesus alive. "We love him.". . . The children love Jesus. "We love him."**

Have a classroom Bible available in a learning center, at the giving table, or wherever the children will see it. Also have it on your lap or at your side as you tell the Bible story. Highlight the Bible words so the children can see them, point to them, and "read" them.

Things to Do for This Unit

- Make copies of the Parents' Letter (page 214) and the Unit Planning Sheet (pages 319 and 320).
- Copy Learning Center Cards (pages 199-204); cut apart on solid lines and glue side 1 of each card to cardboard and side 2 to back of cardboard. Laminate for durability (optional).
- Gather/prepare materials listed on Learning Center Cards.
- Obtain a Polaroid® camera for Lesson 9, or take regular snapshots during the first two weeks of the unit.
- Enlarge and color pictures from pages 205-7 for teaching pictures.
- For Lesson 6, ask a man to portray Nicodemus, using script from the lesson.
- For Lesson 8, purchase or prepare palm branches (page 213).
- For Lesson 7, photocopy and color the figure of Jesus (page 210).
- Prepare the children figures, one per child (page 210).

Use These Songs and Action Rhymes During Unit 2

Let's Be Very Quiet

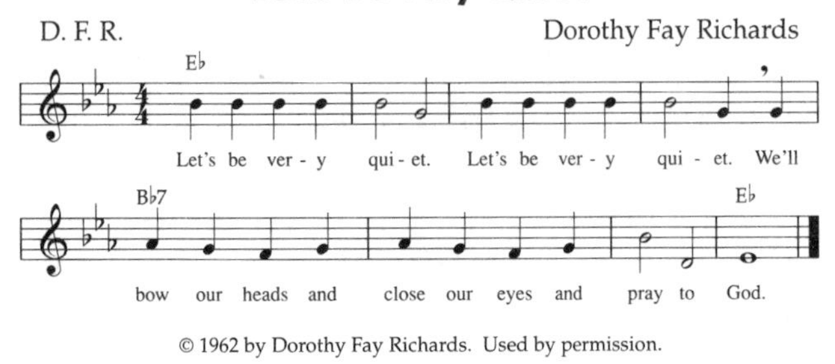

I Love Jesus

(Tune: "Jesus Loves Me")

"I love Jesus," I can say; I will love Him ev'ry day!
While I work and while I play, I will love Him ev'ry day!

Jesus is alive I know, for the Bible tells me so.
He is with me every day, and He hears me when I pray.

I'm Very Special to Jesus

(Tune: "Mulberry Bush")

I'm very special to Jesus.
He hears me when I talk* to Him.
I talk* to Him; He hears my words.
I'm very special to Jesus.
*sing

Jesus Loves Little Ones

We Are Happy

(Tune: "London Bridge")

We* are happy Jesus lives, Jesus lives, Jesus lives.
We* are happy Jesus lives. We* love Jesus.
*Use children's names.

Chant

We love Him. We love Him.
He's alive, and we love Him!

talked together. Jesus' friends were happy because Jesus was alive. They were happy that Jesus was there to talk to them and to listen to them.

Let's Apply the Story

Show me how Jesus' friends felt because He was alive. . . . Show me how you feel because Jesus is alive. Yes, we are happy because Jesus is alive!

Who talked to Jesus in the Bible story? . . . We can talk to Jesus too. We are happy because we can talk to Jesus, and He hears us. Lead children to pray, **We love You, Jesus. We like to talk to You. We are happy that You are alive.** Then sing, "We Are Happy," from page 188.

Learning Activities

(20 minutes)

Let's Play Awhile

Have children stand, clap, and sing "We Love Him" to the tune of "This Old Man."

We love Him. We love Him. He's alive, and we love Him.
Jesus is our special friend, and He hears us pray.
We will talk to Him each day.

Then take children to the God's Wonders Center. Since this activity involves a snack, plan for every child to participate.

Let's Go Home

Zach says, "It's time to clean up after our snack." Gather the children in a circle. Choose one child to be "It." Give that child a copy of the fish from page 208 to use in place of a handkerchief in this version of "Drop the Handkerchief." When a new "It" is chosen, say, **Point to someone in the room who is happy Jesus is alive. . . . Yes, Molly is happy Jesus is alive.**

Make sure the children take home their letters to parents.

Jesus Is Alive!

John 18–21

Bible Words: "We love him" (1 John 4:19, *KJV*).

Lesson Value: Jesus is alive! Today's Bible passage clearly shows this. After His death and resurrection, Jesus ate breakfast with His disciples. It is proof that Jesus rose from the dead. Jesus' disciples were happy because Jesus was alive. Your children will recognize that Jesus' resurrection is a reason for them to be happy too!

Know: Know that Jesus is alive.
Feel: Feel happy that Jesus is alive.
Do: Sing and talk to Jesus.

Children will accomplish the goals when they:

1. Say the Bible words, "We love him."
2. Pray, "We love You, Jesus. We like to talk to You."
3. Sing about Jesus. Sing to Jesus.
4. Point to or tell who ate breakfast with Jesus.
5. Tell how Jesus' friends felt when they talked to Him.
6. Name or point to someone in the room who is happy Jesus is alive.

Let's Get Ready

For the Bible story, you will need the classroom Bible, puppet Zach, picture #1 (enlarged) from page 205, and a boat outline made from blocks or crepe paper streamers.

Prepare the Game Center, the Family Living Center, and the Book/Picture Center. If you are the only teacher, use just the Family Living Center now. Have materials ready for the God's Wonders Center to use after the Bible story.

Note: For Lesson 9 you will need a picture of each child, as well as a group picture. If you do not have access to a Polaroid® camera, take snapshots this week and/or next week.

Learning Activities

(30 minutes, including 10 minutes presession)

Let's Get Started

Have Zach greet each child by name. "Jenny, what did you eat for breakfast this morning? What is your favorite breakfast? Jesus ate breakfast with His friends."

After you have taken care of the usual preliminaries, direct each child to a learning activity. Give a child two choices, either of which will be acceptable to you. **Sarah, would you like to cook breakfast in our family living area or would you like to look at books awhile?** Then make sure Sarah enters into her chosen activity.

Worship and Bible Story

(15 minutes)

Let's Worship God

Have Zach tell the children, "It's time to put our things away so we can sing and pray to God." Begin singing as soon as the first child sits in the circle with you. Sing "Jesus Loves Me." **The Bible is God's special book.** Show the classroom Bible. Do the action rhyme, "My Bible." **The Bible tells us that Jesus is alive!** Sing "Jesus Is Alive" to the tune of "Farmer in the Dell."

Jesus is alive. Jesus is alive.
I'm so very happy that Jesus is alive.

We are happy because Jesus is alive. We are happy because we can sing and talk to Jesus. Let's pray, Dear Jesus, we love You. We are so happy You are alive. Thank You for listening to us when we talk to You and sing to You.

Let's Learn From the Bible

Introduction: Jesus' friends were happy too. They were happy because Jesus was alive. But they weren't always happy. They were sad before they were happy. What happened to change their sadness to happiness? Let's find out. Put Zach aside and hold your Bible on your lap.

The Bible Story: *(Have blocks or crepe paper streamers placed in the outline of a boat shape large enough for everyone to fit inside.)*

Jesus' friends were fishing. They were in a boat on the lake. Let's pretend to be Jesus' fishermen friends. Let's get into our boat. *(Do so.)* Now, let's shove off and row to the middle of the lake. *(All pretend to row.)*

It was very early in the morning. The bright yellow sun was just coming up. Jesus' friends had been fishing all night long. They were tired, and they hadn't caught any fish. *(All yawn and stretch as if tired.)*

Just a few days before, Jesus' friends had seen Jesus die. They were very sad! But this morning, they weren't sad anymore. Jesus had risen from the dead. He was alive! The fishermen were happy. They knew Jesus would come to visit them soon. They were fishing while they were waiting for Jesus.

Just as the fishermen were pulling in their nets, a man yelled to them from the shore. *(Pretend to pull in nets.)* "Cast your nets on the other side of the boat," the man said.

The fishermen obeyed. *(Pretend to throw nets on the other side of the boat.)* They caught 153 fish! Do you know who the man on the shore was? Yes, it was Jesus! The fishermen hurried to see Jesus. *(Pretend to row.)*

(Show picture #1.) Jesus had fixed bread and fish for everyone to eat. Jesus and His fishermen friends ate their breakfast and

Show picture #2. **Point to Nicodemus talking to Jesus. Show me how Nicodemus felt when he talked to Jesus. . . . Show me how you feel when you talk to Jesus.**

Point to Jesus listening to Nicodemus. Show me how Jesus listened to Nicodemus. Show me how Jesus listens to us when we talk to Him.

Nicodemus was happy when he talked to Jesus and Jesus listened to him. We are happy because we can talk to Jesus, and Jesus hears us when we talk to Him.

Learning Activities

(20 minutes)

Let's Play Awhile

Our Bible words say, "We love him." Have children chant and clap to the following rhyme:

We love Him. We love Him.
Everybody here says, "We love Him."

Have materials ready for the God's Wonders Center. If your group is large and you have multiple teachers, use the other activities from the beginning of class as well.

Let's Go Home

Have Zach tell the children that it's time to clean up.

Gather the children in a circle. Sing "Children Talk to Jesus" to the tune of "Row, Row, Row Your Boat."

Talk, talk, talk to Jesus, children talk to Jesus.
Happily, happily, happily, happily, children talk to Jesus.

Also use the words *run, walk, skip,* and *pray.* Have children act out each stanza.

Nicodemus Talks to Jesus

John 3:1-21

Bible Words: "We love him" (1 John 4:19, *KJV*).

Lesson Value: A child's early prayer experiences always involve another person. The child's prayers are directed by parents, teachers, ministers, and others. Nicodemus is an example of someone who talked to Jesus alone. No one else was present. Children need to know that they can talk to Jesus when they are alone. And Jesus will do with children just as He did with Nicodemus—He will take time to listen, no matter when they talk to Him.

Know: Know that Jesus is alive.
Feel: Feel happy that Jesus is alive.
Do: Sing and talk to Jesus.

Children will accomplish the goals when they:

1. Say the Bible words, "We love him."
2. Pray, "We love You, Jesus. We like to talk to You."
3. Sing about/to Jesus.
4. Point to or tell who came to talk to Jesus.
5. Tell how Nicodemus felt when he talked to Jesus.
6. Tell why Jesus' friends are happy.

Let's Get Ready

For the Bible story, you will need the classroom Bible, puppet Zach, an actor prepared to present the Bible story as

Nicodemus, an enlarged copy of picture #2, and the picture of Jesus from the Family Living Center.

Prepare the Music/Drama Center, the Book/Picture Center, and the Family Living Center. If you are the only teacher, use just the Music/Drama Center now. Prepare to use the God's Wonders Center after the Bible story.

Learning Activities

(30 minutes, including 10 minutes presession)

Let's Get Started

Have Zach hold the picture of Jesus and greet each child as he arrives. "Ryan, here's a picture of Jesus. Our Bible words say, 'We love him.' We love Jesus! We are happy we can talk to Jesus."

Direct the children to complete their attendance charts, to deposit their offerings, and to get involved in the learning activities.

Worship and Bible Story

(15 minutes)

Let's Worship God

Have Zach tell the children, "It's time to put our things away so we can sing and pray to God." Begin singing as soon as the first child sits in the circle with you. Sing both stanzas of "I Love Jesus" followed by "We Love Him," used last week after the Bible story. **Our Bible words say, "We love him."** Show the words in the classroom Bible and let each child "read" them. **We love Jesus. We like to talk to Him.** Sing "Let's Be Very Quiet." Then say, **Now we are ready to pray, "Jesus we love You. We like to talk to You. Thank You for listening to us when we talk to You."** Then pray aloud in those same words.

Let's Learn From the Bible

Introduction: Do you see someone in this room who is happy when he talks to Jesus? Point to someone who is happy to talk to Jesus. **Adam, Jessica, and Molly are happy when they talk to Jesus.** Name each child. **We're going to meet a man from our Bible story who was also happy to talk to Jesus.** Put Zach aside, open the classroom Bible, and point to the text. **This man's name was Nicodemus. Let's welcome Nicodemus.**

The Bible Story: *(Have an adult dressed in a Bible-times costume and ready to present the following first-person narrative as Nicodemus. He should sit down with the children.)*

Hi, boys and girls. My name is Nicodemus. I know that all of you like to talk to Jesus. I want to tell you about one time when I talked to Jesus.

It was nighttime. Do you talk to Jesus at nighttime? Nighttime is a good time to talk to Jesus.

Because it was nighttime, the city was quiet. Everyone was home and the children were asleep. I felt happy because I was going to talk to Jesus. Are you happy to talk to Jesus? Show me what you look like when you are happy. Yes, we smile and laugh when we are happy. I was smiling as I was walking to the house where Jesus was staying.

At the house, I knocked on the door. Knock, knock, knock. "I want to talk to Jesus," I said. Jesus and I went up on the roof of the house to talk. We were alone. Do any of you talk to Jesus when you are alone? Anytime you are alone is a good time to talk to Jesus.

I asked Jesus some questions. Jesus said, "God loves you, Nicodemus." Jesus told me many important and wonderful things. I felt happy to talk to Jesus.

Let's Apply the Story

Let the children ask the actor Nicodemus questions. Then help them tell the actor good-bye.

figures toward the figure of Jesus.) They sat in His lap. Jesus put His arms around them. Jesus was happy to see the children. The children were happy to see Jesus. Jesus loved the children, and the children loved Jesus.

Let's Apply the Story

How did the children feel about seeing Jesus? . . . Yes, they felt happy. How did the children feel when they talked to Jesus? . . . Yes, the children felt happy. They felt happy because they knew that Jesus loved them.

Lead the children in singing "Children Talk to Jesus," from Lesson 6. Sing additional stanzas using "sing, run, walk, skip," and "pray" in place of "talk."

When can we talk to Jesus? . . . That's right. We can talk to Jesus anytime we want. And He will listen to us.

Learning Activities

(20 minutes)

Let's Play Awhile

Lead the children in singing "Jesus Loves the Little Ones." Then direct the children to the Art Center. If your class is large and you have multiple teachers, use the other activities from the beginning of the lesson as well.

Let's Go Home

Have Zach tell the children that it's time to clean up. Gather the children in a circle. Have Zach lead them in saying the Bible words. Use this rhyme.

Listen to what I can say.
I've learned some Bible words today. "We love him."

Give each child several happy-face stickers. **Find someone in this room who loves Jesus. Give him or her a happy-face sticker.** Sing songs from this unit until all the children have been picked up.

Children Come to Jesus

Mark 10:13-16

Bible Words: "We love him" (1 John 4:19, *KJV*).

Lesson Value: Jesus loves children; they are important to Him. Jesus called the children to come to Him. He hugged them. They sat on His lap. They talked. The children knew they were important to Jesus. Today's children need to know how important they are to Jesus too. Children are so important to Jesus that He hears every word they sing and pray!

Know: Know that Jesus is alive.
Feel: Feel happy that Jesus is alive.
Do: Sing and talk to Jesus.

Children will accomplish the goals when they:

1. Say the Bible words, "We love him."
2. Pray, "We love You, Jesus. We like to talk to You."
3. Sing about/to Jesus.
4. Point to or tell who came to talk to Jesus.
5. Tell how the children felt when they talked to Jesus.
6. Tell why Jesus' friends are happy.

Let's Get Ready

For the Bible story, you will need the classroom Bible, puppet Zach, and figure of Jesus and prepared children with circle legs (page 210). Have children's figures for everyone. Purchase happy-face stickers for use at the beginning and end of class.

Prepare the Game Center, the Book/Picture Center, and the Music/Drama Center. If you are the only teacher, use just the Book/Picture Center now. Have materials ready for the Art Center to be used after the Bible story.

Learning Activities

(30 minutes, including 10 minutes presession)

Let's Get Started

Put several happy-face stickers on Zach. As children arrive, have Zach greet each one by name. Show them the happy-face stickers and let each child choose one. Place the sticker on the child's clothing. Say, **Jesus loves children. Children are important to Jesus. We are happy because Jesus loves us.**

Direct the children to the attendance chart and offering center. Then direct them to get involved in one of the learning activities. Always make sure that each child takes part in one activity or another and stays with it until it is completed. A bored or restless child can become a problem child!

Worship and Bible Story

(15 minutes)

Let's Worship God

Have Zach tell the children, "It's time to put our things away so we can sing and pray to God." Begin singing as soon as the first child sits in the circle with you. Sing the following words to the tune of "London Bridge":

Head and shoulders, knees and toes,
Knees and toes, knees and toes.
Head and shoulders, knees and toes.
All run to see Jesus.

Use the phrase, "all sing to Jesus," in place of the last line as you sing the song again. Have puppet Zach sing along and do the motions. Then sing "Jesus Loves the Little Ones." **Children are important to Jesus. We love Jesus. Our Bible words say, "We love him." Point to someone in this room who loves Jesus. . . . Yes, we all love Jesus. Let's talk to Jesus and tell Him that we love Him.** Lead children to pray, **Dear Jesus, we love You. We like to talk to You. Thank You, for listening to us when we pray.**

Let's Learn From the Bible

Introduction: Jesus said something very important about children. The Bible tells us what Jesus said. Show the classroom Bible opened to Mark 10:14. **What did Jesus say that was so important? He said, "Let the children come to me." Can you say that with me? . . . Good! Now you are ready to help me with today's Bible story. We will find out why Jesus said, "Let the children come to me."**

The Bible Story: *(Before class, prepare the figure of Jesus and the children with running legs.)*

(Show figure of Jesus.) Here is Jesus. He is tired. Jesus friends knew that Jesus was tired. So Jesus and his friends stopped to rest.

Soon, many people started coming to see Jesus. Children were on their way to see Jesus. Yes, boys and girls and mommies and babies were coming to see Jesus. The children were running; they were skipping; they were hopping to see Jesus. They were happy because they were going to see Jesus. *(Distribute the children figures with circles.)* Show me how the children were going to see Jesus. *(Have children roll the figures to move the legs.)*

Jesus' friends thought Jesus was too tired to see children. They said, "Jesus is tired. Come see Him another day."

But Jesus was not too tired to see the children. Jesus loves children. What did Jesus say to his friends? *(Have children answer.)* Yes, Jesus said, "Let the children come to me."

The children ran to Jesus. *(Have children roll their children*

Let's Apply the Story

Show picture #4. Ask the following questions:

- **How did Jesus get to Jerusalem?** (He rode a donkey.)
- **Why was Jesus' donkey special?** (Jesus was the first one to ride him.)
- **What did the children do when they saw Jesus riding on a donkey?** (They shouted "Hosanna." They made a path from palm branches and coats.)
- **Why were the children happy?** (They loved Jesus.)

We love Jesus too. We are happy because we love Jesus. Our Bible words say, "We love him." Can you say that with me? . . . Let's sing a song to tell Jesus that we love Him. Sing the following words to the tune of "London Bridge." On the second stanza, sing children's names in place of "boys and girls."

Boys and girls sing Hosanna! Sing Hosanna! Sing Hosanna!
Boys and girls sing Hosanna. We love Jesus.

Learning Activities

(20 minutes)

Let's Play Awhile

Have the children stand and do the following action rhyme:

Jesus rode a donkey *(Pretend to ride a donkey.)*
One day to Jerusalem. *(Hold up index finger.)*
The people shouted, "Hosanna!" *(Cup hands over mouth.)*
And showed their love for Him. *(Cross arms over heart.)*

Direct the children to the God's Wonders Center. Since this activity involves eating a snack, involve all the children in it.

Let's Go Home

Have Zach tell the children that it's time to clean up.

Gather children to wave palm branches and to sing "I Love Jesus," as well as other songs learned during this unit.

People Praise Jesus

Mark 11:1-10

Bible Words: "We love him" (1 John 4:19, *KJV*).

Lesson Value: Children love to celebrate, and today's lesson is about celebration. The people who welcomed Jesus into Jerusalem showed their love for Jesus. Today, your children will have the opportunity to celebrate their love for Jesus. Your children will sense the excitement of Jesus' arrival in Jerusalem when they wave their palm branches and shout "Hosanna!" They will understand that joyful celebration is a way to tell Jesus that they love Him.

Know: Know that Jesus is alive.
Feel: Feel happy that Jesus is alive.
Do: Sing and talk to Jesus.

Children will accomplish the goals when they:

1. Say the Bible words, "We love him."
2. Pray, "We love You, Jesus. We like to talk to You."
3. Sing about/to Jesus.
4. Point to or tell who sang to Jesus.
5. Tell how the children felt when they sang to Jesus.
6. Tell why Jesus' friends are happy.

Let's Get Ready

For the Bible story, you will need the classroom Bible, puppet Zach, palm branches (purchased or made from pattern on page 212), garments or towels, picture #4 (enlarged) from page 207.

Prepare the Music/Drama Center, the Art Center, and the Game Center, If you are the only teacher, use just the Art Center now. Have materials ready for the God's Wonders Center to be used after the Bible story.

Learning Activities

(30 minutes, including 10 minutes presession)

Let's Get Started

Spread out palm branches and garments in a path from the doorway to the attendance and offering centers. As children arrive, have Zach welcome them with a wave of the palm branch. "Hello, Mary Ann. The Bible tells us that Jesus' friends made a path for Him much like the path we have in our room today. Can you walk on the path to the attendance center and offering center?" Make sure that children do not trip over the things on the floor. After children have marked the attendance chart and put in their offerings, direct them to get involved in the learning activities.

Worship and Bible Story

(15 minutes)

Let's Worship God

Make a path with the palm branches and towels from the centers to the group area. Have Zach tell the children, "It's time to put our things away so we can sing and pray to God. Follow the path to the group area." Begin singing as soon as the children come to the circle. Sing "Jesus Loves Me" and "I'm Very Special to Jesus." **We are special because Jesus loves us. And we love Jesus. Our Bible words say, "We love him."** Point to the words in the classroom Bible. Let children "read" the words from the Bible. Sing "I Love Jesus." Pray, **We love You, Jesus. We like to talk to You.**

Let's Learn From the Bible

Introduction: We love Jesus. We show Jesus that we love Him when we sing to Him. We can sing "Jesus, we love You." In our Bible story today, children told Jesus they loved Him. They said, "Hosanna!" Can you say, "Hosanna"? Help the children do so several times. **Now you are ready to help me tell the Bible story.** Place the classroom Bible in your lap and Zach behind you.

The Bible Story: *(Give each child a palm branch. On cue, have children wave the palm branches and shout, "Hosanna.")* "Hosanna! Hosanna!" the children shouted. "Hosanna! Hosanna!" the moms and dads shouted. "Hosanna! Hosanna!" all the people shouted.

Jesus was coming to Jerusalem, and He was riding on a donkey. *(Show picture #4.)* The children hurried to see Jesus. Moms and dads hurried to see Jesus. Grandmas and grandpas hurried to see Jesus. Everyone wanted to see Jesus.

Jesus' trip to Jerusalem was very special so Jesus chose a very special donkey to ride. Why was Jesus' donkey special? Jesus was the first one to ride him.

As Jesus rode the donkey to Jerusalem, the people came to greet Him. The people knew Jesus was special. They loved Jesus. They wanted to show Jesus how much they loved Him. They cut big palm branches and laid them on the road. Some of the people took off their coats and laid them on the road. They made a soft path for Jesus. Jesus rode His donkey over the soft path that was made of palm branches and coats.

"Hosanna! Hosanna!" the children shouted. "Hosanna! Hosanna!" the moms and dads shouted. "Hosanna! Hosanna!" all the people shouted. Jesus was here. Perhaps the children waved their arms and their palm branches. Maybe the grandmas and grandpas waved their arms and palm branches. Probably, everyone waved. Everyone celebrated and thanked God for Jesus. The people were happy because they loved Jesus!

It's all of us here. It's you and it's me!

Let's Apply the Story

Show each picture and ask the following questions:

- **Point to the people who sang or talked to Jesus.**
- **How did these people feel when they sang or talked to Jesus?**
- **Why are Jesus' friends happy?**

We are happy because Jesus is alive! How do we look when we are happy? Ask the children to pray with you, **We love You, Jesus. We like to talk to You.**

Learning Activities

(20 minutes)

Let's Play Awhile

Bring a mirror to the circle. Let children look at themselves in the mirror. Also have the picture of Jesus visible to the children. Lead them in saying the following rhyme:

I look in the mirror. What do I see? *(Look in the mirror.)*
I see someone who talks and sings to Jesus. *(Point to Jesus.)*
That someone is me! I love Jesus. *(Point to self.)*

Have materials ready for the Art Center. If your group is large and you have multiple teachers, use the other activities from the beginning of class as well.

Let's Go Home

Have Zach tell the children that it's time to clean up. Gather the children in a circle to play this version of "London Bridge." Two teachers or helpers make the bridge. Children parade under the bridge as you sing "We Are Happy," (page 188).

Use the name of the child "caught" by the bridge in place of the words *we are.* Play as long as time permits, catching a different child each round.

I Know Jesus Is Close to Me

Review of Lessons 5–8

Bible Words: "We love him" (1 John 4:19, *KJV*).

Lesson Value: Through the lessons in this unit, the children have discovered that when they sing and talk to Jesus, He hears them. This lesson will remind them that singing and talking to Jesus are a celebration that Jesus is alive. This lesson will reinforce that children can sing and talk to Jesus about many different things and at many different times.

Know: Know that Jesus is alive.
Feel: Feel happy that Jesus is alive.
Do: Sing and talk to Jesus.

Children will accomplish the goals when they:

1. Say the Bible words, "We love him."
2. Pray, "We love You, Jesus. We like to talk to You."
3. Sing about/to Jesus.
4. Point to/name Bible people who talked or sang to Jesus.
5. Tell how Jesus' friends felt when they talked to Him.
6. Tell why Jesus' friends are happy.
7. Talk to Jesus.

Let's Get Ready

For the Bible story, you will need the classroom Bible, puppet Zach, pictures from pages 205-207, toy piano (optional), music for "Farmer in the Dell," and Polaroid®

camera to take a picture of the group. Also have a small unbreakable mirror and a picture of Jesus.

Prepare the Game Center, the Music/Drama Center, and the Family Living Center. If you are the only teacher, use just the Music/Drama Center. Prepare materials for the Art Center to be used after the Bible story.

Learning Activities

(30 minutes, including 10 minutes presession)

Let's Get Started

Have Zach play the toy piano and sing "Jesus Is Alive" to the tune of "Farmer in the Dell." As children arrive, Zach should call them by name and invite them to join him by the piano to sing. **Garrett, I love to sing about Jesus. Come and sing about Jesus with me.**

Let each child sing the song one time through. Then direct the children to complete their attendance charts and deposit their offerings, and then make sure they get involved in the learning activities.

Worship and Bible Story

(15 minutes)

Let's Worship God

Have Zach tell the children, "It's time to put our things away so we can sing and pray to God." Begin singing as soon as the first child sits in the circle with you. Sing "Jesus Loves the Little Ones" followed by "We Love Him," from Lesson 5. When all the children have gathered, take a snapshot of the group to use during the Bible story. Have children suggest other songs to sing. Sing "I'm Very Special to Jesus" to the tune of "Mulberry Bush." Then sing "Let's Be Very Quiet" before you pray, **We love You, Jesus. We like to talk to You.**

Let's Learn From the Bible

Introduction: Play this version of "Name That Tune." Use several familiar songs from this unit. Hum the melody to a song. Children raise their hands when they recognize the song. For extra help, sing the words. **Who likes to sing these songs about Jesus? . . . I like to sing about Jesus, too. Point to someone who likes to sing and talk to Jesus. . . . Yes, we all like to sing and talk to Jesus. We've met some others who like to sing and talk to Jesus. Let's meet them again. The Bible tells us about these people.** Put Zach aside; open the classroom Bible and place it in your lap.

The Bible-story Review: *(Show picture #1.)*

Someone is talking to Jesus. Someone is happy He's alive.
Someone is eating with Jesus.
It's His fishermen friends by the sea

(Show picture #2.)

Someone is talking to Jesus. Someone is happy He's alive.
Someone is walking to see Jesus.
It's Nicodemus who talked to Jesus alone.

(Show picture #3.)

Someone is talking to Jesus. Someone is happy He's alive.
Someone is waiting to see Jesus.
It's the children Jesus told, "Come to me."

(Show picture #4.)

Someone is talking to Jesus. Someone is happy He's alive.
Someone is praising Jesus.
It's the people who shouted, "Hosanna!"

(Show snapshot of the class.)

Someone is talking to Jesus. Someone is happy He's alive.
Someone is talking to Jesus.

Family Living Center

Unit 2—We Can Know Jesus Is Close to Us

Items to Include:

Lessons 5 and 9
Play dough
Paper plates
Pans
Cups
Plastic food

Lesson 6
Copy of page 209
Folding tables
Blankets to cover tables

Purpose: The child will talk to Jesus.

Things to Do and Say

Lessons 5 and 9

Have housekeeping equipment set up. Allow children to play on their own but guide their thoughts with your conversation.

Jesus' friends discovered that breakfast time was a good time to talk to Jesus. Jesus and His friends ate fish and bread for breakfast. What do we eat for breakfast? . . . Yes, we eat cereal, toast, and eggs. We will make breakfast, and we will talk to Jesus.

Children may make a breakfast of fish and bread or of cereal, toast, and eggs, etc. While children work, talk about what they could say to Jesus at breakfast time.

When Jesus and His friends ate breakfast together, they talked about many things. Jesus' friends told Him how much they loved Him. What can we say to Jesus when we eat breakfast?. . . We can say, "We love You, Jesus. We like to talk to You." Let's eat breakfast and talk to Jesus.

Lesson 6

Arrange blankets over tables to make a large house. Set up the picture of Jesus inside the house.

Nicodemus was happy. He was on his way to see Jesus. He was going to talk to Jesus. Let's pretend to be Nicodemus. We are going to the house where Jesus is. We

Book/Picture Center

Unit 2—We Can Know Jesus Is Close to Us

Items to Include:

Books listed on page 187

Lesson 5
Picture #1 (page 205)
Picture of Jesus (page 209)

Lesson 6
Picture #2 (page 206)

Purpose: The child will point to or tell who talked or sang to Jesus.

Things to Do and Say

Lesson 5

Make puzzles from pages 205 and 209 if you wish. Use two copies of a picture for each puzzle. Enlarge picture #1 if possible. Use one copy for the puzzle base. Color and glue the other copy onto cardboard before cutting it into four or five large puzzle pieces.

If possible, have a book that tells of Jesus' resurrection. Also have books/pictures that show Jesus talking to and associating with people, especially children.

Our Bible story tells about a time when Jesus and His friends had a happy breakfast together. Jesus' friends were happy that He was alive and was there for them to talk to.

We can talk to Jesus anytime we want. He likes for us to talk to Him, and He listens to us. Let's talk to Him right now. Pray, Dear Jesus, we like to talk to You. We love You.

As a child works the puzzle of Jesus and His friends eating breakfast, ask the child to tell you who talked to Jesus. If the child is shy, let her point instead of telling you.

Lesson 6

Have books displayed where children can pick them up and start looking at them. Make puzzles using picture #2 on page 206. Follow the directions given for Lesson 5.

Book/Picture Center, continued

Someone is talking to Jesus. Who is it? Let's find out. Help children put the puzzles together. When complete, point to Jesus and Nicodemus and say, **This is Jesus, and this is Nicodemus. Laylah, can you point to Jesus? Good! Now point to the man who is talking to Jesus. . . . Aaron, who is talking to Jesus? Yes, Nicodemus is talking to Jesus.**

Point to someone in this room who can talk to Jesus. Yes, we can talk to Jesus. Where is Nicodemus talking to Jesus? . . . That's right, they are talking at home. Where can we talk to Jesus? . . . You may need to help children suggest places. **Nicodemus was alone when he talked to Jesus. Do you talk to Jesus when you are alone? What is Nicodemus saying to Jesus? What can we say to Jesus? . . . Let's talk to Jesus.** Lead children to pray, **We love You, Jesus. We like to talk to You.**

Lesson 7
The Boy Who Couldn't

Lesson 7

Show the children the book, *The Boy Who Couldn't.* **Benjamin was sad. He thought he was too little to do anything. But he wasn't too little to talk to Jesus. Let's find out what happened.**

Read the book. Then ask, **Who was happy to talk to Jesus? . . . Yes, Benjamin was happy to talk to Jesus. Point to someone like Benjamin in this room who is happy to talk to Jesus. . . . That's right, all of us are happy to talk to Jesus.** Pray, **We love You, Jesus. We like to talk to You.** Sing "Jesus Loves the Little Ones."

If you do not have access to the book suggested, use another one that is appropriate, perhaps one about a child who is getting big enough to do things, such as *Look, I'm Growing Up.* Read the book and ask questions at the end, such as, **What else are you big enough to do? . . . Yes, you are big enough to talk to Jesus. Let's do that right now.** Do so.

Family Living Center, continued

are going to talk to Jesus. What will we say to Jesus when we see Him? Our Bible words say, "We love him." We could tell Jesus that we love Him.

Have children walk to the table house and knock. **Knock, knock, knock. We have come to see Jesus. May we talk to Jesus?** Have children talk to the picture of Jesus.

Music/Drama Center

Unit 2—We Can Know Jesus Is Close to Us

Items to Include:

Purpose: The child will sing about or sing to Jesus.

Things to Do and Say

Lessons 6 and 9

Nicodemus came to talk with Jesus. "God loves you," Jesus said to Nicodemus. Nicodemus was happy to talk to Jesus. Lead the children to sing the following words to the tune of "Mulberry Bush":

Nicodemus walked to see Jesus, see Jesus, see Jesus. *(Walk fingers up arm.)*
Nicodemus walked to see Jesus. *("Walk" fingers.)*
And they had a happy talk. *(Draw a smile on face.)*

Who came to talk to Jesus? . . . Yes, Nicodemus. How did Nicodemus feel about talking with Jesus? . . . That's right, happy! Point to someone who can talk to Jesus. Yes, all of us can talk to Jesus. How do we feel when we talk to Jesus? . . . We feel happy!

Continue by singing these words:

We are happy to talk to Jesus, talk to Jesus, talk to Jesus.
We are happy to talk to Jesus. He listens to our prayers.

Add the following stanza for Lesson 9: "We are children who talk (or sing) to Jesus, etc. . . . We talk about God's world" (our friends, our food, the animals, and so on). Have children name things they can talk or sing to Jesus about.

Art Center

Unit 2—We Can Know Jesus Is Close to Us

Items to Include:

Lesson 7
Copies of page 211
Red construction paper
Glue sticks
Scissors (for teacher)
Crayons

Lesson 8
Cardboard tubes
Stickers from page 208

Purpose: The child will tell how Jesus' friends felt when they sang or talked to Jesus.

Things to Do and Say

Lesson 7

Cut large hearts from red construction paper. The scenes from page 211 can be prepared as stickers or can be glued on the hearts. Don't cut out the scenes until after the children have had time to color them.

Show a completed picture from page 211. **Jesus said, "Let the children come to me." Jesus loves children. Children are important to Jesus. The children came to see Jesus. They talked to Jesus. How did the children feel when they were talking to Jesus? . . . Yes, the children were happy. They loved Jesus. How do we feel when we talk to Jesus? . . . We are happy when we talk to Jesus. Point to places where you can talk to Jesus.**

Have children scribble-color their papers. Cut out the scenes and the Bible words. Help children lick and stick (or glue) them to their hearts.

Lesson 8

The cardboard tubes may be covered with construction paper ahead of time. Or, if you prefer, make megaphones in place of the tubes. *(See the sketch on page 213.)* Have the stickers ready for the children to color.

Let the children color their stickers. Then cut them apart and let the children lick

Art Center, continued

Construction paper and glue (optional)

and stick them to the tubes. As the children work, talk about the pictures on the stickers. Have children point to those who could sing or talk to Jesus.

We are making "Hosanna Tubes." The Bible tells about a time when Jesus rode into town on a donkey. The people were very glad to see Him. Even the children shouted "Hosanna! Hosanna! We love You, Jesus." No doubt they even sang those words! When the "Hosanna Tubes" are finished, show the children how to use them to say, "Hosanna! Hosanna! We love You, Jesus!" or sing a song from this unit.

Lesson 9
Copies of pages 205-207
Cellophane tape
Paper punch
Yarn
Construction paper
Scissors (for teacher)
Crayons
Polaroid® camera

Lesson 9

Before class, cut sheets of construction paper in half, two per child. Make one front cover for each child by gluing the cover art (page 205) in the center of a half-sheet of construction paper. Photocopy the five pages of the book.

In class, distribute the sheets and covers. As children are coloring their papers, take one Polaroid® snapshot of each child. Tape the pictures into the picture-frame pages. Help children put the pages of their books together in order, with the picture page last. Add a construction-paper back cover to each book. Punch holes on the left sides of the pages. Tie the books together with yarn. Then read the books together.

As children work, ask the following questions: **Can you point to someone who sang or talked to Jesus? . . . How did Jesus' friends feel when they talked to Him? . . . Name a time when you can sing or talk to Jesus. . . . Tell me something that you can sing or talk to Jesus about.**

Music/Drama Center, continued

Lesson 7

Jesus said, "Let the children come to me." Jesus was happy to talk to children. We feel happy to talk to Jesus. We are going to sing and pretend to get ready to see Jesus.

Gather the children in a circle. Sing these words to the tune of "Mulberry Bush":

This is the way I wash my hair, wash my hair, wash my hair.
This is the way I wash my hair. I'm going to see Jesus.

Lead children to act out what they are singing. Sing the following stanzas: "This is the way I wash my face; brush my teeth; tie my shoes; zip my coat; smile when I'm happy."

Lesson 8
Rhythm instruments
Palm branches

Lesson 8

Either use purchased palm branches or make some from the pattern on page 213.

We love Jesus. We show Jesus that we love Him when we sing to Him. We can sing, "Jesus, we love You." Our Bible tells us about some children who told Jesus they loved Him. They said, "Hosanna!" Can you say "Hosanna"? Let's sing to Jesus. Lead the children in singing the following words to the tune of "London Bridge":

The children shouted, "Hosanna! Hosanna! Hosanna!"
The children shouted, "Hosanna! We love Jesus."

Let the children wave their palm branches as they sing. **The children in our story sang to Jesus when He was riding a donkey into Jerusalem. When can we sing to Jesus?** As children name places, have them pretend to be at that place. Then sing these words:

Boys and girls sing Hosanna! Sing Hosanna! Sing Hosanna!
Boys and girls sing Hosanna! We love Jesus.

God's Wonders Center

Unit 2—We Can Know Jesus Is Close to Us

Items to Include:

Lesson 5
Bread
Peanut butter
Plastic knives
Milk or water
Cups
Raisins
Napkins
Wet wipes

Lesson 6
Picture #2 (page 206)
Black marker

Purpose: The child will name or point to those who sang or talked to Jesus and will feel happy that Jesus is alive.

Things to Do and Say

Lesson 5

Who was happy that Jesus was alive? Yes, Jesus' fishermen friends were happy that Jesus was alive again after He died. Point to someone in this room who is happy that Jesus is alive. Yes, we are all happy that Jesus is alive!

Spread peanut butter on bread that has been cut into circles. Give each child a slice of bread on a napkin and about ten raisins. **Let's use our raisins to make a face on our bread that shows how we feel because Jesus is alive.** Have a finished happy face to show the children.

Pray, **We love You, Jesus. We are happy that You are alive. We like to talk to You. Thank You for listening to us.** Then let the children eat their happy faces. Serve milk or water with the snack.

Lesson 6

Write each child's name on the outside of a small plastic self-sealing bag.

Show picture #2. Point to Nicodemus. **Nicodemus liked to talk to Jesus about many wonderful things. How does Nicodemus feel to be talking to Jesus? Yes, he is happy.**

Game Center

Unit 2—We Can Know Jesus Is Close to Us

Items to Include:

Lessons 5 and 9
Copies of page 208
Masking tape
Taped children's music
Cassette tape player
Classroom Bible

Lesson 8
Page 212
Bulletin board
Blindfold
Tape

Purpose: The child will say the Bible words, "We love him."

Things to Do and Say

Lessons 5 and 9

Make eight copies of the fish (page 208) on white paper and four copies on colored paper. Tape the fish to the floor in a large circle. Distribute the four colored fish evenly among the white ones. In class, have the children walk around the circle of fish as the music plays. When the music stops, the children standing on the colored fish say the Bible words or "read" them from the Bible: "We love him."

Lesson 7

Gather the children in a large circle. Stand in the middle. Say, **Jesus loves children.** The children answer, "We love him." Then say, **Jesus said, "Let the children walk to me."** Then have children walk to the center of the circle and back. Repeat the game using the following actions: run, skip, crawl, hop, tiptoe.

Lesson 8

Make one copy of the donkey. Make one copy of the donkey's tail for each child. Enlarge the patterns if possible. Pin the donkey to the bulletin board. Put a circle of tape on the reverse side of each tail.

Here is a donkey. What's wrong with this donkey? . . . Yes, this donkey is missing

God's Wonders Center, continued

Small self-seal bags

How do you feel when you talk to Jesus? . . . I feel happy too. Because Jesus is alive, we can talk to Jesus about wonderful things. Let's take a walk and look at some of the wonderful things we have to talk to Jesus about.

Take a walk outside and name things to talk to Jesus about. Let children gather a few small items such as twigs, leaves, and grass to put in their bags.

We can talk to Jesus about the things in His world. We can talk to Jesus about anything. We are happy Jesus is alive, and we can talk to Him. Let's talk to Jesus. . . . We love You, Jesus. We like to talk to You. We like to talk to You about things in Your world. Thank You for listening to us when we talk to You.

Lesson 8
- Graham crackers
- Frosting
- Plastic knives
- Small round candies
- Sprinkles
- Sheet-cake pan
- Milk or water
- Cups
- Napkins
- Wet wipes

Lesson 8

"Hosanna!" the children shouted. "We love Jesus!" How did the children feel when they saw Jesus? . . . Yes, the children felt happy. They loved Jesus. How do we feel about Jesus? . . . Yes, we feel happy. We love Jesus too. The children showed their love for Jesus by shouting, "Hosanna!" They laid palm branches and coats on the road to make a path for Jesus.

Let's make graham-cracker coats to lay on the road to welcome Jesus. We will show Jesus that we are happy to be His friends and that we love Him. Spread each graham cracker with frosting. Give each child a few small round candies and a small amount of sprinkles. Allow them to decorate the graham crackers to look like coats. Help them place the candies down the middle for buttons and spread the sprinkles over the frosting.

What a beautiful coat you have made, Jeremy! Let's lay our coats on the road and welcome Jesus to Jerusalem. Lay the "coats" in the sheet-cake pan. **Let's welcome Jesus by saying, "Hosanna! We love You, Jesus!"** Do so. Then pray for the snack and let children eat their "coats." Serve milk or water with the snack.

Game Center, continued

his tail. Jesus rode a donkey to Jerusalem. The people were happy because Jesus was coming. Jesus was their friend. We'll help Jesus get to Jerusalem by helping this donkey find his tail.

Have children take turns taping the tail on the donkey. As each child is blindfolded, ask him to say the Bible words with you.

Our Bible words say, "We love him." Can you say that with me? We are happy because Jesus is our friend. "We love him."

Jesus' fishermen friends talked to Him at breakfast time.

1

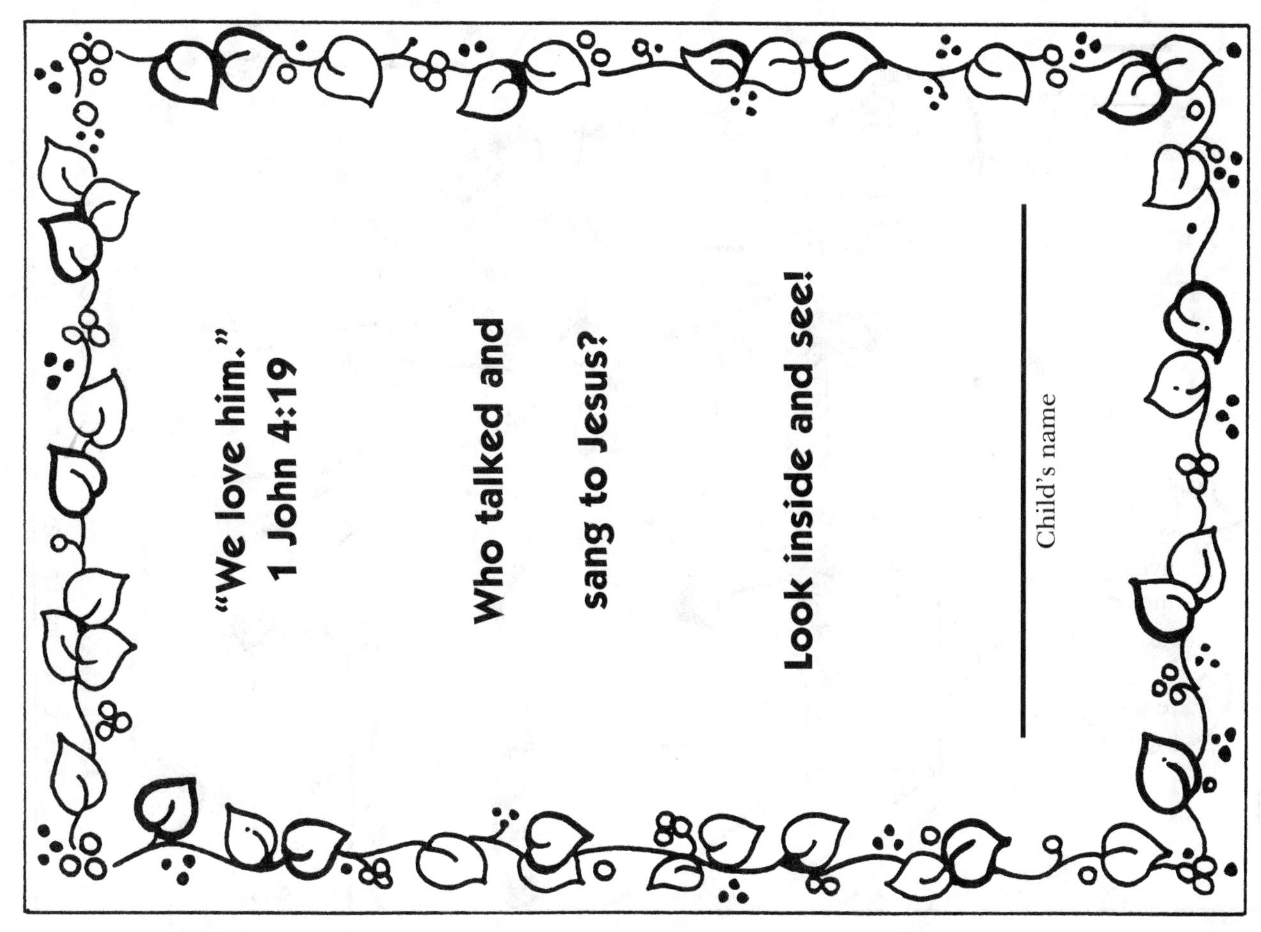

cover

Jesus said, "Let the children come to me."
The children talked to Jesus.

2

Nicodemus talked to Jesus at nighttime.

3

The children said, "Hosanna! We love You, Jesus!"

4

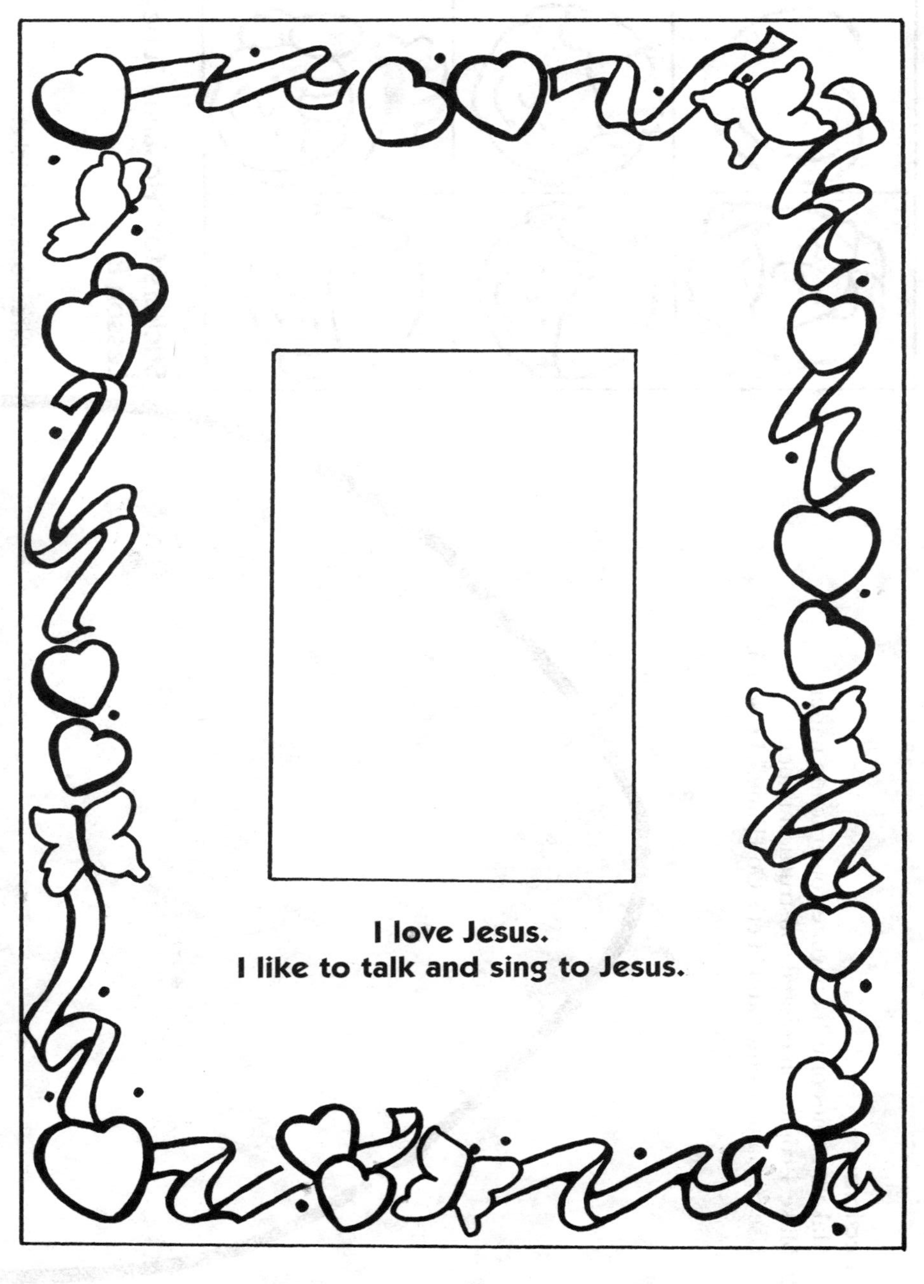
I love Jesus.
I like to talk and sing to Jesus.

5

Spring, Unit 2—Lesson 5 Game Center

Directions:

1. Make 8 copies of fish on white construction paper.
2. Make 4 copies on colored construction paper.
3. Use in Game Center and "Let's Go Home," Lesson 5.

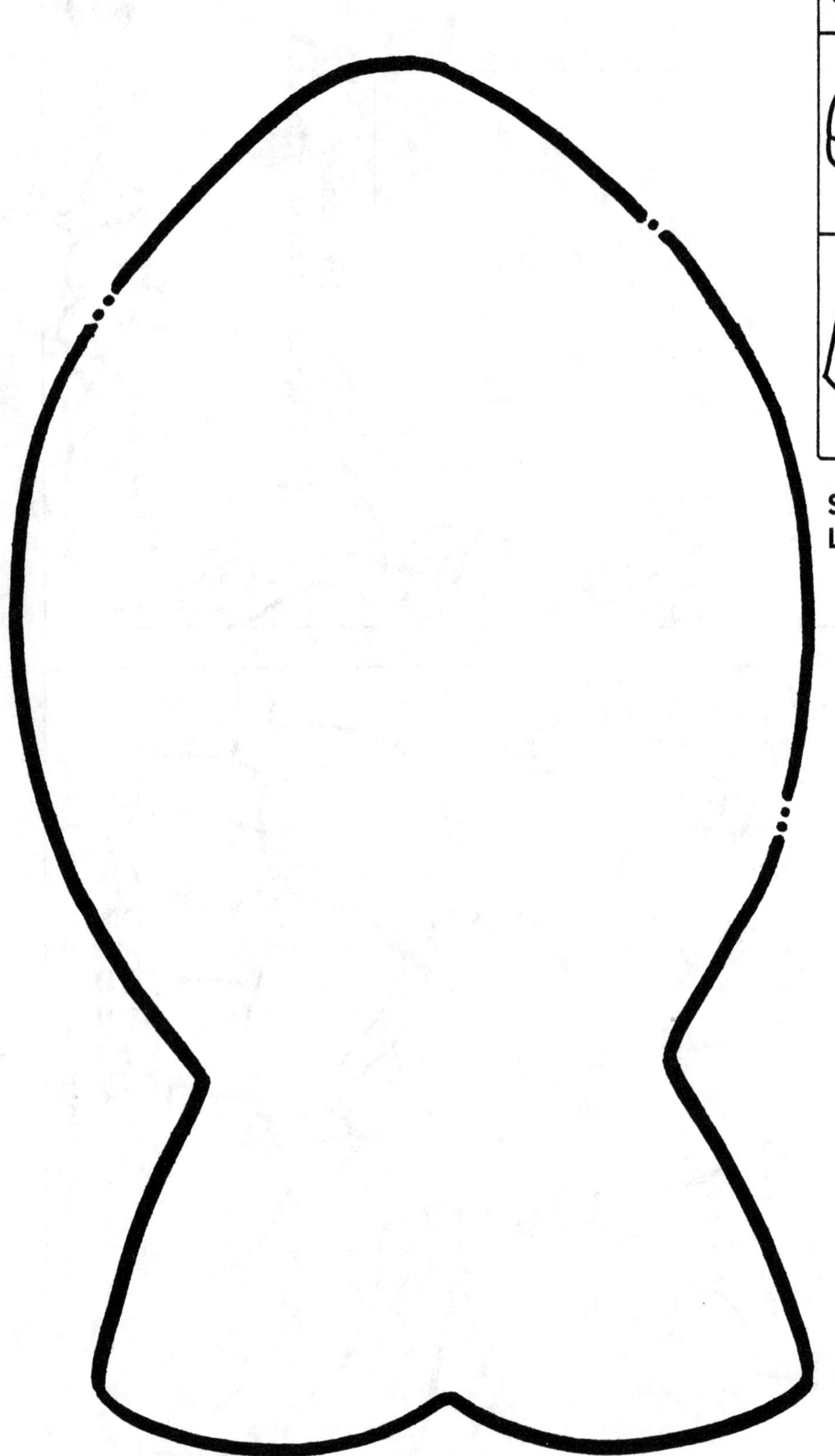

Stickers for "Hosanna Tube," Lesson 8

Directions for Stickers:

1. Mix two parts white glue and one part vinegar.
2. Add a few drops of peppermint extract if desired.
3. Lightly "paint" mixture onto backs of uncut stickers. Let dry.
4. Allow children to color (or print these on colored stock).
5. Cut stickers apart and let children lick and stick.

My friend, Jesus

Spring, Unit 2—Lesson 7 Visual

Directions:

1. Copy, color, and cut out one figure of Jesus.
2. Copy and cut out a boy figure for each boy and a girl figure for each girl.
3. Attach copies of feet to figures with paper fasteners.

Spring, Unit 2—Lesson 7 Art Center

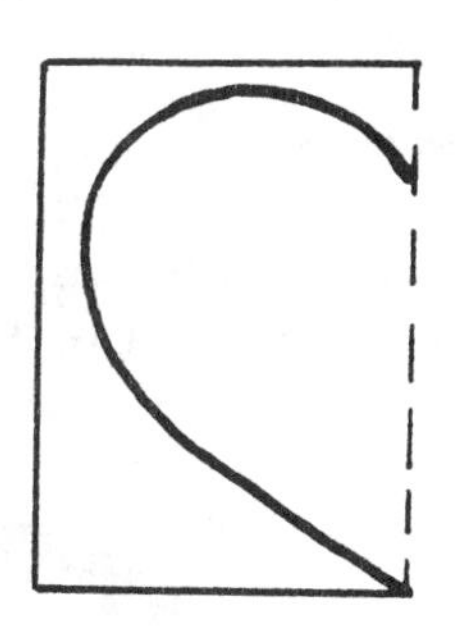

Directions:

1. Make one copy of page for each child.
2. Cut hearts from 9" x 12" sheets of construction paper, folded in half. (See sketch.)
3. Allow children to color pictures in class.
4. Cut out pictures and glue to hearts.

We love him.

1 John 4:19

Spring, Unit 2—Lesson 8 Game Center

Directions:

1. Copy donkey onto gray construction paper.
2. Copy donkey tails onto brightly colored paper, one tail per child. Enlarge patterns, if possible.

Spring, Unit 2—Lesson 8

Directions:
1. Copy palm branch onto green construction paper.
2. Cut on heavy lines.
3. Reinforce backs with strips of heavy cardboard (optional).

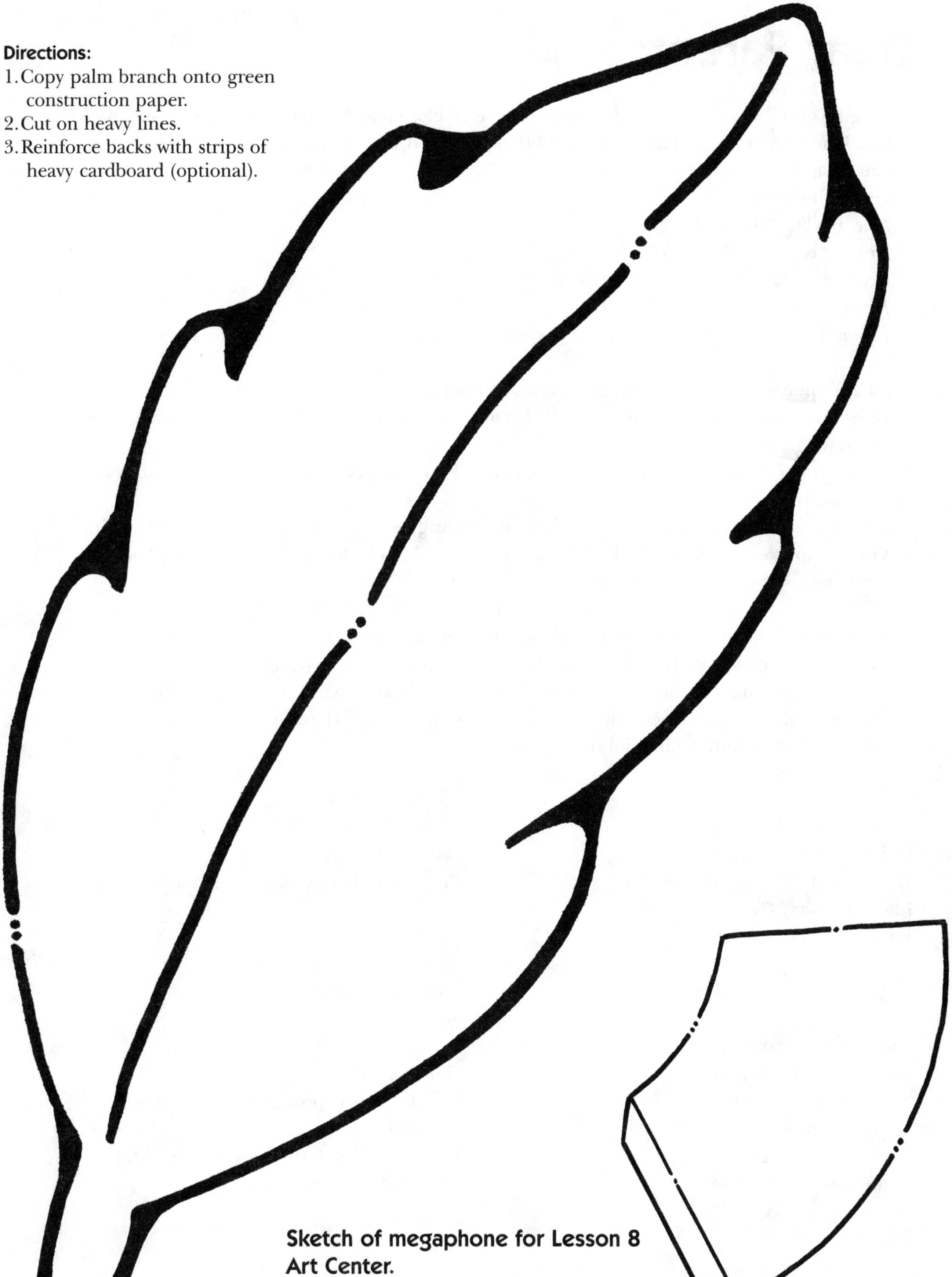

Sketch of megaphone for Lesson 8 Art Center.
1. Cut each megaphone from 9" x 12" sheet of construction paper.
2. Roll and hold together with clear tape.

Dear Parent:

During this unit, your child will learn that Jesus is so close that He hears us when we sing and talk to Him. Your child will learn about Bible people who sang and talked to Jesus. He or she will feel happy because Jesus is alive, and will sing and talk to Him because He is alive. These are our Bible stories:

Jesus Is Alive! (John 18—21)
Nicodemus Talks to Jesus (John 3:1-21)
Children Come to Jesus (Mark 10:13-16)
People Praise Jesus (Mark 11:1-10)
I Know Jesus Is Close to Me (review of previous lessons)

Here are some ways to reinforce these lessons at home:

- Point out times your child can sing and talk to Jesus (morning, night, when we are together, when we are alone).
- Tell your child why you are happy to sing and talk to Jesus. Say, "I'm happy to talk to Jesus because He loves me."
- Play "I know something I can tell Jesus." Take turns guessing what the other one is thinking.
- Pray this prayer with your child, "We love You, Jesus. We like to talk to You. Thank You for listening to us when we talk to You."
- Before bedtime, ask your child what he or she can tell Jesus about the day.
- Show your child a picture of Jesus and have him or her talk to Jesus.
- Remind your child that Jesus loves children. Children are very important to Jesus.
- Remind your child that because Jesus is alive, He can hear us when we sing and talk to Him.
- Say the Bible words with your child every day: "We love him," (1 John 4:19).
- Sing these songs with your child during the unit:

(Tune: "Mulberry Bush")
I'm very special to Jesus.
He hears me when I talk* to Him.
I talk* to Him; He hears my words.
I'm very special to Jesus
*sing

(Tune: "Row, Row, Row Your Boat")
Talk*, talk, talk to Jesus.
______ talks to Jesus.
Happily, happily, happily, happily,
______ talks to Jesus.
(*run, walk, skip, pray)

(Tune: "Farmer in the Dell")
Jesus is alive. Jesus is alive.
I'm so very happy that Jesus is alive.

Chant: We love Him. We love Him.
He's alive, and we love Him!

(Tune: "London Bridge")
We* are happy Jesus lives, Jesus lives,
Jesus lives.
We* are happy Jesus lives. We* love Jesus.
*Use child's name.

Your child's teacher,

Unit 3: We Can Be Jesus' Helpers

Lessons 10–13

By the end of the unit, the children will

Know ways to help others.
Feel able to help others.
Help others willingly.

Unit Bible Words:
"We . . . are helpers" (2 Corinthians 1:24, *KJV*).

Books
from Standard Publishing
All About Hands (24-03591)
Busy Feet (24-03592)
Look, I'm Growing Up (24-04233)

This Unit at a Glance

10 The Samaritan Man Is a Helper — **Luke 10:30-37**
A Samaritan helps a man who has been beaten and left to die.

11 Timothy Is a Helper — **2 Timothy 1:5; 3:15**
Timothy helps at home because he loves God.

12 Peter Is Jesus' Helper — **Acts 3**
Peter sees a man in need and stops to help in a way the man could never have dreamed possible.

13 I Know I Can Be Jesus' Helper — **Review of Lessons 10–12**

Why Teach This Unit to Young Children?

Jesus told a story about a Jew who needed help and two Jewish leaders just passed by. A Samaritan, a man from a race hated by the Jews, saw the man and immediately stopped and did all he could to help the man.

Timothy was raised by his mother and grandmother to love and obey God. Because of the kind of young man he became, we can safely assume that he was taught at a young age to be helpful to others.

When a lame man asked Peter for money, Peter gave the man far more than he ever expected—healing! Peter did this in the name of Jesus.

These stories will help the young child understand how and why they need to help others. Young children love to please. Up until now, they have been living in a very self-centered world of their own, but now they are learning that other people also have feelings and needs. Through these lessons, your children will start to see how they can be helpers in the world about them. They will discover the good feelings they can get from helping others, and understand that when they help others they are also helping Jesus.

The Bible words should be used over and over in conversation, in Bible stories, at the learning centers, and in prayers. **Timothy was a helper and "We are helpers." . . . The Bible tells us "We are helpers."**

Have a Bible available in a learning center, at the giving table, or wherever the children will see it. Also have it on your lap or at your side as you tell the Bible story. Have the Bible words highlighted or underlined so the children can see them, point to them, and "read" them.

Things to Do for This Unit

- Photocopy Parents' Letter (page 237) and Unit Planning Sheet (pages 319 and 320).
- Copy the Learning Center Cards (pages 225-230); cut apart on solid lines; glue side 1 on cardboard and side 2 on back of cardboard. Laminate for durability (optional).
- Gather/prepare materials listed on Learning Center Cards.
- Copy and prepare teaching pictures (pages 231, 233, and 235).
- For Lesson 10, obtain a first-aid kit and adhesive bandages.
- For Lesson 11, have a supply of cleaning materials.
- For Lesson 12 obtain a cane, crutches, and/or a wheelchair.
- For Lesson 13, magazine pictures of people helping others.

Use These Songs and Action Rhymes During Unit 3

It's Time to Put the Toys Away

(Tune: "Mary Had a Little Lamb")

It's time to put the toys away, toys away, toys away.
It's time to put the toys away,
so we know where to find them.

I Love Jesus

(Tune: "Jesus Loves Me")

"I love Jesus," I can say; I will love Him ev'ry day!
While I work, and while I play,
I will love Him ev'ry day!
* Use "help" in place of "love."

I will use my helping hands. *(Repeat.)*
Pick up toys and share with friends.
I'll be Jesus' helper.

I will use my helping eyes. *(Repeat.)*
Look for things to do to help.
I'll be Jesus' helper.

I Want to Help

I want to help in every way!
With ears, and eyes, and mouth, *(Point to each.)*
With feet, *(Bend down and touch feet.)*
And hands. *(Clap hands.)*
I want to help today. —*Dorothy Fay Richards*

Listening Rhyme

First our feet go tap-tap-tap, *(Tap feet on floor.)*
Then our hands go clap-clap-clap. *(Clap hands.)*
We look with both our eyes,
(Make glasses by circling fingers around eyes.)
We hear with both our ears,
(Cup hands behind ears.)
And then our hands fall in our laps.
(Fold hands in lap.) —*Dorothy Fay Richards*

Let's Be Very Quiet

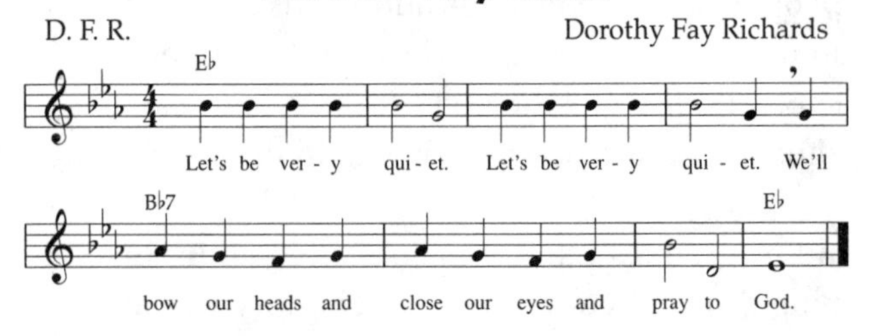

It's Time to Worship

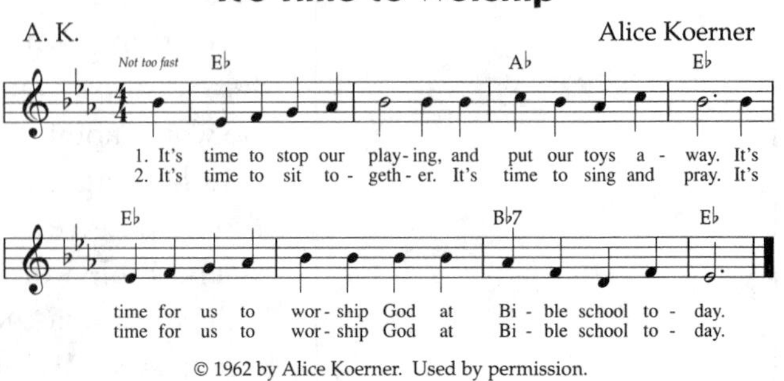

doll, wrap it in a blanket, and hug it to make it feel better, as the children suggest.

Bring an older willing child up beside you. **Let's pretend that Maria fell down and got hurt. How could we help her? . . . Getting an adult to help her is a good idea. When you help someone you are doing what our Bible words say, "We are helpers." All of you are getting big enough to help others. And Jesus is pleased when we help others.**

Learning Activities

(20 minutes)

Let's Play Awhile

Have the children stand and do the action rhyme, "I Want to Help." Then send the children to the Family Living Center. If you have a large class use the other centers as well. If everyone has completed the art, don't offer it again.

Let's Go Home

Let Zach sing "It's Time to Put the Toys Away." If some children are reluctant to pick up, give simple instructions such as, **Joshua, be a helper and put these two blocks in the box. . . . Mallory, you can help by putting the bandages on the counter. What good helpers we have!**

As soon as most of the toys are picked up and there is one child with nothing to do, start this activity. Divide the children in two groups. Line the groups up for a relay. Talk about how the children can help their teammates as they play. Set up two chairs, one for each team, at the other end of the room. Two children run to the chairs, sit down, run back, then the next children go. Let the game continue until every child has been picked up by a parent. There is no winner to this game—it's just for fun and for practice in helping others!

Make sure the children take home their parent letters and the pictures they made in the Art Center.

The Good Helper

Luke 10:30-37

Bible Words: "We . . . are helpers" (2 Corinthians 1:24, *KJV*).

Lesson Value: Jesus chose twelve men to be His helpers. Jesus himself helped people—sick people, blind, lame, and emotionally hurt people. And He wants us to help others too. Jesus told a story about a man who had been beaten, robbed, and left to die. Two men—Jewish leaders, well known and respected—saw him but preferred not to get involved. A Samaritan—a race despised by the Jews—saw him and immediately helped him. Children enjoy helping. Knowing that Jesus also wants them to be helpers will encourage them to begin now to make helping others a lifetime habit.

Know: Know ways to help others.
Feel: Feel able to help others.
Do: Help others willingly.

Children will accomplish the goals when they:

1. Say the Bible words, "We are helpers."
2. Sing about helping.
3. Help someone in the classroom.
4. Tell how the person in the Bible story helped.
5. Name or point to ways to help.

Let's Get Ready

For the Bible story, you will need the classroom Bible, the picture from page 231, puppet Zach, a first-aid kit or a box of adhesive bandages, a doll, and a blanket.

Prepare the Art Center, the Block Center, and the Game Center. If you are the only teacher, use just the Art Center now. Have materials ready in the Family Living Center to use after the Bible story.

Learning Activities

(30 minutes, including 10 minutes presession)

Let's Get Started

Use Zach to greet each child. "Jazmine, you can be a helper and put your money in the offering." Help the child with the usual routine, then offer her a choice of two activities. **Jazmine, would you like to color a picture or do some building?** This allows Jazmine to make a choice and either choice will be acceptable to you. Then gently lead her to the chosen area, if necessary, and make sure she enters into the activity with the others.

Worship and Bible Story

(15 minutes)

Let's Worship God

Use Zach to sing "It's Time to Worship." By now, the children probably know that this song signals a change in the program. As soon as the toys are picked up and the first child comes to the worship/story area, start singing "Jesus Loves Me." Then sing "I Love Jesus." Use "Let's Be Very Quiet" to introduce prayer time. Then say, **Now we are ready to tell God, "We love You. Help us to be good helpers."** Then pray those same words. The children will soon learn to say them along with you. Open the classroom Bible and say, **The Bible tells us "We are helpers." Can you say our Bible words with me?** If you have sufficient time, allow each child to hold the Bible and "read" the words with your help.

Let's Learn From the Bible

Introduction: Have Zach come in carrying a first-aid kit or bandage box. **Where are you going with that first-aid kit, Zach?** Have Zach point to a doll or stuffed animal that is ripped or looks hurt. **Oh, Zach is on his way to help a friend who is hurt. Today our Bible story is about a hurt man and the person who helped him. Let's listen very quietly and find out what happened.** Put Zach and his equipment behind you and set the Bible on your lap or beside you.

The Bible Story: A man was walking along a road one day *(Have children pat their legs to make stepping sounds.)*, when suddenly some bad men jumped out of the bushes and hurt him. The bad men ran away and left the hurt man on the road. The man moaned. His head hurt. *(Children moan and rub their heads.)*

(Children pat legs.) What did the man hear? Someone was coming. Maybe the man would stop and help him. *(Stop patting.)* The person went right on by. He didn't stop to help.

(Children pat legs again.) Oh, more steps. Someone was coming again. Maybe this person would stop. *(Stop patting.)* No, the person walked right past the hurt man. He moaned again. *(Children moan; then pat their legs.)*

Someone else was coming. Would this person stop? *(Stop patting.)* The hurt man looked up. This man had stopped! The kind man bent down and gently wrapped up the hurt man's wounds. Then very carefully he put him on his own donkey and took him to a house where people would take care of him until he got well.

Let's Apply the Story

Pick up the "hurt" doll. **This doll is hurt. What could we do for her?** Be prepared to put an adhesive bandage on the

Let's Apply the Lesson

Bring out your bag of helping supplies. Let one child at a time reach into the bag and pull out an item. **Josie, tell me what you pulled out of the bag. How could you help with a broom? Who might you be helping?** Use the items more than once and let each child have a turn. **When you help your parents you are helping the way Timothy probably helped his mother and grandmother. All of you are big enough to be helpers. And Jesus is happy when we help others! Let's say our Bible words together, "We are helpers."** If you have time, allow each child to hold the Bible and "read" the words.

Learning Activities

(20 minutes)

Let's Play Awhile

Have the children do the rhyme, "I Want to Help." Let the children go to the various centers, if your class is large and you have enough teachers. Make sure each child has a turn in the Family Living Center since that activity involves food.

Let's Go Home

Have Zach lead the children in the song, "It's Time to Put the Toys Away." Make up your own tune (just up and down the first five notes of the scale will do) and sing, "Susie is a helper and so is Cameron." As soon as most of the toys are picked up, gather the children in a circle and sing the following words to the "Mulberry Bush" tune:

This is the way we sweep the floor, sweep the floor, sweep the floor.
This is the way we sweep the floor, so early in the morning.

Also sing, "dust the furniture, set the table, wash the windows, pick up toys, go to bed." Change the ending to fit the action—"late in the evening," etc.

If you did not use the helping picture from page 234, let the children take copies home to color.

Timothy Is a Helper

2 Timothy 1:5; 3:15

Bible Words: "We . . . are helpers" (2 Corinthians 1:24, *KJV*).

Lesson Value: We don't know many details of Timothy's life as a child, other than the fact that his mother and grandmother loved the Scriptures and taught them to Timothy "from infancy." In that kind of setting we can only suppose that they also taught him to be good, kind, loving, and to be a helper. Timothy, as a young child, probably helped with simple chores. This story of a child from the Bible who helped his parents is a good example for young children and one to which they can relate.

Know: Know ways to help others.
Feel: Feel able to help others.
Do: Help others willingly.

Children will accomplish the goals when they:

1. Say the Bible words, "We are helpers."
2. Sing about helping.
3. Name/point to the helper in the teaching picture.
4. Help someone in the classroom.
5. Name/point to ways they can help others.

Let's Get Ready

For the Bible Story, you will need the classroom Bible, puppet Zach, a copy of page 233, and a bag of helping supplies such as a dust cloth, a small broom, a plate and plastic glass.

Prepare the Art Center, the Game Center, and Book/Picture Center. If you are the only teacher, use just the Book/Picture Center. Have materials ready in the Family Living Center to be used after the Bible story.

Learning Activities

(30 minutes, including 10 minutes presession)

Let's Get Started

Have Zach greet each child by name. As the children come in tell them Zach is your helper today and that they can be helpers too. **Rachel, you are a helper when you hang up your jacket. The Bible tells us about a boy named Timothy. He was a helper. Would you like to make a picture of Timothy or look at books now?** When Rachel decides, direct her to the learning center of her choice and make sure she becomes involved in the activity.

Worship and Bible Story

(15 minutes)

Let's Worship God

Have Zach lead the children in the song, "It's Time to Worship." As children are picking up the toys, say something like, **Jeremy is a good helper. He picked up the books and put them away.** This will encourage the children to help as well as give them a concrete example of helping others. Begin singing as soon as children start coming to the circle. Sing "I Love Jesus" and "I Am Jesus' Special Friend" (page 162). Do the "Listening Rhyme," if children are a bit restless. Hold up your Bible and open it to the Bible words. **We just sang two songs about our friend Jesus. Jesus wants us to be helpers. In our Bible it says, "We are helpers." Let's say our Bible words together. Now we are ready to pray, "Thank You, God, for loving us. Please help us to be good helpers."** Pray in those same words, pausing to allow children to say the words with you.

Let's Learn From the Bible

Introduction: Have Zach hiding behind you with your Bible. **Zach, can you bring me the Bible? Thank you, Zach, for bringing our Bible to me. Zach is a good helper, isn't he. Today our story is about a young boy who was a helper in his home. You can be a helper right now by listening to the story and watching very carefully so you will know what actions to do with me.** Put Zach behind you and the Bible on your lap.

The Bible Story: The Bible tells us about a boy named Timothy. When Timothy was a small boy, maybe about your age, he probably liked to help his mother and grandmother. Perhaps sometimes Timothy would help his mother sweep the floor. *(Let the children stand up and pretend to sweep the floor.)*

Timothy liked to hear his grandmother read the big Bible-scroll. She might have said, "Timothy, please bring me the Bible-scroll so I can read you a Bible story." Timothy probably hurried to get the scroll. Then his grandmother would read the Bible-scroll to him as he sat very quietly and listened. *(Hold hands together as a book and pretend to read.)*

Sometimes Timothy's mother needed sticks to build her fire so she could cook. Perhaps she would say, "Timothy, please bring me some sticks for a fire. Thank you, Timothy, for being such a good helper!" *(Let children pretend to pick up sticks.)*

Timothy was a good helper. He was always ready to do what his mother and grandmother needed him to do. He liked being a helper! *(Show the picture from page 233 and let children name/point to the helper in the picture.)*

Let's Apply the Lesson

Show the children the cane or crutches and demonstrate how a person uses them. If it is possible, let the children practice using them also. **What do you think it would be like to use this as the only way to get around? Would it be easy or hard? Could you run fast using crutches? It would not be fun not to be able to walk or run or jump. How can you help someone in a wheelchair? . . . How can you help someone on crutches? . . . You have suggested good ways to help. You are all big enough to help. Let's say our Bible words, "We are helpers." Jesus is pleased when we help others.**

Learning Activities

(20 minutes)

Let's Play Awhile

Do the action rhyme, "I Want to Help." The children may want to do it a couple of times. Take the children to the Game Center and help them get started.

Let's Go Home

Have Zach sing "It's Time to Put the Toys Away." Encourage the children to be helpers by singing the song from last week, "Tommy is a helper and so is Alicia." As soon as there is one child without something to do, sing the following song with actions to the tune of "London Bridge":

Jesus' helpers set the table, set the table, set the table.
Jesus' helpers set the table. We are Jesus' helpers.

Let the children think of things they do at home to help and sing about these. Continue until parents have picked up all the children.

Make sure each child has his happy/sad puppet to take home. If you did not use the helping picture from page 236 in class, let the children take copies to color at home.

Peter Is Jesus' Helper

Acts 3

Bible Words: "We . . . are helpers" (2 Corinthians 1:24, *KJV*).

Lesson Value: In Jesus' day, begging was very common because there was no welfare, and no jobs for people who were handicapped. One day, as Peter and John went to worship in the temple, a lame man asked them for money. Peter didn't have money, but he gave the man something he would never have thought to ask for—the ability to walk. No amount of money could have done that for the lame man! Peter helped the lame man in the name of Jesus. Your children will learn that they too can help Jesus by helping others. Helping others at this young age gives children a great deal of satisfaction and joy. And knowing that Jesus is pleased when they help others is a concept that can last the rest of their lives!

Know: Know ways to help others.
Feel: Feel able to help others.
Do: Help others willingly.

Children will accomplish the goals when they:

1. Say the Bible words, "We are helpers."
2. Sing about helping others.
3. Name/point to the helper in the teaching picture.
4. Name/point to ways to help others.
5. Help someone in the classroom.

Let's Get Ready

For the Bible story, you will need the classroom Bible, the teaching picture from page 235, puppet Zach, a happy/sad face puppet from the Art Center, and crutches, a cane, and/or a wheelchair.

Prepare the Art Center, the Block Center, and the Book/Picture Center. If you are the only teacher, use just the Block Center. Have materials ready for the Game Center to be used after the Bible story.

Learning Activities

(30 minutes, including 10 minutes presession)

Let's Get Started

As Zach greets the children today, look for ways they are helping and comment on how each is a helper. After the child has put in his offering and put his sticker on the attendance chart, guide him to a learning activity that he will enjoy doing.

Worship and Bible Story

(15 minutes)

Let's Worship God

Have Zach sing "It's Time to Worship." After the children have picked up most of the toys, and a few children are ready, sing "I Am Jesus' Special Friend" and "I Love Jesus." Open your Bible and say, **Jesus is our special friend and He wants us to help others. In the Bible it says, "We are helpers." Let's say our Bible words together.** Then pray, **Thank You, Jesus, for being our friend. We want to please You by helping others.** Do the "Listening Rhyme" before beginning the Bible story.

Let's Learn From the Bible

Introduction: Have Zach help someone bring in the cane, crutches, or wheelchair. If your Zach puppet can sit, let him ride in the wheelchair. If you teach alone, have a cane where you can reach it but where it is not obvious. **Have any of you seen someone using one of these?** Hold up or point to the object. **A person uses this when he can't walk or if he has trouble walking. Our Bible story today is about a man who couldn't walk. This poor man didn't have a wheelchair to help him get around. All he could do was sit at the door of the temple-church and beg for money.**

Put Zach and the cane, etc., away and have your Bible on your lap or at your side. Have the happy/sad puppet ready to hold up at the appropriate time. If your children have all made puppets, allow them to use these as you tell the story. Explain that the children are to smile when they see the happy face, and look sad when they see the sad face.

The Bible Story: One day Peter and John were going to the big temple-church to pray to God. As they were walking through the gate, a man who couldn't walk was sitting in the way. *(Show sad-face. Children look sad.)* This man sat here every day asking people for money to buy food.

When the man held out his hand and asked Peter and John for money, Peter said, "I don't have any money *(sad face)*; but I do have something I can give you." *(Happy face.)*

Peter said to the man, "In the name of Jesus, get up and walk!" Then Peter reached down his helping hand and took the man's hand. As Peter helped the man up, the man's legs and feet were made strong and he stood up! The man began to walk. *(Show the teaching picture.)* The man began to jump! And then the man praised God! *(Show happy face. Have children smile. Let children stand up, walk in place, jump up and down, and say, "Praise God!")* Peter helped the lame man because Peter loved God and wanted to help. Peter was Jesus' helper.

someone else we are also helping Jesus, and that makes Him very happy. Do you remember our Bible words? Let's say them together, "We are helpers."**

Learning Activities

(20 minutes)

Let's Play Awhile

Have the children stand up and do the action rhyme, "I Want to Help." They may enjoy doing this several times. Then go to the Family Living Center. If you have a large class you will probably want to have all of the learning centers again. If everyone has already made the art activity, don't offer it now.

Let's Go Home

Have Zach lead the children in singing "It's Time to Put the Toys Away." Remember to sing the helper song, "Jason is a helper and so is Amy." Children like to hear their names and be recognized, especially when they are helping. Make sure you include each child as you see him or her help even in a very small way.

As soon as most of the toys are picked up, start the following activity. Have each child pull a chair to the middle of the room, making a long line of chairs. This will be your traveling train. As the children are helping to do this comment on how they are such good helpers to work together and accomplish this big job. Talk about where they want their pretend train to go. Help the children make the "choo-choo" and "chug-chug" sounds for their train. As the children play, point out ways that they are helping, even when they help to make a loud noise! Continue to play until the last child has been picked up by a parent.

I Know I Can Be Jesus' Helper

Review of Lessons 10–12

Bible Words: "We . . . are helpers" (2 Corinthians 1:24, *KJV*).

Lesson Value: The Samaritan who helped the Jew who hated Samaritans, Timothy who learned from his mother and grandmother and helped them, and Peter who helped a lame man demonstrate to us the importance of helping others in need. Have you ever noticed the gleam in a young child's eyes as she discovers she has done something to please you or to help you? This is the instant gratification that Jesus wants each of us to feel when we help someone. These three Bible stories help the child to realize that Jesus does want all of us to help others and that by helping them we are pleasing Jesus.

Know: Know ways to help others.
Feel: Feel able to help others.
Do: Help others willingly.

Children will accomplish the goals when they:

1. Say the Bible words, "We are helpers."
2. Sing about helping others.
3. Name/point to ways to help others.
4. Help someone in the classroom.
5. Name/point to Bible people who were helpers.

Let's Get Ready

For the Bible story, you will need the classroom Bible, puppet Zach, a small bucket of pebbles, pictures from Lessons 10–12 and the modern-day helping pictures, mounted pictures of people helping others (from magazines, etc.), and any of the previous props you want to use to help the children remember the stories.

Prepare the Art Center, Block Center, and the Book/Picture Center. If you are the only teacher, use just the Art Center now. Have materials ready for the Family Living Center to use after the Bible story.

Learning Activities

(30 minutes, including 10 minutes presession)

Let's Get Started

As the children come in and hang up their coats, have Zach greet them. Zach can comment on how the child is helping by hanging up his coat all by himself. Help the child to put in his offering and attach his sticker on the attendance chart. Let Zach help the child to pick out a learning center.

Worship and Bible Story

(15 minutes)

Let's Worship God

Have Zach sing "It's Time to Worship." After the children have picked up most of the toys and a few children are ready, start singing "I Love Jesus." Then sing "I Am Jesus' Special Friend." Use "Let's Be Very Quiet" and then pray, **Thank You, God, that Jesus is our special friend. Help us to help others.** Then open the classroom Bible and say, **We are Jesus' friends when we help others. The Bible says, "We are helpers." Can you say our Bible words with me?**

Let's Learn From the Bible

Introduction: Have Zach come in carrying a small bucket of pebbles. **Look, Zach has been helping his neighbor pick up rocks in his yard. That is being a good helper, Zach!** Ask the children, **Do you remember our Bible stories about three helpers? I need you to help me remember these Bible stories.** Put Zach and the bucket of pebbles behind you. Hold the Bible pictures on your lap. Put the modern-day helping pictures on the floor or table in front of you.

The Bible-story Review: Some bad men hurt another man and left him. Two men walked right on by the hurt man. But then a kind man stopped and helped the hurt man. He took the hurt man to some people who could look after the hurt man until he was well. *(Show the teaching picture; have children identify picture of hurt child.)*

The next helper was Timothy, who was just a little boy who knew he could help. He probably helped his mother around the house. He helped his grandmother by getting things for her that she needed. Sometimes he got the Bible-scroll so she could read to him. *(Show picture of Timothy; have children identify picture of child helping at home.)*

The third helper was Peter. He saw a man who was begging for money. The man could not walk. Peter didn't have any money, but he knew God could help the man. Peter said, "In the name of Jesus, get up!" The man got up and he walked and he jumped and he praised God! *(Show picture of man; have children identify picture of child helping at church.)*

Let's Apply the Lesson

Show a mounted helping picture to the children. Ask questions such as, **How is the person in this picture helping? What is this person doing to help? Have you ever helped to set the table? How is this person helping? What have you done to help your mother? father? brother? sister? You all know how to help. That is wonderful, because when we help**

Art Center

Unit 3—We Can Be Jesus' Helpers

Items to Include:

Lesson 10
Copies of page 232
Crayons
Small adhesive bandages

Lesson 11
Copies of page 233
Broom sticker from page 229
Crayons

Purpose: The child will better understand how to be a helper.

Things to Do and Say

Lesson 10

Make copies of page 232. As the children color their pages, ask questions about the picture, such as, **What is this little boy doing? What do you think has happened to him? What does he need? Have you ever fallen and hurt your knee like that? What did you do? Did someone make you feel better? Have you ever helped someone who was hurt?**

When the children have finished coloring, ask, **How can you help this little boy? . . . Yes, Michael, you could put a bandage on his hurt knee. That is a good idea.** Give each child a bandage to put on the picture of the child. Let him put the bandage wherever he wishes. **A kind man in our Bible story took time to help a hurt man. He was a good helper. You can be a helper too. Our Bible words say, "We are helpers." That's what the words on your paper say.** Point to the words, then have the children say them with you.

Lesson 11

Make copies of page 233 and the broom from page 229. Follow the directions on page 229 to make stickers. Let the children color the stickers first, then cut them out while the children color their pictures.

This is Timothy, the boy in our Bible story. He looks like he needs a broom. Let's put the broom in his hands. Give one child at a time a broom and help her lick and

Block Center

Unit 3—We Can Be Jesus' Helpers

Items to Include:

Lesson 10
Large cardboard blocks
Small baby blankets
Small dolls

Purpose: The child will help others in the classroom.

Things to Do and Say

Lesson 10

Suggest that the children build the outline of a house with several rooms. Use a block for a bed and put a blanket on the "bed" and lay a doll on it. **Our Bible story is about a hurt man who needed someone to help him. A kind man stopped to help him. I think this baby is sick. Would could you do to help take care of her?** Help the children think of ways to help, such as, getting things for Mommy to use for the baby, giving an older person a drink of water, bringing flowers to a sick person, and so forth. Help them realize that they are big enough to help.

Older children could build a hospital. Some children may not know what you would find in a hospital. Others will at least know that hospitals have doctors, nurses, beds, ambulances and patients. Help the children think of these things and create their own "hospital." (Be sensitive to a child who may be afraid of hospitals, doctors, etc.) Point out ways various children help others. Be specific in your praise. **Jonathan, you helped Matthew build that wall. You are a helper. Our Bible words are, "We are helpers." You are all big enough to help. And Jesus is happy when we help others.**

Art Center, continued

Lesson 12
Paper plates
Stapler
Crayons
Colored tape

Lesson 13
Construction paper
Felt marker
Crayons
Dust cloths
Glue sticks

stick it in place. **What is he doing to help his mother? . . . Yes, he's sweeping the floor. What can you do to help your mother?** Offer suggestions if children can't come up with some. **These are our Bible words. Let's read them together. "We are helpers."**

Lesson 12

To make Happy/Sad faces, put two paper plates together facing each other. Staple around the edges, leaving a space for a hand to slip inside. Cover the staples with colored tape. Have the plates ready ahead of time. Draw a happy face on one side and a sad one on the other side for a sample.

Help the children draw the faces on their plates, and then let them color the faces. Draw the faces on plates for 2's and let them just color the faces. Show the children how to slip their hands inside the plates.

Our Bible story is about someone who was sad. Have children hold up their sad faces. **Peter helped the person and made him happy.** (Happy faces.) **What do you look like when you are sad?** (Sad faces.) **What do you look like when you are happy?** (Happy faces.) **When you help someone what does he look like? Sad or happy?** (Happy faces.) **How does he feel?** (Happy faces.)

Lesson 13

Draw around each child's hand or copy the small hand from page 230 before class. Let each child color his hand, and then glue a dust cloth on the hand. Use just a small amount of glue so the child can remove the cloth and use it when he gets home. **What do you do at home to help? Have you ever dusted furniture? You can use this dust cloth to help clean house! It is fun to help at home! Our Bible words say, "We are helpers." You are big enough to help!**

Block Center, continued

Lesson 12
Blocks
Cars

Lesson 12

Build a church building with the children. As the children play, find opportunities to point out helping acts. **Kalika, thank you for handing Brett those blocks. You were a helper! The Bible says, "We are helpers." Jesus is pleased when we help others.**

In our Bible story, Peter helped a man who could not walk. The man was very sad. Peter made him glad. What do you suppose Peter did for the man? I'll tell you in a few minutes. Peter was a good helper! . . . You are getting big enough to help in our classroom. I like the way you pick up the toys when it is time to go home. Hanging up your coats is another way to help. How else can you help in our classroom?

Lesson 13

Repeat either of the activities suggested above. Young children enjoy repetition and learn from it! Encourage them to think of ways to help at home and at church.

Family Living Center

Unit 3—We Can Be Jesus' Helpers

Items to Include:

Lesson 10
Housekeeping supplies
Dolls and blankets
Doctor and/or nurse kits
Ace bandages
Men's shirts

Lesson 11
Sugar cookies
Frosting
Sprinkles
Raisins
Chocolate chips
Plastic knives

Purpose: The child will feel able to help others.

Things to Do and Say

Lesson 10

Add the medical equipment to your family living area. The children will enjoy dressing up in the shirts to be doctors and nurses, wrapping each other with the ace bandages, and taking care of sick "children." Make sure the children take turns playing the various roles. Encourage them to help each other when dressing up, bandaging another child, and working together.

Thank you, Maria, for helping Mallory put on the doctor shirt. You are a good helper. . . . When doctors and nurses work with sick or hurt people, they are helping them to get well. In our Bible story, a kind man stopped to help a hurt man. The kind man was a good helper. Our Bible words say, "We are helpers." You are getting big enough to be good helpers!

Lesson 11

Show the children how to frost their cookies with the plastic knives. Then let them decorate the cookies with sprinkles and other decorations. Make sure you know any allergies your children may have before you start this project! As the children work, suggest ways to help as well as point out those who are helping. Be specific so children will know what they did to help.

Game Center

Unit 3—We Can Be Jesus' Helpers

Items to Include:

Lesson 10
Large ball

Purpose: The child will name ways he can help.

Things to Do and Say

Lesson 10

Have the children sit down in a circle with their legs spread out in front of them. Say a child's name and roll the ball to him. When the child catches the ball have him say, "We are helpers." Have 2's roll the ball back to you and start all over. Older children can say another child's name and roll the ball to that child. Remind the children that we want to let everybody have a turn. After the children have had turns to say the Bible words, when they get the ball have them tell ways they can help at home.

Lesson 11

Have the children stand in a circle. Using the tune to "Row, Row, Row Your Boat," sing these words:

Timothy helped at home. Timothy helped at home.
He was growing up. Timothy helped at home.

Let the children think of ways Timothy might have helped and act these out as they sing the first line. For example, "Timothy swept the floor; picked up toys; made his bed," and so forth.

Family Living Center, continued

Jordan, please pass the raisins to Stephen. You are a good helper. . . . Jeff, you can help Sean by handing him this napkin. . . . Taylor, have you ever helped your mom bake cookies at home? What do you do to help her? Jesus wants us to help others. Our Bible words are, "We are helpers."

Lesson 13
Sponges
Dust cloths
Spray bottles
Small brooms

Lesson 13

Provide damp sponges, dust cloths, and spray bottles of water for the older children. All young children enjoy cleaning. They will clean the same chair over and over. If you use the spray bottles, be prepared to dry up the classroom afterwards. Make sure the children understand that they are to use just a little water at a time.

I need some good helpers to help me clean our classroom. Point out jobs to be done. **When we clean our room we are taking care of the things we have. We are also helping the janitor who cleans our room for us every week. When we help others we are making Jesus feel happy. We are doing what our Bible words tell us—"We are helpers"!**

Game Center, continued

Then sing these words. Let children suggest ways they can help and then pretend to do them.

I can help at home. I can help at home.
I am growing up. I can help at home.

You thought of lots of good ways to help! You are big enough to do these things.

Lesson 12
Tape player
Tape of children's music
Beanbag

Lesson 12

Have the children sit on the floor in a circle. Turn on the taped music, preferably music without words so the children are not confused with what they are to do. Hand a beanbag to the child next to you and show how to pass the beanbag around the circle. After the children catch on tell them, **When I stop the music, the person holding the beanbag will hold it while he tells a way he can help someone.** Make sure each child gets an opportunity to do this.

If the children have never played a game like this it may be hard for them to pass the beanbag and also hard to hold on to it when the music stops. Encourage these actions by saying, **Keep the beanbag moving. Don't let it stop. Hand the beanbag to Thomas. Sarah, the music has stopped. Hold on to the beanbag and tell us one way you can help.**

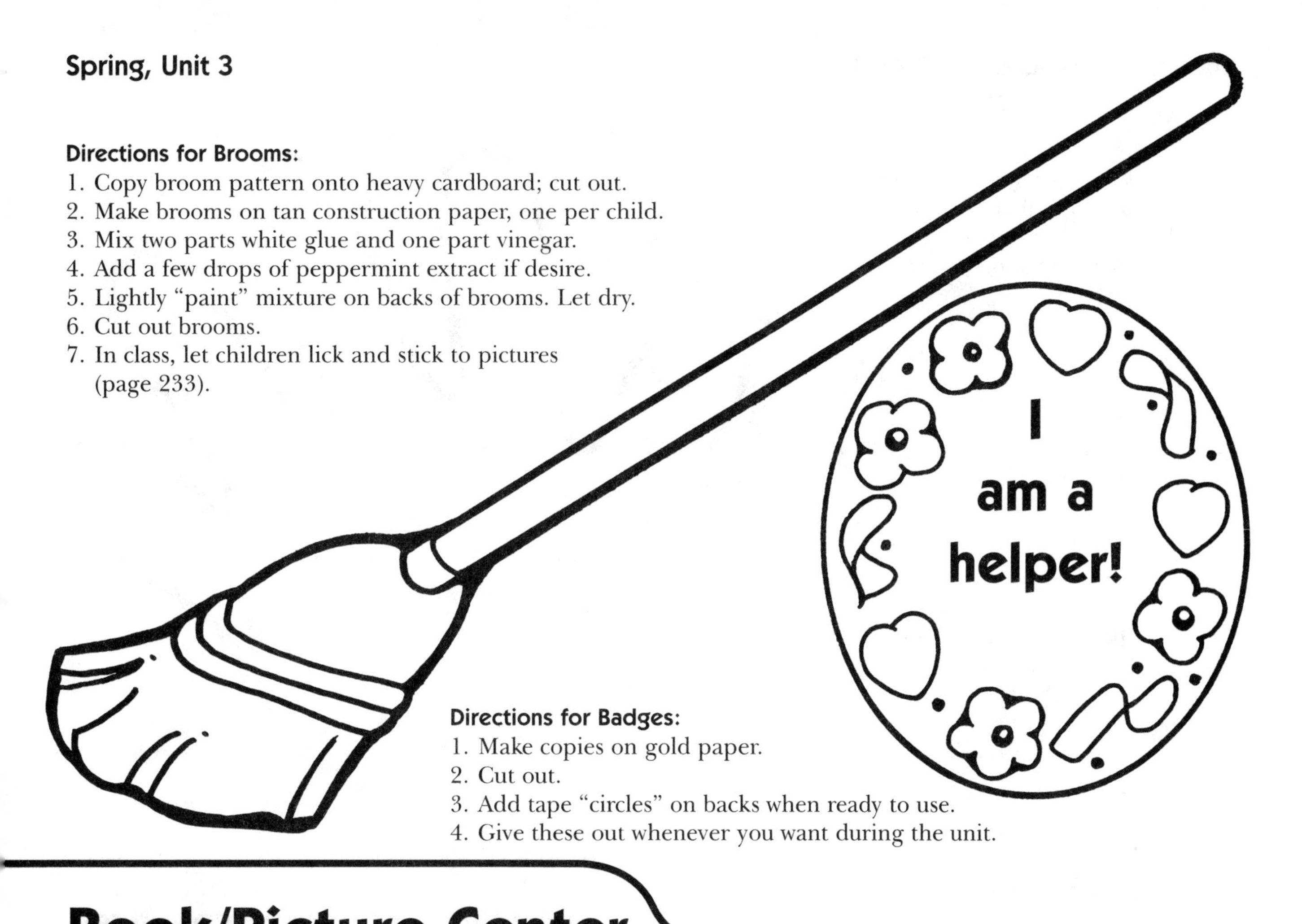

Directions for Brooms:

1. Copy broom pattern onto heavy cardboard; cut out.
2. Make brooms on tan construction paper, one per child.
3. Mix two parts white glue and one part vinegar.
4. Add a few drops of peppermint extract if desire.
5. Lightly "paint" mixture on backs of brooms. Let dry.
6. Cut out brooms.
7. In class, let children lick and stick to pictures (page 233).

Directions for Badges:

1. Make copies on gold paper.
2. Cut out.
3. Add tape "circles" on backs when ready to use.
4. Give these out whenever you want during the unit.

Book/Picture Center

Unit 3—We Can Be Jesus' Helpers

Items to Include:

Lesson 11
Books (See list on page 215.)
Pictures of children helping at home
Copies of page 234

Lesson 12
Books
Pictures of children helping at church

Purpose: The children will name or point to ways to help.

Things to Do and Say

Lesson 11

Make a puzzle of the picture on page 234. To make a puzzle, use two copies of the picture. Use one copy for the puzzle base. Color and glue the other copy onto cardboard before cutting it into four or five large puzzle pieces.

If you do not have suitable books to read to the children, use books that have pictures of children in situations in which they could help. Talk about what the child could do in this situation. Encourage the children to suggest ways to help. Do the same with pictures.

As a child works the puzzle, ask her, **What is this child doing? Have you ever helped that way? What else do you do for your mom?** If a child refuses to answer, ask her to point to the helper in the picture. **Yes, that girl is a helper. You can be a helper by making sure that the puzzle pieces are all in place when you put the puzzle back.**

Lesson 12

Make puzzles of the picture on page 236. See Lesson 11 directions. Direct your conversation toward helping at church or in the classroom. Encourage the children to make suggestions for helping. Also point out ways they are helping as they look at the books and work the puzzle. Suggest ways to help when it is time to put away the books

Directions:
1. Use this handprint if you need to prepare papers ahead of time.
2. Make copies on construction paper.
3. Add Bible words at bottom of page.

Book/Picture Center, continued

Copies of page 236

and pictures and the puzzle. Commend children for being helpers. Be genuine about this. Even young children can see through hypocrisy!

Lesson 13

Use the books, pictures, and puzzles as you did in Lessons 11 and 12. This is a good time to review and reinforce the things you talked about during the unit.

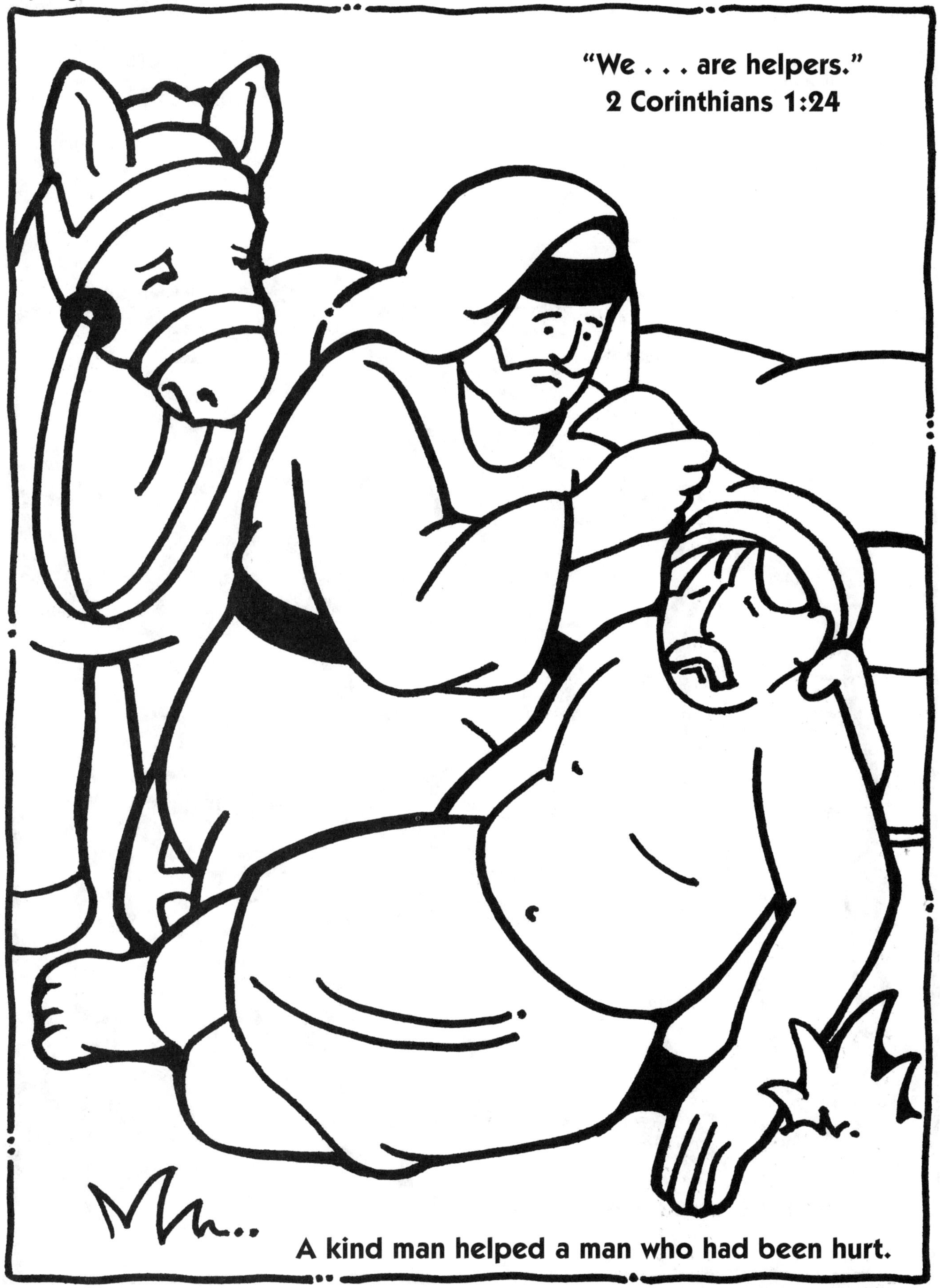
"We . . . are helpers."
2 Corinthians 1:24
A kind man helped a man who had been hurt.

"We . . . are helpers."
2 Corinthians 1:24
I can help someone who is hurt.

"We . . . are helpers."
2 Corinthians 1:24
Timothy was a good helper.

I can help at home.

"We . . . are helpers."
2 Corinthians 1:24

The lame man praised God when Peter helped him to walk!

I can help at church.

"We . . . are helpers."

2 Corinthians 1:24

Dear Parent:

This unit your child will be learning that Jesus wants us to be helpers and that helping others makes Jesus happy. Through songs, action rhymes, varied learning activities, and the Bible stories your child will be encouraged to help others. The lesson titles and Scriptures are:
The Samaritan Man Is a Helper (Luke 10:30-37)
Timothy Is a Helper (2 Timothy 1:5; 3:15)
Peter Is Jesus' Helper (Acts 3)
I Know I Can Be Jesus' Helper (review of previous lessons)

Our Bible words are, "We . . . are helpers," from 2 Corinthians 1:24 *(KJV)*. Young children learn best by repetition. It is good if you get your Bible out at home and read the Bible words to him. This way he learns the Bible is a special book to you and that the words he learned in class are important to you too. Jesus wants us all to be helpers, and He is pleased when we help.

At some time during the month plan to do something special for an elderly person, a relative, or a neighbor. Perhaps you and your child could bake cookies, or take some fresh fruit to the person, or visit the person and take a bouquet of flowers. Your child could also scribble-color a picture for that person. As you work together on your project, talk about how both of you are helping that person by doing something special. You are making the person happy with your gift and your time, and you will receive a blessing in return.

Here are other ways to reinforce what your child is learning:

- Look for ways your child can help at home—dusting furniture, picking up toys and clothing, folding laundry, putting away silverware, setting the table, and so forth.
- Point out when he is helping you at home. Give sincere, specific praise for your child's efforts.
- Sing "Head and Shoulders," ending with the Bible words, "We are helpers."
- Do this action rhyme with your child this month.

I Want to Help

I want to help in every way!
With ears, and eyes, and mouth, *(Point to each.)*
With feet, *(Bend down and touch feet.)*
And hands. *(Clap hands.)*
I want to help today.

—Dorothy Fay Richards

Have a great month enjoying your little helper!

Your child's teacher,

Summer Quarter

Learning to Know How We Grow in God's Family

These young children are growing! They are growing taller, wiser, mastering new skills, developing a concept of "me," learning to be independent. They are becoming big enough to do the things that bigger people do, and that's important to 2's and 3's. Being big enough to do new things motivates a child to learn!

This quarter's lessons are planned to help 2's and 3's see that they are "big enough" to help, to share, and to show love for God. Unit One, "We Can Learn to Help," is based on lessons about Bible people who helped others—Joseph, Miriam, Ruth, and Samuel. Young children love to help and need to be encouraged to channel that enthusiasm into constructive helping acts. The learning activities will offer many opportunities to do this.

Unit Two, We Can Learn to Share," introduces the concept of sharing with others. This is a difficult one for young children, who are naturally self-centered. Along with the Biblical examples of those who shared, provide plenty of opportunities for children to share without being pressured. When the children see that a simple act of sharing the crayons with a neighbor gets your attention and approval, they will begin to understand that their sharing pleases you and that God is pleased also. Be patient! Teach this difficult concept in very small steps. It will be a beginning that others will build upon as the children grow.

"We Can Learn to Love God," Unit Three, concerns our response to God's love—worship. These children are big enough to know that they can listen to God's Word, that they can talk to God, and sing to Him, all elements of worship. Josiah, Daniel, and Hezekiah will be the Biblical examples. Your example will be the present-day lesson! Make sure you take time for frequent spontaneous worship throughout the lesson—a song, a short prayer of thanks, saying the Bible words—whenever there is an appropriate moment. This will often mean more to a young child than a planned worship time does.

As a result of these lessons, the children will

KNOW

Know that they are big enough to help, to share, and to love God (listen to His Word, talk and sing to Him).

FEEL

Feel willing to help others, to share, and to show love for God

DO

Help others, share with others, and show love for God in specific ways.

Note to those who teach alone: Prepare the learning center suggested in each lesson, but also have one or two others ready to use when the children tire of the first one.

Use these songs and action rhymes throughout the quarter, in addition to those specifically mentioned in the units.

The Marching Song

I'm So Happy Today

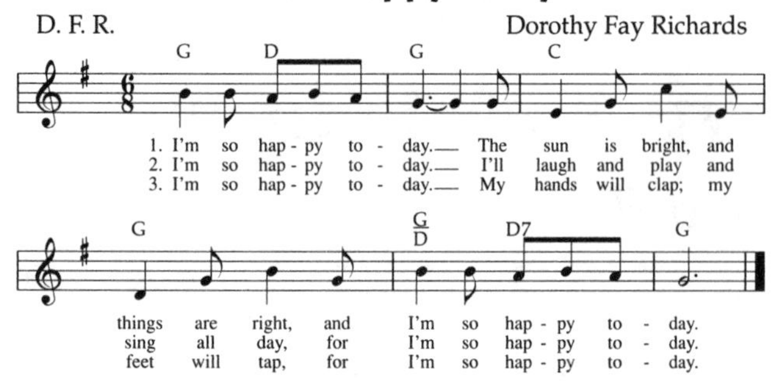

The Growing Song

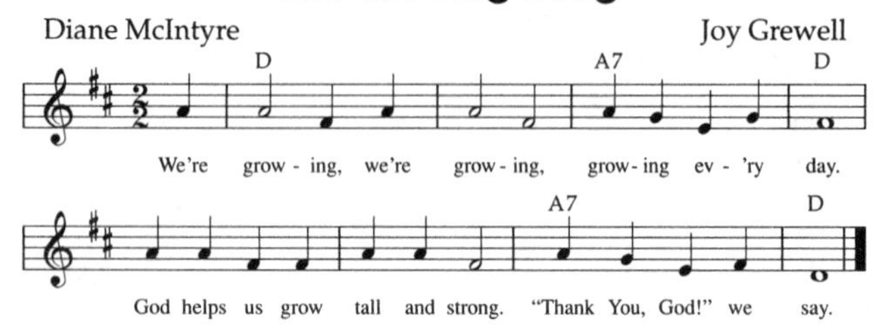

Birds and Bugs

God teaches a bird to fly high, high, high.
(Stretch arms overhead; swoop them up and down.)
God teaches a bug to go slow, slow, slow.
(Squat with hands on ankles and take one step for each word "slow.")

—Dorothy Fay Richards

Sharing

This is my book; I'll open it wide,
To show you the pictures that are inside.

This is my ball, so big and round.
We can toss it in the air or roll it on the ground.

This is my umbrella; it can keep us both dry
When raindrops fall from the cloudy sky.
(Do motions the words suggest.)

—Adapted

Summer Party Suggestions

June—Father's Day Party

Purpose: To help children show Dad he's special!
When: During class time
Preparation: Cut out tie shapes with knots from construction paper, 5" at widest part. Punch holes on each side of "knots" and string yarn through so dads can wear their ties. Let the children decorate ties with crayons or seals.
Food: Decorated cupcakes and water
Story: Joseph's love for Jesus—what he would have done for Jesus as He grew. Thank God for each father.

July—Ice Cream Party

Purpose: A time for parents, teachers, and children to interact
When: Sunday afternoon
Activity: Making sundaes!
Craft: Make ice cream cones. Cut circles from a variety of colored paper and long triangles from light brown paper for cones. Let children glue the ice cream circles to the cones and decorate with glitter or colored sugar.
Food: Ice cream, toppings, sprinkles, plastic bowls, etc.
Devotion: God gives us good food. Let children thank God for food.

August—Sprinkler Party

Purpose: Fun!
When: Saturday or Sunday afternoon
Activity: Sprinkler fun
Preparation: Have one or two parents bring sprinklers and garden hoses to the churchyard or a home and let the children run through the sprinklers.
Food: Ice cream sandwiches or popsicles
Devotions: A "water" story—Jesus helps the disciples catch fish.

Unit 1: We Can Learn to Help

Lessons 1–5

By the end of the unit, the children will

Know that God is helping them grow big enough to help.
Feel big enough and willing to help.
Help in specific ways (at home, with friends, at church).

Unit Bible Words

"I will . . . help"(2 Samuel 10:11, *KJV*).

Resources

from Standard Publishing
All About Hands (24-03591)
Busy Feet (24-03592)
Families (24-03584)
I'm Glad I'm Me (24-04209)
Jesus Grew (24-03115)
Little Lamb (24-03120)
Look, I'm Growing Up (24-04233)
Moses in the Bulrushes (24-03707)
My Family and Friends (24-03114)
Sharing Makes Me Happy (24-04214)
Where Are We Going Today? (24-03116)
Happy Face Seals (22-01255)

This Unit at a Glance

1 We Are Growing — Genesis 37:2, 3, 14
When Joseph grew big enough, his father sent him to find his brothers who were caring for the sheep .

2 We Can Help at Home — Exodus 2:1-10
Miriam helped her parents by watching baby Moses in the river. She helped the princess by getting her mother to be the baby's nurse.

3 We Can Help Our Friends — Ruth 1, 2
Ruth traveled to Bethlehem with Naomi, and picked grain so she and her friend would have food.

4 We Can Help at Church — 1 Samuel 1:24-28; 2:11, 18, 19; 3:15
Hannah took her son Samuel to help Eli in the tent-church.

5 We Are Big Enough to Help — Review of Lessons 1–4

Why Teach This Unit to Young Children?

People are a wonderful creation of God. Help the children in your class be thankful to God for their eyes, ears, noses, mouths, hands, and feet. Three's are more aware of growing and being big enough to help than two's are. You will be helping your class learn that children in the Bible grew up just like they are growing. As these Bible children grew they were given jobs to do at home, for friends, and at church (actually, the tabernacle).

There are important ways children can help as they grow bigger. Plan your room so that children will feel successful in the jobs they do. Use simple and specific words when you give them jobs to do. Through you, the teacher, they will know that God is pleased when they obey His Word and help. Place a Bible in every learning center for the children to hold and use. Use the Bible words often in conversation and song. Encourage the children to say them with you. Use bookmarks and highlighted words to attract attention.

Things to Do for This Unit

- Photocopy the "Growing Joseph" (page 259) onto the back of each Parents' Letter (page 266). Copy the Unit Planning Sheet (pages 319 and 320).
- Photocopy the Learning Center Cards (pages 253-258); cut pages on solid lines. To make each card, glue side 1 to cardboard and side 2 on opposite side of cardboard; laminate for durability (optional).
- Gather/prepare materials listed on Learning Center Cards.
- Obtain a growth chart or make one using shelf paper. Mark off feet and inches and hang on wall in an accessible place. Add pictures of children to decorate (optional).
- Make visual for Lesson 1 from page 259.
- Gather visuals listed at beginning of each lesson under "Let's Get Started."

Use These Songs and Action Rhymes During Unit 1

We Are Helping

(Tune: "Are You Sleeping?")

We are helping, we are helping,
Putting toys away, putting toys away.
(Sing names of six children.)
Are helping today, helping today.

I Love You, God

(Tune: "This Old Man")

I love You. I love You.
I love You, God. I love You.
I can read my Bible, sing, and talk to You.
I love You, God. I love You.

We Are Growing Big Enough

(Tune: "Oh, Be Careful")

We are growing big enough to help. (I will help!)
We are growing big enough to help. (I will help!)
We are growing big enough. We are growing big enough.
We are growing big enough to help. (I will help!)

I Will Help

(Tune: "Row, Row, Row Your Boat")

I will help at home.* I will help at home.
I am big enough to help. I will help at home.
*For Lesson 3, "my friends"; Lesson 4, "at church."

A Helper I Will Be

(Tune: "Farmer in the Dell")

A helper I will be, a helper I will be.
There's work to do, there's work to do,
In my family.*
*For Lesson 4, "I'll help happily."

I love to help my mom. I love to help my dad.
I love to help; it makes God glad.
A helper I will be.

The Busy Fingers

Busy little finger people, *(Wiggle all fingers.)*
Who will (or "helped to") put the toys away?
(Look at hands.)
"I will" (or "did"), "I will," "I will," "I will," "I will,"
(Raise fingers one at a time.)
All the fingers say (or "said"). *—Louise M. Oglevee*

I Want to Help

I want to help in every way!
With ears, and eyes, and mouth, *(Point to each.)*
With feet, *(Bend down and touch feet.)*
And hands, *(Clap hands.)*
I want to help today. *—Dorothy Fay Richards*

Let's Apply the Lesson

Have the children squat as you show Joseph's head. **Could baby Joseph go away from home to find his brothers?** (No.) Now have children sit on their knees as you show the middle of the picture. **Could little boy Joseph go away from home to find his brothers?** (No.) **Could the grown-up Joseph go away from home to find his brothers?** (Yes.) Children stand as you show the open picture.

Have Zach help you use a tape measure to measure a baby doll. **Let's find someone who has red on to measure.** As you name a new color, have Zach sniff the child's clothes and help you measure the child. Help each child mention a way he or she helped at clean-up time. **You are growing to be helpers just like Joseph did.** Zach growls and barks at you. **Oh, yes, Zach, you are growing to be a helper too. I see that all your toys are put in their box.**

Learning Activities

(20 minutes)

Let's Play Awhile

Have the children pretend to be sheep as you lead them around the room looking for cool water and grass. Have God's Wonders Center ready. Lead the children to the measuring chart mounted on the wall. If you have a large class with multiple teachers, use the centers you had earlier as well.

Let's Go Home

Sing "Small, Tall!" and the first stanza of the "Review Song" from the Music/Game Center card as children are waiting for their parents.

Each child should take home a Parents' Letter with "Growing Joseph" on the back, along with his sack coat. Remind the children to be good helpers at home.

We Are Growing

Genesis 37:2, 3, 14

Bible Words: "I will . . . help" (2 Samuel 10:11, *KJV*).

Lesson Value: Joseph was growing, and as he grew his father gave him jobs he was able to do. What expectations do you have of the young children in your class? They can be wonderful helpers! Allow and expect them to help in their classroom. Plan and direct the children so they can be independent and successful. They will understand how good Joseph felt when he completed his jobs. They will feel good when they do their jobs.

Know: Know that God helps me grow big enough to help.
Feel: Feel big enough and willing to help.
Do: Help in specific ways.

Children will accomplish the goals when they:

1. Say the Bible words, "I will help."
2. Sing about growing and helping.
3. Tell Joseph's name and how he helped.
4. Do specific jobs in the classroom.
5. Pray, "Thank You, God, that we are growing big enough to help."

Let's Get Ready

For the Bible story, you will need the Bible with Bible words highlighted and a bookmark in place, puppet Zach, bell, small toy box with dog toys, tape measure, doll, and the "Growing Joseph" visual (colored and folded) from page 259, used as a bookmark for the Bible story.

Prepare the Art Center, the Family Living Center, and the Book/Puzzle Center. If you are the only teacher, use just the Family Living Center now. Have materials ready for the God's Wonders Centers to use after the Bible story.

Learning Activities

(30 minutes, including 10 minutes presession)

Let's Get Started

Zach will greet each child as he stands beside the growth chart. "My, you are growing tall, Eric! You might need a new coat like Joseph's since you're growing so big. Your hand is bigger than my paw." Have Zach measure his paw with a child's hand. Help children with offering and attendance stickers. Direct each child to one of the centers. Try to keep groups evenly divided.

Worship and Bible Story

(15 minutes)

Let's Worship God

Have Zach choose a helper to ring his bell at each center. "Gru-uff, gru-uff. Almost time to pick up." In three minutes start singing "We Are Helping." As children finish their jobs, sing "I Love You, God" to call them to the story area. Then sing "The Growing Song" from page 240. **Now we are ready to pray, "Thank You, God for helping us to grow big enough to help."** Pray aloud in those same words. Have children stand up and sing "We Are Growing Big Enough," clapping on "I will help!" Explain that those words are from the Bible. Have a child find the bookmark and open to the words. Repeat the Bible words together.

Let's Learn From the Bible

Introduction: Have Zach work hard to put his bone and toys into a box. **My, you surely are working hard, Zach!** Zach shakes his head and continues working. **Last year you were not able to pick up that big bone or reach over the side of the box.** Have Zach stretch up tall to show how much he has grown. **Zach, you remind me of someone in the Bible who was growing up and could help his family more and more. Boys and girls, I want you to help me. This is a story from God's Word. Every time you hear me say, "Sheep," I want you to "Baa-a-a" two times. Let's practice. Joseph's father had many sheep.** (Baa-a-a, baa-a-a.) **Joseph's brothers took care of the sheep.** (Baa-a-a, baa-a-a.) **You are good "Baa-a-a-ers"! Now be good listeners to our story from God's Word.**

The Bible Story: *(Open the Bible on your lap to "Growing Joseph.")* Joseph was a little boy whose father loved him very much. *(Show Joseph's head.)* Joseph probably liked to go outside and watch his brothers take care of the sheep. *(Wait for children to baa-a-a.)*

When Joseph was older, his father gave him a beautiful coat with many colors. *(Unfold to show middle section of picture.)* Joseph was big enough to help his brothers watch the sheep. *(Baa-a-a.)* He probably wore his new coat when he went out to watch the sheep. *(Baa-a-a.)*

Joseph continued growing and helping his father. By the time Joseph was a young man, he had grown tall and could help even more. *(Unfold last section.)* His father said, "Joseph, you are big enough to help in a special way. Your brothers have been gone a long time trying to find green grass for our sheep. *(Baa-a-a.)* I want you to go and see if your brothers and the sheep *(baa-a-a)* are all right. Then come back and tell me."

God had helped Joseph grow big enough to help. I think the sheep *(baa-a-a)* grew fat on the green grass too!

Let's Apply the Story

Have the doll and baby items ready for children to show you how they would help with a baby. **We can only hold babies when Mommy and Daddy help us. How did Miriam help at home?** Show a "Moses" book if you have one. **Let's pretend to make a basket-boat and lay a baby in it. Now let's tiptoe along the river and peek through the tall grasses. Sh-h-h! Be very quiet. Now let's run to get the "mother" to take care of the baby for the princess.**

Review the Bible words. Then do this rhyme:

Here is baby Moses, *(Hold up thumb.)*
Sleeping in his bed. *(Cover thumb with fingers.)*
Here is sister Mir-ri-am, *(Lift up pointer finger.)*
Peeking up her head. *(Bend finger and peek up.)*
Here comes the princess, walking by the Nile.
(Walk two fingers on arm.)
Miriam brought her mother. *(Bring two pointer fingers together.)*
Now everybody smile! *(Point to smile.)*

Learning Activities

(20 minutes)

Let's Play Awhile

Sing "A Helper I Will Be" as you march around. Then stop and pray, **Thank You, God, that we can be helpers like Miriam.** Have the Book/Puzzle Center prepared. Use the activities from earlier in the session if you need more to do.

Let's Go Home

Have Zach sing "We Are Helping," then suggest simple jobs to individual children. Make sure everyone has an opportunity to place a sticker on the chart. Do the first stanza of the "Review Song" and add stanza 2 as parents arrive.

Send the Parents' Letter with new children. Remind the children to be good helpers at home.

We Can Help at Home

Exodus 2:1-10

Bible Words: "I will . . . help" (2 Samuel 10:11, *KJV*).

Lesson Value: This lesson about Miriam's helpfulness to her family will help your children learn that God's Word teaches them to help. It will also give you opportunities to talk about ways the children can help their parents. The children need to know that they are old enough to begin to assume some responsibility at home. This concept is an important one for young children to learn. Helping is fun at this age and should be encouraged. Continue to offer opportunities in the classroom to practice helping. Use repetition in conversation and examples to direct and encourage the children to help in their homes.

Know: Know that God helps me grow big enough to help.
Feel: Feel big enough and willing to help.
Do: Help in specific ways at home.

Children will accomplish the goals when they:

1. Say the Bible words, "I will help."
2. Sing about growing and helping.
3. Tell Miriam's name and how she helped.
4. Pray, "Thank You, God, that we are growing big enough to help."
5. Do specific jobs in the classroom.

Let's Get Ready

For the Bible story, you will need the Bible with bookmark; Zach puppet with bell, box dog house, duster, little broom; cattails or papyrus type grass; sample from the Art Center; doll, blanket, basket, spoon, bottle, and bib.

Prepare the Art Center, Family Living Center, and the Block Center. If you are the only teacher, use just the Family Living Center now. Prepare materials for the Book/Puzzle Center to be used after the Bible story.

Learning Activities

(30 minutes, including 10 minutes presession)

Let's Get Started

Display cattails/grass and use Zach to greet the children, "Gr-rass, gr-rass. Miriam picked grass for a basket. Feel the gr-rass." Continue to refer to the Growth Chart. Direct each child to a center by offering her a choice between two activities, either of which is acceptable to you.

Worship and Bible Story

(15 minutes)

Let's Worship God

Choose a helper to ring Zach's bell at each center then have the child choose a sticker to place by his hands on the "I Will Help" chart (Lesson 1). Sing "We Are Helping" to signal clean-up time. As children complete tasks, let them choose stickers for the chart. Call children to the worship/story area with "I Love You, God" and "The Growing Song." Have children stand and do the rhyme, "I Want to Help." **Who would like to help say a prayer to God?** Commend any effort. **As we grow up we pray to God.** Pray, **Thank You, God, that we are growing big enough to help.** Sing "I Will Help" (at home).

Let's Learn From the Bible

Introduction: Zach is furiously sweeping and dusting his dog house. **Zach, you are certainly a good helper at home!** Zach barks his agreement and whispers in your ear. **You know a good helper in the Bible!** Zach nods his head; whispers again. **Her name is Miriam!** Zach nods in agreement and whispers. **She had a baby brother!** Zach nods even more excitedly, and whispers. **Now the boys and girls can help by listening to God's Word.** Put Zach down. Place the open Bible on your lap. Have the papyrus grass behind you.

The Bible Story: Miriam loved to watch her baby brother. When Moses was born, he had a tiny cry. *(Ask for a helper to cry like a tiny baby.)* As He grew, his cry became louder and he made funny baby sounds. *(Ask several children to give examples.)* Miriam watched as her parents tried to hide Moses, so the soldiers of the mean king would not hear him and take him away.

Miriam watched as her mother made a basket-boat. Miriam was big enough to help bring the papyrus grass. Perhaps Miriam asked, "Mother, may I help take care of baby Moses?"

"Yes," her mother answered, "I am going to hide baby Moses in this basket-boat and float it in the river. I want you to stay and watch it very carefully."

Miriam peeked through the tall grass so she could see baby Moses. *(Hold grass in front of your face. Have children peek through their fingers.)* She watched carefully. Just then Miriam saw the princess coming. Miriam watched as the princess found baby Moses, picked him up, and gave him a soft kiss. *(Pretend to kiss "lollipop Moses"; have children cup hands and pretend to kiss baby Moses.)*

Miriam asked the princess, "Do you want someone to take care of this baby?"

The princess said, "Yes," and Miriam ran to get her mother.

The princess said to Miriam's mother, "Please take care of this baby until he grows up." Miriam was happy she had helped her mother take care of baby Moses!

Let's Apply the Lesson

Have two children help teachers pass out croutons. **M-m-m, these are good. Who made bread? Who was the friend who picked the grain? What did Boaz do? What did Naomi say to God? And who were the friends who passed out croutons?** Choose a friend big enough to find the Bible words bookmark. Say the Bible words together. Sing, "We Are Growing Big Enough." **Did anyone hear our Bible words in that song?** Have all the helpers put stickers on the "I Will Help" chart. Talk about ways friends have helped in class today.

Learning Activities

(20 minutes)

Let's Play Awhile

Use this activity in the Music/Game Center. To begin the song/game, choose a friend to walk around the circle with you.

With each stanza, add appropriate motions as you continue going around in a circle. Sing to the tune of "Mulberry Bush." Have a short prayer at the end of the last stanza.

This is the way we walk with friends, . . . early in the morning.
This is the way we pick up grain, . . . early in the morning.
This is the way we bake our bread, . . . early in the morning.
This is the way we pray to God, . . . early every morning.

Let's Go Home

Zach will sing, "We Are Helping" ("fr-r-riends" in place of "we") to signal clean-up time. Make sure everyone has a new sticker on the "I Will Help" chart. Sing all three stanzas of the "Review Song" from the Music/Game Center.

As a child leaves, tell her, **Thank you for helping your friends.** Name a specific job if you can remember. **Remember to tell your family who the friend helper was in our Bible story.**

We Can Help Our Friends

Ruth 1, 2

Bible Words: "I will . . . help" (2 Samuel 10:11, *KJV*).

Lesson Value: Many of your children are moving from parallel play to cooperative play. They are more aware of those around them and are beginning to have special "friends." They already know that you, the teacher, are a friend. And as you teach about Ruth they will hear that God helps us to be friends and expects us to help each other. Make sure that they have many opportunities to help each other and offer honest praise for specific acts of helpfulness.

Know: Know that God helps me grow big enough to help.
Feel: Feel big enough and willing to help.
Do: Help in specific ways with friends

Children will accomplish the goals when they:

1. Say the Bible words, "I will help."
2. Sing about growing and helping.
3. Tell Ruth's name and how she helped.
4. Pray, "Thank You, God, that we are growing big enough to help."
5. Do specific jobs in the classroom.

Let's Get Ready

For the Bible story, you will need the Bible with bookmark; puppet Zach with bell, blanket, two dog treats, water bowl;

two small baskets with croutons.

Prepare the Art Center, the Family Living Center, and the God's Wonders Center. If you are the only teacher, use just the Family Living Center now. Use the Music/Game activity suggested after the Bible story.

Learning Activities

(30 minutes, including 10 minutes presession)

Let's Get Started

Zach will greet children and help with the usual routine. "Hello, fr-r-riend, let me help you with your name tag. I like to help my fr-r-riends."

Ruth and Naomi were friends in our Bible story. Ruth gathered grain for her friend. Zach repeats, "Gr-r-rain." **Let's go feel some grain or make snow-cones. Which would you prefer?**

Worship and Bible Story

(15 minutes)

Let's Worship God

Let Zach choose a "fr-r-riend" to "r-r-ring" his bell to "r-r-remind" children to finish their work. Let the "fr-r-riend" add a sticker to the "I Will Help" chart for being a friend helper. Look for other friend helpers during your class time, so all will have new stickers. Sing, "We Are Helping" to signal clean-up time. Say the rhyme, "Busy Fingers." Encourage friends to work together.

Sing, "I Love You, God" to call children to the worship/story area. Then sing "The Growing Song." **Now let's fold our hands and close our eyes and talk to God.** Pray, **Thank You, God, that we are growing big enough to help our friends.** Sing "I Will Help" (my friends), and then "Small, Tall!" to get children seated.

Let's Learn From the Bible

Introduction: Have Zach struggle to pull his blanket and water pan in front of the circle. **Tori, will you help Zach spread out his blanket? Thank you, friend. Austin, will you help Zach fill his pan?** Child pretends to pour out of empty pitcher. **Thank you, friend**. Zach gets two little dog treats. **Zach, is something special going to happen?**

Zach says, "My fu-uzzy fr-r-riend is coming. One tr-r-reat for him and one tr-r-reat for me."

Zach, you are such a good friend and almost big enough to fix your own blanket and pan. Did you see our friends feeling the grain awhile ago? Discuss experiences at centers. **Zach, lie down on your blanket. The children are going to listen to a Bible story about Ruth who helped her friend Naomi.**

The Bible Story: Naomi was so sad. She did not have a husband. She did not have any children. *(Look sad and wave good-bye.)* "Good-bye, friend Ruth. I am going back to Bethlehem." *(Have children walk hands on legs.)* Walk-walk-walk, Naomi started to go.

(Hold up hand.) "Stop, stop!" said friend Ruth. "I will go to Bethlehem with you. I love your God." *(Walk hands on legs.)* Walk-walk-walk. Walk-walk-walk. It was a long way, but Ruth stayed with her friend, Naomi.

In Bethlehem, Ruth took a big basket and went to pick up grain for bread. *(Have children stand; do bend and picking actions.)* Bend and pick, bend and pick. Friend Ruth worked hard all day.

(Sit down and pretend to drink.) Nice Boaz gave friend Ruth a drink while she was resting. Drink, drink, drink. It tasted so good! *(Lick your lips.)* "Thank you for being such a good helper-friend to Naomi," said Boaz. "Come pick grain anytime you want to." Boaz was a friend too.

(Walk hands on legs.) Walk-walk-walk. Ruth took the grain to Naomi to bake bread. Perhaps Naomi gave Ruth a big, happy hug. *(Hug yourself; then fold hands to pray.)* Naomi may have prayed, "Thank You, God, for my friend Ruth; thank You for my friend Boaz; and thank You for good bread."

Let's Apply the Lesson

Ethan, stand up and show us a job Samuel did. Yes, he pulled the curtain. Thank you for being my helper at church. . . . Molly, point to a picture and show us another job Samuel did. Thank you for being my helper at church. . . . Casey, can you point to a different picture and show us the job? Thank you for being my helper at church. If your class is large, have one child point and another do the action. Remember that every helper gets to add a new sticker to the chart. Ask if anyone would like to tell or show a job he did today in church.

Let's all be helpers and pretend to open our Bibles and read our Bible words. Some children may be ready to stand by the teacher to say the Bible words. Make sure this is a successful experience.

Learning Activities

(20 minutes)

Let's Play Awhile

Walk children around the room and pretend to do various jobs—straighten books, stack blocks, wash windows, scrub tables, vacuum rug, pick up trash and throw it away, wash hands, wrap dolls, dust chairs. Have the Art Center ready.

Let's Go Home

Sing "I Will Help" (at church) as you put your supplies away. Do "The Busy Fingers" rhyme while children finish. Sing four stanzas of the "Review Song," from the Music/Game Center as parents arrive. The children may want to take turns showing the curtain box. Each child should have a window picture and perhaps a paint hat.

As a child leaves, say, **Maria, you were a very good helper at church. God is helping you grow big enough to help. Tell your family what Samuel did. And tell them what you did too.**

We Can Help at Church

1 Samuel 1:24-28; 2:11, 18, 19; 3:15

Bible Words: "I will . . . help" (2 Samuel 10:11, *KJV*).

Lesson Value: A child's world revolves around his home and family. Last week the lesson emphasized friends. This lesson encourages children to help in the classroom. Church should be a safe, happy place where children can be successful in helping. Make pick-up a pleasant relaxed time of teaching. Samuel's mother wanted him to be a good helper at the tent-church when he grew big enough. Help your children be successful helpers at church.

Note: Do not emphasize that Hannah left Samuel permanently at the tent-church with Eli. That is a frightening idea to most children, some of whom worry that Mommy won't come back for them.

Know: Know that God helps me grow big enough to help.
Feel: Feel big enough and willing to help.
Do: Help in specific ways at church.

Children will accomplish the goals when they:

1. Say the Bible words, "I will help."
2. Sing about growing and helping.
3. Tell Samuel's name and how he helped.
4. Pray, "Thank You, God, that we are growing big enough to help."
5. Do specific jobs in the classroom.

Let's Get Ready

For the Bible story, you will need the Bible with bookmark; Zach with bell, church-shaped bank, small paint brush and bucket; and the box visual from the Block Center.

Prepare the God's Wonders Center, the Family Living Center, and the Block Center. If you are the only teacher, just use the Block Center now. The Art Center will be used after the Bible story.

Learning Activities

(30 minutes, including 10 minutes presession)

Let's Get Started

Have Zach greet children and help with your usual routine. "I'm sur-r-re glad you came to church. We need lots of helpers." **Samuel helped in his tent-church. Would you like to help clean up our room or work with the blocks?** Let each child choose which activity she wants to do first.

Worship and Bible Story

(15 minutes)

Let's Worship God

Choose a helper to ring Zach's bell as a reminder to finish activities. "You are a helper at church just like Samuel was. Choose a sticker for the 'I Will Help' chart," says Zach. Sing "We (Friends) Are Helping" to start clean-up time. Remember to watch for helpers and have them add stickers to the "I Will Help" chart.

As children finish, sing "I Love You, God," Then sing "The Growing Song"and do the rhyme, "I Want to Help." **Now, let's fold our hands and pray, "Thank You, God, that I am growing big enough to help in my church."** Pray aloud in those same words.

Let's Learn From the Bible

Introduction: Have Zach hum "Rock-a-bye Baby" as he pretends to paint the church wall or some furniture. **My, Zach, you are a happy church helper. You are big enough to reach the very top.** Zach stops to nod his head and then reaches up to paint some more. Watch Zach paint for a few minutes. Suddenly he stops, looks around, and begins to point toward you. Point to yourself. **Me? You want me to do something?** Zach looks at the children and begins nodding his head. "Tell her yes, boys and girls, tell her yes!" Zach whispers in your ear, puts his paint away, and lies down on his blanket. **Zach wants me to be a helper and tell you about Samuel.** Open the Bible on your lap. **Before we begin the story, let's all say the Bible words together.** Do so.

The Bible Story: Samuel's mother and father taught him to be a good helper. Perhaps his father said, "Samuel, help me chop the wood." *(Have everyone make chopping action.)*

Maybe Samuel's mother asked him, "Samuel, help me roll up the blankets." *(Pretend to roll up blankets.)*

When Samuel was big enough, Hannah took him to the tent-church to work and pray. Samuel was big enough to help Eli the priest. *(Choose two helpers to put the curtain box in front.)*

Samuel was Eli's good helper. Every morning he may have opened the tent-church curtain. *(Open curtain to show Eli. Have children pretend to pull curtain.)* Pull, pull.

Samuel helped Eli with other jobs in the tent-church. *(Open curtain to scroll.)* Pull, pull. Maybe Samuel carefully took the Bible-scroll and laid it out for Eli to read.

(Open to candlestick) Pull, pull. Samuel probably kept the candlesticks shiny and bright. Rub, rub; polish, polish.

(Open to table with bread.) Pull, pull. Samuel may have helped lay the fresh bread on the table. Samuel loved God and was a good helper. Every year his mother made him a new coat because Samuel was growing bigger. Eli probably said, "Samuel is a good helper in the tent-church."

Let's Apply the Lesson

Hold up the enlarged review sheet and read with the children. Go over each statement; then end with how the children can help. **Rebecca, show me how to stack blocks. Let's pretend to stack blocks with our friend. . . . John, what can you show us?** Choose children and pretend to do various jobs (wash dishes, make beds, feed pets, pick up toys).

Learning Activities

(20 minutes)

Let's Play Awhile

Sing "We Are Growing Big Enough." Then sing all stanzas of the "Review Song." Play the following game, or, if you prefer, use the one from Lesson 3.

Play this game like you do "Duck, Duck, Goose," using "Small, small, tall." Children sit in a circle. "It" walks on the outside tapping each child on the head, saying, "Small." When he says, "Tall!" the child tapped jumps up and chases "It" back to the empty spot. Clap and encourage runners.

Keep circles very small. This will work better with older children.

If your class is large and you have multiple teachers, use other activities from this unit that the children especially enjoyed.

Let's Go Home

Let Zach sing "We (friends) Are Helping"as children clean up. Have children stand by their "I Will Help" pictures. Cut apart each child's section to take home. Sing "I Will Help" as you march around the room. Sing, "Small, Tall!" with papers in the children's hands. **Can you roll up your papers like Samuel rolled up his blanket?** Young children may need help.

As children leave, have Zach place his paw on each child's head and say, "You've gr-r-rown to be a big helper like (Joseph, Miriam, Ruth, or Samuel)!"

We Are Big Enough to Help

Review of Lessons 1–4

Bible Words: "I will . . . help" (2 Samuel 10:11. *KJV*).

Lesson Value: Children learn through repetition and reinforcement. They also love repetition! This is your opportunity to review and reinforce this unit's Bible stories and see what the children are learning. Let the children repeat familiar names and words back to you. They should enjoy doing some of the routine tasks they have learned. They should be able to recognize some of the items, even if they cannot verbalize very well. God is pleased with growing children who are learning to help.

Know: Know that God helps me grow big enough to help.
Feel: Feel big enough and willing to help.
Do: Help in specific ways.

Children will accomplish the goals when they:

1. Say the Bible words, "I will help."
2. Sing about growing and helping.
3. Tell what each person did to help.
4. Pray, "Thank You, God, that we are growing big enough to help."
5. Do specific jobs in the classroom.

Let's Get Ready

For the Bible story, you will need the Bible with bookmark

and visual by each story (Growing Joseph, lollipop baby, grain basket, and curtain box); Zach with bell, bowl, toy sheep, doll, basket, church, and tape measure; and enlarged review sheet (page 262).

Prepare the Art Center, the Family Living Center, and the Book/Puzzle Center, or your favorite ones. If you are the only teacher, do the Art Center first. Use the Music/Game activity after the Bible story.

Learning Activities

(30 minutes, including 10 minutes presession)

Let's Get Started

Let Zach greet each child and help with the usual routine. "Hello. Here's a good helper, my friend Michael. Let's see how tall you are." Let the child stand in front of the Growth Chart. "You are certainly big enough to help!" **What are you going to do today? You enjoyed washing dolls. Would you like to do that again or would you rather work on our art activity first?** Direct the child to the center of his choice and make sure he becomes involved in it.

Worship and Bible Story

(15 minutes)

Let's Worship God

Let Zach choose his bell helper. Ask children at the centers if they know what it means. Continue to let children put stickers on the "I Will Help" Chart. Sing "We (Friends) Are Helping" to signal clean-up time. **Everyone look around the room to see how neat it looks. You are all good helpers!** Sing "I Love You, God" to call children to the worship/story area. **God loves you too. He helps you grow.** Sing "The Growing Song." **Let's fold our hands and close our eyes and talk to God now. Thank You, God, for helping us grow big enough to help.** Let children take turns holding the Bible and "reading" the Bible words. Then sing "Small, Tall!"

Let's Learn From the Bible

Introduction: Zach starts dragging out all his things. **Zach, do you need some help?** Zach shakes his head and pants. "I could sure use a drink of water! Gr-r-ruff, gr-r-ruff." Choose a helper to get his bowl as well as helpers to get his other items. Line them in a row. **What is all this about?** Zach whispers in your ear. **You want to help the boys and girls remember some Bible friends who grew up!** Zach nods his head. **OK, you point to your things as we talk about the stories.** Place the open Bible on your lap.

The Bible-story Review: Joseph was a boy who grew up and watched his father's . . . sheep. *(Wait for children to help answer. Zach will point to sheep.)* Joseph's father gave him a special present. Who can tell me what it was? *(Let someone find visual in Bible.)* A new coat. That's right. His father also gave him a hard job. What was it? To go look for his brothers and the sheep.

Who helped watch her baby brother? Yes, Miriam was big enough to help. What did baby Moses hide in? *(Zach points to basket.)* What did the princess find in the river? *(A helper finds visual in the Bible.)* What did Miriam do? Yes, she brought her mother to take care of the baby.

What did Ruth do for her friend Naomi? She picked up grain. Where did she put the grain? *(Zach points to basket.)* What did Naomi do with the grain? That's right, she made bread to eat. She was a good friend too.

Where did Samuel go to help? *(Zach points to the little church as children answer.)* It was a tent-church. *(Choose a helper to open each curtain and review what you find.)* Eli was the priest. Maybe Samuel brought the scroll for Eli to read; Samuel may have polished the candlestick, and brought the bread to the table. What a good helper Samuel was and what good helpers you are!

Family Living Center

Unit 1—We Can Learn to Help

Items to Include:

Bible
Child-size furniture
Dolls, blankets
Dishes
Dress-up clothes
Toy telephones
Aprons

Lesson 1
Oranges
Hand juicer
Small cups

Lesson 2
Water tubs
Bath towels
Baby towels/wash

Purpose: The child will help in specific ways.

Things to Do and Say

Lesson 1

Help children use orange-juice squeezer. Make sure each child has a turn at this. Pour juice into cups and have a taste.

Orange juice is good for our bodies. It helps us grow. Can you name other foods God gives us to help us grow? Joseph grew up and helped his father. You are getting big enough to help too.

If you have time after this, allow the children to pretend to "keep house." Talk about ways to help and point out helpful actions you see.

Lesson 2

Cover tables with bath towels. Put one inch of water in tubs. Children will wash and dry dolls and taste baby food. Make sure you have water-proof dolls. If not, give the children damp washcloths with which to wipe the dolls clean.

Kelsey, you are being a good helper to wash the doll. Conner, thank you for taking turns with the baby food. Do you remember eating baby food when you were a baby? You don't eat that any more. You are big enough to eat grown-up food. . . . The girl in our Bible story was big enough to feed her baby brother. She was a helper. You are big enough to be helpers too.

Art Center

Unit 1—We Can Learn to Help

Items to Include:

Lesson 1
Crayons
Paper sacks
Scissors (teachers)

Lesson 2
Copies of page 260
Flat lollipops
Happy-face stickers
2" fabric squares
Glue
Yarn
Self-stick name tags

Lesson 3
Ingredients for play dough:

Purpose: The child will know that God helps him grow big enough to help.

Things to Do and Say

Lesson 1

Cut up the center of each sack and across the bottom. Cut a neck hole in the bottom and arm holes in the sides to make a sack coat.

As children color, say, **Our Bible story is about a boy named Joseph who grew big enough to help. His father gave him a pretty coat with lots of colors in it. Maybe it looked something like this.** Hold up a completed coat. **God is helping you grow. You are big enough to be helpers. Let's thank God for helping you grow big enough to help.**

Lesson 2

Before class glue fabric to name tags. Have a completed page ready. Children will glue the yarn to the basket, add a happy-face sticker to the lollipop, and insert it in basket. Help each child peel off the tag backing and stick the blanket on top of the lollipop baby.

Miriam was big enough to help her mother. You are big enough to help too. God is helping you grow. How do you help at home?

Lesson 3

To make play dough, dissolve drink mix in 1 1/2 cups boiling water. Add to dry ingredients in bowl and mix well. This recipe makes enough for 6-8 children. Put small

Art Center, continued

2 1/2 cups flour
1/2 cup salt
1 Tbl. cream of tartar
2 pkgs. unsweetened drink mix
seal-top bags

Lesson 4
Copies of frame (page 261)
Waxed paper
Black paper
Liquid starch
Brushes
Multi-colored tissue paper

Lesson 5
Copies of page 262

amounts in the seal-top bags and let the children knead until smooth.

As the children use the play dough, say, **The Bible tells about Ruth who gathered grain for bread. Bread smells so good when it is baking. Smell your play dough. It smells good too. Do you think you could make loaves of bread with your dough? . . . Ruth was a good helper to her friend Naomi. You are big enough to help your friends too. God is helping you to grow.**

Lesson 4

Cut pieces of waxed paper 17 1/2" long; fold these in half. Cut black window frames from pattern on page 261. Cut tissue into 2" squares.

Place tissue paper in foil pans or paper plates; open the waxed papers and pour a tablespoon of starch in the center of each. Children will brush starch around their waxed paper and add tissue paper squares. Fold waxed papers and staple frames on top.

These pretty windows look like they could be in a church building. You are big enough to help at church. God is helping you to grow.

Lesson 5

Read each review statement and help children name the missing word. Glue one item after each answer—sheep/cotton ball, baby/2" squares of cloth, grain/crouton, curtain/yarn rope, child's name/happy-face stickers.

How will you help? Do you have animals to care for like Joseph did? Is there a baby at your house? Can you help a friend like Ruth did? How can you help at church? Let's say our Bible words, "I will help." Thank You, God, for helping us grow big enough to help.

Family Living Center, continued

cloths
Baby food, fruit
Plastic spoons
Small cups

Lesson 3
Snow-cone machine (optional)
Ice crusher
Powdered juice drink
Wide-mouthed container
Plastic spoons
3 oz. cups

Lesson 4
Small mops and brooms
Dustcloths
Spray bottles

Lesson 3

Always offer general play in this center. Try to have a separate table for the special activity. Help children take turns crushing the ice. Let them fill their cups half full and spoon a little powdered juice on it. If you do not have time/facilities to make the snow-cones, have a small pitcher of water and some plain cookies. Allow the children to pour (with help) and to serve their friends.

Friends work together and take turns. Boaz gave Ruth a nice cool drink. He was a friend. . . . Thank you, Rachel, for being a helper when you threw your cup in the trash. You may choose a sticker to put on the "I Will Help" chart.

Lesson 4

Have some things obviously out of place in this area, along with paper scraps for the children to see and pick up. Show them how to sweep or mop the floor, and dust furniture. You may need to point out specific things for younger children to do. If your group is small, you may want to take them out into the hallway or outdoors to help make the church building look neat.

This area needs cleaning. Here are the tools to use. . . . Tony, you are doing a good job with the broom. . . . You did a good job picking up scraps, Emily. . . . The boy in our Bible story grew big enough to help in the tent-church. He helped Eli. You are all big enough to help clean up our room (church building). You have done a good job!

Lesson 5

Allow free play here, or use an activity from previous weeks. Talk about being big enough to help, and commend helpful acts that you see.

Block Center

Unit 1—We Can Learn to Help

Items to Include:

Unit blocks or Blockbusters
People figures

Lesson 2
Dollhouse furniture
Fabric pieces
Barn animals

Lesson 4
Copy of page 261
Cardboard box, 3' square
4 yds. of cord
8 large safety pins
8 pieces of fabric, 5" x 12"

Purpose: The child will feel big enough and willing to help.

Things to Do and Say

Lesson 2

Help the children set up several blocks with some furniture and people to suggest homes. Start about four areas so children will have room to build and work.

I see your baby sleeping in a bed, Brittany. In our Bible story, baby Moses slept in a basket-boat. His sister was big enough to watch carefully. You are big enough to help at home. . . . What do you do for your mommy, Aaron? Do you help her take care of your baby brother? . . . Taylor, can you tell me something you do to help at home? . . . It is time to pick up now. You are big enough to put the people in the blue box. Have specific, identifiable containers so children can understand jobs and feel good about helping.

Lesson 4

Before class, enlarge each object on page 261 to fit 8 1/2" x 11" paper, color objects, and glue to sides of a box for windows. Cut cord into 36" pieces. Poke holes into box at upper corners of windows (pictures). Thread cord to the inside and tie ends securely. Tape inside to keep from slipping. Pin upper inside corner of fabric to cord to make curtain that will slide. Tape outside corner of curtain to box.

Show the children how to open and close the curtains. Help them build walls and

God's Wonders Center

Unit 1—We Can Learn to Help

Items to Include:

Lesson 1
Newsprint or shelf paper
Camera
Scales
Tape measure
Crayons
Note pad
Glue sticks

Lesson 3
Shower curtain
Tub or flat suitcase
Corn, rice, or

Purpose: The child will feel big enough to help.

Things to Do and Say

Lesson 1

Before class tape a length of newsprint or shelf paper on the wall. Print "I will help" (2 Samuel 10:11) at the top.

Draw around one hand of each child on the paper. Then draw second hand and use a note pad sheet on which to draw around the feet. While children color hands and feet, print names and mark and write height and weight underneath name and above hands. Glue feet at the bottom. Take pictures of a group of children's faces. These can be cut apart and glued above their names when developed.

Look how tall you are growing, Luke. Joseph was this tall before he grew up. As we grow, we become big enough to be helpers. Repeat the Bible words and sing "I Will Help" as children work on the chart.

Lesson 3

Place a plastic shower curtain on the floor with a tub or suitcase (good for storage and reuse) in the center. Put about 1" of corn and rice or cornmeal in the container. As children touch, feel, pour, and scoop, periodically have them help pick up the corners of the plastic to slide the grain back to the center. It can be funneled easily by removing

Block Center, continued

Masking tape
Glue

roads around the "church" building.

You are opening the curtain like Samuel probably did. Can you pretend to take the scroll Bible to Eli? . . . Samuel's mother walked on the road to the tent-church to give Samuel his new coat. . . . Who can open the curtain and pretend to polish the candlestick like Samuel may have done? How can you help around our church building or in our room? . . . Yes, you can clean up and put away toys when it is time.

God's Wonders Center, continued

cornmeal
Drink scoops
Berry baskets
Toilet paper tubes
Small plastic jars
Tablespoons

the container and picking up all four corners of the plastic. (A good helping project.)

This grain makes me think of Ruth, the helper in our Bible story, who walked with Naomi to Bethlehem. Ruth went out every day to pick up grain and Naomi baked bread with it. They were friends and helpers.

What friend do you walk with? You are growing big enough to help your friends. What might you pick up together? Yes, toys. When we have finished playing in this grain, you can help me pick up the grain that is on the floor. You are big enough to help me do that!

Lesson 4
Plastic buckets
Full-size paint brushes
Paint hats (optional)
Self-stick labels

Lesson 4

Obtain disposable hats from the paint store if possible. Have one bucket for every two children to share. Print the Bible words on the labels.

Let children put the labels on their hats as you add their names. Practice saying the Bible words. Take children outside to a brick or concrete wall. Put 1" of water in each bucket. You can refill as needed. **Samuel may have helped clean the outside of his tent-church. You are all very good helpers.**

Sing to the tune of "Mulberry Bush," "This is the way we paint our church . . . We're big enough to help!"

Book/Puzzle Center

Unit 1—We Can Learn to Help

Items to Include:

Books listed on page 241

Lesson 1
Socks
Shoes
Gloves
Hats

Lessons 2 and 5
3 flat boxes or lids
Copies of pages 263-265
3 x 5 file cards

Purpose: The child will feel big enough and willing to help.

Things to Do and Say

Lesson 1

Display the books on a table or bookrack. Have some child-size chairs, a large soft rug, or pillows on the floor. While some children look at books, others will want to try on the items you have brought. Have a variety of sizes and textures of socks, shoes, gloves, and hats, both men's and women's. As you help children try on the items, talk about who wears them and what jobs they help with.

Do those garden gloves fit you? Have you helped plant a garden? How can you help your dad or mom work in the yard? You are big enough to do that. . . . These socks are to be worn by someone who has to go out in the cold. They are made of wool. Where do we get wool? Yes, from sheep. The boy in our Bible story, Joseph, was big enough to help with the sheep. God is helping you grow big enough to help too.

Lessons 2 and 5

Make copies of pages 263-265, color them, and glue each one inside a box or lid. Cut appropriate, easily identified items from catalogs and magazines and glue to 3 x 5 cards.

Have children take turns selecting a card and talking about how and where the item is used. Have the child choose a box to place it in. **Does your Daddy keep his tools in the garage? . . . That's right. Our toothbrushes are kept in the bathroom. . . . Do you**

Music/Game Center

Unit 1—We Can Learn to Help

Items to Include:

Purpose: The child will sing about growing and helping.

Things to Do and Say

Lessons 1-5

Use this song throughout the unit. Start slowly and go faster.

Small, Tall!
(Tune: Sing up and down the scale.)

We are grow-ing tall,
(Stoop down, then slowly rise as you sing up the scale.)
We are not so small.
(Go back down as you sing down the scale.)
(Repeat first two lines.)

Small! . . . Tall!
(Stoop! . . . Stand!)
(Repeat.)
Now we all will fall!
(Fall down as you sing down scale.)

—Peggy DaHarb

Music/Game Center, continued

Lessons 1-5

Use this "Review Song" throughout the unit. Sing the song with actions or do as a game. Children form a circle, then lie down and curl up to sleep. Child chosen to be the Bible character tiptoes around the inside of the circle, watching. On "YOU," he claps his hands and everyone jumps up. Choose a new Bible character and repeat. Use the tune of "Rock-a-bye Baby."

Joseph's a helper; watching the sheep. *(Watch with hand above eyes.)*
While Joseph watches; gently they sleep. *(Lay head on folded hands.)*
Joseph is helping; God watches too. *(Watch with hand above eyes.)*
Joseph's a helper. YOU be one too! *(Point to someone on "YOU.")*

Rock-a-bye Moses, in your bed boat. *(Cradle arms to rock.)*
While Miriam watches, gently you float. *(Watch with hand above eyes.)*
Miriam is helping watch over you. *(Watch with hand above eyes.)*
Miriam's a helper; YOU be one too! *(Point to someone on "YOU.")*

Ruth helped Na-o-mi, not be alone. *(Hug yourself.)*
They walked together all the way home. *(Stand and walk or walk fingers.)*
While Ruth is helping, God watches too. *(Watch with hand above eyes.)*
Ruth is a helper; YOU be one too! *(Point to someone on "YOU.")*

Samuel's a helper with the scroll book, *(Make fists, hold together.)*
He pulled the curtain, so Eli could look. *(Look at open palms.)*
While Samuel's helping, God watches too. *(Watch with hand above eyes.)*
Samuel's a helper; YOU be one too! *(Point to someone on "YOU.")*

Book/Puzzle Center, continued

Magazine pictures of kitchen, garage, and bathroom items

have a scale to see how much you are growing? . . . You can help put the spoons away in the kitchen.

Use appropriate books to suggest where and how the children can help in their homes.

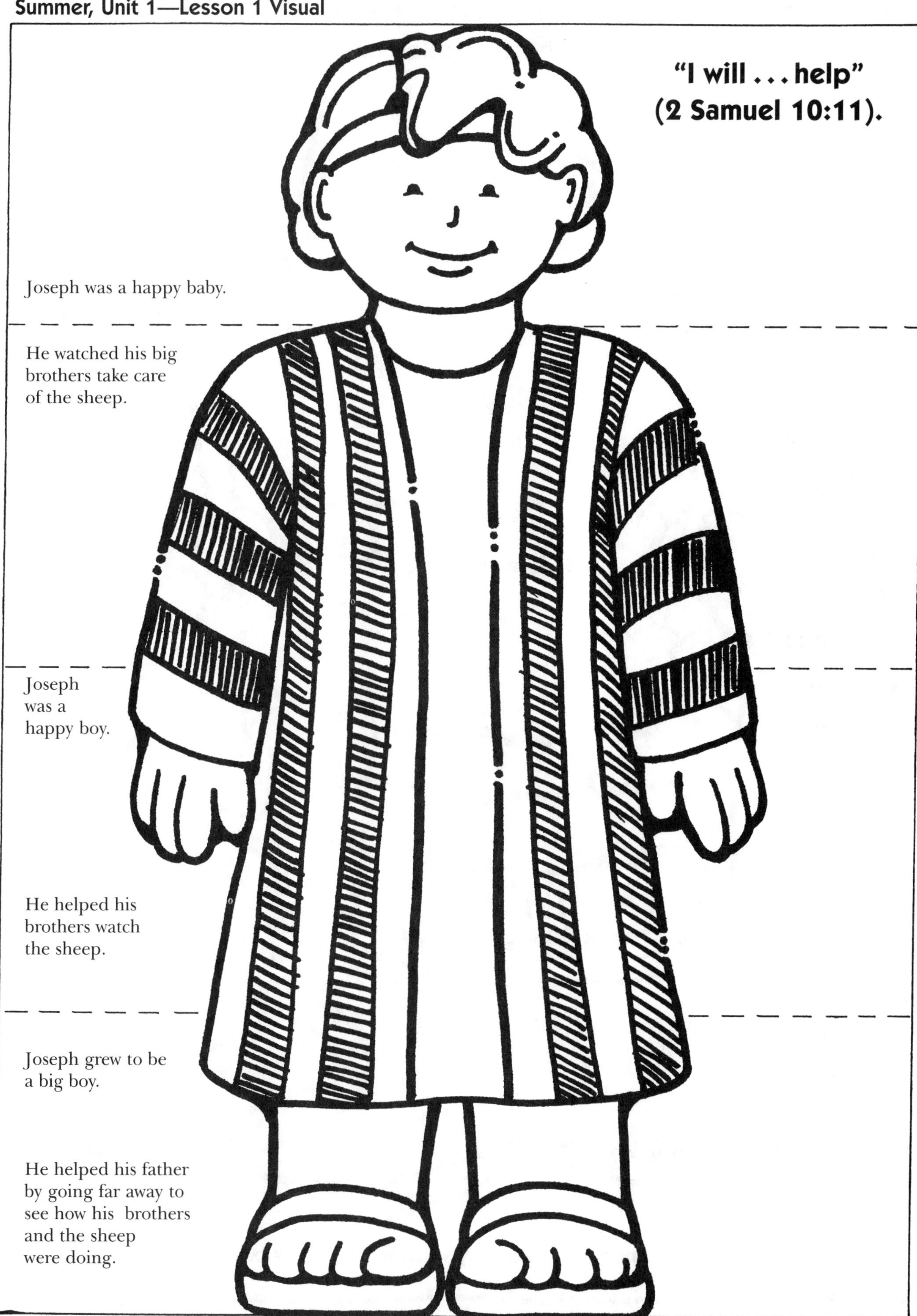
"I will . . . help"
(2 Samuel 10:11).
Joseph was a happy baby.
He watched his big brothers take care of the sheep.
Joseph was a happy boy.
He helped his brothers watch the sheep.
Joseph grew to be a big boy.
He helped his father by going far away to see how his brothers and the sheep were doing.

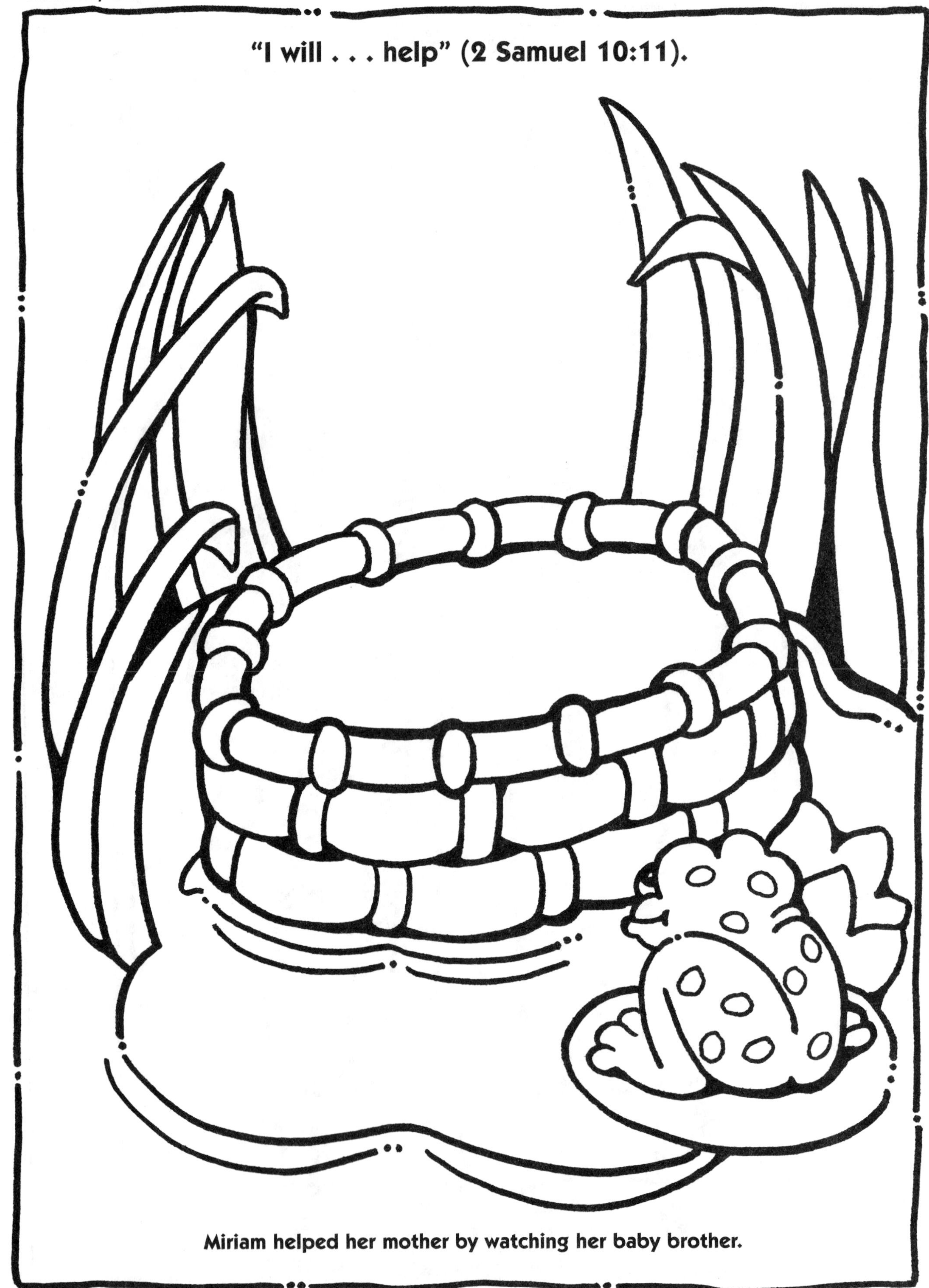
"I will . . . help" (2 Samuel 10:11).
Miriam helped her mother by watching her baby brother.

Enlarge window frame pattern to fit on 9" x 12" sheet of black construction paper. Follow directions on Art Center Card, page 254, to make completed picture.

Lesson 4 Block Center

Follow directions on Block Center Card, page 255.

Who Will Help?

"I will help," said Joseph."

"I will watch the ______________."

"I will help," said Miriam.

"I will watch the ______________."

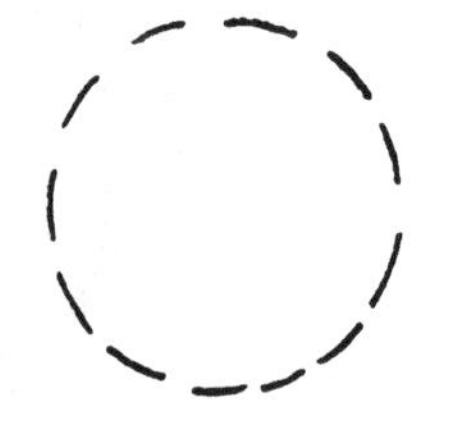

"I will help", said ______________.

"I will ______________."

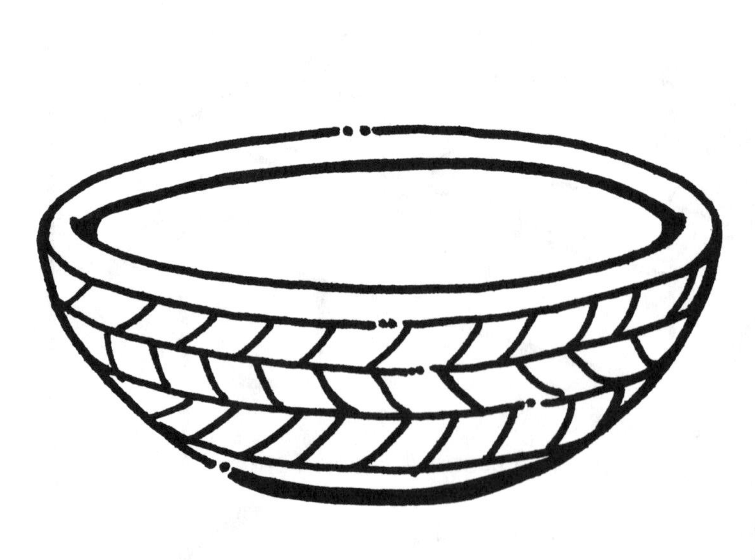

"I will help," said Ruth.

"I will pick up ______________."

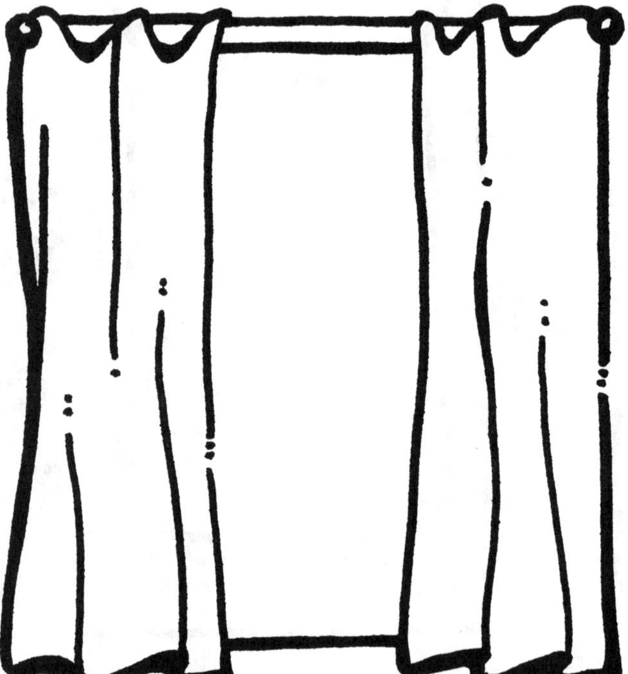

"I will help," said Samuel.

"I will pull the ______________."

Kitchen

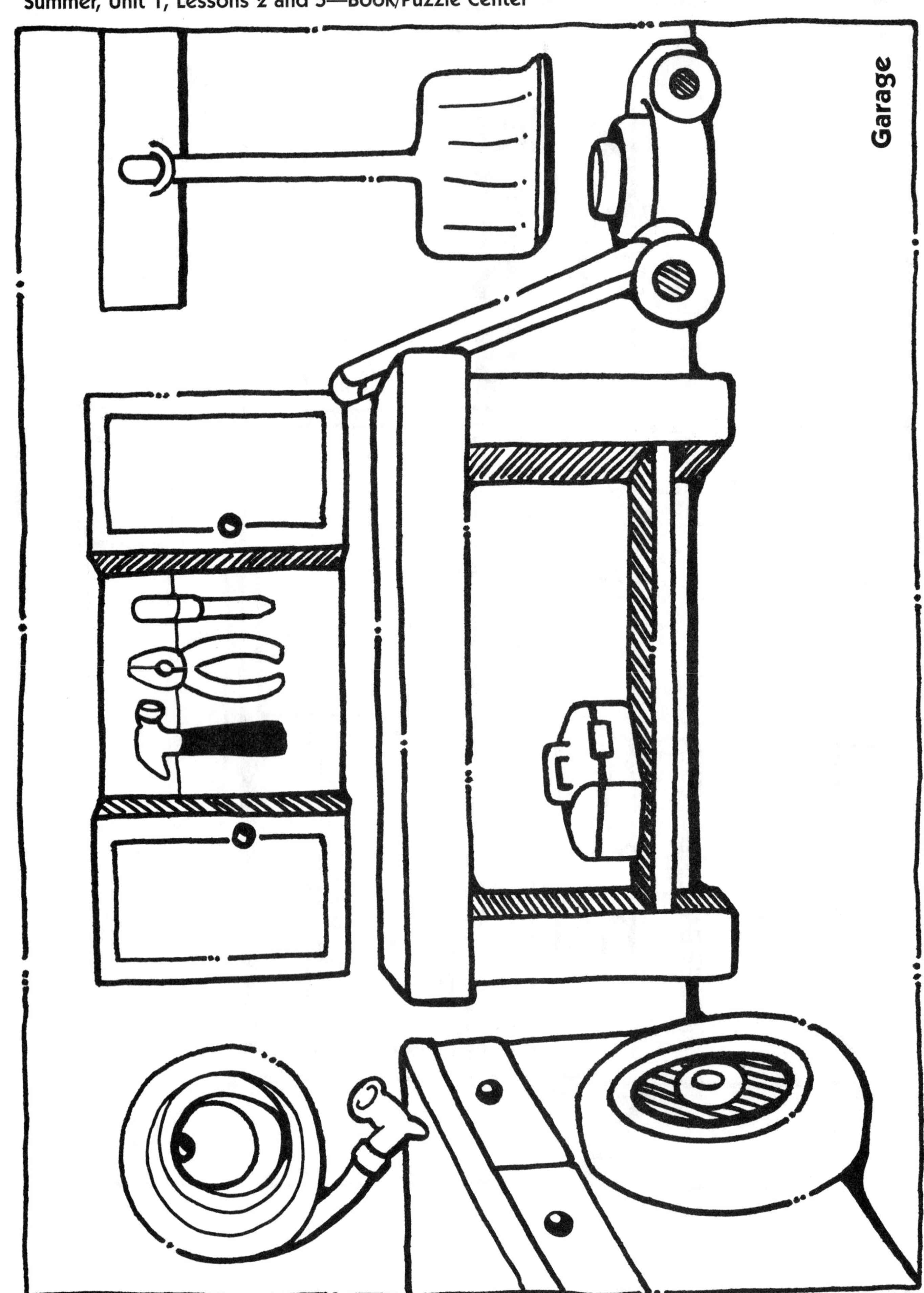
Garage

Bathroom

Dear Parent:

I appreciate the opportunity to have your child in class. Our unit theme is, "We Can Learn to Help." Your child will learn about helping by example and encouragement from teachers, as well as through the following Bible stories:

- *We Are Growing*—Joseph helps his father (Genesis 37:2, 3, 14).
- *We Can Help at Home*—Miriam watches baby Moses (Exodus 2:1-10).
- *We Can Help Our Friends*—Ruth stays with Naomi (Ruth 1, 2).
- *We Can Help at Church*—Samuel helps Eli the priest (1 Samuel 1:24-28; 2:11, 18, 19; 3:15).

Mark the Bible words, "I will . . . help" (2 Samuel 10:11), with a ribbon. Keep the Bible in a special place to read and to learn the verse.

The following activities will reinforce the truths learned in class:

- Look at your child's baby book or picture album. Contrast his footprint with his baby footprint. Talk about growing the way Joseph did.
- If you have baby clothes your child once wore, get these out and show her how small they were and talk about her growth.
- Put a tub of water in the yard to play in. Draw a face on a little scoop and place it in a margarine tub. Talk about how Miriam watched baby Moses.
- Take a walk in your neighborhood. Point out friends' homes. Talk about Ruth who traveled a long way with her friend Naomi to find a new home.
- Make cookies with your child and take a plate to a friend.
- Allow your child to use a dustcloth, a small broom, or a mop to do little cleaning jobs. Tell her she is helping the way Samuel probably did.
- Pray, "Thank You, God, for helping (child's name) grow bigger."

- Sing the following song to the tune of "Row, Row, Row Your Boat":

  I will help at home.* I will help at home.
  I am big enough to help.
  I will help at home.
  *For Lesson 3, "my friends"; Lesson 4, "at church."

- Sing these words to the tune of "Farmer in the Dell":

  A helper I will be, a helper I will be.
  There's work to do, there's work to do,
  In my family.*
  *For Lesson 4, "I'll help happily."

  I love to help my mom, I love to help my dad.
  I love to help; it makes God glad.
  A helper I will be.

Sincerely,

Unit 2: We Can Learn to Share

Lessons 6–9

By the end of the unit, the children will

Know that God helps them grow big enough to share.
Feel big enough and willing to share.
Share in specific ways (at home, with friends, and at church).

Unit Bible Words

"Be . . . kind" (Ephesians 4:32, *KJV*).

Books

from Standard Publishing
My Family and Me (24-03701)
Families (24-03584)
Sharing Makes Me Happy (24-04214)
Look, I'm Growing Up (24-04233)

This Unit at a Glance

6 We Can Share at Home — 2 Kings 4:8-11
A kind couple shares a room, a bed, and food with Elisha.

7 We Can Share With Friends — 1 Samuel 18:1-4
Jonathan shares his most prized possessions with his friend, David.

8 We Can Share at Church — Exodus 35:4-29; 39:42, 43
The Israelites share their possessions to help build the tabernacle.

9 We Are Big Enough to Share — Review of Lessons 6–8

Why Teach This Unit to Young Children?

This unit introduces your children to the concept of sharing—at home, with friends, and at church. Sharing is not an easy concept to understand at this age, however, because young children are naturally self-centered. Their idea of sharing may be, "You share with me!" The degree to which the children will accept or "catch" the concept of sharing will be as varied as are the personalities and developmental levels of your 2's and 3's. There is one concept, however, that can be "caught" easily at any age—happiness is a result of sharing. Your children will delight in being able to master successfully the attitude of "happy faces." Although their sharing skills will sharpen with age, help them now to master the most fundamental of beginning steps—a glad heart.

Have a Bible available in your classroom with the Bible words highlighted. Point to the words in the Bible as you say them so that the children begin to associate the words with the Book. Include the words frequently as you talk with the children about sharing.

Things to Do for This Unit

- Make copies of the Parents' Letter (page 289) and a copy of the Unit Planning Sheet (pages 319 and 320).

- Photocopy the Learning Center Cards (pages 277-282); cut apart on heavy lines. Glue side 1 to cardboard, and then side 2 to the back of the cardboard. Laminate for durability (optional).
- Prepare/collect materials listed on the Learning Center Cards.
- For Lesson 6, obtain non-spring clothespins, 1 per child and adult.
- For Lesson 7, have a small gift box with fabric or a doll's robe inside.
- For Lesson 8, make paper-bag coats according to directions given in Lesson 7, page 272.
- Locate a picture of David and Jonathan together.
- For Lesson 8, you will need a sheet, costume jewelry and shiny metal objects, scarves, and spices in cheesecloth.

Use These Songs and Action Rhymes During Unit 2

I Love You, God

(Tune: "This Old Man")

I love You. I love You. I love You, God, I love You.
I can read my Bible, sing, and talk to You.
I love You, God, I love You.

I'm Big Enough to Share

(Tune: "Row, Row, Row Your Boat")

I will share at home.* I will share at home.
I am big enough to share. I will share at home.
* Lesson 7, "with friends"; Lesson 8, "at church."

We Are Growing Big Enough

(Tune: "Oh, Be Careful")

We are growing big enough to share. (Be kind!)
We are growing big enough to share. (Be kind!)
We are growing big enough. We are growing big enough.
We are growing big enough to share. (I will "be kind"!)

We Are Helping

(Tune: "Are You Sleeping?")

We are helping, we are helping,
Putting toys away, putting toys away.*
(Sing names of six children.)
We're helping today, helping today.
*Clean up the room, etc.

I Will Share

(Tune: "She'll Be Comin' 'Round the Mountain")

I will share at my home. I will share. *(Repeat line.)*
I will share my tricycle.* I will share chocolate cookies.*
I will share at my home. I will share.

I will share with my friends. I will share. *(Repeat line.)*
I will share cars and trucks.* I will share my new doll.*
I will share with my friends. I will share.

I will share at my church. I will share. *(Repeat line.)*
I will share glue and crayons.* I will share paint and paper.*
I will share at my church. I will share.
*Substitute other items your children can share.

This Is the Way

(Tune: "Here We Go 'Round the Mulberry Bush")

This is the way we share our work,
Share our work, share our work.
This is the way we share our work, in our class today.

I will share with my friends,
With my friends, with my friends.
I will share with my friends, in my class today.

Jesus is happy when I share,
When I share, when I share.
Jesus is happy when I share, ev'ry day.

Did you like your bed? Zach nods again. **Who can point to the person who had a new bed in our Bible story?** Display your clothespin. **Who can show me how Elisha felt when the kind woman and her husband shared with him?** Encourage the children to make happy faces. **Do I see anyone who is growing big enough to share?** Encourage children to point to themselves or to others. **Zach, help us sing "We Are Growing Big Enough."**

Learning Activities

(20 minutes)

Let's Play Awhile

Teach the children the "Sharing" rhymes (page 240). Then sing "This Is the Way." Lead the children to the Game Center for some bubble blowing and sharing. If your class is large you may wish to repeat other learning activities as well.

Let's Go Home

Sing "We Are Helping" using Zach to sing children's names during the appropriate places. Give children specific tasks to help them complete classroom cleanup. As children finish putting away toys sing, "We Are Growing Big Enough."

Make sure each child takes home a letter to parents and his completed coloring page from the Art Center.

When I Pray

When I pray, I fold my hands *(Fold hands.)*
And close my eyes; *(Close eyes.)*
I think about God, and He hears me.

—*Jean Katt*

We Can Share at Home

2 Kings 4:8-11

Bible Words: "Be . . . kind" (Ephesians 4:32, *KJV*).

Lesson Value: Sharing is a very important, yet difficult, value for children to learn. Children are encouraged from an early age to share. We are pleased when they demonstrate good "sharing skills." But children are best taught desirable behaviors by observing positive adult role models. How wonderful then to have a story of a husband and wife who chose to share not only their food and their home with God's prophet, but also their resources in providing for him a room of his own. Sharing is a desirable behavior—no matter the age! Sharing also produces the same result regardless of the giver's age—a happy friend.

Know: Know that God helps me grow big enough to share.
Feel: Feel big enough and willing to share.
Do: Share in specific ways (at home).

Children will accomplish the goals when they:

1. Say the Bible words, "Be kind."
2. Pray, "Thank You, God, that we are growing big enough to share."
3. Sing about growing and sharing.
4. Name or point to someone who is growing big enough to share.
5. Act out sharing at home.

Let's Get Ready

For the Bible story, you will need the Bible, puppet Zach, doll pillow and blanket, and non-spring clothespins, one per child and adult. If you want, wrap a small piece of cloth around your clothespin and tie a piece of yarn around the middle. Draw a face on the "head" with a black marker.

Prepare the Family Living Center, the Art Center, and the Book/Picture Center. If you are the only teacher, use just the Family Living Center now. Use the Game Center after the Bible story.

Learning Activities

(30 minutes, including 10 minutes presession)

Let's Get Started

Use Zach to greet each child by name. Zach may hand each child a sticker to put on the attendance chart or other appropriate place. Say, **Zach would like to share a sticker with you, Courtney! We're going to be doing lots of sharing today. Would you like to work on a picture in the Art Center or share some play dough in the Family Living Center?** Encourage each child to get involved in the activity she chooses.

Worship and Bible Story

(15 minutes)

Let's Worship God

Let Zach tell the children, "It's time to be big helpers and put our things away! Let's get ready to sing and pray to God." Sing "We Are Helping" as the children work. To prepare the children for worship, begin singing "I Love You, God" as soon as children come to the circle. Sing "The Growing Song" (page 240), and "I'm Big Enough to Share." Use the rhyme on page 269, "When I Pray," and then pray, **Thank You, God, that we are growing big enough to share.** Do the rhyme, "My Bible" (page 273), adding the Bible words, "Be kind," at the end. Encourage the children to say the words with you.

Let's Learn From the Bible

Introduction: Invite Zach to join the children in listening to the Bible story. Say, **Zach, would you like to listen to a Bible story with us?** Bring Zach into the circle carrying the doll pillow and blanket. Help Zach make a bed. Say, **What do you think Zach wants to do with this bed?** (Take a nap, sleep, etc.) **We'll let Zach lie on his bed while we listen to a Bible story about someone else who had a bed.** Put Zach to one side. Open your Bible to today's story.

The Bible Story: This is Elisha. *(Display clothespin.)* He was one of God's helpers. *(Distribute clothespins to children.)* Let's help Elisha walk to the town of Shunem. *(Demonstrate Elisha "walking" on the floor; encourage children to follow your example.)* Elisha walked to tell people what God wanted them to do.

When Elisha got to Shunem a woman asked Elisha to come to her house. "Please come have dinner with my husband and me," she said. So Elisha went home with the woman. *(Help Elisha "walk" to the woman's house.)*

Every time Elisha came to Shunem he stopped to eat with the kind woman and her husband.

One day the kind woman said to her husband, "I want to share with God's helper Elisha. Let's build a room in our house where he can stay when he visits us."

So the kind woman and her husband built a room just for Elisha. He could sleep in this room when he visited his friends. Elisha was happy that the kind woman and her husband shared with him. *(Put Elisha to "sleep" on the floor; then collect all clothespins.)*

Let's Apply the Lesson

Bring the "sleeping" Zach into the circle. Say, **Zach, it's time to wake up! Did you have a good nap?** Zach nods yes!

Let's Apply the Lesson

Who is wearing something Jonathan shared? . . . I see Kara wearing a robe. Judah is wearing a bow and arrow. Continue with the other gifts. **How did David feel when his friend Jonathan shared these gifts with him? . . . Yes, David felt happy! And how did Jonathan feel when he shared with his friend David? . . . He felt happy too!**

Let's practice being big enough to share. Assist each child who wore a bag to choose a friend to share with. Help the child take the bag off and give it to another child. **You are big enough to share with your friends just like Jonathan was. . . . How do you feel when your friend shares with you? . . . How do you feel when you share with your friend? . . . Yes, you all feel happy!**

Learning Activities

(20 minutes)

Let's Play Awhile

Have the children stand and do the song, "We Are Growing Big Enough," then go to the Game Center. If your class is large and you have multiple teachers you may wish to repeat the activities used earlier in this session.

Let's Go Home

Have Zach sing "We Are Helping," using the children's names. Encourage them to listen and do what Zach is singing about. Give children specific tasks to help them clean up. **Anastasia, please put the ball in the toy closet. Peter, you can put that book on the shelf.**

Begin singing "I Will Share" (with my friends) as children complete picking up the toys. Allow children to offer ideas of what to share in the song. Continue to sing as long as children are interested.

Make sure the children have their "Sharing Tubes" from the Art Center when they leave with parents.

We Can Share With Friends

1 Samuel 18:1-4

Bible Words: "Be . . . kind" (Ephesians 4:32, *KJV*).

Lesson Value: Two's and 3's have an earned reputation of being self-centered. Sharing is not an easily acquired trait at this stage of development. Sharing qualities, however, are not automatically acquired with age! When Jonathan shared with David he gave up possessions that under certain circumstances had the power to save his life. Jonathan shared even when it was costly. Many adults find these lessons more difficult than will your classroom of children. Encourage and reward with smiles and positive conversation the sharing of good things in your session today.

Know: Know that God helps me grow big enough to share.
Feel: Feel big enough and willing to share.
Do: Share in specific ways (with friends).

Children will accomplish the goals when they:

1. Say the Bible words, "Be kind."
2. Pray, "Thank You, God, that we are growing big enough to share."
3. Sing about growing and sharing.
4. Name or point to someone who is growing big enough to share.
5. Act out sharing with friends.

Let's Get Ready

For the Bible story, you will need a Bible, the puppet Zach, a small gift box with cloth or doll's robe inside (for Zach). Prepare a "sword," "belt," "coat," and "bow and arrow" from grocery sacks. Cut an opening in the bottom of a grocery sack to fit easily over a child's head. Draw the picture of the appropriate object(s) on the front. If possible, locate a picture of David and Jonathan to show during the Bible story.

Prepare the Family Living Center, the Art Center, and the Book/Picture Center. If you are the only teacher, use just the Family Living Center now. The Game Center will be used after the Bible story.

Learning Activities

(30 minutes, including 10 minutes presession)

Let's Get Started

Use Zach to greet each child by name. Zach can say, "I see Katie! She is growing big enough to share with her friends!" If you have provided stickers and an attendance chart, Zach may hand each child a sticker saying, "I want to share a sticker with you, Betsy!" Give the children any help they need, then see that they become involved in the learning centers. A child who is allowed to roam from place to place in the classroom is not learning and will distract those who are.

Worship and Bible Story

(15 minutes)

Let's Worship God

Let Zach begin singing, "We are Helping." Zach can sing out the children's names as you move from center to center. As children enter the worship circle sing, "I Will Share," and "I'm Big Enough to Share" (with friends). Use the "Sharing" rhymes from page 240. **We have been singing about sharing with our friends. Our Bible words tell us, "Be kind."** Use the rhyme from page 269, "When I Pray," then pray, **Thank You, God, that we are growing big enough to share.**

Let's Learn From the Bible

Introduction: Ask Zach to come to the worship circle. As you bring him in front of you with one hand, use your other hand to give him the gift-wrapped package containing the robe or cloth. Say, **I have something I want to share with you, Zach. Shall I open it for you?** Open the box and place the robe/cloth on Zach. Say, **We are going to learn a Bible story about someone who shared a coat with his friend. Let's listen!** Lay Zach aside and place your Bible on your lap open to today's Bible story.

The Bible Story: *(Place grocery-sack "shirts" on the floor beside you. Display the picture of David and Jonathan.)* David and Jonathan were friends. One day Jonathan said, "David, you are my friend and I am your friend. We will always be good friends. I love you and I want to give you some gifts."

So Jonathan took off his robe and put it on David. *(Choose a child to stand and place "robe" on him/her.)*

Jonathan also wanted to give David his belt and his sword. *(Choose two more children to stand and wear the belt and sword bags.)*

David put on the belt. He put on the sword. He said, "Thank you, Jonathan for these gifts."

"I have one more gift I want to share with you. Please take my bow for shooting arrows." *(Choose a child to stand and wear the bow-and-arrow bag.)*

David was happy. He told Jonathan, "Thank you for sharing with me."

Jonathan was happy too. He was glad to share with his friend David.

What can you share at church? Help the children think of books, crayons, blocks, and so forth. **How do you feel when someone shares a book with you? . . . Yes, happy. And how do you feel when you share something with someone else? . . . Happy! Sharing makes everyone feel happy!**

Learning Activities

(20 minutes)

Let's Play Awhile

Have the children stand and do the song, "This Is the Way," adding items. Then sing "We Are Growing Big Enough." Go to the Music Center. If your class is large and you have multiple teachers, repeat learning activities used earlier in this session.

Let's Go Home

Use Zach to sing "We Are Helping" to encourage children to put toys and materials away. Give specific jobs to children during the clean-up time. **John, please put this book on the shelf. . . . Karen, that drum needs to be put in the box.**

Begin singing "I Will Share" as children complete their tasks. Allow children to use the Bible story props to pretend taking gifts to the tent-church as you sing "I will share at my church." Continue singing until all the children have been picked up by their parents.

My Bible

This is my Bible; *(Palms held together.)*
I'll open it wide *(Open hands; keep them touching.)*
And see (or say) what is written on the inside!
(Say Bible words: "Be kind.") —*Jean Baxendale*

We Can Share at Church

Exodus 35:4-29; 39:42, 43

Bible Words: "Be . . . kind" (Ephesians 4:32, *KJV*).

Lesson Value: The greatest story that will ever be presented to 2's and 3's about sharing at church will come through the living example of a dedicated teacher. A teacher who is kind and compassionate, prepared and involved, enthusiastic and consistent, brings riches to his/her church of a far greater value than the material things brought to the tabernacle by the children of Israel. Live out the lesson brought by today's Bible story by bringing the best of yourself to your children.

Know: Know that God helps me grow big enough to share.
Feel: Feel big enough and willing to share.
Do: Share in specific ways (at church).

Children will accomplish the goals when they:

1. Say the Bible words, "Be kind."
2. Pray, "Thank You, God, that we are growing big enough to share."
3. Sing about growing and sharing.
4. Pretend to be the Bible people sharing.
5. Name or point to someone who is growing big enough to share.
6. Act out sharing at church.

Let's Get Ready

For the Bible story, you will need the Bible, a large blanket or sheet, costume jewelry, scarves, potpourri/spices in cheesecloth, and shiny metal objects.

Prepare the Art Center, the Family Living Center, and the Book/Picture Center. If you are the only teacher, use just the Art Center now. Use the Music Center after the Bible story.

Learning Activities

(30 minutes, including 10 minutes presession)

Let's Get Started

Use Zach to greet each child by name. As children give their offerings Zach may say, "I see someone who is big enough to share at church!" Assist children as needed at this time. Offer a child a choice between two learning centers. **Jose, would you like to work on a coloring page now, or look at pictures and books?** Then make sure that Jose gets involved in the center of his choice. Making a choice is a good learning experience for a young child. Staying with that choice is also an important learning experience.

Worship and Bible Story

(15 minutes)

Let's Worship God

Have Zach sing "We Are Helping," using children's names. Begin singing "This Is the Way" as soon as children come to the worship circle. Do the rhyme, "My Bible." If you have time, let the children take turns holding the Bible and "reading" the highlighted Bible words. Sing "I Love You, God," and then use the rhyme, "When I Pray." Tell the children, **Now we are ready to pray, "Thank You, God, that we are growing big enough to share."** Then pray aloud in those same words.

Let's Learn From the Bible

Introduction: Use Zach to whisper a message in your ear. **Zach says he wants to share something with me.** Help Zach place a necklace (or something similarly appropriate) around your neck. **Thank you, Zach, for sharing! I am happy that you shared with me.** Let Zach say, "I'm happy too!"

Good-bye Zach! Lay Zach aside. **Let's listen to a story from the Bible about a time when people brought pretty things to share at God's house.**

The Bible Story: God told a man named Moses, "Tell my people to build a big tent-church. It will be called a tabernacle. After the people build the tent-church, they can go there to sing and pray to me." *(Drape a blanket or sheet over a table or several chairs to build a "tabernacle.")*

Moses told the people that God wanted them to build a beautiful tent-church where people would come to pray and sing to Him. Moses said, "Everyone who wants to help build this beautiful tent-church should bring a gift."

So the people brought gold, silver, and sparkling jewels. They brought earrings and bracelets. Some people brought beautiful cloth. Some people brought oil and spices that smelled good. *(Hand each child a "gift." Keep one for yourself.)* Let's share our gifts just like those people did. *(Take your gift and lead the children to the "tabernacle." Leave the gifts inside.)*

The people built the beautiful tent-church with their gifts just as God had told them. The people were happy. They were glad to share.

Let's Apply the Lesson

Use Zach to enter the tent and bring out a gift that was placed inside. **What does Zach have?** (Gift, necklace, cloth, etc.) **We pretended to take our gifts to help build a tent-church for God. Who can point to what the people of God shared? . . . Point to the place where the people shared their gifts. . . . Show/tell me how sharing made the people feel.** (Happy.)

Children point to clothespin. **How did Elisha feel when the kind people shared with him? How did they feel?** Children show happy faces or say, "Happy!"

Put on Zach's coat or robe. **What did Jonathan share with David?** Children point to coat. **How did David feel when Jonathan shared with him? How did Jonathan feel when he shared with David?** Children show happy faces or say, "Happy!"

Put on or display jewelry item. **What did the people share to help build God's special tent-church?** Children point to jewelry. **How did the people feel when they shared?** Children show happy faces or say, "Happy!"

What can you share at home? . . . What can you share with a friend? . . . What can you share when you are at church? Allow children to answer these, then ask, **How do you feel when you share? . . . Yes, you feel happy! Sharing makes everyone feel happy!**

Learning Activities

(20 minutes)

Let's Play Awhile

Have the children stand and do the rhyme, "Sharing," then go to the Music Center. If your class is large, you will want to repeat learning centers used earlier in the session.

Let's Go Home

Let Zach sing "We Are Helping," adding children's names. Use this time to encourage and praise sharing skills you have observed. **Sarah, when you gave Jeremy that book you were showing that you are big enough to share!**

When the toys are put away begin singing "We Are Growing Big Enough." Play a game used in the Game Center during this unit until all children have left with parents. If you can, take time to mention sharing actions each child has shown during this session and previous ones.

We Are Big Enough to Share

Review of Lessons 6–8

Bible Words: "Be . . . kind" (Ephesians 4:32, *KJV*).

Lesson Value: Because the concept of sharing is a new and sometimes puzzling one for your 2's and 3's, reviewing and reinforcing the lessons used previously is especially important! Use the learning opportunities previously provided by these lessons as a showcase for your own sharing talents. The best learning process is often a combination of what is heard, spoken, and practiced. But the learning experience of sharing is at its best when it can be seen in the teacher. Make use of every opportunity to practice sharing in front of your 2's and 3's. The visual impact of a teacher practicing the lesson is the most valuable tool in your classroom.

Know: Know that God helps me grow big enough to share.
Feel: Feel big enough and willing to share.
Do: Share in specific ways.

Children will accomplish the goals when they:
1. Say the Bible words, "Be kind."
2. Pray, "Thank You, God, that we are growing big enough to share."
3. Sing about growing and sharing.
4. Tell what each Bible person shared.
5. Act out sharing.

Let's Get Ready

For the Bible story, you will need the Bible, props used in Lessons 6-8, and puppet Zach.

Prepare the Art Center, the Family Living Center, and the Book/Picture Center. If you are the only teacher, use just the Art Center. Use the Music Center after the Bible story.

Learning Activities

(30 minutes, including 10 minutes presession)

Let's Get Started

Use Zach to greet each child by name. "I see Heather! She is growing big enough to share! . . . Here's Brian; he is big enough to share with his friends. Sharing makes us happy!"

Assist children with attendance stickers and offering. **When you bring your offerings to church you are growing big enough to share at church!** Encourage each child to participate in one of the learning centers. Keep groups small and as even as possible.

Worship and Bible Story

(15 minutes)

Let's Worship God

Let Zach begin singing "We are Helping," using children's names in the appropriate places. Some children may need to be told that this song is a reminder to help clean up any toys or supplies used in their learning centers and begin coming to the worship circle.

As children enter the worship circle begin singing "I Love You, God." Then sing "I Will Share," and "I'm Big Enough to Share." Use the rhyme, "My Bible," reading the Bible words from your Bible. Then say the rhyme, "When I Pray," and pray, **Thank You, God, that we are growing big enough to share.**

Let's Learn From the Bible

Introduction: Use Zach to carry the clothespin Elisha to the center of the worship circle. Repeat this process with the robe or coat from Lesson 7 and a piece of jewelry from Lesson 8. **Why do you suppose Zach has brought these things? . . . Yes, they are from our Bible stories. They will help us remember the people who shared. Thank you, Zach, for helping us remember!** Lay Zach aside.

The Bible-story Review: *(Pick up the clothespin.)* Who is this? *(You may need to help the children remember Elisha's name.)* A kind woman and her husband shared their food with God's helper, Elisha. Then the woman and her husband built Elisha his very own room. Elisha was happy that they shared with him. What did Elisha do in his new room? *(Children may lie down to show Elisha "sleeping.")* How did Elisha feel because the kind woman and her husband shared? *(Lay clothespin aside.)*

(Pick up cloth or robe.) David and Jonathan were friends who loved each other very much. Jonathan gave David his robe, his belt, his sword, and his bow. David was very happy that his friend Jonathan shared with him. Who can point to someone who is big enough to share with a friend? Who can show how you feel when a friend shares with you? Who can show me how Jonathan felt when he shared with David?

(Pick up the jewelry item.) God wanted His people to build a special tent. They would pray and sing to God at this special tent-church. The people brought beautiful gifts such as jewelry, gold, and silver to help build God's special tent-church. The people were happy they could share. What did the people share? Who can point to someone who is big enough to share at church? Who can show me how you feel when you share at church?

Let's Apply the Lesson

Display clothespin Elisha. **Name/point to the person who was happy that the kind woman and her husband shared.**

Art Center

Unit 2—We Can Learn to Share

Items to Include:

Lesson 6
Copies of page 283
Crayons
Red felt or construction paper
Glue sticks

Lesson 7
Short cardboard tubes
Self-stick seals
Crayons or washable markers

Purpose: The child will feel big enough and willing to share.

Things to Do and Say

Lesson 6

Cut small circles from the felt or construction paper. In class, distribute copies of page 283, crayons, and red circles. Some children may wish just to color their pictures while others will enjoy adding the apples. Assist those who would like to glue the red circles on the apples by adding a small amount of glue on one apple on the tree at a time.

Who is big enough to share in this picture? Who else is big enough to share? . . . Yes, you are! Have you ever shared an apple with someone, Ashley? . . . Mommy cut it in half? Yes, that's a good way to share! When we share we are doing what our Bible words tell us, "Be kind." Sharing makes you feel happy. It makes the other person feel happy too.

Lesson 7

Use toilet-paper tubes or cut long tubes in half. Let the children decorate their "Sharing Tubes" with crayons or washable markers. Have self-stick happy-face seals available for those who want to add them. These will adhere to the tubes better than those you make. When the children have finished their tubes, take a "trip" around the room. Have them look for objects they can share and for people who are big enough to share with their friends.

Game Center

Unit 2—We Can Learn to Share

Items to Include:

Lesson 6
Bubble solution in jars
Bubble wands

Lesson 7
Balloons

Purpose: The child will name or point to someone big enough to share.

Things to Do and Say

Lesson 6

Group children in a circle. Assist one child at a time to dip the wand in the bubble solution and blow. Ask each child to pass the wand to the child seated/standing beside her.

When you give the wand to someone you are sharing. I see someone big enough to share! Point to child who is passing the wand. **Yes, it is Corey. He is sharing with Rachel. . . . Can you see someone who is big enough to share? You can share like this at home too.**

Lesson 7

Group children in a circle. Begin by tapping the balloon to a child on the other side of the circle. Say, **I am big enough to share with James.** As each child passes the balloon encourage him to say (or say for him), "I am big enough to share!" Then have the other children name those who are big enough to share.

If your class is composed of very young children, you may prefer to have them seated on the floor in a circle and roll a ball back and forth. You will need to say the words each time a child rolls the ball. Some children may roll the ball to you rather than to another child.

Joshua sees a puzzle he could share. . . . Sarah sees Abby, who is sharing a book with her friend Nicholas. Abby is big enough to share! . . . I see Karen who is growing big enough to share. I think she is going to share a napkin with her friend Emily. She is doing what our Bible words tell us to do, "Be kind"!

Lesson 8
Copies of page 284
Crayons
Stickers from page 281

Lesson 8

Prepare the stickers from page 281 according to directions. Let children color these, and then cut them apart while the children color their pictures. Place a container of crayons between two children so they will have to share.

Here is a picture of a church building. You are getting big enough to share at church. Jared, you will be sharing these crayons with Ian. When you share at church you are doing what our Bible words say, "Be kind." I see many children today who are big enough to share! Sharing makes us feel happy! Let's add pictures of children who are big enough to share.

Lesson 9
Copies of page 288
Stickers from page 282
Crayons

Lesson 9

Make copies of page 288 and stickers from page 282. Let the children color the stickers before you cut them apart.

This says, "I am big enough to share at home." Here is a picture of some blocks. Are you big enough to share blocks with someone at home? Yes, you are! Help the children add their blocks stickers. Continue in the same way with the other two stickers. Then help the children "read" the Bible words. **When you share with someone you are being kind. That makes everyone happy!**

Family Living Center

Unit 2—We Can Learn to Share

Items to Include:

Lessons 6 and 9
Play dough (recipe on page 318)
Plastic rolling pins
Cookie cutters

Lesson 7
Tablecloth or blanket
Paper plates
Paper cups
Napkins
Picnic basket or grocery bag

Purpose: The child will share in specific ways.

Things to Do and Say

Lessons 6 and 9

Give each child a portion of play dough. Distribute plastic rolling pins and cookie cutters. There should not be enough for each to have one. As children work with their play dough, perhaps making food of some kind, direct their thinking to sharing.

When you have finished with the rolling pin, Jack, please share it with Austin. . . . Julie is big enough to share this cookie cutter with you, Tyler. Thank You, God, for helping these children grow big enough to share. . . . When we share we are doing what our Bible words say, "Be kind." Sharing makes us feel happy too! . . . You can share like this at home with your brother, Nathan. You are big enough.

Lesson 7

Explain to the children that they will be going on a picnic. Gather supplies into the basket or bag and pretend to hike to a certain area of the room (or outside, weather permitting). Arrange the blanket or tablecloth on the floor. Hand out items, giving one child the plates, one the cups, and so forth.

When we have a picnic we can share with our friends. Marci has just plates. She can't have a picnic that way. Marci is going to share her plates with everyone. Continue in this way until each child has shared something. Explain that you will share

Music Center

Unit 2—We Can Learn to Share

Items to Include:

Rhythm instruments

Purpose: The child will sing about growing and sharing.

Things to Do and Say

Lesson 8

Have a variety of simple rhythm instruments, either bought or homemade. See page 318 for directions for making some instruments.

Distribute two or three instruments to the children. After you have sung one song, ask children to share the instruments with others. Do this each time a song is sung. Make sure that each child gets to use an instrument. You may want to give each child an instrument for the last song. Choose songs from this unit; also sing these words to the tune of "If You're Happy and You Know It":

We are growing, we are growing every day!
We are growing, we are growing every day!
We can sing, we can pray, we can share at church today.
Thank You, God, that we are growing every day!

Lesson 9

Do as you did in Lesson 8. Ask the children to play as the song (over) is being sung. After each stanza, encourage children to give the instruments to others. **You are growing big enough to share when you let your friends take turns with the instruments!**

Family Living Center, continued

Graham crackers
Juice or water

juice (water) with them.

Thank you, Marci, for sharing paper plates with your friends. Tressa is big enough to share crackers with her friends. Before eating pray, **Thank You, God, for helping these children grow big enough to share with their friends.**

Lesson 8
Baby dolls
Blankets
2 small rockers (optional)

Lesson 8

Seat children in a circle. Hand baby dolls and blankets to two children. **Let's sing a song about baby Jesus!** Encourage children with babies to rock while a lullaby is sung. Sing these words to the tune of "Are You Sleeping?"

I love Jesus, I love Jesus. He's God's Son! He's God's Son!
Mary rocked Him gently, Mary rocked Him gently.
He's God's Son! He's God's Son!

When the song is finished encourage children with dolls to share by letting other children rock the babies while the group sings the lullaby again. Repeat as needed. **I see Elizabeth sharing her doll with Lori! God is helping her grow big enough to share. When we share with our friends at church we are listening to our Bible words, "Be kind."**

Music Center, continued

I Can Share

(Tune: "Deep and Wide")

I can share. *(Point to self.)* You can share. *(Point to others.)*
We are growing big enough to share. *(Spread arms wide.)*
I can share. *(Point to self.)* You can share. *(Point to others.)*
We are growing big enough to share! *(Clap hands in rhythm.)*

Share at home. *(Make house with fingers.)*
Share with friends. *(Point to a friend.)*
We are growing big enough to share. *(Stand up big and tall!)*
Share at home. *(Make house with fingers.)*
Share with friends. *(Point to a friend.)*
We are growing big enough to share! *(Clap hands in rhythm.)*

Book/Picture Center

Unit 2—We Can Learn to Share

Items to Include:

Classroom Bible
Books on sharing

Lesson 6
Copies of page 285
Pictures of objects to be shared or people sharing
Sharing Makes Me Happy (24-04214)

Lesson 7
Pictures of children
Copies of page 286

Purpose: The child will know that God is helping him grow big enough to share.

Things to Do and Say

Lesson 6

Make several copies of page 285. Color and mount on construction paper. Cut out and mount magazine pictures of objects to share (apple, umbrella, jump rope, book, etc.) or people who are sharing. Display pictures on a low table or mount several small ones on poster board.

These children are sharing at home. Do you see something you can share, Mary? . . . Stephen, point to someone in this picture who is big enough to share. Very good! Yes, God is helping you grow big enough to share too. Have your Bible open to the Bible words. Read them aloud. Ask the children to point to them as you help them "read" the words. If time allows read the book, *Sharing Makes Me Happy.*

Lesson 7

Open your Bible and point to the Bible words. Display the pictures of children. Ask a child to point to someone in the picture who is big enough to share with a friend. As a child points ask, **Jenna, could you share a toy with that child? Yes, you are big enough to share with your friends! . . . . Brian, could you share a puzzle with that boy? God is helping you grow big enough to share.**

Include last week's pictures of objects to share. Let children look at these, then ask a

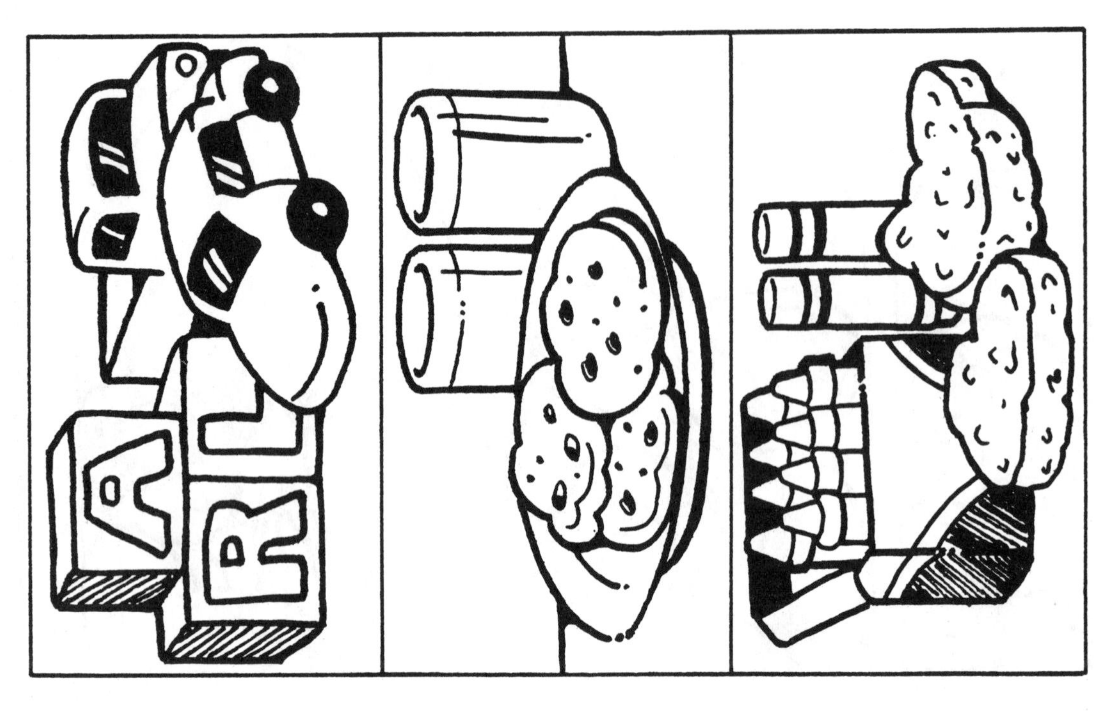

Directions for stickers:

1. Mix 2 parts glue with 1 part vinegar.
2. Add a few drops of peppermint extract (optional).
3. Lightly paint mixture on backs of uncut stickers. Let dry.
4. Let children color before cutting stickers apart.
5. Lick and stick!

Book/Picture Center, continued

child to pick out something he could share and point to a friend with whom he might want to share the object. This could be a child in a picture or one in the room. Read an appropriate book on sharing if children show interest in it.

Lesson 8
Picture of church building
Copies of page 287
Look, I'm Growing Up (24-04233)

Lesson 8

Display a picture of a church building and copies of the picture on page 287. **We're learning to share. Where can we share? Yes, we can share at church.** Display pictures of children participating in church. **Daniel, point to someone in this picture who is big enough to share. . . . Cara, what do you share at church?** Help her think of something, such as crayons or books.

Read *Look, I'm Growing Up* to children. **God is helping you grow big enough to do so many things. You are even getting big enough to share!** Ask children to point to the Bible words as you read them aloud. Encourage children to say the Bible words with you.

Lesson 9

Use pictures, books, and conversation from previous lessons to reinforce the unit goals.

I am big enough to share.

"Be . . . kind" (Ephesians 4:32).

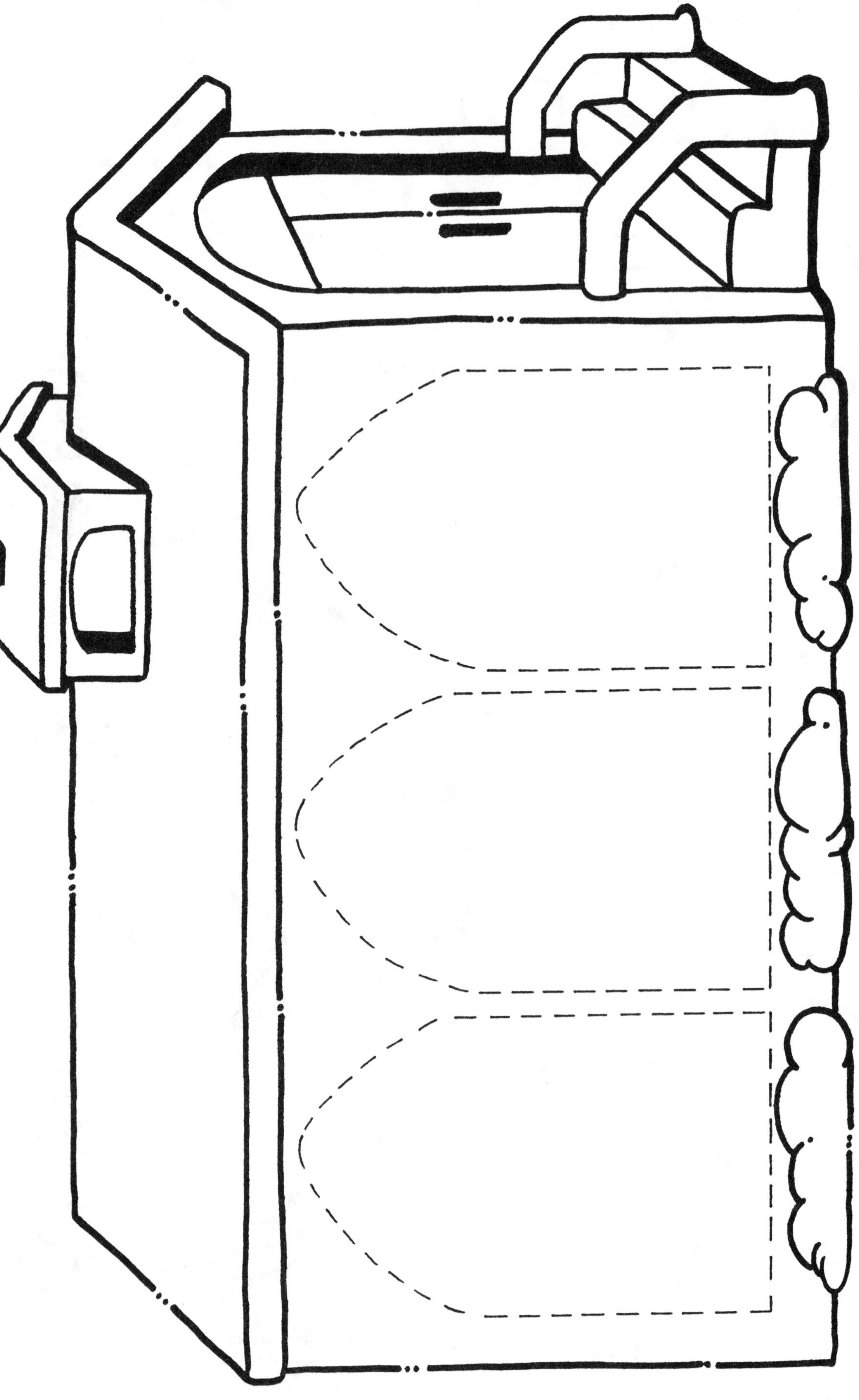

I am big enough to share at church.

"Be . . . kind" (Ephesians 4:32).

I am big enough to share at home.
"Be . . . kind" (Ephesians 4:32).

"Be . . . kind" (Ephesians 4:32).
I am big enough to share with my friends.

I am big enough to share at church.
"Be . . . kind" (Ephesians 4:32).

I am big enough to share at home.

I am big enough to share with my friends.

I am big enough to share at church.

"Be . . . kind" (Ephesians 4:32).

Dear Parent:

During this unit your child will be learning that . . .
. . . *We Can Share at Home* (2 Kings 4:8-11);
. . . *We Can Share With Friends* (1 Samuel 18:1-4);
. . . *We Can Share at Church* (Exodus 35:4-29; 39:42, 43); and that
. . . *We Are Big Enough to Share* (review of previous lessons)

The main goal for this unit is to introduce the concept of sharing—through the use of Bible stories, songs, and learning activities. This is a difficult concept for young children, and they will not master it in one month! They can begin to understand, however, that sharing makes others happy. And we will encourage them to know that when they choose to share they will feel happy too!

Here are some ways to cultivate happy attitudes about sharing at home:

- Say, "You looked happy when you shared your doll with me. I feel happy that you shared with me!"
- At the end of the day pray with your child, "Thank You, God, that (child's name) is growing big enough to share."
- Highlighting the Bible words, "Be . . . kind" (Ephesians 4:32), in your family Bible will create additional opportunities for you and your child to communicate about happy sharing. Using the Bible and the Bible words at home also gives your child an opportunity to know that the Bible is an important book at home as well as at church. It's never too early for children to realize that God's Word is important outside the church building—parent's read it too!
- Use the following song and action rhyme throughout each week with your early learner. They will help to encourage your child to practice sharing or cooperating skills that are being reinforced at church.

Big Enough to Share

(Tune: "Row, Row, Row Your Boat")

I will share at home.* I will share at home.
I am big enough to share. I will share at home.
*(2) With a friend. (3) At church.

I Will Share

(Tune: "She'll Be Comin' 'Round the Mountain")

I will share at my home.* I will share. *(Repeat.)*
I will share my tricycle. I will share chocolate cookies.**
I will share at my home. I will share.
*(2) With my friends. (3) At my church.
**Substitute appropriate items your child can share.

Your child's teacher,

Unit 3: We Can Learn to Love God

Lessons 10–13

By the end of the unit, the children will

Know that God helps them grow big enough to love Him.
Feel big enough and willing to love God.
Love God in specific ways (listen to and "read" the Bible, talk to God, sing to God).

Unit Bible Words

"We love him" (1 John 4:19, *KJV*).

Resources

from Standard Publishing
Alexander's Praise Time Band (24-03826)
Families (24-03584)
I Can Pray to God (24-04208)
Lost and Found, Stories Jesus Told (24-03655)
My Bible Story Pals (24-02749)
Thank You, God 24-03820
The Big Book of Noah's Ark (24-03655)
Where Are We Going Today? (24-03116)

This Unit at a Glance

10 We Can Listen to the Bible — **2 Kings 22:1-10; 23:1-3**
King Josiah listened to God's Word when it was found and read it to his people.

11 We Can Talk to God — **Daniel 6:1-10**
Daniel prayed to God three times a day to show his love for God.

12 We Can Sing to God — **2 Chronicles 29:28-30**
King Hezekiah gathered all the people at the temple to sing to God in worship.

13 We Are Big Enough to Worship God — **Review of Lessons 10–12**

Why Teach This Unit to Young Children?

Throughout this quarter, the children have been learning to love God for helping them grow. They have learned that they are getting big enough to help and to share. Now they will learn that they are also getting big enough to worship God. They will learn three ways to show their love to God—by "reading" the Bible (listening to God's Word), talking to God (praying), and singing to God. While these three ways to love God make up our worship time, they can also be incorporated into every activity of the session. Give the children opportunities to say and listen to God's Word—**You are showing your love to God by being a good listener;** to talk to God in prayer—**Let's tell God we are glad He helps us grow;** and praise God in song—**You showed God you loved Him when you sang to Him.** The children will also have the opportunity to model your example of loving God through your praise and worship, and by your attitude toward God's Word.

Help children connect God's Word with everything they do by displaying and referring to the Bible in the welcome area and every learning center, as well as the worship/story time. Insert in the Bible pictures of children reading, praying, and singing. Also use pictures of the

Bible people. Mark the Bible words and stories with matching colors of highlighters and bookmarks. Use the Bible words frequently and statements such as, **God's Word says, "Be loving, kind, helpful, . . ."** (relate to children's actions and behavior).

Things to Do for This Unit

- Make photocopies of the Parents' Letter (page 313) and the Unit Planning Sheet (pages 319 and 320).
- Photocopy the Learning Center Cards (pages 301-306); cut pages on solid lines. To make each card, glue side 1 to cardboard and side 2 on opposite side of cardboard; laminate for durability (optional).
- Gather/prepare materials listed on Learning Center Cards.
- Make a heart attendance chart and stickers for each child (page 307).
- For Lesson 12, invite a guest musician for the Book/Picture Center.

Use These Songs and Action Rhymes During Unit 3

Bible Time

(Tune: "London Bridge")

Gather 'round, it's Bible time, Bible time, Bible time.
Gather 'round, it's Bible time; come and listen.

We Love Him

(Tune: "This Old Man")

We love Him. We love Him.
We love Him, yes, we love Him.
We can read our Bibles, sing, and talk to Him.
We love Him, yes, we love Him.

We can read. We can pray.
We can sing to God today.
We can read and pray and sing to God today.
We love Him, yes, we love Him.

God's Word

(Tune: "She'll Be Comin' 'Round the Mountain")

I am big enough to see God's Word. (With my eyes!)
I am big enough to hear God's Word. (With my ears!)
I am big enough to pray. I am big enough to sing.
I am big enough to pray and sing God's Words. (With my mouth!)

Praise Him

(Tune: "Jesus in the Morning")

Praise Him. Praise Him.
Praise Him in the morning, praise Him in the noontime.
Praise Him. Praise Him.
Praise Him when the sun goes down.

Pray to Him! Pray to Him!
Pray in the morning; pray in the noontime.
Pray to Him! Pray to Him!
Pray when the sun goes down.

I Have

I have two eyes to see God's Word. *(Circle eyes.)*
I have two ears to hear it read. *(Cup ears.)*
I have one mouth to sing His praise. *(Point to mouth.)*
I have two hands to fold in prayer. *(Fold hands.)*

My Bible

This is my Bible; *(Palms together.)*
I'll open it wide *(Open hands; keep them touching.)*
And see (or say) what is written
On the inside! *(Say Bible verse, "We love Him.")*

—Jean Baxendale

in place.) King Josiah loved God and read His good words. The people loved God and listened carefully. Sh-h-h. *(Have children sit down. Point to Bible words.)* God's Word says, "We love him."

Let's Apply the Lesson

There should be several Bibles and scrolls around the room. Pass out the "glasses." **Joel, please find the Bible by the door.** Have Joel stand by you with the Bible. **How can you show God you love Him?** (Read His Word, listen, obey.) Help the child say, "My Bible." Continue choosing children until all have had a turn using their glasses to find and "read" a Bible. Sing, "God's Word" and collect the "glasses."

God is helping you grow big enough to love Him. What was the name of the king who loved God? . . . What was found in the temple-church? . . . Who listened to God's words when King Josiah read them? Say "I Have" and then pray, **Dear God, thank You for Your good words in the Bible. We love You.**

Learning Activities

(20 minutes)

Let's Play Awhile

Stand and sing, "God's Word." Have the Block Center prepared. If you have a large class and several teachers, also use the activities from earlier in the session.

Let's Go Home

Sing "Praise Him," to signal clean-up time. Help children get their crowns on. Sing "We Love Him" and say "My Bible." Hide a scroll. When it is found, say the Bible words and hide it again. Continue doing this as long as children are interested.

As children leave, make sure they have their "glasses," their crowns, and copies of the Parents' Letter. **You look like King Josiah with your crown on. You are growing big enough to love God.**

We Can Listen to the Bible

2 Kings 22:10; 23:1-3

Bible Words: "We love him" (1 John 4:19, *KJV*).

Lesson Value: King Josiah was one of the few Jewish kings who was faithful to God throughout his life. The emotions he felt when he learned that the scroll containing God's law given to Moses had been found tell us of his great desire to please God. Not only did he listen to God's Word, he also read it to all the people so they, too, could obey God. Use the example of this courageous young king to help the children see that they are big enough to listen to God's Word, to "read" it, and to tell others about it.

Know: Know that God helps me grow big enough to love Him.
Feel: Feel big enough and willing to love God.
Do: Love God in specific ways (listen to and "read" Bible words).

Children will accomplish the goals when they:

1. Say the Bible words, "We love him."
2. Sing about growing and loving God.
3. Tell what King Josiah did.
4. Act out loving God by listening to and "reading" the Bible.
5. Pray, "Thank You, God, that we are growing big enough to love You."

Let's Get Ready

For the Bible story, you will need the classroom Bible (Bible words highlighted in yellow with ribbon to match), crown and glasses for Zach, toy trumpet, Bible-scroll (see page 308), "glasses" for each child, cut from plastic six-pack soft drink holders. Also have the attendance hearts and Bible stickers from page 307.

Prepare the Art Center, the Family Living Center, and the Book/Picture Center. If you are the only teacher, start with the Book/Picture Center. Have materials ready for the Block Center to use after the Bible story.

Learning Activities

(30 minutes, including 10 minutes presession)

Let's Get Started

Place a Bible near the door with a cloth over it. Help with offering, name tags, and Bible stickers on the hearts. As Zach greets the children he will ask them to peek under the cloth and tell what they see. "Some workers found a Bible-scroll in the temple. King Josiah read God's words from the Bible-scroll. These words say, 'We love him.' I have a crown like King Josiah had. Would you like to make one?" Direct each child to a center.

Worship and Bible Story

(15 minutes)

Let's Worship God

Zach blows the trumpet at each center and tells the children, "Hands up, hands up. Everyone, hold up your hands."
Repeat the rhyme, "The Busy Fingers" (page 306), several times encouraging children to help with specific jobs. Sing "Bible Time" to call children to the worship/story area. Sing "We Love Him." Then use "My Bible" to introduce the Bible words. **We love God when we listen to His Word. Now we can tell God, "Thank You that we are growing big enough to love You."**

Let's Learn From the Bible

Introduction: Zach is wearing his glasses and crown. He sticks his nose into the Bible on your lap, and then looks up at the children and says, "Um-m-m. Good words." He looks down, then looks up and says, "Y-i-i-i-ip! Mighty good words! God's words are good words!" **Zach, why do you have on those big glasses?** "Well, I have big ears to *listen* to God's good words, so-o-o-o, I thought I should have big glasses to *see* God's good words. Sa-a-ay, boys and girls, do you know any of God's good words?"

Help children say, "My Bible." **Now Zach, why do you have a crown on?** "We-l-l-l, there's this king who listened to God's good words and I want to be just like him. I'll listen while you tell us about King Josiah. **I will, Zach. But first I need a helper to find the yellow ribbon in our Bible.** Choose a child.

The Bible Story: Josiah was only eight years old when he became king. *(Have the children clap eight times.)* He loved God very much. He always tried to do what was right.

One day when he grew up he said to his helper, "Go to the temple and see how the workers are doing." So the helper walked over to the temple. *(Have children walk hands on their legs and say, "Walk, walk, walk.")* But the helper did not walk back, he ran back! *(Have class run hands and say, "Run, run, run.")*

"King Josiah, King Josiah!" the helper called. "Look what the workers found!" *(Hold up scroll.)* "The Bible-scroll—God's good words!"

King Josiah said, "Read me all of God's good words. I want to hear them." King Josiah listened carefully then said, "I want all the people to hear God's good words. Tell them to come and listen while I read God's good words."

"Hurry, everyone, the king is going to read God's good words. Come and listen." So the people hurried to the temple to hear King Josiah read God's good words. *(Have children stand and run*

everyone to pray to him. But Daniel loved God. Daniel went up to his room *(have children stand and pretend to walk up)* and kneeled *(kneel)* right in front of the window and prayed to God. Three times every day he prayed. Whether it was sunny, or rainy, or snowy *(do actions),* Daniel still prayed. Even when the king said, "No!" Daniel still prayed three times a day. Daniel loved God more than he loved the king. Daniel always prayed to God.

Let's Apply the Lesson

Have Zach start howling. **Zach, what are you doing? This is still Bible story time!** "I know. I just want people to know I love God and want to talk to Him three times a day just like Daniel did." **That's very good, Zach, now bring your thank-you bag over here.** Zach drags the bag over. Sing, "The Growing Song" (page 240). **There are some things in Zach's bag for which we can say thank-you.** Let each child choose an item and say a thank-you prayer. **D.J., you are big enough to pray like Daniel did!**

Learning Activities

(20 minutes)

Let's Play Awhile

Stand and sing "God's Word." Have Music/Game Center ready. **Daniel prayed to God three times each day. We're going to play a game to help us remember times we can pray.**

Let's Go Home

When the children have almost finished cleaning up their areas, have Zach start singing "Praise Him." As the children gather, sing "Small, Tall!" (Game/Music Card).

Make sure the children take home their prayer reminders from the Art Center and their matching games from the Book/Picture Center. First-time children should take a Parents' Letter also. Have Zach help you say good-bye. **Remember to say thank-you to God like Daniel did.** "And pray three times every day!"

We Can Talk to God

Daniel 6:1-10

Bible Words: "We love him" (1 John 4:19. *KJV*).

Lesson Value: Some children, since they were babies, have watched and listened as their parents prayed. This lesson on Daniel will give them an opportunity to learn of a Bible person who loved God and prayed to Him. Daniel's faithful prayer life is an important example to all of us. Seeing and hearing teachers pray throughout each session will encourage the children to pray regularly and spontaneously. Help the children learn to express their love for God by providing many opportunities for them to talk to Him in prayer.

Know: Know that God helps me grow big enough to love Him.
Feel: Feel big enough and willing to love God.
Do: Love God in specific ways (talk to God).

Children will accomplish the goals when they:

1. Say the Bible words, "We love him."
2. Sing about growing and loving God.
3. Tell what Daniel did.
4. Act out loving God by talking to God.
5. Pray, "Thank You, God, that we are growing big enough to love You."

Let's Get Ready

For the Bible story, you will need the Bible with green highlights and ribbon, puppet Zach, thank-you bag with item for each child (include a heart for God's love, plastic food, toy, picture of friends, bed, and blanket), toy trumpet, and telephone.

Prepare the Art Center, the Family Living Center, and the Book/Picture Center. Start with the Art Center if you have just one teacher. Prepare to use the Music/Game Center after the Bible story.

Learning Activities

(30 minutes, including 10 minutes presession)

Let's Get Started

Zach will greet each child with a big "Go-o-od evening. Didn't God give us a great day today!" Take care of offering, name tags, and attendance. Zach then asks, "Would you like to pick something from my thank-you bag? Let's say thank-you to God for the (item)." Pray; then ask the child to place the item next to the bag. Direct children to the centers. **Would you like to cook, or would you prefer to make a prayer reminder in the art area?** Make sure each child gets involved in an activity.

Worship and Bible Story

(15 minutes)

Let's Worship God

Have Zach blow the trumpet at each center. Allow a little time for children to finish before Zach says, "Hold up your hands, everyone. Listen to Miss Carol's words." Say "The Busy Fingers" (page 306) as you direct children in their picking up. As they finish, start singing "Bible Time" to gather at the worship/story area. Children will model your actions as you place your hands together and say "My Bible." Sing "We Love Him," clapping on "Yes." **Now we are ready to talk to God. Let's pray, "Thank You, God, that we are growing big enough to pray."**

Let's Learn From the Bible

Introduction: Zach comes in talking on a telephone. **Zach, who are you talking to?** "I'm just talking to God." **Zach, you don't need a phone to talk to God. He hears you wherever you are.** Zach looks around and up and down. "Is God behind you?" Have Zach look over your back. You laugh. **Oh, no, Zach. God is everywhere.** Zach flops his ears as he looks again. "Well, can I pretend to talk to God on my telephone?" **You surely can! It's a good way to practice talking to God in prayer. We have a Bible friend who practiced talking to God in prayer. He loved God and always talked to God three times every day. Put your phone down and choose a helper to find our Bible story.** Let the child help you find the green marker.

The Bible Story: Three times. *(Hold up three fingers each time you say three.)* Three times every day. If it was sunny *(make round sun over your head),* if it was rainy *(make rainfall with fingers),* if it was snowy *(hug self and shiver);* it did not matter. Daniel still prayed three times every day. When Daniel woke up *(Have children stretch and yawn with you.)* he stopped and prayed. *(Fold hands.)* Maybe Daniel prayed, "Thank You God, for watching over me.Thank You for this new day. I love You."

Before Daniel ate his food *(have children pretend to eat with you),* he stopped and prayed. *(Fold hands.)* Perhaps he said, "Thank You, God, for my food."

Before Daniel went to bed *(have children lie down or lay heads on hands),* he stopped and prayed. *(Fold hands.)* He probably said, "Thank You for all the things You have given me today—my clothes, my bed, my room, and my work. Thank You for taking care of me."

Daniel was a good worker. The king liked Daniel's work, but he did not like Daniel's praying. *(Shake head.)* The king wanted a happy sound. *(Have everyone "too-too-too-too" through their fists.)* The instruments were played *(rhythm instruments)* and made a happy sound. All the people said, "We love God!"

Let's Apply the Lesson

Have children stand and march around singing "We Love Him," using "God" in place of "Him." **You are singing and praising God just like Hezekiah and his people did. Zach, let's get the rhythm instruments out and sing some more.** Pass out instruments. Do the warm-up procedure and then tap instruments to the rhythm of the Bible words, "We love Him, yes, we love Him." Let the children suggest favorite songs to sing to God. Take turns with the instruments and then collect them. **What did King Hezekiah do? What did the people do? What can you do to show you love God?** Say "I Have" and then thank God for singing voices.

Learning Activities

(20 minutes)

Let's Play Awhile

If there is an older group having choir practice, take a walk to the area and listen. Visit the choir area and look at any musical instruments you might use for worship services. Let the children sing a song in the choir area. Have the Music/Game Center ready for when you return.

Let's Go Home

Have Zach help you sing "Praise Him" and ask the children to clean up their things. Have Zach blow his trumpet or ring a bell when each child leaves. **Tell your family why the trumpets blew in our story. Sing a song with your family to show you love God.**

We Can Sing to God

2 Chronicles 29:28-30

Bible Words: "We love him" (1 John 4:19, *KJV*).

Lesson Value: There isn't anything quite like the "joyful noise" of young children praising God in song. King Hezekiah sang in "joyful" song with his people to show their love for God and this is what you will do with your class. Children need to know that praying and singing to God can be done at any time and any place, but there are special times of worship when God's people come together. Your "joyful noise" is also welcomed by God, so be a great example of happy, not perfect, singing to your class. We are never too young or too old to express our love for God in song.

Know: Know that God helps me grow big enough to love Him.
Feel: Feel big enough and willing to love God.
Do: Love God in specific ways (sing to God).

Children will accomplish the goals when they:

1. Say the Bible words, "We love him."
2. Sing about growing and loving God.
3. Tell what King Hezekiah and the people did.
4. Act out loving God by singing to Him.
5. Pray, "Thank You, God, that we are growing big enough to love You."

Let's Get Ready

For the Bible story, you will need a Bible marked with pink, Zach puppet, trumpet, crown, baton, soft background music and "Praise Him," temple transparency, overhead projector (optional), and rhythm instruments.

Prepare the Block Center, the Family Living Center, and the Book/Picture Center. Start with the Book/Picture Center if you are the only teacher. Prepare to use the Music/Game Center after the Bible story.

Learning Activities

(30 minutes, including 10 minutes presession)

Let's Get Started

Have Zach greet children and help them with offering, attendance, and name tags. Have Zach sing to the tune of "Mulberry Bush"—"This is the way we sing at church, sing at church, sing at church. This is the way we sing at church and I'm so glad you came." **Zach has his crown on again, because we're going to hear about another king. Can you say Hez-e-ki-ah? Hezekiah liked to sing in church like Zach does. Would you like to use an instrument or take an "obstacle" walk? You are big enough to choose.**

Worship and Bible Story

(15 minutes)

Let's Worship God

Have Zach go to each center and blow his trumpet or use one of the real instruments. "Do you know what to do next, boys and girls? That's right, hold up your hands, everyone." Say "The Busy Fingers" and direct children in picking up their toys. Start singing "Bible Time" as a signal to gather at the story area. Sing several other songs from this unit. Then put your hands together and say "My Bible." See if anyone is willing to say it by himself, with your help. Pray, **Thank You, God, that we are growing big enough to love You.**

Let's Learn From the Bible

Introduction: Have Zach come in singing, "We Love Him" with a box of rhythm instruments. **Looks like we're going to have a rhythm band. Put your hands on your legs until everyone has an instrument.** Have Zach pass out instruments and lay his baton in front of him. "Make your instrument lay like my baton stick. When I pick up my stick you start playing." **First we'll warm up, Zach.** Have Zach pick up the baton and wave exuberantly as children warm up. Lay the baton down and wait until all is quiet. Then start singing "We Love Him" as Zach picks up the baton and gently directs. **My, that was a lovely praise song!** Have everyone trade instruments. Do another song, and then collect instruments. **The people sang and the trumpets blew in our Bible story. Listen while I tell you the story.** Choose a child to find the pink marker.

The Bible Story: King Hezekiah woke up. He got up and hurried to get dressed. He was so happy and excited. The special day had finally come. The temple workers said, "We have cleaned up the temple. It is all ready to worship God."

King Hezekiah probably put on his finest robe and his shiniest crown. *(Pretend to put on robe and crown.)* He loved God and wanted this to be a very special day at the temple. King Hezekiah said, "Call all the people to God's temple. We are going to sing and praise God." *(Show the temple transparency if you can.)* The helpers passed out the instruments and trumpets. *(Pass out rhythm instruments again.)* Everyone waited for the king to give the order.

King Hezekiah stood up and said, "Let everyone worship God. Play your instruments *(turn on tape recorder)*. Blow your trumpets. Sing to the Lord." *(Turn off recorder.)*

King Hezekiah sang a happy song to God. The people sang a happy song to God. The trumpeters blew their horns and made

Boys and girls can sing to God, sing to God, sing to God.
Boys and girls can sing to God. They love Him.

(Have children sit down and sing a favorite song or play the tape recorder; use instruments. Then put them away.)

Let's Apply the Lesson

Ask the following questions and have a child act out the answer using the review items.

- How did King Josiah show he loved God? *(Use crown and scroll to act out reading. Say the Bible words.)*
- How can you be like King Josiah? *(Use Bible, pictures, or books to act out reading.)*
- How did Daniel show he loved God? *(Kneel and pray.)*
- How can you be like Daniel? *(Help child kneel and word a prayer.)*
- How did King Hezekiah show he loved God? *(Use crown; sing.)*
- How can you be like King Hezekiah? *(Play instrument; sing.)*

Learning Activities

(20 minutes)

Let's Play Awhile

Stand and sing the last stanza of "We Love Him" and then go to the Music/Game Center. If there was an activity the children especially enjoyed use it again. Also, use activities from the beginning of the session if you have a large class.

Let's Go Home

Have Zach help you sing "Praise Him" to signal clean-up time. Be specific in your directions and expect everyone to help. Have children bring their puppets to the worship/story area. Have their puppets sing "God's Word." Invite two or three children to stand and sing with Zach. Let the children take home their attendance hearts as a reminder of this unit. **This will remind you to show you love God by listening, singing, and praying. Have your little puppet help you sing and pray at home.**

We Are Big Enough to Worship God

Review of Lessons 10–12

Bible Words: "We love him" (1 John 4:19, *KJV*).

Lesson Value: Children learn through repetition and routine. They feel secure and grown up when they hear and see familiar words and pictures. This lesson will give them the opportunity to name the Bible people and the ways they showed love for God. Reinforce the children's loving actions, especially as they share God's Word in prayer and song. Evaluate your love and dependence upon God as you model your love for God to the children.

Know: Know that God helps me grow big enough to love Him.
Feel: Feel big enough and willing to love God.
Do: Love God in specific ways ("read" the Bible, pray, sing to God).

Children will accomplish the goals when they:

1. Say the Bible words, "We love him."
2. Sing about growing and loving God.
3. Point to or tell what each Bible person did.
4. Act out loving God.
5. Pray, "Thank You, God, that we are growing big enough to love You."

Let's Get Ready

For the Bible story, you will need a Bible with all three markers and orange marker at Bible words, puppet Zach with scroll and glasses, toy trumpet, Matching Game (page 305), rhythm instruments, and crown. Also have the small puppet from the Art Center.

Prepare the Art Center, the Family Living Center, and the Book/Picture Center. If you are the only teacher, start with the Art Center. Use the Music/Game Center after the Bible story.

Learning Activities

(30 minutes, including 10 minutes presession)

Let's Get Started

Have Zach greet each child by name. "Am I g-g-glad you came. It's gr-r-reat to see you, Brittany. Did you pray and sing this week? I want you to meet a friend of mine." Show the small puppet. Direct the child to the Art Center.

Worship and Bible Story

(15 minutes)

Let's Worship God

Zach says, "My new friend is going to help today." Use a squeaky voice for the little puppet, "Hands up everyone, hands up." Say "The Busy Fingers" as you direct clean-up time. Sing "Bible Time" to gather the children at the worship/story area. **You are all being such good helpers! I can tell you love God very much too. I need a helper to find the orange marker. Let's stand up like the people did with King Josiah and King Hezekiah.** Sing "We Love Him." Sing "Small, Tall!" to get children to sit down; then use the rhyme, "I Have." **Who would like to worship God by saying our prayer?** Help the child say, "I love You, God" or "thank-you" for something named.

Let's Learn From the Bible

Introduction: "Help, help," barks Zach, "I need someone big enough to help me." **What are you doing Zach?** "Well, I'm getting ready to worship God and I need some help." **OK, let's see what you have.** Ask several helpers to lay the review items in the middle of the circle. **Are you ready now, Zach?** "Just about. I need one more helper to stand in the middle of the circle." Choose a child to act out the words for each verse.

The Bible-story Review: *(Sing the following words to the tune of "London Bridge.")*

King Josiah read God's Word, read God's Word, read God's Word. King Josiah read God's Word. He loved God.

(Child should pick-up scroll and pretend to read.)

What made King Josiah so happy? (They found the Bible-scroll.) What did King Josiah do with the Bible-scroll? (Listened and read it to the people.) *(Have class stand and sing.)*

Boys and girls can read God's Word, read God's Word, read God's Word. Boys and girls can read God's Word. They love God. *(Have children sit down.)*

Daniel talked to God each day, God each day, God each day.
Daniel talked to God each day. He loved God. *(Child kneels.)*

When did Daniel pray to God? *(Use Matching Board.)* What did the king tell Daniel? (Pray to me.) What did Daniel do? (Prayed by his window.) *(Have class kneel and sing.)*

Boys and girls can pray to God, pray to God, pray to God.
Boys and girls can pray to God. They love God.

(Have children sit down.)

Hezekiah sang to God, sang to God, sang to God.
Hezekiah sang to God. He loved God.

(Child sings and plays instrument.)

Where did Hezekiah go to sing? (Temple) Who sang with him? (The people) Why did they all sing? (To show their love) *(Have class stand and sing. Pass out rhythm instruments.)*

Art Center

Unit 3—We Can Learn to Love God

Items to Include:

Bible
Supplies for cleaning up
Glue
Crayons
Stapler
Transparent tape

Lesson 10
Copies of crown (page 306)
Shoe boxes
Yellow, red, blue tempera paint
Marbles
Adding machine tape
Aprons

Purpose: The child will know that God helps him grow big enough to love Him.

Things to Do and Say

Lesson 10

Before class make crowns and print the Bible words on them.

Let a child place a crown in a box, add a handful of marbles, and choose a paint color. Pour 1/4 to 1/2 teaspoon of very thin paint on the crown. Show the child how to move the box to make the marbles roll in the paint. Add colors until the child has all three. Allow the crown to dry. Tape a piece of the adding machine tape to the crown to fit the child's head.

The Bible tells about a young man named Josiah who was a king. He wore a crown. When some men found a Bible-scroll in the temple, Josiah listened to God's words. Then he read the Bible-scroll to the people. Everyone listened to the words on the Bible-scroll. . . . God is helping you grow big enough to listen to Bible words. Show the highlighted Bible words in the Bible. Help each child "read" them. Then point to the words on a crown and read them. **These words are from the Bible.**

Family Living Center

Unit 3—We Can Learn to Love God

Items to Include:

Lesson 10
Bible scroll
Wooden or plastic hammers
Large Styrofoam pieces
Golf tees
Masking tape
Sandpaper
Square blocks
Pieces of wood
Aprons with pockets
Shower curtain

Lesson 11
Bread
Margarine

Purpose: The child will feel big enough and willing to love God.

Things to Do and Say

Lesson 10

Make a scroll and print the Bible words on the inside. Tape sandpaper to square blocks. General play items should be available. Place the shower curtain on the floor to work on. Children will pound tees into Styrofoam and sand wood pieces. Place tees in the apron pocket. Keep track of tees with young two's. Encourage some children to play with the regular equipment while others will want to be "carpenters." Help them to enact the Bible story in a very simple manner.

The Bible tells about some men who were fixing the big temple-church. One day, they found a Bible-scroll there. They took it to King Josiah. The king loved God. He wanted to hear the words from the Bible-scroll. Then He read the words to all the people. . . . Would you like to be King Josiah, Nathan? Emily and Aaron, you can be the workers who find the Bible-scroll. . . . Now, King Josiah can read from the Bible-scroll.

Lesson 11

Place the skillet where the children can see it but not touch it. Discuss safety rules. Work on plates. Have the children cut shapes from bread then spread margarine on the bread cutouts. Let a child place a shape on the spatula. Toast both sides of the bread. The

Family Living Center, continued

Paper plates
Cookie cutters
Plastic knives
Electric skillet
Spatula

Lesson 12
Enlarged copy of page 309
Tape player
Child-size furniture
Dolls
Dress-up clothes
Dishes

children can eat the scraps while shapes toast. **The Bible tells us that Daniel prayed to God three times a day. When can we talk to God?** Help the children think of various times. **What can we say to God?** You may need to give a few examples of this. **Let's stop and thank God for hands to work with. . . . When our toast is done, we will thank God for it. You are big enough to pray to God about many things!**

Lesson 12

Have everything ready for the children to play house. Place a tape player at a little distance, ready to play music. Encourage the children to get the babies up, dress and feed them, and so forth. Explain that everyone is going to the temple-church to sing to God.

After awhile start the music. **Listen! Do you hear music? It's time to go to the temple-church to sing to God.** Designate an area near the tape player. Have an enlarged copy of page 309.

The temple-church might have looked something like this. In our Bible story, many people went to the temple-church to sing to God. They were glad they could show their love for God by singing to Him.You are big enough to show God you love Him by singing to Him. Sing "We Love Him" and other familiar songs with the children.

Lesson 13

Suggest that the children get ready to "go to church." **Suzi is ironing the clothes and Jon is getting breakfast. We'll all be ready to worship God at church. We can sing to God while we're all getting ready.** Sing, "I Will Help," adding phrases according to what children are doing. **Before we eat our breakfast, we will stop and pray like Daniel did. . . . Nicole is "reading" God's Word like King Josiah did. You are all getting big enough to show God you love Him.**

Art Center, continued

Lesson 11
Copies of page 310
Paper fasteners
Stickers from page 310

Lesson 11

Cut out the "clocks" from page 310 and mount them on construction paper or card stock. Mount the pointers on card stock and cut out. Attach these to the clocks with paper fasteners. Make stickers according to directions on page 307. Cut these apart after the children color them, or print on colored paper and cut apart ahead of time.

Give the child one sticker at a time and show where it goes on the clock. When the children have finished adding their stickers, ask them to turn to a time when they can pray. **Yes, Adam, you can pray at breakfast time. . . . Michelle, can you pray before you go to bed? Yes, you are big enough to do that. The Bible tells about Daniel who prayed three times a day. God is helping you grow big enough to pray many times a day!**

Lesson 13
Copies of page 312
Nylon hose

Lesson 13

Make copies of page 312, fold on broken lines, and cut puppet where indicated. Cut legs of hose 14" long for ears. Let children help you do as much as time and abilities allow.

As children color their dogs, take turns stapling ears and taping edges (on the inside of the puppets). Show the children how to place their fingers in the puppets and have little Zach say the Bible words.

What does Zach have in his mouth? Can you point to God's words? Can you say the words? . . . King Josiah listened to God's words; then he read God's words to all the people. . . . God is helping you grow big enough to listen and say God's words. Can you have Zach go sing "We Love Him" to a friend?

Music/Game Center

Unit 3—We Can Learn to Love God

Items to Include:

Lesson 11
Copies of page 310
Paper fastener
Glue
Stop sign (page 306)

Lesson 12
Tape player
Tape of children's music

Purpose: The child will show love for God in specific ways.

Things to Do and Say

Lesson 11

Print the circle on page 310 on green construction paper. Add the stickers and pointer as indicated. Make the stop sign (page 306) out of red paper and add the praying figure. The children will use these to play the "Stop and Pray" game. This is played like "Red Light, Green Light."

Have the children line up by a wall. One child holds a red stop sign and one holds the green sign. Hold up the green sign and move the arrow to the wake-up picture. **Wake up and walk.** Hold up the red sign. **Stop and pray.** Children will kneel and fold their hands. Green sign up. **Walk to breakfast.** Red sign up. **Stop and pray.** Green—**Walk to play**. Red—**Stop and pray.** Continue in this way around the "clock." Let children take turns holding the signs.

Lesson 12

The children will play "Musical Chairs." Have the children make two lines of chairs back to back. Choose one child to be the music helper and take one chair away. The helper will push the button to start and stop the music when you say it is time.

In our Bible story, the king wanted to have a big celebration to praise God. He asked many helpers to play their musical instruments. When the people heard the

Book/Picture Center

Unit 3—We Can Learn to Love God

Items to Include:

Bible with markers
Books (see list on page 291)

Lessons 10 and 13
Enlarged copy of page 308
Shelf paper
Cardboard pants hanger bars
Ribbon or cord

Lesson 11
Copies of page 305

Purpose: The child will learn to love God in specific ways (read the Bible, talk to God, sing to God).

Things to Do and Say

Lessons 10 and 13

Make the Bible-scroll according to the directions on page 308. Place bookmarks in the Bible at the Bible words and at the story of King Josiah.

Many years ago, people did not have Bibles. They had Bible-scrolls that might have looked something like this. Let's open it and look at the pictures. Why do you suppose that boy is wearing a crown? Yes, he is a king. . . . What do you see in the next picture? It looks as though the big temple-church needed some cleaning and fixing! Look! King Josiah's helper has found a scroll with God's words written on it. . . . What is King Josiah doing with the Bible-scroll? Yes, he is reading it to all the people. They are listening to God's words.

Let's read God's words in our Bible. Help the children find the Bible words, point to them, and "read" them. Then find the story of Josiah. **We can read about King Josiah in our Bible. You are looking at God's words in the Bible. You are big enough to listen to God's words. You are showing you love God like Josiah did.**

Lesson 11

For each child, make two copies of page 305; glue each on card stock and cut one board

Music/Game Center, continued

music they all went to the temple-church and sang to God. When you hear the music pretend to walk to the temple-church. When the music stops find an empty chair and sit down. Say the Bible words, "We love Him," each time the children sit down. The child without a chair is your new music helper.

All Lessons

Use this song whenever you need a song and/or some exercise.

Small, Tall!

(Tune: Sing up and down scale.)

We are grow-ing tall,
(Stoop down, then slowly rise as you sing up the scale.)
We are not so small.
(Go back down as you sing down the scale.)
(Repeat the first two lines.)
Small! . . . Tall!
(Stoop! . . . Stand!)
(Repeat.)
Now we all will fall! *(Fall down as you sing down scale.)*

Book/Picture Center, continued

Card stock
Glue
Quart self-sealing bags
Crayons

into cards. Let the children color the pictures on the cards.

The man in our Bible story, Daniel, prayed three times every day. Can you find Daniel on your card? Can you find the matching picture of Daniel? Very good! Now put it on top of the other one. You are big enough to pray three times a day too! . . . Perhaps Daniel prayed in the morning. Can you find a picture that looks like morning? Yes, the one with the big sun! We can pray when the sun is in the sky. We can say, "Thank You, God, for this new day." Continue this way with each picture. **You are big enough to show God you love Him by praying to Him.** Children may enjoy singing "Praise Him" as they point to the pictures. Use the plastic bags for storage. If there is time, look at/read other books that have to do with prayer or things/people to pray for.

Lesson 12
Copies of page 311
Card stock
Red and blue yarn
Guest musician
Recorder/wind instrument
Rhythm instruments
Wet wipes
Tape recorder
Blank tape

Lesson 12

Before class make several copies of page 311. Mount these on card stock. On each picture, thread three pieces of blue yarn through the hole beneath the hands and knot on back of board. Do the same beneath the mouth with two pieces of red yarn. Include a recorder or similar wind instrument as well as several rhythm instruments.

Have your guest explain and demonstrate the recorder/wind instrument. Help the children sing a familiar song. Tape record the instrument and singing. Let the children try various instruments. (Clean the mouth piece after each child uses the recorder.) **What does our guest use to play her instrument? Her mouth, that's right!** Show the children how to match a piece of red yarn to the trumpet on the page. Do the same with other pictures. **Some people used instruments to praise God in the temple-church while others sang. Listen to the praise music you just made.** Play the tape. **You are big enough to sing to God.** Read books that illustrate times and places for praising/singing to God.

Block Center

Unit 3—We Can Learn to Love God

Items to Include:

Unit blocks or blockbusters
Figures of people
Cars and trucks
Church pictures
Bible

Lessons 10 and 13

Doll-house furniture
Bible(s)
Bible-scroll(s) (See page 308.)
Photo of your church building

Purpose: The child will feel big enough and willing to love God.

Things to Do and Say

Lessons 10 and 13

Set up several areas with a few blocks, furniture, people, and cars to indicate neighborhoods with churches and streets. Make these areas inviting so that children will want to add to them. Place a Bible-scroll, a Bible, and a photo of your church building in each area.

Kaitlyn, you are building a good house. We can listen to Bible stories in our houses. . . . Michael is working on a church building. In our Bible story, some men worked on the big temple-church. They found a Bible-scroll and took it to King Josiah. . . . Can you find a picture of a Bible-scroll? a church building? a Bible? . . . King Josiah listened to the words from the Bible-scroll. Then he read them to all the people. They all listened to the words. You are big enough to listen to God's words too. Our Bible words say, "We love him." We love God!

Summer, Unit 3—
Lesson 10, Art Center

Directions for Crown:

1. Make a cardboard pattern.
2. Lay broken line of pattern on fold of paper.
3. Cut out crowns; print Bible words on each.
4. See Art Center Card for finish (page 301).

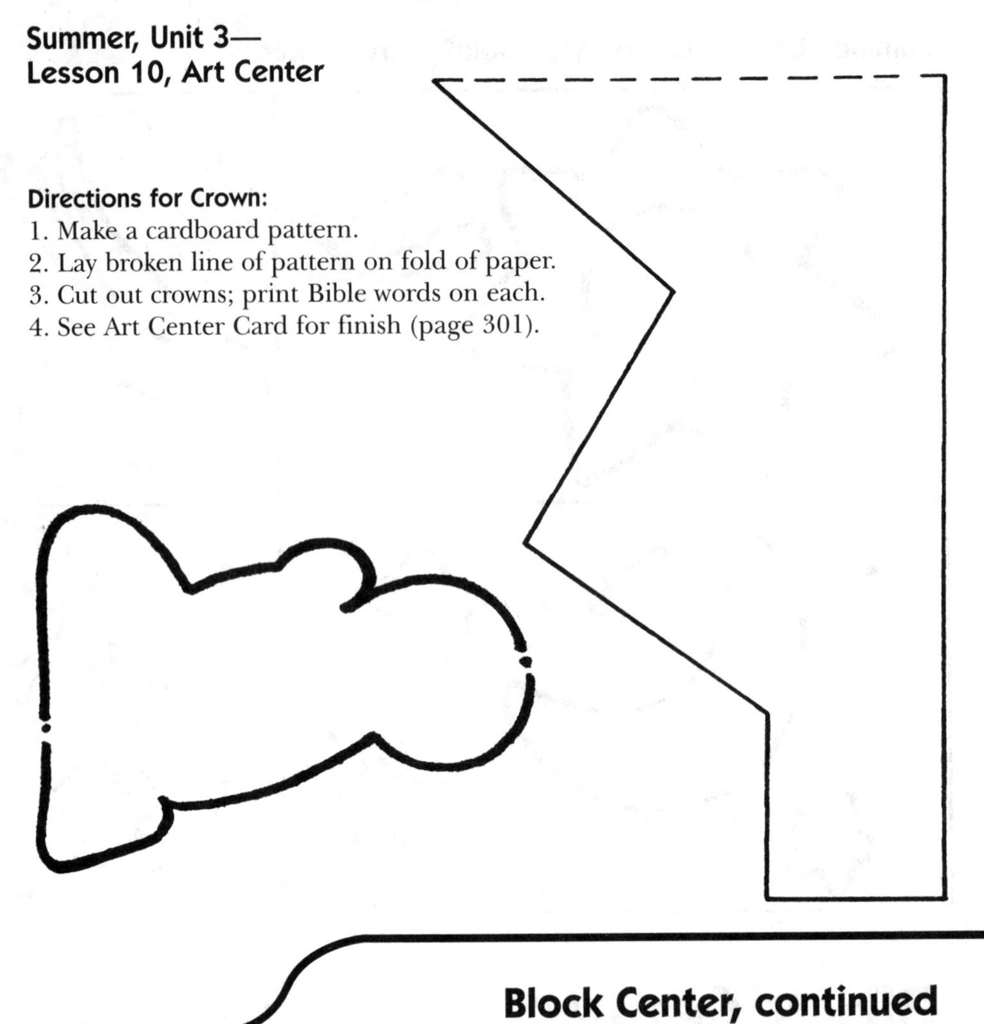

Lesson 11, Music/Game Center

Directions for Stop Sign:

1. Cut red construction paper into 9" square.
2. Cut corners as shown in sketch.
3. Glue enlarged copy of praying figure to stop sign as shown.
4. Attach a craft stick to back of sign for a handle.

Block Center, continued

Lesson 12
Carpet pieces
Plastic bubble wrap
Small inner tube
Balance beam
Temple picture (page 309)

Lesson 12

Make an enlarged copy of the temple picture on page 309 and color it. Lay out a simple obstacle course with the materials—a short balance beam made with 2x8's, block stepping stones, a path between blockbusters, interspersed with the carpet samples, and so forth—that leads to the picture of the temple. Have the children remove their shoes so they can feel the different textures.

Let's all walk to the temple-church. King Hezekiah has called all the people to the temple-church to sing to God. We can sing and pray to God when we reach the temple-church. Sing "We Love Him" and "Praise Him." **Thank You, God, for legs to walk and voices to sing. We love You.** Sing, "God's Word." **Now we can walk back and invite a friend to come with us.**

Use this action rhyme when it is time to pick up blocks, etc.

The Busy Fingers

Busy little finger people, *(Hold up closed hands.)*
Who will put the toys (blocks, etc.) away? *(Look at hands.)*
"I will," "I will," "I will," "I will," "I will," all the fingers say.
(Raise fingers one at a time beginning with thumbs.)
—*Louise M. Oglevee*

Summer, Unit 3—Attendance Heart

Directions for Stickers:

1. Mix two parts white glue and one part vinegar.
2. Add a few drops of peppermint extract if desired.
3. Lightly "paint" mixture onto backs of uncut stickers. Let dry.
4. Allow children to color (or print these on colored stock).
5. Cut stickers apart and let children lick and stick.

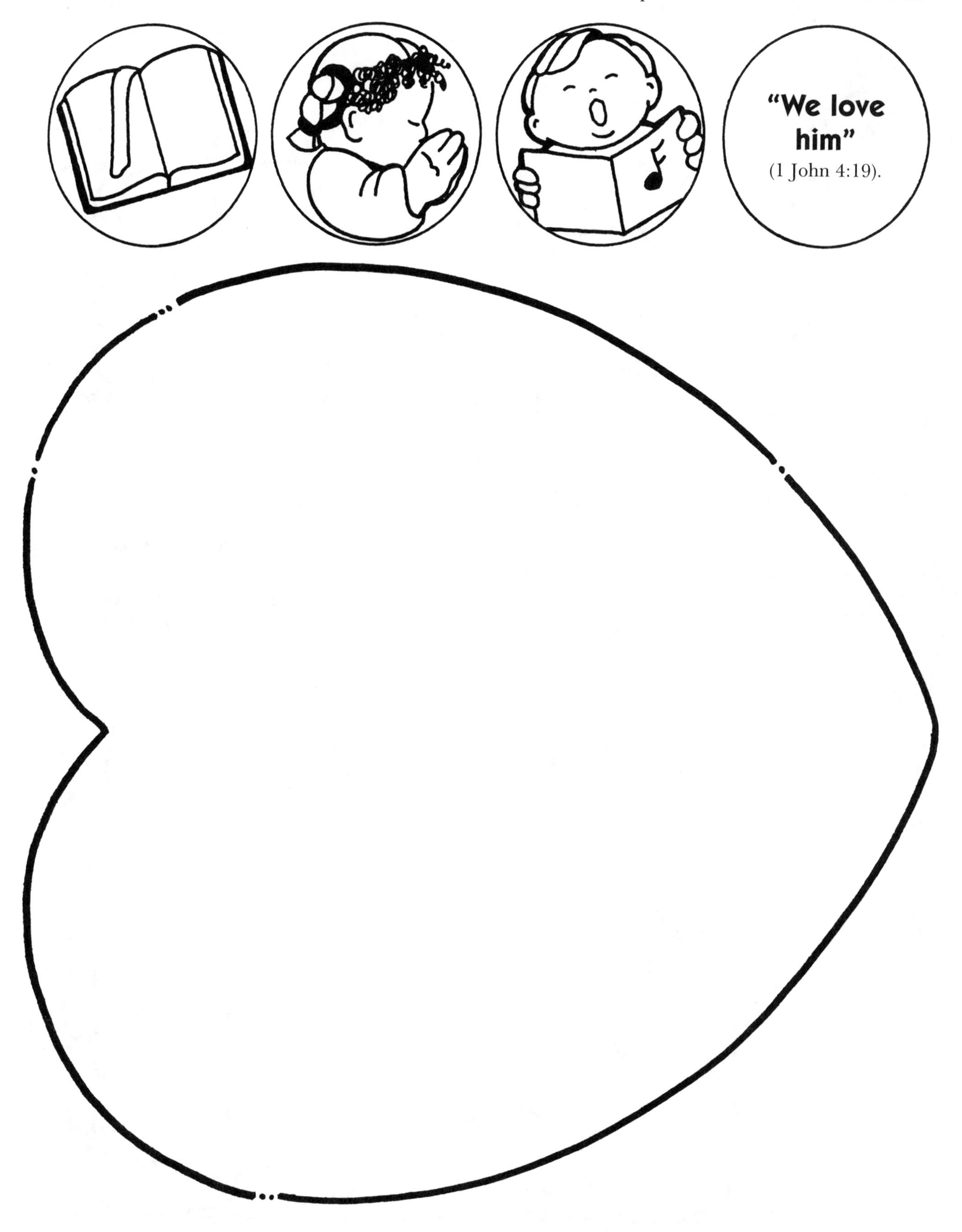

Directions for Bible-scroll:

1. Cut a length of shelf paper (about 24").
2. Enlarge pictures on this page.
3. Color pictures; cut out.
4. Glue these to paper in order, from left to right, with Bible words at the end.
5. Glue ends of paper to cardboard pants hanger bars (or tape to dowel rods).
6. Roll each end to the middle; tie with ribbon or cord.

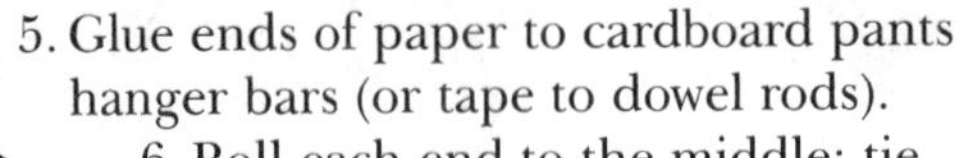

"We love him"
(1 John 4:19).

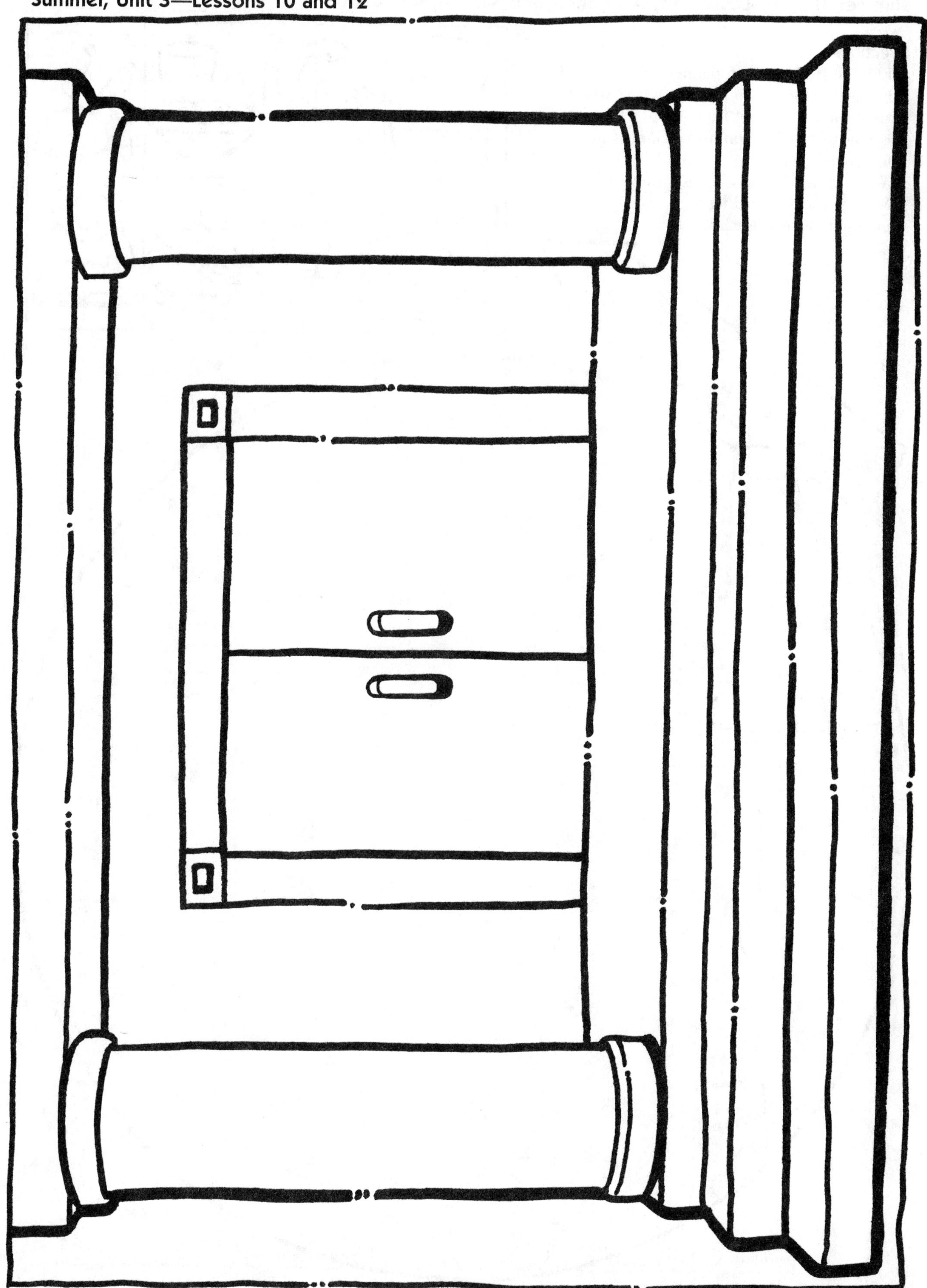

Directions:

1. Enlarge circle to 9" in diameter.
2. Follow instructions on Art Center Card for art project (page 302).
3. Follow instructions on Music/Game Card for game (page 303).
4. Add a craft-stick handle for game.
5. Make stickers according to instructions on page 307.

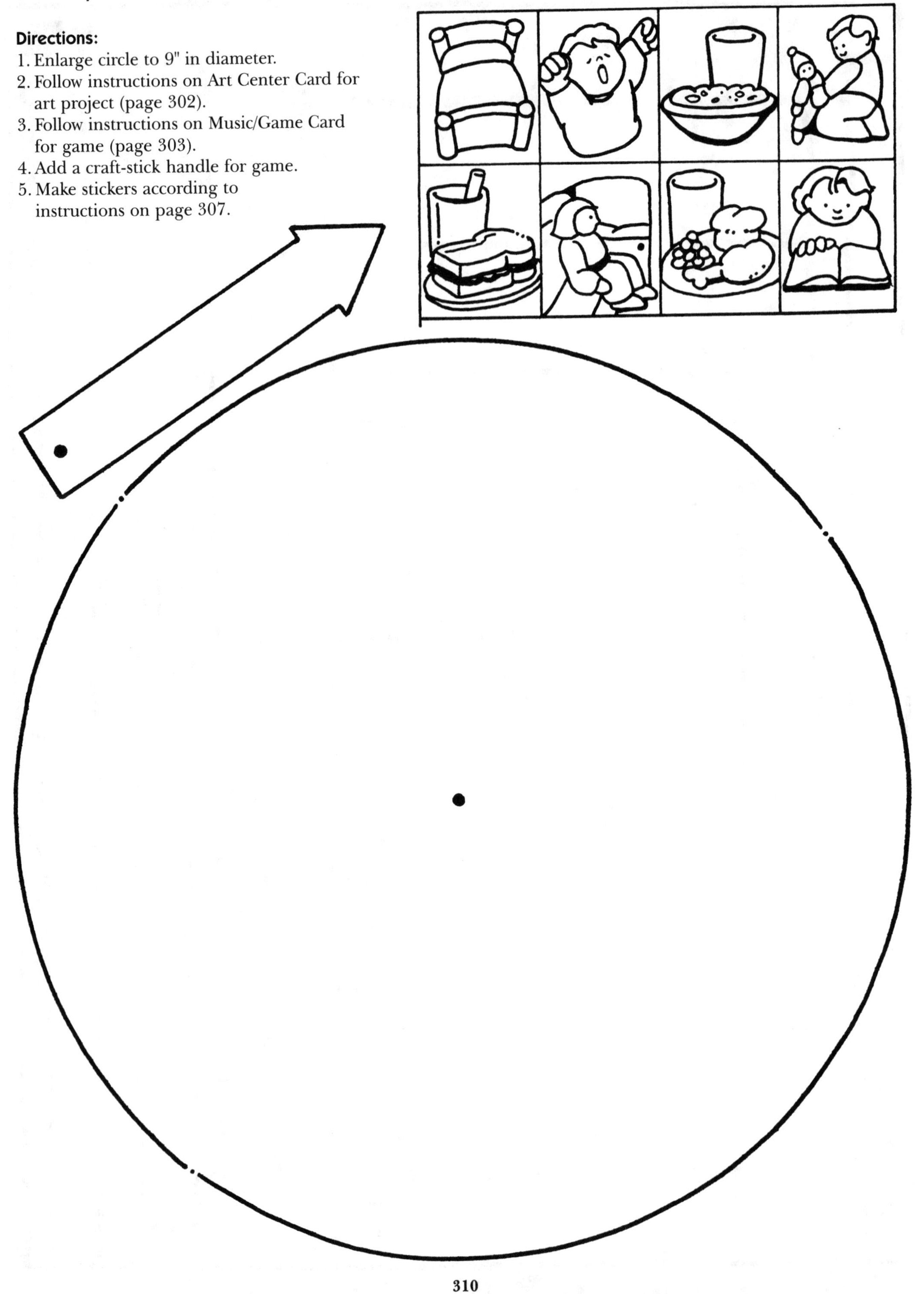

I can worship with my—

Thread 2 pieces of red yarn through hole under mouth. Match red line to worship with mouth.
Thread 3 pieces of blue yarn through hole under hands. Match blue line to worship with hands.

"We love him"
(1 John 4:19).

6. Staple or tape.

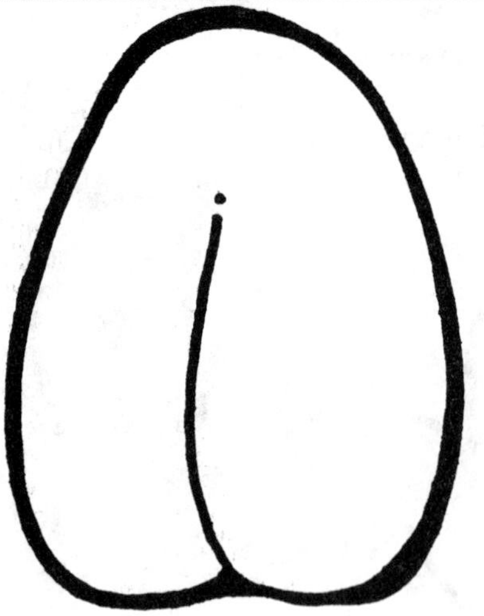

"We love him"

(I John 4:19).

5. Tape edges together.

2. Fold and cut (top only).

3. Reinforce with tape.

4. Staple ears; tape over backs of staples.

Directions for Puppet:

1. Enlarge pattern to fit on 9" x 12" construction paper.
2. Fold on broken line; then fold on solid line.
3. Cut on solid line; use tape to reinforce at ends of dotted line.
4. Tape at bottom and sides where indicated.
5. Finish according to directions on Art Center Card (page 302).

7. Tape edges together.

1. Fold lengthwise.

8. Staple or tape.

Dear Parent:

There's nothing quite like the sound of a young child saying the "Bible words" or making a "joyful noise" praising God in song! This unit gives your child many opportunities to listen to and "read" the Bible, talk to God, and sing to Him—ways we show love for God. These are the lessons we are using:

- *We Can Listen to the Bible* (2 Kings 22:1-10; 23:1-3)
  King Josiah listened to God's Word when the Bible-scroll was found in the temple, and then read it to all his people.
- *We Can Talk to God* (Daniel 6:1-10)
  Daniel prayed to God three times a day to show his love for God.
- *We Can Sing to God* (2 Chronicles 29:28-30)
  King Hezekiah gathered all the people at the temple to sing to God in worship.
- *We Are Big Enough to Worship God* (review of previous lessons)

Our Bible words are, "We love him [God]" 1 John 4:19. You can help your child learn these words by singing this song to the tune of "This Old Man."

We love Him. We love Him. We love Him, yes, we love Him.
We can read our Bibles, sing, and talk to Him.
We love Him, yes, we love Him.

We can read. We can pray. We can sing to God today.
We can read and pray and sing to God today.
We love Him, yes, we love Him.

Enjoy the following activities with your child as the truths of the Bible are applied to life:
- Choose a regular time to read a short Bible story to your child.
- Have family members take turns praying at mealtimes. Help your child, if necessary, when it is his turn. "Thank You, God, for food" is enough for a young child to say.
- At bedtime, simple prayers such as, "I love You, God. Thank You for my day," help a child learn to word her own prayers.
- Sing praise songs with your child to show your love for God. Remember, God loves a "joyful noise." Listen to or sing along with a tape in your car.
- Plan ahead for worship. The night before lay out clothes and help your child set out breakfast items. "We want to be ready for our special day to worship God!"

I appreciate the opportunity to work with your child and pray that this unit will help your family grow in their love for God.

Sincerely,

Zach

Zach is a cute, short-legged dog. His full name is Zaccheus. He is the mascot for this course. He will be helping with many of the activities in the classroom. To make him even more appealing to the children, you may want to make a pretend doghouse, such as the one below. Make this on a large piece of cardboard or poster board. Fasten this to a cardboard box and cut open the door. If you are not artistic, enlist the aid of someone who is.

Zach, the Puppet

Zach, the puppet, is meant to be the class mascot—the children's friend. Two's and 3's love puppets, and are fascinated by one even though they can see you holding the puppet on your hand and talking for him. Having Zach give instructions, suggestions, or warnings can be more effective than your telling the children what to do.

Zach should not be used to tell the Bible story, however, because the Bible story should be real, not a tale told by an animal. Also, make sure that Zach is used only by adults. He will lose his effectiveness if the children are allowed to treat him like a toy.

If you already have a dog puppet, or you can find one ready-made, by all means use it. If you need to make one, however, here are several suggestions.

Materials to make puppet using these patterns:

Scissors
Cardboard
Felt—tan, off-white, or light brown (features won't show up on dark colors)
Markers
Fabric glue

Directions to make puppet using these patterns:

1. Photocopy patterns onto paper. Enlarge patterns when you copy.
2. Trace pieces onto felt.
3. Go over features with markers.
4. Cut out pieces.
5. Glue front and back head pieces around edges, leaving a small opening in which to stuff cotton. Let dry.
6. Stuff head with cotton; glue opening closed. Let dry.
7. Glue front and back body together around edges, leaving bottom open for operator's hand. Let dry.
8. Glue neck to back of head piece. Lower part of head should not be glued tight to body.
9. Glue ears to sides of head.

Note: The puppet can also be made from a soft fabric such as fake fur, velour, or velveteen. You may have to embroider features onto the fabric rather than use markers.

You can also make a puppet one of these ways:

1. Purchase or find a toy stuffed dog. Rip a seam at lower back of dog. Pull out some stuffing so you can insert your hand into toy, with fingers in the front legs. Make sure you can manipulate dog well. Push stuffing up far enough so it won't come out. If necessary, finish seam to keep it from raveling. (Whip edges with needle and thread, or use fabric glue on edges.) You may find the toy dog will work better if you cut off the lower part of the body so that you have a larger opening for your hand. (You don't need the back legs for the puppet.) Finish the bottom edges as suggested previously.

2. Obtain stuffed toy dog. Purchase or find a piece of fabric to match the dog as closely as possible. Cut out a pocket that will allow you sufficient room to put your hand into and manipulate the dog like a puppet. Turn under edges of pocket and sew around pocket by hand onto back of dog. Or, attach with fabric glue.

Make It Yourself

Recipes

Play Dough: Mix 1 C. flour, 1/2 C. salt, and 2 tsp. cream of tartar in saucepan. (Do not omit cream of tartar.) Add 1 C. water, 1 Tbs. cooking oil, and food coloring. Cook, stirring, for three minutes or until mixture pulls away from pan. Knead immediately. Store in airtight container. Makes enough for about six children.

Finger Paint: Mix 1 C. mild powdered soap or detergent with 1/3 C. liquid starch (or 1/4 C. water). Beat with rotary beater until mixture is like frosting. (Add more liquid or more soap if necessary. Starches and soaps vary.) Add food coloring last.

"Sticker" Glue: Mix 2 parts white glue and 1 part vinegar. Add a few drops of peppermint extract if desired. Lightly "paint" mixture onto backs of uncut stickers. Let dry. Color stickers if needed. Cut out stickers. Apply by moistening backs of stickers just as you would ready-made ones.

Rhythm Instruments

Sand Blocks: Sand lumber scraps (about 5" x 3"). Cover one side with fine sandpaper, tacked or glued to the ends of the blocks.

Shakers: Use cardboard or metal boxes (bandage or spice cans) or plastic bottles and fill with seeds, small rocks, dry beans, rice, macaroni, etc. Tape boxes closed and cover with colorful self-adhesive plastic. Glue on lids of bottles. May be used singly or in pairs.

Drum: Remove both ends of a one-, two-, or three-pound coffee can. Make sure there are no rough edges. Cover can with colorful self-adhesive plastic, if desired. Cover ends by gluing on plastic lids. Use hands or short dowels to beat drums. Ice cream cartons (round), large shortening cans, or waste baskets also make good drums.

Bells: Sew five or six jingle bells to a 6" length of 1/2" elastic. Sew ends of elastic together to form a bracelet.

Maracas: Put dry beans in salt boxes and tape spouts shut. Use 1/4" dowel rods for handles. Poke these through bottom and glue at each point where dowel and box touch. Cover boxes after you glue handles in place.

Triangle: Obtain a 6" to 8" piece of brass pipe and string through it heavy twine 3 times as long as the pipe. Tie securely at top. Use a spoon to play the triangle.

Clap sticks (rhythm sticks): Half-inch doweling cut into 12" lengths and sanded on ends should be used in pairs. Use a nontoxic, nonlead base paint if you wish to paint them.

Accessories

Books: Mount pictures on cardboard, cover with clear self-adhesive plastic, and punch holes. Put these together with chicken rings or yarn or place in a loose-leaf notebook. Or, mount pictures in a magnetic photo album. For a touch-and-feel book, stitch cloth together and cut objects from felt or other textured cloth and glue to pages.

Appliances: Make stoves, refrigerators, and sinks from large cardboard boxes. Paint the outsides or cover with appropriate colors of self-adhesive plastic if you wish. Use a waterproof marker to indicate burners, handles, etc. Cut a hole in top of sink and insert a plastic dishpan. The appliances may be as simple or as elaborate as you wish.

Play Food: Glue pictures of food to cardboard and cover with clear, self-adhesive plastic and cut out.

Blocks: Make blocks using various sizes of cardboard milk or juice cartons. Wash and dry cartons; cut off tops. Place one carton over another of the same size. Cover with colorful self-adhesive plastic if desired. Blocks can also be covered with appropriate pictures and then covered with clear plastic.

Unit Planning Sheet

Quarter: ______________________

Unit: ______________________

Bible Words: ______________________

Unit Aims:

KNOW

____

FEEL

____

DO

____

To Do Ahead

Lesson One: ______________________

Learning Activities:

1. ______________________

Materials needed: ______________________

____

____

2. ______________________

Materials needed: ______________________

____

____

3. ______________________

Materials needed: ______________________

____

____

4. ______________________

Materials needed: ______________________

____

____

Materials for the Bible story: ______________________

____

____

2. ______________________

Materials needed: ______________________

____

____

3. ______________________

Materials needed: ______________________

____

____

4. ______________________

Materials needed: ______________________

____

____

Materials for the Bible story:

____

____

Unit songs/action rhymes to learn and/or tape:

____

____

____

Special arrangements for unit:

____

____

____

Room/bulletin board decorations:

____

____

____

Materials for unit party:

____

____

____

Lesson Two: ______

Learning Activities:

1. ______

Materials needed: ______

2. ______

Materials needed: ______

3. ______

Materials needed: ______

4. ______

Materials needed: ______

Materials for the Bible story:

Lesson Three: ______

Learning Activities:

1. ______

Materials needed: ______

2.

Materials needed: ______

3.

Materials needed: ______

4. ______

Materials needed: ______

Materials for the Bible story:

Lesson Four: ______

Learning Activities:

1. ______

Materials needed: ______

2.

Materials needed: ______

3. ______

Materials needed: ______

4. ______

Materials needed: ______

Materials for the Bible story:

Lesson Five: ______

Learning Activities:

1. ______

Materials needed: ______